Social History of the
United States

Titles in ABC-CLIO's
Social History of the United States

Social History of the United States
The 1970s

Laurie Mercier

Series Editors
Daniel J. Walkowitz and Daniel E. Bender

A B C · C L I O

Santa Barbara, California   Denver, Colorado   Oxford, England

Library of Congress Cataloging-in-Publication Data

Mercier, Laurie.
Social history of the United States : the 1970s / Laurie Mercier.
    p.   cm.
Includes bibliographical references and index.
ISBN 978-1-85109-923-8 (alk. paper) — ISBN 978-1-59884-127-5 (set)
EISBN 978-1-85109-924-5 (ebook)
1. United States—Social conditions—1960–1980.   2. United States—Social life and customs—1971–   I. Title.
HN59.M43   2009
306.0973'09047—dc22   2008032813

12 11 10 09   1 2 3 4 5

Production Editor: Kristine Swift
Production Manager: Don Schmidt
Media Editor: Julie Dunbar
Media Resources Manager: Caroline Price
File Management Coordinator: Paula Gerard

This book is also available on the World Wide Web as an eBook.
Visit www.abc-clio.com for details.

ABC-CLIO, Inc.
130 Cremona Drive, P.O. Box 1911
Santa Barbara, California 93116–1911

This book is printed on acid-free paper ∞
Manufactured in the United States of America

Contents

Series Introduction

Ordinary people make history. They do so in ways that are different from the ways presidents, generals, business moguls, or celebrities make history; nevertheless, the history of ordinary people is just as profound, just as enduring. Immigration in the early decades of the 20th century was more than numbers and government policy; it was a collective experience of millions of men, women, and children whose political beliefs, vernacular cultural expression, discontent, and dreams transformed the United States. Likewise, during the Great Depression of the 1930s, President Franklin Delano Roosevelt advanced a broad spectrum of new social policies, but as historians have argued, ordinary Americans "made" the New Deal at the workplace, at the ballot box, on the picket lines, and on the city streets. They engaged in new types of consumer behavior, shifted political allegiances, and joined new, more aggressive trade unions. World War II and the Cold War were more than diplomatic maneuvering and military strategy; social upheavals changed the employment patterns, family relations, and daily life of ordinary people. More recently, the rise of the Christian Right in the last few decades is the expression of changing demographics and emerging social movements, not merely the efforts of a few distinct leaders.

These examples, which are drawn directly from the volumes in this series, highlight some of the essential themes of social history. Social history shifts the historical focus away from the famous and the political or economic elite to issues of everyday life. It explores the experiences ordinary Americans—native-born and immigrant, poor and rich, employed and unemployed, men and women, white and black—at home, at work, and at play. In the process, it focuses new attention on the significance of social movements, the behavior and meanings of consumerism, and the changing expression of popular culture.

In many ways, social history is not new. American historians early in the 20th century appreciated the importance of labor, immigration, religion, and urbanization in the study of society. However, early studies shared with political history the emphasis on leaders and major institutions and described a history that was mostly white and male—in other words, a history of those who held power. Several cultural shifts combined to transform how social history was understood and written in the last half of the 20th century: the democratization of higher education after World War II with the GI Bill and the expansion of public and land grant universities; the entry of women, children of immigrants, and racial minorities into the universities and the ranks of historians; and the social movements of the 1960s. Historians created new subjects for social history, casting it as "from the bottom." They realized that much was missing from familiar narratives that stressed the significance of "great men"—presidents, industrialists, and other usually white, usually male notables. Instead, women, working people, and ethnic and racial minorities have become integral parts of the American story along with work, leisure, and social movements.

The result has not simply been additive: ordinary people made history. The story of historical change is located in their lives and their struggles with and against others in power. Historians began to transform the central narrative of American history. They realized that—in the words of a popular 1930s folk cantata, "Ballad for Americans"—the "'etceteras' and the 'and so forths' that do the work" have a role in shaping their own lives, in transforming politics, and in recreating economics. Older themes of study, from industrialization to imperial expansion, from party politics to urbanization, were revisited through the inclusion of new actors, agents, and voices. These took their place alongside such new topics as social movements, popular culture, consumption, and community. But social history remains socially engaged scholarship; contemporary social issues continue to shape social historians' research and thinking. Historians in the 1970s and 1980s who focused on the experiences of working people, for instance, were challenged by the reality of deindustrialization. Likewise, historians in the 1990s who focused on popular culture and consumer behavior were influenced by the explosion of consumerism and new forms of cultural expression. Today's historians explore the antecedents to contemporary globalization as well as the roots of conservatism.

The transformation of the questions and agendas of each new era has made it apparent to historians that the boundaries of historical inquiry are not discrete. Social history, therefore, engages with other kinds of history. Social history reinterprets older narratives of politics and political economy and overlaps both areas. Social historians argue that politics is not restricted to ballot boxes or legislatures; politics is broad popular engagement with ideas about material wealth, social justice, moral values, and civil and human rights. Social historians, naturally, remain interested in changing political affiliations. They have, for example, examined the changing political allegiances of African Americans during the 1930s and the civil rights movement of the 1960s. So too have they examined the relationship of socialist and communist parties to working-class and immigrant communities. At the same time, social historians measure change by looking at such issues as family structure, popular culture, and consumer behavior.

For the social historian, the economy extends far beyond statistical data about production, gross domestic product, or employment. Rather, the economy is a lived experience. Wealthy or poor, Americans have negotiated the changing reality of economic life. Social historians ask questions about how different groups of Americans experienced and resisted major economic transformations and how they have grappled with economic uncertainty. The Great Depression of the 1930s, for example, left both urban workers and rural farmers perilously close to starvation. During the 1970s and 1980s, factories in the Rust Belt of the Midwest and Northeast shuttered or moved, and many Americans began laboring in new parts of the country and working new kinds of jobs, especially in the service sector. Americans have also grappled with the unequal distribution of wealth; some people advanced new ideas and engaged with emerging ideologies that challenged economic injustice, but others jealously guarded their privilege.

As social history has broadened its purview, it has transformed our sense of how historical change occurs. Social history changes our conception of chronology; change does not correspond to presidential election cycles. Social history also changes how we understand sources of power; power is constituted in and challenged by diverse peoples with different resources. Social historians, then, look at the long history of the 20th century in the United States and examine how the terrain has shifted under our feet, sometimes slowly and sometimes dramatically and abruptly. Social historians measure change in complex ways, including but also transcending demographic and geographic expansion and political transformation. How, for example, did the institution of the family change in the face of successive waves of immigration that often left spouses and children separated by national borders and oceans? Or during years of war with rising rates of women's wage and salary employment? Or following moralist reaction that celebrated imagined traditional values, and social movements that focused on issues of sexuality, birth control, homosexuality, and liberation? Historical change can also be measured by engagement with popular culture as Americans shifted their attention from vaudeville and pulp novels to radio, silent films, talkies, television, and finally the Internet and video games. The volumes in this series, divided by decades, trace all these changes.

To make sense of this complex and broadened field of inquiry, social historians often talk about how the categories by which we understand the past have been "invented," "contested," and "constructed." The nation has generally been divided along lines of race, class, gender, sexuality, and ethnicity. However, historians have also realized that analysts—whether in public or professional discourse—define these "categories of analysis" in different ways at different moments. Waves of immigration have reconfigured understandings of race and ethnicity, and more recent social movements have challenged the meanings of gender. Similarly, to be working class at the dawn of the age of industry in the 1900s meant something very different from being working class in the post-industrial landscape of the 1990s. How women or African Americans—to cite only two groups—understand their own identity can mean something different than how white men categorize them. Social historians, therefore, trace how Americans have always been divided about the direction of their lives and their nation, how they have consistently challenged and rethought social and cultural values and sought to renegotiate relationships of power, whether in the family, the workplace, the university, or the military. Actors do this armed with differing forms of power to authorize their view.

To examine these contestations, social historians have explored the way Americans articulated and defended numerous identities—as immigrants, citizens, workers, Christians, or feminists, for example. A post–World War II male chemical worker may have thought of himself as a worker and trade unionist at the factory, a veteran and a Democrat in his civic community, a husband and father at home, and as a white, middle-class homeowner. A female civil rights worker in the South in the 1960s may have seen herself as an African American when in the midst of a protest march or when refused service in a restaurant, as working class during a day job as a domestic worker or nurse, and as a woman when struggling to claim a leadership role in an activist organization.

Social historians have revisited older sources and mined rich new veins of information on the daily lives of ordinary people. Social historians engage with a host of materials—from government documents to census reports, from literature to oral histories, and from autobiographies to immigrant and foreign-language newspapers—to illuminate the lives, ideas, and activities of those who have been hidden from history. Social historians have also brought a broad "toolbox" of new methodologies to shed light on these sources. These methodologies are well represented in this series and illustrate the innovations of history from the bottom up. These volumes offer many tables and charts, which demonstrate the ways historians have made creative use of statistical analysis. Furthermore, the volumes are rich in illustrations as examples of the new ways that social historians "read" such images as cartoons or photographs.

The volumes in this series reflect the new subject matter, debates, and methodologies that have composed the writing of the United States' 20th-century social history. The volumes have unique features that make them particularly valuable for students and teachers; they are hybrids that combine the narrative advantages of the monograph with the specific focus of the encyclopedia. Each volume has been authored or co-authored by established social historians. Where the work has been collaborative, the authors have shared the writing and worked to sustain a narrative voice and conceptual flow in the volume. Authors have written the social history for the decade of their expertise and most have also taught its history. Each volume begins with a volume introduction by the author or authors that lays out the major themes of the decade and the big picture—how the social changes of the era transformed the lives of Americans. The author then synthesizes the best and most path-breaking new works in social history. In the case of the last three volumes, which cover the post-1970 era, scholarship remains in its relative infancy. In particular, these three volumes are major original efforts to both define the field and draw upon the considerable body of original research that has already been completed.

The ten volumes in the series divide the century by its decades. This is an avowedly neutral principle of organization that does not privilege economic, political, or cultural transformations; this allows readers to develop their own sense of a moment and their own sense of change. While it remains to be seen how the most recent decades will be taught and studied, in cases such as the 1920s, the 1930s, and the 1960s, this decadal organization replicates how historians frequently study and teach history. The Progressive Era (ca. 1890–1920) and postwar America (ca. 1945–1960) have less often been divided by decades. This highlights the neutrality of this division. In truth, all divisions are imposed: we speak of long decades or short centuries, and so forth. When historians teach the 1960s, they often reach back into the 1950s and ahead into the 1970s. The authors and editors of these volumes recognize that social processes, movements, ideas, and leaders do not rise and fall with the turn of the calendar; therefore, they have worked to knit the volumes together as a unit.

Readers can examine these texts individually or collectively. The texts can be used to provide information on significant events or individuals. They can provide an overview of a pivotal decade. At the same time, these texts are designed to allow readers to follow changing themes over time and to develop their own sense of chronology. The authors regularly spoke with one another and with the series editors to establish the major themes and subthemes in the social history of the century and to sustain story lines across the volumes. Each volume divides the material into six or seven chapters that discuss major themes such as labor or work; urban, suburban, and rural life; private life; politics; economy; culture; and social movements. Each chapter begins with an overview essay and then explores four to six major topics. The discrete essays at the heart of each volume give readers focus on a social movement, a social idea, a case study, a social institution, and so forth. Unlike traditional encyclopedias, however, the narrative coherence of the single-authored text permits authors to break the decade bubble with discussions on the background or effects of a social event.

There are several other features that distinguish this series.

- Many chapters include capsules on major debates in the social history of the era. Even as social historians strive to build on the best scholarship available, social history remains incomplete and contested; readers can benefit from studying this tension.

- The arguments in these volumes are supported by many tables and graphics. Social history has mobilized demographic evidence and—like its sister field, cultural history—has increasingly turned to visual evidence, both for the social history of media and culture and as evidence of social conditions. These materials are not presented simply as illustrations but as social evidence to be studied.

- Timelines at the head of every chapter highlight for readers all the major events and moments in the social history that follows.

- A series of biographical sketches at the end of every chapter highlights the lives of major figures more often overlooked in histories of the era. Readers can find ample biographical material on more prominent figures in other sources; here the authors have targeted lesser known but no less interesting and important subjects.

- Bibliographies include references to electronic sources and guide readers to material for further study.

- Three indices—one for each volume, one for the entire series, and one for all the people and events in the series—are provided in each volume. Readers can easily follow any of the major themes across the volumes.

Finally, we end with thanks for the supportive assistance of Ron Boehm and Kristin Gibson at ABC-CLIO, and especially to Dr. Alex Mikaberidze and Dr. Kim Kennedy White, who helped edit the manuscripts for the press. But of course, these volumes are the product of the extraordinary group of historians to whom we are particularly indebted:

The 1900s: Brian Greenberg and Linda S. Watts
The 1910s: Gordon Reavley
The 1920s: Linda S. Watts, Alice L. George, and Scott Beekman
The 1930s: Cecelia Bucki
The 1940s: Mark Ciabattari
The 1950s: John C. Stoner and Alice L. George
The 1960s: Troy D. Paino
The 1970s: Laurie Mercier
The 1980s: Peter C. Holloran and Andrew Hunt
The 1990s: Nancy Cohen

Daniel J. Walkowitz, Series Editor
Daniel E. Bender, Series Associate Editor

Volume Introduction

THE 1970S AND THE TRANSFORMATION OF AMERICA

The decade of the 1970s is remembered in many ways. In popular memory, it is a "forgettable" decade, characterized by insipid music, tasteless fashions, and political apathy overshadowed by the more remarkable 1960s and 1980s. A frequently quoted *Doonesbury* cartoon character seemed to have the last word at the end of the 1970s as he celebrated the passing of a "kidneystone of a decade." According to much retrospective popular culture, Americans spent a good deal of their time either longing for the 1960s or anxious about the future. The recently popular *That '70s Show,* which focuses on the antics and relationships of a teenager and his friends, mostly in the basement of his parents' suburban home, affirms the idea that nothing much happened in the "Me Decade." Although the show has helped revive interest in the period, especially in retro dress and music among young people, much of this recent attention, as a review of Web sites about the 1970s reveals, emphasizes the foolish fads of the decade, from pet rocks to platform shoes.

If many Americans have mocked or even romanticized the carefree 1970s, commentators past and present have mourned the selfishness and superficiality of the decade. After Tom Wolfe wrote about the "Me Decade" in 1976, and Christopher Lasch described "The Culture of Narcissism" in 1979, the media seized these labels to lament the purposeless and loss of community the decade embodied. Pundits saw a generation of hedonists and narcissists who abandoned visions of a more just society to pursue a self-indulgent culture. Although some descriptions of the excesses of sexual liberation, drug experimentation, and self-help may be accurate, most generalizations of the decade have exaggerated their extremity. As critic Gene Seymour asks, "When has *any* decade lacked narcissists, gratuitous excesses, or, even, malaise?" (Seymour 2004, 28).

As popular culture, the media, and commentators have collectively distorted the image of the 1970s, historians have been slow to size up this period that seems so paradoxical and less neatly pegged than the 1930s, 1950s, or other decades of the 20th century. Historians have not so much dismissed as avoided confronting its meaning. Scholarship about the 1970s is still in its embryonic stages, and there are surprisingly few written surveys or college courses about the decade.

For many scholars, the story of the 1970s is one of declension: the Kent State tragedy of 1970 ominously portended the end of youthful optimism for revolutionary change, confirmed by the 1980 presidential election of the retrograde Ronald Reagan. In *Decade of Nightmares*, Philip Jenkins reaffirms the view that growing fears and anxieties during the 1970s fed a conservative counterrevolution. Andreas Killen also argues in *1973 Nervous Breakdown* that by the end of that year, former ideals of the 1960s succumbed to a national malaise and the rise of a punitive conservative atmosphere. Many have remembered the 1970s with disappointment, their analyses colored by their own politics, hopes, and expectations. The 1960s promised radical transformation; the 1970s seemed to highlight the excesses and failures—drugs, violence, sexual promiscuity, a corrupt political system—all of which gave the conservative Right reasons to mobilize and challenge 1960s movements and principles.

Other historians have insisted that the 1970s were more significant to the 20th century—that "something" did happen. From Peter Carroll's 1982 book, *It Seemed Like Nothing Happened*, which argues that a search for alternatives permeated the decade of crises, to Edward Berkowitz's recent *Something Happened*, these scholars have called for a reconsideration of the "forgotten" decade. Elsebeth Hurup's 1996 edited collection, *The Lost Decade*, also focuses on the diversity and dynamism of the decade. Beth Bailey and David Farber call the 1970s "our strangest decade" and focus on the uncertainties generated by economic decline and an "age of limits" as expressed in popular culture. For conservative David Frum, *How We Got Here* acknowledges the pivotal and welcome role of the 1970s in redirecting subsequent decades away from the protest-filled and "statist" 1960s.

This volume, too, adds to the ongoing reassessment of the 1970s and its importance in shaping late-20th-century America. The key unsettling events of our times—U.S. integration into the global economy, growing disparities in incomes, the abuses of presidential power, record high oil prices, a plummeting dollar, an expensive and seemingly endless war, environmentalist warnings of a global ecological crisis—echo the grim headlines of the 1970s. Yet as this book reveals, the roots of the nation's economic decline and position in the world are not all that we learn from studying the period. Americans' determination to make a better society is reflected in the persistence of social movements to address the environment; sexual identity; and labor, civil, and women's rights. Along with the anxieties that economic decline and the loss of global pre-eminence produced emerged enormous creativity in African American arts and Hollywood film, for example. Large numbers of people asserted new confidence in staking a claim in American society, whether Latino politicians, major league ball players, single women, Native American activists, or public employees. The decade is also marked by experimentation in ways of living and in commercial and cultural production.

This is a social history that examines how Americans experienced and shaped the 1970s—how they made a living and voted; how they participated in their communities and national life; and what they thought, read, played, bought, and created. The book includes people who were popular and influential—such as Shirley Chisholm, Bruce Springsteen, and Phyllis Schlafly—but for the most part focuses on lesser-known individuals, groups, and events that represented major social trends and illustrate major themes of the era. Readers will be introduced to associations as diverse as Pittsburgh's Group against Smog and Pollution (GASP), the Mexican American Education Council of Houston, the Montana Equal Rights Amendment Ratification Council, and the South Boston antibusing group Restore Our Alienated Rights (ROAR), among many others.

As the editors of this series note, events are embedded in historical processes that rarely begin or end with the turn of the calendar, making the analysis of any one decade difficult. Historians even debate the beginning and ending dates of the "seventies" as a coherent era. Bruce Schulman's book, *The Seventies,* for example, begins in 1968 with radical upheavals and the election of Richard Nixon, and concludes with the end of Reagan's first term in 1984. Elsebeth Hurup divides the chronological seventies into two halves, with the first belonging to the sixties. Edward Berkowitz begins the decade in 1973, after the U.S. pullout from Vietnam. Some have left out the seventies altogether. Historians of the "sixties" refer to the "long decade" that runs to 1975; scholars of the "eighties" often begin their narrative in the late 1970s. Recognizing the fluidity of boundaries, this series nonetheless respects the organizational value of chronology; hence, this book focuses on the 10 years between 1970 and 1979.

Two central themes dominate the chapters in this volume: the perceptible shifts in values, attitudes, and ways of living that occurred during the 1970s, and the nation's vigorous social movements that organized to improve working and living conditions, expand opportunity, curb government abuse, and advance or resist social change. This book contests the popular assessment of the decade as the end of a radical era. The media generalized about a generation based on the visible actions of a few, like former radical Yippie-cum-Yuppie Jerry Rubin, who famously became a New York stockbroker in 1980. Yet social movements continued and flourished into the 1970s, permanently changing American life. Many Americans sought to realize some of the more abstract goals of the 1960s through experimental communities and cooperatives, community-based social movements, and government legislation and regulation. As sociologist Doug McAdam found in his study of the hundreds of mid-1960s Freedom Summer volunteers, the activists remained politically committed in the 1970s.

Movement historians have often analyzed this period as representing a retreat from multicoalition politics that sought civil rights or an end to war in order to pursue single-issue "identity" politics. The latter focused on individual identity and "difference" at the expense of sharing larger collective goals that often involved compromise. But viewed from another angle, what might appear as fragmentation can also be seen in the context of the 1970s as confidence and experimentation, where the explosion of new movements was part of the mix of identifying new struggles, frustration with state and corporate power that led to different strategies, and the liberating atmosphere that made all kinds of social change seem possible.

Many concluded that the assassination of Martin Luther King Jr. in 1968 ended the progression of the civil rights movement, but in the 1970s, struggles for civil rights moved in many directions. Many felt triumph with the first African American southerners elected to Congress, some southern school desegregation, the courts initiating busing as a way to alleviate segregation, and the launching of Equal Employment Opportunity Commission (EEOC) lawsuits to enforce nondiscriminatory hiring. By the early 1970s, black poverty had declined, and access to new degrees and jobs expanded the size of the African American middle class. The election of African American mayors in major cities represented another assertion of African American political strength. George Clinton expressed this hope for black America in his 1975 song "Chocolate City" that celebrated the growth of African American–dominated cities such as Washington, D.C: *We didn't get our forty acres and a mule, but we did get you CC. . . .*

But others had reason to be frustrated with the nation's slow progress toward equality. Significant desegregation had not occurred in casual areas of contact, workplaces, schools, or housing, and after the mid-decade recession, economic decline affected African Americans and other minorities disproportionately. Population growth and political power shifted from the Northeast to the Sunbelt, from the cities to the suburbs. A majority of African Americans, Latinos, and new immigrants lived in central cities in a much higher proportion than whites. Industrial and white flight from the central cities squeezed burdened infrastructures and, along with the bitter antibusing protests in Boston in 1974, signaled white resistance to the ideals of racial justice.

In the face of this resistance, African Americans adopted new forms of protest that embraced cultural pride. In abandoning an integrationist ideal, they adopted diaspora-influenced fashions and hairstyles, and strengthened the arts, literature, and music, making the 1970s the "black decade" in cultural production. African American theater groups, film, and university Afro-American studies also flourished.

Other Americans were emboldened by African American assertions of political and cultural autonomy in the 1970s. Native Americans demanded greater tribal sovereignty, revitalized traditional practices, and expanded the American Indian Movement to demand from the federal and tribal governments services, cultural facilities, and control over tribal resources. Recognizing their rising demographic clout as the nation's fastest-growing ethnic group, Latinos and Chicanos mobilized around "brown power" to demand land reparations, agricultural workers' rights, improved education, and political representation. Asian Americans also created pan-Asian political alliances and cultural journals, and Japanese Americans pressed for redress for the 120,000 Japanese immigrants and their American-born children who were interned during World War II.

A host of other social movements gathered momentum in the 1970s, drawing attention to the needs of the disabled, senior citizens, and consumers. In asserting their rights to access, respect, and safety, these groups initiated legislative changes and dramatically changed public attitudes.

At the end of the 1970s, the country also had a profoundly different attitude toward the physical environment due to the work of citizens who drew attention to the reality of finite natural resources, disappearing wildlife, the impacts of industrial and auto pollution, and the disproportionate impacts of toxins on the working class and poor. The first Earth Day celebration in 1970, which involved 20 million people, led to an upsurge in environmental activism. Americans questioned the safety of and halted the construction of nuclear plants, passed legislation to improve the quality of air and water, and demanded inspections of hazardous workplaces. Environmentalism also resulted in changes in daily habits and practices in the 1970s, such as purchasing organic foods and recycling.

Social struggles, the counterculture, and economic decline converged in the 1970s labor and poor people's movements. In the early 1970s, many thousands of young working-class veterans protested the war; their defiance while wearing military fatigues and throwing away war medals made it difficult to claim that draft-dodging, privileged hippies dominated the antiwar movement. Youthful working-class militance was again expressed in GM's Lordstown, Ohio, plant and in the blue-collar suburb of Levittown, Pennsylvania. Unionized workers reacted against new employer offenses and their slipping standard of living through an unprecedented number of strikes. Unions also organized new African American, Latino, women, and public-service workers and formed new alliances with environmental groups and others. The working poor and welfare mothers also organized in the 1970s against rising poverty and job insecurity, forming Arkansas Community Organizations for Reform Now (ACORN) and expanding the National Welfare Rights Organization.

The movement most associated with 1970s social change affected half the nation's population. Feminists identified gender inequalities in American society and sought to transform politics, culture, and the sexes. Many feminists who joined groups such as the National Organization for Women (NOW) stressed the need for equal rights in American society and believed this could be achieved through legislation and the courts. Economic changes went hand-in-hand with a rising feminist consciousness: by the 1970s, a majority of women worked outside the home, and women union members pushed to end discrimination in the workplace and campaigned for comparable worth. Younger women's liberationists believed that equality could only occur once private lives were transformed, and focused energies on consciousness-raising, challenging family roles, respecting sexual identities and difference, and creating institutions that directly addressed women's concerns such as reproductive rights, health and child care, and racial justice. Cultural feminists built such women-only institutions as bookstores, retreat centers, and battered women's shelters.

At the end of the decade, one could see pronounced and radical changes in women's lives. Reflecting their independent status, many women preferred to remain single longer, often kept their maiden names upon marriage, and "Ms." rather than "Miss" or "Mrs." became the standard form of address. More women moved into political office, new laws prohibited sex discrimination, Title IX forced schools to devote resources to girls' and women's sports, and rape statutes were revised to improve prosecution. Contraceptives, the women's health movement, and changing attitudes toward marriage and divorce gave millions of American women the freedom to choose when and if to mother, and their increasing participation in college and the workforce put them in public roles even if they did not overtly embrace the feminist revolution that surrounded them.

If feminists inspired the maxim "the personal is political," many Americans during the 1970s turned toward new ways of living, believing that they could not change society until they changed themselves. They experimented with creating their own self-sufficient urban and rural communes, alternative institutions, and spiritual and health centers. New religious sects, the New Age movement, experimental therapies, and self-help groups flourished.

Others sought personal liberation through new sexual and fashion mores or gender identities. In an era before AIDS, sex had few consequences, and sexual experimentation reached new heights and acceptance. The gay rights and feminist movements transformed gender ideals and assumptions. New definitions of masculinity and fatherhood were symbolized by the popularity of Robert Bly's men's groups and the film *Kramer vs. Kramer.*

This experimental atmosphere, which broke down social and cultural boundaries, extended into American popular culture. Although the 1970s have often been dismissed as the synthetic "polyester age," the decade produced important, influential new music, film, television, and literature. The era's social movements and the lifting of censorship restrictions pushed these art forms to consider critical social issues and explore formerly taboo subjects. Even the world of professional sports took a dramatic turn in the 1970s, with athletes asserting themselves in labor actions and embracing the racial and countercultural politics of the times. Leisure pastimes and popular culture teetered between the impulses of experimentation and independence and the pressures of increasing commercialization, blockbusters, and narrowing distribution.

Technological innovations in the 1970s excited imaginations and offered hope for improving lives. Apollo landings on the moon and robotic explorations of planets vastly increased knowledge of space even as NASA funding declined. New electronics, from calculators to personal computers, made easier information gathering and processing, and other consumer products, from CB radios to VCRs, provided new leisure-time pleasures. The alternative technology movement initiated more efficient and self-sufficient practices, such as solar and wind energy use, that promised to rescue an endangered planet.

The tremendous vitality and creativity behind these innovations, expressions, and movements nervously contended with the decade's dramatic political and economic changes. The resignation of a president and the end of the Vietnam War, which left millions dead, a country devastated, and the United States reeling from the economic consequences—all without achieving the U.S. war aims of a noncommunist state—marked a watershed in how the country viewed its place in the world. The oil crisis and an economic recession whacked communities that had only recently gained access to the American Dream.

Three presidential administrations of the 1970s struggled with righting the sinking American economy, and their policies, along with new grassroots conservative movements, stymied efforts of workers, women, African Americans, and others to narrow the gaps between rich and poor. Workers and their advocates faced difficult obstacles, including stagflation, deindustrialization, rising oil prices, and rising employer strength. Congressional supporters passed the Humphrey Hawkins Full Employment Act, but it lacked enforcement teeth. Declining industrial jobs hurt workers as well as their unions, reducing the political clout they had enjoyed since the 1930s.

Many had turned to the federal government to help alleviate poverty through wealth redistribution in jobs and welfare programs, end sex and race discrimination through enforcement of civil rights laws, and improve the environment through regulation. Although President Nixon expanded some federal activities, created new regulatory agencies such as OSHA and EPA, and even proposed a guaranteed income floor, he pioneered "devolution"—moving power from the federal government to the states—to undermine New Deal liberalism and reduce dependence on government programs.

Although Nixon was driven from office in 1974 for illegal activities, the impeachment proceedings, which demonstrated that government "worked," had the ironic effect of discrediting government and strengthening conservative forces that supported Nixon's privatization efforts. Despite the Watergate crisis, Democrats were unable to revive the liberal New Deal/Great Society coalition and the idea that government could serve the people. The 1976 election of President Jimmy Carter symbolized a new political and social trend, representing the power of the New South, religious evangelicals, and an approach to government that shared little with the old liberal consensus. Carter called for a balanced budget, deregulation of industry, and a moratorium on social spending.

Believing that 1960s and 1970s social change had led to government overreach, new movements organized to reduce taxes, end busing, and overturn affirmative action. In 1978, tax rebels led a successful fight in California that enacted Proposition 13, thus reducing state services. That same year, in *Regents of the University of California v Bakke*, the Supreme Court ruled against quotas in university admissions policies. The case symbolized a rising white backlash and belief, amid growing economic competition, that African Americans and other minorities were gaining unfair advantages.

Other groups emerged to limit gay rights, restore the traditional patriarchal family and gender roles, and end abortions. As mainstream moderate religious denominations declined across the United States, conservative evangelical churches rose in popularity. Evangelical preachers tapped into the possibilities of cable television to launch Christian programs that reached many millions, and Jerry Falwell's group, the Moral Majority, and others organized evangelical Christians into a powerful new political force. The election of openly religious Jimmy Carter in 1976 paved the way for the closer integration of religion and politics in American life, with a decidedly conservative bent.

These new conservative movements made impressive advances by the late 1970s. In 1972, Congress and a majority of states enthusiastically endorsed the Equal Rights Amendment. By the end of the decade, the anti-ERA movement led by conservative activist Phyllis Schlafly successfully linked an expansive government to an antifamily agenda, and the amendment failed to attain ratification in the necessary final states. Abortion in particular galvanized religious groups and others to roll back the 1973 Supreme Court's *Roe v. Wade* decision. The National Right to Life Coalition fought to restrict women's access to abortions at the state level. By 1977, the antiabortion movement successfully lobbied Congress to pass the Hyde amendment to disallow federal funding of abortions except in the case of extreme danger to a woman's life.

Media activists strengthened community access to public airwaves on television and radio, but their diverse voices and perspectives were drowned out by a more powerful commercial media that continued to shape Americans' understanding of society and the world. Latent nationalism, tamped down after the U.S. loss in Vietnam and the exposure of CIA abuses around the world, emerged again at the end of the decade as gas shortages imperiled Americans' favorite symbol of freedom: the automobile. Television programming repeated the theme "America Held Hostage" with Iranian students shockingly burning effigies of Uncle Sam and the American flag. Media highlights of youthful excesses, prison riots, urban discontent, the agitation of gays and other minorities contributed to a general unease.

If conservative social movements built significant media, financial, organizational, and political muscles through the 1970s, liberal and left movements suffered from their own success and bureaucratization. For example, once mobilizing millions, by the end of the decade, many environmental groups focused on attaining environmental legislation and defending regulation in the courts, rather than sustaining the earlier activism of constituents. The success of these movements, too, inspired conservatives who learned from their creativity and persistence.

At the end of the 1970s, America was a changed place. Americans lived and thought differently. Two impulses competed for the nation's ideological identity. One looked to improve American society through expanding rights to disenfranchised citizens, improving the environment, and radically changing America's culture; the other sought to shrink government, face off perceived enemies, embrace the market to meet the country's declining economic hegemony, and resist social changes that threatened family roles and conservative Christian traditions. It is not surprising that the nation approached its Bicentennial in 1976 with some indifference. In accentuating the contradictions, divisions, and optimism embedded in American life, the 1970s illustrate perhaps better than other decades how these paradoxical tendencies coexist, conflict, and coalesce to explain our own more recent times.

ACKNOWLEDGMENTS

Many people helped with the production of this book. Robert Schimelpfenig and John Hryciuk provided essential research assistance and in our many lively discussions sustained my intellectual interest in the 1970s over the past four years. I am deeply indebted to them for their contributions and support. Josh Ashenmiller also stepped in to provide a critical chapter on politics for this volume. The extraordinary librarians at Washington State University Vancouver (WSUV) accommodated my every request. I am particularly grateful to colleagues Linda Fredericksen and Pavithra Narayanan for sharing resources about the period. WSUV also provided a mini-grant to help with research costs. Many in my extended family remembered the 1970s and shared my interest in the period; others, especially Adam Larue Hryciuk, patiently endured and supported another book project. The editors and production crew of ABC-CLIO are to be commended for organizing and directing this large collaborative project on the 20th century social history of the United States. Finally, this book depends on the work of many scholars, whose books, articles, and electronic publications are mentioned in the References section following each chapter.

REFERENCES AND FURTHER READING

Bailey, Beth, and David Farber, eds. 2004. *America in the Seventies.* Lawrence: University Press of Kansas.

Berkowitz, Edward D. 2006. *Something Happened: A Political and Cultural Overview of the Seventies.* New York: Columbia University Press.

Carroll, Peter N. 1990. *It Seemed Like Nothing Happened: America in the 1970s.* New Brunswick, N.J.: Rutgers University Press.

Frum, David. 2000. *How We Got Here: The 70s: The Decade That Brought You Modern Life (For Better or Worse).* New York: Basic Books.

Hurup, Elsebeth, ed. 1996. *The Lost Decade: America in the Seventies.* Aarhus, Denmark: Aarhus University Press.

Jenkins, Philip. 2006. *Decade of Nightmares: The End of the Sixties and the Making of Eighties America.* New York: Oxford University Press.

Killen, Andreas. 2006. *1973 Nervous Breakdown: Watergate, Warhol, and the Birth of Post-sixties America.* New York: Bloomsbury.McAdam, Doug. 1988. *Freedom Summer.* New York: Oxford University Press.

Schulman, Bruce J. 2001. *The Seventies: The Great Shift in American Culture, Society, and Politics.* New York: Free Press.

Seymour, Gene. 2004. "The Black Decade: Why the 1970s Were a Turning Point in African-American—and all American—Culture." *American Legacy* 10 (3): 28–36.

Issues of the 20th Century

The Legacy of the 1960s: 1970s Activism

OVERVIEW

The momentum for social change in the 1960s continued into the next decade. In fact, what is generally called "the sixties," a period of remarkable activism, extended through the 1970s. Americans worked to end the Vietnam War, expand civil rights to all, and protect consumers and the environment. Although the social movements of the 1970s were large, like other movements in American history, they involved a minority of citizens; yet they had a lasting impact on the nation's political, social, and cultural landscape.

Many scholars refer to the "sixties" as ending in 1975, when two important developments affected movements for change: the fall of Saigon ended the Vietnam War, which had linked many diverse social movements in protest, and a revolution or a collapse of the American system did not occur, as many radicals had anticipated. The "seventies" then begin mid-decade, when many goals of social movements became institutionalized, activists either retired from public life or began working in electoral politics to bring about change, and a new conservative era was launched.

But as the examples in this chapter demonstrate, instead of ending, American social movements in the 1970s took new forms. The New Left of the late 1960s brought together a variety of constituencies that sought fundamental political and social change in the United States. But different interests and goals of antiwar activists, lesbians, African Americans, feminists, and others invariably led to splits and the formation of new movements, many of which gained maturity

1

and strength in the 1970s. The demise of Students for a Democratic Society (SDS), which had been the leading student organization of the 1960s, over sectarian arguments did not mean that student mobilizations fell apart. On the contrary, the early 1970s witnessed some of the largest demonstrations in U.S. history, including the antiwar Mobilization and Earth Day events. Women critical of the sexism they experienced in the civil rights and New Left movements produced the dynamic feminist movement of the 1970s; lesbians critical of both gay rights and feminist movements created their own counterculture; activists in the antiwar and civil rights movements inspired and participated in new environmental and low-income movements.

Young people were often at the forefront of movements for change in the 1970s as they were in the 1960s. The expansion of diverse college student bodies including more women and students of color affected the size and nature of student protests in the 1970s. Some were motivated by recognitions of historic and persistent discrimination against them or the examples of Third World movements. Although the seeds of brown power, gay rights, environmentalism, and other social movements were planted decades earlier, the vitality of so many movements in the 1970s can be attributed to the large numbers of young people who had more leisure time to participate in the cultural revolution that they created. In 1971, the passage of the 26th Amendment to the Constitution lowered the voting age to 18, significantly increasing young peoples' potential political power.

Antiwar protests continued to occupy college campuses until the end of U.S. involvement in Vietnam in 1975. John Paul Filo's famous 1970 photo of a college girl crying out next to the dead body of a Kent State University student shot by the Ohio National Guard symbolizes the "end" of the 1960s and youthful optimism and the continued execution of a bloody war that millions had protested for half a decade. Students were enraged at the expansion of the war into Cambodia and the Kent State killings, and the 1970–1971 school year saw half of the nation's campuses engaged in, and periodically shut down from, significant protests. But with President Nixon's "Vietnamization," or gradual withdrawal of U.S. troops and reliance on the South Vietnamese army, and with the decline of draft calls of young men, students felt less compelled to protest the war.

Even by the early 1970s, student antiwar movements were combining issues by calling for larger reforms of American society and universities, such as ending racism and economic inequality. By the late 1970s, student movements were preoccupied with numerous global and local issues, including campaigns to rein in the CIA, halt nuclear proliferation, support civil rights and ethnic and women's studies curricula on campus, and oppose tuition hikes.

Through the influence of the African American civil rights and black power movements, many Americans realized they had not been granted equal status because of their ethnicity, identity, or abilities, and they organized to demand change or explore their own cultural history. Michael Novak called the 1970s the "decade of the Ethnics," when, influenced by minority assertions of rights,

Catholic white ethnics also realized they did not need to submit to a dominant WASP (White Anglo-Saxon Protestant) culture. But much of this white Euro-American ethnic identity emerged as a backlash against other civil rights movements and ignored the historic patterns of discrimination based on race and the privilege of whiteness.

By the late 1970s, the intensity of democratic social movements began to diminish. Historians have pointed to the depressed economy, an increasingly powerful conservative backlash, and the necessity for many low-income and minority peoples to focus on survival rather than expanding democratic rights as major factors influencing this decline. Movements struggled with whether to organize locally or nationally, finding funding, and tensions over which strategies and issues should take precedence.

After a decade of struggle, too, young people had become frustrated, disillusioned, and alienated from American institutions. Terry Anderson has noted that optimistic baby boomers at the beginning of the decade had graduated "into a sea of frustration." Believing that their elders failed to embrace democracy and reform a corrupt, hypocritical system, many young people dropped out and formed new alternative societies and enterprises separated from mainstream America. They talked less of politics and more of cultural revolution.

It was this cultural revolution that made its mark on the 1970s. At the outset of the decade, many believed the "Woodstock Nation" would create a new country. Charles Reich wrote in *The Greening of America* (1970) that a revolution was brewing, but that it would "originate with the individual and with culture," not with the political structure. He saw the nation's youth rejecting the corporate state and its "metal and plastic" world and embracing a new consciousness that would create a better world, "a veritable greening of America." Young people created thousands of "counterinstitutions" such as day care and food cooperatives, free schools and health clinics, and urban and rural communes. They created new communities and culture in rock festivals, street and mural art, and alternative businesses.

These ideas and experiments in new ways of living also translated into new forms of social activism. It was the cultural impulses of the New Left that persisted in the 1970s, Barbara Epstein argues, that revived attention to nonviolence as a method of achieving social change. As the more militant wing of the antiwar movement declined by the early 1970s, nonviolent direct action gained more preeminence as a strategy. Many movements of the period sought not only workplace justice and an end to war, discrimination, nuclear power, and pollution but also to completely change the way society and lives were organized. The direct action movements that evolved in the late 1970s included a new sense of egalitarianism, moved away from a focus on the state, and believed in a cultural revolution that would transform the nation's politics (Epstein 1991).

Many have viewed the decade of the 1970s through the lens of the late-20th and early 21st centuries and have emphasized pessimistic and conservative tendencies. But in reviewing the enormous quantity and vitality of local movements for change, it is apparent that optimism also characterizes the decade. The legacy of 1960s activism is clear: many Americans believed that change was possible, that it was one's civic duty to improve American society and carve out new possibilities for a better life. Radicals and others working for social change did not believe that ills in society, whether war, racism, or other injustice, were inevitable outcomes. Rather, they still optimistically assumed that suffering and inequality could be overcome through different social and political arrangements. Activists in the 1970s recognized that revolution was not likely to occur soon in the United States but that basic incremental social change was attainable and possible, and they set their sights on local issues that had larger national implications. Movements for gay and sexual liberation had not yet faced the AIDS crisis or yet lost a number of leaders to that devastating disease. Feminist and environmental movements flourished in the 1970s, transforming ideas about gender roles and the limitations of modern development and winning significant legislative and judicial gains.

The intensity and media coverage of social movements may have waned by the mid-1970s, but the United States had clearly changed from activists' determination to end the war, clean up the environment, and obtain respect as women, gays, or ethnic/racial minorities. Young people had recognized that the mainstream press reflected the values of the establishment they were seeking to change, and created hundreds of alternative or underground newspapers that by 1970 reached over 5 million. They established noncommercial, listener-sponsored FM radio stations. They also communicated through thousands of posters, leaflets, tracts, and protests, which foreshadowed the alternative media movement of the 21st century.

Government repression, including counterintelligence activities, and a conservative backlash may have thwarted 1970s social movements, but many of the struggles resulted in legislative gains and the mainstreaming of issues that had formerly appeared radical. Dissent continued to flourish, and many Americans sustained a passion to imagine and implement social change.

TIMELINE

1970   The Native American Rights Fund is founded.

The Gray Panthers is founded.

The first Gay Pride March, Christopher Street, Greenwich Village, takes place.

Millions participate in the first Earth Day events in thousands of locations.

The American Indian Movement (AIM) holds a sit-in at the Bureau of Indian Affairs (BIA) office in Washington, D.C.

President Nixon creates the Environmental Protection Agency (EPA), which consolidates federal environmental activities.

Congress passes the Clean Air Act.

President Nixon creates the Occupational Safety and Health Administration (OSHA).

Moratorium and Mobilization antiwar protests take place on tax day, April 15.

The shootings of four students by Ohio National Guardsmen at Kent State and two students by police at Jackson State in Mississippi trigger riots and protests at college campuses across the country.

A federal court orders the Internal Revenue Service (IRS) to tax segregated schools in Mississippi.

The U.S. Senate extends the Voting Rights Act of 1965 by banning literacy tests.

The first gay couple attempts to wed legally in Minneapolis.

The Rolling Quads form the Disabled Students' Program on the University of California, Berkeley, campus.

1971   The U.S. Supreme Court rules desegregation is constitutional.

The 26th Amendment to Constitution grants 18-year-olds the right to vote.

The U.S. Supreme Court says employers cannot use job tests that discriminate against African Americans if those tests are not related to the work.

The U.S. Supreme Court in *Swann v. Charlotte-Mecklenburg Board of Education* approves the use of extensive busing to promote school desegregation.

The Natural Resources Defense Council and the Sierra Club Legal Defense Fund are established.

The last big mobilizations against the Vietnam War and the largest civil disobedience protest in U.S. history are held in April and May in Washington, D.C.

1972   Congress passes the Indian Self-Determination and Education Act.

The Strategic Arms Limitation Talk (SALT) treaty is signed.

The EPA bans DDT.

Congress passes the Federal Water Pollution Control Act Amendments (amended as Clean Water Act in 1977).

The Equal Employment Opportunity Act of l972 provides Commission with litigation authority to enforce the Civil Rights Act of 1964; two executive orders require contractors and institutions receiving federal funds to develop affirmative action programs.

The Supplemental Security Income (SSI) program is enacted to ensure minimum income for elderly and disabled poor.

1973

The 71-day AIM occupation of Wounded Knee, South Dakota, protests violations to American Indian treaties over the past centuries.

The American Psychiatric Association drops the old listing of homosexuality as a mental disorder and urges abolition of legal inequalities.

The Endangered Species Act (ESA) is passed.

The National Gay and Lesbian Task Force forms in New York City.

The Heritage Foundation is established to formulate and promote conservative public policies.

Congress passes the Rehabilitation Act, the first national civil rights legislation for the disabled.

1974

Congress passes the Age Discrimination Act.

Beverly Johnson is the first African American model to appear on the cover of a major fashion magazine, *Vogue*.

Congress abolishes the Atomic Energy Commission and establishes the Nuclear Regulatory Agency.

Susan Sygall and Deborah Kaplan form the Disabled Women's Coalition at the University of California, Berkeley.

1975

Congress passes the Resource Conservation and Recovery Act.

The Federal Civil Service Commission announces that homosexual identity cannot bar a person from federal employment.

South Vietnam surrenders to North Vietnam. The United States reneges on its pledge to pay Vietnam $3 billion in war reparations and instead imposes an economic embargo.

The Energy Policy and Conservation Act of 1975 sets importation quotas on petroleum.

1976   The parents of Karen Ann Quinlan win court fight to remove the life support equipment that keeps their comatose daughter alive.

1977   Red Dye No. 2, found to cause cancer, is banned.

President Jimmy Carter officially pardons all those who avoided the draft during the Vietnam War.

1978   Dan White, a former police officer, kills Mayor George Moscone and gay supervisor Harvey Milk in San Francisco.

A Tennessee citizens' group temporarily halts the construction of a Tennessee Valley Authority (TVA) dam under ESA to protect the endangered snail darter fish.

The Supreme Court rules in the *University of California Regents v. Bakke* decision that colleges and universities can consider race as a factor in admissions policies but may not impose quotas.

Unita Blackwell, founding member of the Mississippi Freedom Democratic Party, becomes the first African American woman mayor in the history of Mississippi in Mayersville, a city in which she had once been denied the right to vote.

The Gay Rights National Lobby forms.

The Age Discrimination in Employment Act prohibits mandatory retirement in most occupations.

1979   The first national March on Washington for Lesbian and Gay Rights is held.

The Supreme Court upholds voluntary affirmative action plans by private employers.

The EPA bans PCB production.

SOCIAL MOVEMENTS PERSIST

Antiwar Movement

By 1970, there were literally thousands of local, regional, and national groups organized to protest and end the Vietnam War. But the antiwar movement had

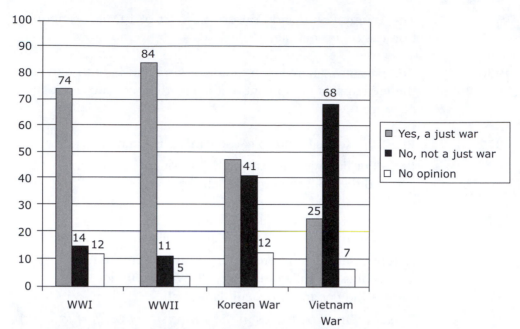

Figure 1.1 *1990 Gallup Survey of Americans' Perceptions of Past Conflicts.* Source: The Gallup Poll Monthly, *May 1990.*

become more fragmented, and it lost the momentum that had been building in the late 1960s. Students for a Democratic Society (SDS), which had been at the forefront of antiwar organizing in the 1960s, had dissolved as a national movement by the 1970s. The two major peace coalitions, the Moratorium and the Mobilization, held large demonstrations across the country on tax day in April 1970, but the Moratorium committee soon disbanded because it was unable to control radicals who repeatedly disrupted demonstrations.

In 1970, President Nixon, pressured by the antiwar movement and seeking to weaken it, stepped up surveillance and harassment of antiwar groups, instituted the nondiscriminatory lottery system for the draft, and began withdrawing troops under "Vietnamization." But on April 30 when Nixon announced the invasion of Cambodia, ostensibly to weaken North Vietnam, his actions symbolized an expansion rather than reduction in the war and reignited the antiwar movement.

As campuses exploded at the news of Nixon's bombing of Cambodia, on May 1, Kent State students gathered to protest. After several hundred students smashed windows in downtown Kent, the mayor declared a state of civil emergency and called in the Ohio National Guard. Students were pushed back to the campus, and on May 2, what began as a peaceful rally turned into a riot, with some students burning the ROTC building. The National Guard, already tense from previous weeks in confrontation with striking Teamsters, occupied the campus and were hostile to students who tried to talk to them about the war. Nonetheless, student activists decided to proceed with holding their May 4 rally. Several thousand students gathered at the Commons while another 10,000 watched. The Guardsmen, claiming they had been hit by rocks, fired tear gas and tried to disperse the crowd. Some students lobbed tear gas canisters back at the Guard, who regrouped, marched up a hill away from the students, turned, and fired 61 rounds into the crowd. Four students were killed and nine wounded. Hysterical, students dropped to the ground; the Guard commander ordered them to leave or be fired on, and students slowly dispersed.

College campuses erupted immediately at the news of the killings. Students and police clashed even at traditionally nonactive campuses, and more than 30 ROTC buildings were burned or bombed. More than four million students at more than 1,300 colleges participated in demonstrations. Protests and strikes led to 500 campuses closing, many for the rest of the semester. Sixteen governors called out their states' national guard units to halt rioting at universities.

Even before the Kent State killings, many campuses were at war. In February 1970, Michigan State University Weathermen led a group to East Lansing City Hall to protest the convictions of the Chicago Seven and began smashing windows. Police attacked both protestors and bystanders and arrested several hundred students. Students and police clashed later that month at SUNY-Buffalo, and the riots resulted in 125 students, faculty, and police hospitalized, and a bitter faculty senate voted to abolish the campus ROTC. Even at relatively quiet campuses like Penn State, antiwar protestors, divided by radical and pacifist factions, met violence from state troopers and police called out by the university president.

Students angry with university administrators, communities, and state governments for employing outside police forces to the university generated additional spontaneous protests at U.S. campuses. Many believed that the U.S. government had deliberately brought the war home. The expansion of student bodies at state universities was ironically tied to military research contracts and the revenue they generated. Students, faculty, and clergy increasingly protested university research related to what they believed an unjust war. However, school administrators, communities, and states that oversaw state university activities believed that such protests were communist-inspired and were therefore less reluctant than their private-school counterparts to enlist the aid of police and state guard troops to halt such dissent.

Ten days after the Kent State shootings, police at Jackson State College in Mississippi opened fire, killing 2 African American men and wounding 12. Media coverage of Kent State overshadowed the killings at Jackson State, a historically African American college, underscoring for many the racist undertones of the media's coverage of student protests and police violence. Disillusioned by the general public silence following the killings at Jackson State, 15 African American college presidents met with President Nixon in the White House to describe the

Poster announcing a strike and march to commemorate the shooting of antiwar and antiracism protesters at Kent State University, the city of Augusta, Georgia, and Jackson State University, May 5, 1970. (Library of Congress)

anger and outrage felt by African Americans at this injustice. But a white grand jury investigating the killings in Mississippi absolved the officers who shot the students and warned students to expect similar responses to their protests.

Despite the tragedies, many Americans reacted more negatively to student protestors than to the guardsmen and state troopers who had killed students. On May 8, several hundred construction workers, prodded by police, attacked peaceful antiwar demonstrators in lower Manhattan. Although many working-class antiwar veterans were participating in the demonstration, the heavily publicized incident affirmed for many Americans that hard-working blue-collar workers supported the president's war and hated the pampered, countercultural war protestors. Nonetheless, the outrage surrounding the college shootings and the invasion of Cambodia led a number of aides in the National Security Council and foreign service officers to resign, and the Senate passed amendments to try to cut off funds for the war if American troops were not withdrawn from Cambodia. President Nixon was forced to address what happened and appointed former Pennsylvania governor William Scranton to lead a commission to investigate the killings. The commission concluded that despite student disruption, the Guard's use of lethal weapons against the Kent State students was completely "unnecessary, unwarranted, and inexcusable," and the incident at Jackson State "an unreasonable, unjustified overreaction."

The Cambodia invasion triggered other protests across the country, and the New Mobe, what remained of the national network of antiwar groups, called for a protest in Washington, D.C., on the weekend of May 9. With such short notice in the days before the Internet, it was astonishing that at least 100,000 demonstrators appeared. Hundreds of federal employees joined the protest, and Peace Corps volunteers took over several offices in their building. Tens of thousands more rallied in dozens of other cities to protest both the escalation of the war and the Kent State shootings.

In the early 1970s, Vietnam veterans infused new energy into the antiwar movement, which had become divided and frustrated by the lack of impact in altering the course of U.S. policies in Southeast Asia. No longer could antiwar activists be painted as antimilitary when so many GIs were among their ranks, who because of their veteran status, enjoyed some protection from police harassment.

Undoubtedly, the veterans' protests emboldened others who had opposed the war but had remained silent. On April 24, 1971, nearly 1,000 active-duty GIs lead 500,000 antiwar demonstrators through the streets of Washington, D.C., and 250,000 in San Francisco to demand "total and immediate withdrawal from Indochina." Billed as the largest protest in American history, almost one-third of the participants were attending their first antiwar rally. By that summer, a large majority of Americans opposed the Vietnam War and 61 percent favored a pullout, even if South Vietnam fell.

GI activism reshaped the military, too. Several hundred underground newspapers appeared on bases and on the front, and soldiers adopted the dress and drugs of the counterculture, many sporting antiwar buttons and slogans on their uniforms. Hollywood stars Jane Fonda and Donald Sutherland attracted GIs to their Free the Army (FTA) visits to West Coast base-area coffeehouses. Nixon's plans of gradual withdrawal may have hindered the domestic antiwar movement's

Vietnam veterans outside the 1972 Republican convention protest Richard Nixon's reelection campaign. (JP Laffont/Sygma/Corbis)

push for immediate withdrawal, but it accelerated discipline and morale problems in the military. Desertions and dishonorable discharges increased dramatically by 1971.

In addition to increasing soldier and veteran protests, more influential opinion shapers spoke out against the war. In spring 1971, *The New York Times* Vietnam correspondent Neil Sheehan called for a war crimes investigation of the Nixon administration, and 400 college student presidents and editors called for the president to end the war. In June 1971, *The New York Times* published excerpts from the "Pentagon Papers," a history of the prosecution of the war prior to Nixon's term, copied by former hawk turned dove Daniel Ellsberg. At the end of the month, the Senate passed a nonbinding resolution calling for the termination of all military operations at the "earliest practicable date." A number of cities and towns passed resolutions calling for withdrawal of troops from Vietnam. Celebrities and other public figures also denounced the war. For example, Kathy Huppe gave up her title as Miss Montana to call for an end to the war.

Just as widespread antiwar sentiment increased throughout the country, the antiwar movement was plagued by disorganization, burnout, ideological divisions, and government surveillance and infiltration. During the week of May 3, 1971, the People's Coalition for Peace and Justice, led by Rennie Davis, planned to shut down Washington and the war machine bureaucracy by blocking bridges and streets into the city. But intelligence agencies had easily infiltrated the diffuse group, and the Nixon administration acted to preempt any major disruptive civil disobedience, even if ignoring the Constitution, by arresting and holding in makeshift detention centers more than 7,000 protestors and bystanders. Protestors managed to block many streets but not shut down the nation's capital.

In addition to the stepped-up surveillance and harassment by the Nixon administration, the lack of media attention on the large antiwar movement weakened its ability to educate and attract other Americans to its cause. By 1971, demonstrations had become so common that unless something dramatic happened, the news media did not report them. The media reported any sensational encounters or violence, but since antiwar groups tried to limit any violent activities, their daily actions went unreported. On the other hand, although it had received a lot of media attention for its violent activities, the revolutionary group Weatherman counted only a few hundred active members, blurring the public's distinction between radical bomb-makers and the scores of more peaceful protestors who dominated the antiwar movement.

Protests continued monthly through 1971, but numbers of participants began to fall, and membership in peace organizations, except for Vietnam Veterans Against the War (VVAW), also fell. The antiwar movement was not active in all parts of the country, especially in the South and in rural areas where a conservative backlash was more potent.

In early 1972, Nixon stepped up the air war against North Vietnam, and antiwar groups focused on the antibombing campaign, organizing demonstrations across the country. Although antiwar activism dropped after the 1973 U.S. pull-out from Vietnam, the peace movement remained involved in raising humanitarian aid for South Vietnamese and in pursuing amnesty for draft evaders.

Vietnam Veterans Against the War

Vietnam Veterans Against the War (VVAW) began as a small group of former servicemen in New York City who protested in the giant April 1967 Spring Mobilization. They formed as a separate group from Veterans for Peace, which included World War II and Korean War veterans. The invasion of Cambodia and shootings at Kent State and Jackson State mobilized thousands of veterans to join the fledgling organization. In the early 1970s, VVAW had over 40,000 members throughout the United States as well as active-duty GIs stationed in Vietnam.

Antiwar veterans engaged in many dramatic actions. During the Labor Day weekend of 1970, 150 veterans marched in Operation RAW (Rapid American Withdrawal) from Morristown, New Jersey, to Valley Forge State Park, Pennsylvania, and engaged in mock search-and-destroy missions. In January 1971, VVAW sponsored the Winter Soldier Investigation in Detroit, where more than 100 soldiers testified about war crimes produced by American war policies in Southeast Asia. After *Playboy* magazine editor Hugh Hefner donated advertising space for a VVAW ad in February 1971, thousands more veterans joined the organization.

In one of the most dramatic protests, Operation Dewey Canyon III, named for a military invasion of Laos by U.S. and South Vietnamese forces, VVAW led protestors in April 1971 on "a limited incursion into the country of Congress." The week of events attracted media publicity and featured Gold Star Mothers (mothers of soldiers killed in Vietnam) leading more than a thousand veterans to the Arlington Cemetery for a memorial service. VVAW members defied Justice Department orders and camped on the Mall, lobbied members of Congress, marched to the Pentagon to try to turn themselves in as war criminals, performed guerrilla theater, and presented Congress with their 16-point resolution for ending the war. More than 800 veterans tossed their medals, ribbons, discharge papers, and other war mementos from the Capitol steps onto the lawn.

VVAW spokesman, John Kerry, who returned from Vietnam with a Silver Star, a Bronze Star, three Purple Hearts, and other medals, testified against the war for two hours in front of the Senate Foreign Relations Committee. He eloquently described how as "winter soldiers" many veterans felt obligated to inform the rest of the country about the horrors of the war, how soldiers were pushed to commit war crimes, and how "we rationalized destroying villages in order to save them." Soldiers saw a civil war, but presidents Johnson and Nixon continued the war, so that neither would be the "first President to lose a war." "To justify the loss of one American life in Vietnam," Kerry claimed, "is that kind of hypocrisy which we feel has torn this country apart" (Kerry 1971). Kerry's speech impressed millions of TV viewers and helped mobilize support for VVAW, but many VVAW activists resented Kerry's privilege, media attention, and moderate appeals.

Historians' Debate:
How Effective Was the Antiwar Movement?

Historians have wrestled with the impact of the antiwar movement on the actual prosecution of the Vietnam War. After all, despite large protests that grew each year after 1965, it took almost another decade of tremendous effort, much destruction, and millions of dead for the United States to end its goal of crushing Vietnamese communism. Some historians of the Left, such as Howard Zinn, have credited the antiwar movement for halting the war and especially for halting other military interventions in the immediate future. Others have been less sanguine about its impact.

Although President Nixon insisted that antiwar demonstrators hurt rather than helped their cause, the president clearly acted in reaction to his rising unpopularity. Like his predecessor, Lyndon Johnson, his own mobility was often constrained, as he could not make public appearances for fear of antiwar protestors. And as more uniformed Vietnam veterans appeared at protests in the 1970s, and the American public increasingly opposed the war, it became more difficult for Nixon to dismiss his critics; therefore, he chose to avoid them. He hoped his policy of "Vietnamization"—gradual withdrawal of American troops and increasing reliance on South Vietnamese troops—would defuse his critics, but the antiwar movement was appalled by the president's accelerated bombing attacks on the North and in neighboring Cambodia and Laos. The movement clearly hampered the president's desires to escalate the war. Yet the antiwar opposition did not prevent the president's reelection in 1972, and after the peace treaty was signed in Paris in January 1973, bringing an end to American combat losses, it was difficult to mobilize large numbers of Americans to protest U.S. policies in Southeast Asia.

As Kenneth Heineman notes in his book about the campus antiwar movement, the "bitter taste of death" from Kent State, though it immediately galvanized campus activists, also ultimately disillusioned student radicals (1993, 256). In the months following the tragedy, the campus Left disintegrated, plagued by ideological divisions, burnout, and the loss of some of its dynamic leaders.

Although historians debate the impact of the antiwar movement on Johnson's and Nixon's prosecution of the Vietnam War, "the movement's greatest importance," notes Melvin Small, "was its legacy" (2002, 1). Subsequent policymakers worried about another powerful antiwar movement and, following Nixon's introduction of the all-volunteer military, knew that a draft and an expansive war would be unpopular.

VVAW also struggled for the rights and needs of veterans. In 1970, it started the first rap groups to deal with postwar trauma. Veterans discovered through discussions with one another that their individual troubling experiences in Vietnam were shared and were due to U.S. policies. They lobbied for better counseling and health care at VA Hospitals. When U.S. combat involvement in Vietnam ended in 1973, VVAW began advocating for amnesty for draft resisters and dissenters. President Carter finally granted an amnesty in 1980. That same year, VVAW activism brought Post Traumatic Stress Disorder (PTSD) to be recognized as a disease to be treated, and in 1982, the group sued herbicide manufacturers for illnesses suffered as a result of exposure to Agent Orange in Vietnam.

Militance and defiance often characterized VVAW, and this often led to uneasy relations with the rest of the antiwar movement. Veterans' eyewitness combat experiences and working-class roots often made many feel more righteous than their stateside counterparts. By 1971, radical anarchist veterans began to vie with antiwar Democrats for control of VVAW. The organization's activities also frightened the Nixon administration and FBI, which recognized the potential power of veterans organizing against the war. They stepped up surveillance and intimidation tactics and installed agents provocateurs and infiltrators to stifle the group's success. Informants controlled most of the southern chapters of VVAW. Petty jealousies among leaders, divisions over tactics, and other strains that typically divided social movements plagued the organization. Yet the VVAW retained its membership, even after the Paris agreement of January 1973 ended U.S. involvement in the war; it transformed into a veterans' advocacy network, outliving other antiwar organizations.

Gay Rights and Liberation

For decades, gay men and women had often hid their sexual identity for fear of persecution and arrest. Since the publication of the Kinsey Reports in the late 1940s, a growing number of Americans knew that homosexual experiences and orientations existed but were concealed and denied. Yet through the 1950s and 1960s, gays were reported as "perverts," "deviates," and "sexual psychopaths." The gay civil rights and liberation movements broke this silence, challenged stereotypes, and forced Americans to recognize a sizable part of the population that was not heterosexual. Along with the women's movement, the lesbian, gay, bisexual, and transgender (LGBT) movements successfully questioned and transformed notions of fixed sex roles in American society during the 1970s.

Gay networks and communities had formed in urban areas in the post–World War II period, and by the late 1960s, gay bars, newspapers, and organizations were functioning more openly. On June 27, 1969, when police raided the Stonewall Inn in Greenwich Village in New York City and beat some of the gay patrons, a crowd of hundreds gathered and began attacking the police. This symbolic moment, when gay people spontaneously organized and militantly defended themselves, marked the beginning of the gay power movement.

The general liberatory atmosphere of the 1970s allowed lesbians and gays to declare their sexual identities and form a common bond. Cities like New York and San Francisco provided the freedom to experiment, create, and party, as well as to pursue political and social rights. Soon after Stonewall, the radical Gay Liberation Front (GLF) formed in New York City and published the newspaper *Come Out!* Influenced by the New Left and the revolutionary ferment of the times, the GLF took its name in solidarity with Vietnamese rebels. In March 1970, activists organized the first Christopher Street parade, which drew up to 10,000 marchers, to commemorate Stonewall and urge people to "come out of the closets and into the streets."

In the years following Stonewall, over a thousand lesbian and gay groups formed to provide a collective sense of community in what became known as the gay liberation movement, a dramatic call for affirming homosexual desire and identity. The civil rights, antiwar, and New Left movements had emboldened gay people to disrupt and demand. Gay liberation activists also admired and borrowed from the Black Panthers, developing gay pride, a more militant stance toward the police, and a self-sustaining community with its own associations and businesses to serve the new openly gay population.

LGBT activists sought to transform Americans' understanding of sexual preference and identity. In 1970, activists disrupted the annual convention of the American Psychiatric Association meeting in San Francisco to protest the inconsistencies in theories about homosexuality. Repeated annual confrontations and greater awareness led the governing board of the organization in 1974 to drop the listing of homosexuality as a mental disorder, a decision with which the membership later concurred.

During the decade, gay activists worked to expand their civil rights, first working to repeal state laws banning homosexual sex, often called sodomy laws. In 1974, gay and lesbian activists convinced New York representative Bella Abzug to introduce a bill in the House that would provide civil rights protections. Similar bills were introduced each year until Congress held committee hearings in 1980. By the mid-1970s the U.S. Civil Service Commission restricted any firing of gay people without just cause related to job performance. In 1976, the Immigration and Naturalization Service (INS) lifted its ban on homosexual immigrants, and the next year the Foreign Service ended its exclusion of gays from employment.

The LGBT movement hardly considered winning the rights to marry or serve in the military, but in 1975, an important case paved the way for subsequent challenges to antihomosexual prohibitions in the military. Tech. Sgt. Leonard Matlovich, a Republican who served three tours of duty in Vietnam, challenged the ban by revealing his gay identity. He appeared on the cover of *Time* and publicly spoke out against the Uniform Code of Military Justice that discriminated on the basis of sexual orientation.

The movement spawned intellectual work as well. In 1973, gay students at Columbia University created the Gay Academic Union, which made as its goal to encourage gay and lesbian scholarship, but it also debated identity, bisexuality, and feminism, and generated multiple subcommittees and study groups. Books such as *Out of the Closets: Voices of Gay Liberation,* an interdisciplinary collection of writings and commentaries exploring sexuality, identity, and radical politics, provided gays coming out with the knowledge and references of a larger literary, activist world (Jay and Young, 1972). Novels, too, such as Andrew Holleran's *Dancer from the Dance* (1978) described the urban sexual revolution and the "gayness" of music, style, and dance.

Just as other social movements divided over politics and strategies, by the mid-1970s, the gay and lesbian movement began to move in different trajectories. The gay rights movement, composed mostly of white, middle-class men, struggled for equality within the existing frameworks of American society, such as gay rights legislation and the repeal of antigay statutes. Gay liberationists sought a much broader critique and transformation of society. Along with the feminist movement, gay liberation became as much about transforming the gendered structure of American society as gaining acceptance and equal rights for a class of people. By the late 1970s, gay liberation had become a movement for sexual freedom.

The movement also divided as lesbians increasingly felt a gender bias in leadership and in forms of activism. Recognizing that men were part of the dominant culture, many lesbians turned away from gay activism to create a lesbian counterculture and influence the feminist movement. In late 1970, many of the women in the Gay Liberation Front created a separate lesbian caucus and later created a new group, the Radicalesbians. Recognizing their own specific needs and cultures, black, Latino, and Asian American gays also created separate organizations.

Like other civil rights movements, the LGBT movement became increasingly divided in the 1970s over tactics. Some believed change could only come about through continued militant actions, others sought mainstream political acceptance. For example, the Gay Activists Alliance (GAA) formed after some members left the Gay Liberation Front in pursuit of more mainstream political action. Gay political participation increased, especially in the Democratic Party and in the cities of San Francisco, New York, and Los Angeles.

The LGBT movement also generated a backlash from the religious Right, which began organizing statewide antigay ballot initiatives in the late 1970s. Gay rights opponents were more successful than LGBT activists in winning ballot measures, although they often lost court challenges. Because of opponents' successes in heightening voters' fears, activists began focusing on education, legislation, and organization.

Still, by the late 1970s, 36 cities and 1 state had enacted policies prohibiting discrimination on the basis of sexual orientation. California voters' rejection of the Briggs Amendment in 1978 revealed the increasing tolerance of gays in American society. John Briggs, a conservative Republican state senator, obtained

*Thousands of gays and lesbians march for equal rights in Washington, D.C., on
October 14, 1979. The march was organized by the National March on Washington
for Lesbian and Gay Rights. (Bettmann/Corbis)*

enough signatures for a referendum that would have required school boards to
fire any teachers who made "pro-gay" comments.

But weeks after California activists celebrated the Briggs defeat, they had to
mourn another setback. Former San Francisco police officer and city supervisor,
Dan White, who had been a critic of "deviates" taking over the city, killed Mayor
George Moscone and gay supervisor Harvey Milk. Businessman Milk had been
elected to the Board of Supervisors in 1977 and helped pass the city's gay rights
ordinance. White was sentenced to just seven years for the killing, triggering a
massive demonstration in San Francisco's gay community that resulted in a police riot.

The vitality of the gay liberation movement in the 1970s had much to do with
the creation of an open, exuberant, and celebratory culture of sexual liberation.
On October 14, 1979, tens of thousands of people turned out for the first national march on Washington for Lesbian and Gay Rights. But this energy was
sapped in the 1980s by the AIDS epidemic. The Reagan administration's inaction and conservative Christians' claim that God was punishing gay men for gay
sex changed the movement from one of celebration and assertiveness to one
that had to defend the right of LGBT people to exist.

New Movements for Change

Many social movements that flowered in the late 1960s and early 1970s, such as the antiwar movement, foundered by the mid-1970s as goals were achieved or repression and divisions limited their effectiveness. Other new movements, such as gay liberation, flourished; some movements took new directions; still others, such as the feminist movement, gained strength in the 1970s. Inspired by the militant ethos of the era, new movements emerged in the 1970s as groups of people recognized their own oppression or saw ills in society that needed attention. When new opportunities promised by Civil Rights legislation of the 1960s failed to materialize, and a changing economic landscape made more desperate the plight of the poor, new groups emerged to challenge poverty and demand welfare rights. Groups of people who had been neglected or dismissed for their lack of political power, such as the disabled and senior citizens, began to assert their rights for dignity and independence. And others recognized that consumers and animals needed protections. New movements often focused on local issues, encouraged broad participation, and relied on nonviolent direct action.

In the early 1970s, Americans with disabilities and their families began to assert their rights to assistance and independent living. In 1971, Ed Roberts and his associates established a Center for Independent Living (CIL) in Berkeley, California. Later, with the University of California, Berkeley Health Center, Roberts formed a group called the Rolling Quads, which then formed the Disabled Students' Program on the Berkeley campus. In 1974, Susan Sygall and Deborah Kaplan founded the Disabled Women's Coalition at Berkeley to run support groups, hold disabled women's retreats, contribute to feminist publications, and lecture on women and disability.

In 1972, the Boston CIL and the Berkeley CIL advocated for the civil rights of individuals with disabilities and for the services that would allow them full roles as citizens. Congress passed the Rehabilitation Act of 1973, the first national civil rights legislation for the disabled, which prohibited discrimination because of disability in any federal program and required those with federal contracts to make efforts to hire disabled Americans. The act transformed the ways in which schools treated the disabled, providing greater access and direct assistance to enable the disabled student to succeed academically.

In his 1976 election campaign, candidate Jimmy Carter promised that his administration would sign regulations that had received extensive input from affected agencies and the disability community nationwide, and which had taken years to finalize. But when Carter's administration took office, the Health, Education, and Welfare Department (HEW) immediately began revising and watering down the regulations, with no input from the disability community. On April 5, 1977, a group of disabled people occupied the San Francisco offices of HEW to protest Secretary Joseph Califano's refusal to sign meaningful

Rally held in Lafayette Park in Washington, D.C., as part of a series of demonstrations against the Department of Health, Education, and Welfare (HEW) in April 1977. National sit-ins and protests did not end until HEW secretary Joseph A. Califano agreed to implement the Rehabilitation Act of 1973, which prohibited programs that receive federal funding from discriminating on the basis of disability. (Mainstream: Magazine of the Able-Disabled)

regulations for Section 504. Activists remained in the office for almost a month, making the action the longest sit-in of a federal building. The historic demonstrations were successful and the 504 regulations were finally signed.

The consumer movement also grew during the 1970s and ushered in significant legislative changes. Inspired by Ralph Nader's call for citizen action in a speech at the University of Oregon in 1970, students created the Oregon Student Public Interest Research Group (OSPIRG). Students at the University of Minnesota launched a similar group, and the two universities provided the model that would initiate PIRGs across the country and in Canada. Students used student fees to finance their work and hired some professional staff to undertake research and specific campaigns with the help of student volunteers. Unlike many movements in the 1970s that focused on single issues, the Nader-inspired network sought to link environmental, labor, and consumer issues to the problem of corporate dominance.

Just as the increased numbers of college students contributed to the dynamism of the youth movements of the 1970s, the increased numbers of elderly (roughly 10 percent of the population), and an increased life expectancy rate made aging a concern of the country. Many older Americans had become active in the 1960s to lobby for Medicare, increased Social Security benefits to match inflation, and nursing home reform. The American Association of Retired Persons (AARP) had been established in 1958 to provide affordable insurance for retirees, but in the 1970s, many in the organization succeeded in changing the leadership to focus on nonpartisan political action. As a result, AARP became a household name with 9 million members in the 1970s. The Gray Panthers became a more militant voice of the elderly during the decade, calling a halt to ageism and more social welfare for seniors.

Growing compassion for the rights of animals grew into a new social movement in the 1970s. Animal rights activity had become more widespread in Britain by 1970, but it did not move to the United States until the end of the Vietnam War. Peter Singer's book *Animal Liberation,* published in 1975, provided the intellectual rationale for recognizing "speciesism" as a form of discrimination and awakened many to the problem of animal abuse. Singer's documentation of animals in research and Tom Regan's work on the moral basis of vegetarianism brought the question of animal rights into academic discussions as well as to a larger public.

In 1976, New York City schoolteacher and civil rights activist Henry Spira, who had been influenced by Singer's arguments, formed Animal Rights International and led campaigns against animal experiments at the American Museum of Natural History. Spira's group obtained details about the government-funded research through the Freedom of Information Act, and when the museum refused to negotiate, the group set up pickets in front of the museum. They convinced New York congressman Ed Koch to question the experiments, and they drew public attention to the mistreatment of cats in research at the museum. Public pressure forced the National Institutes of Health to stop funding the project. Succeeding in their mission, the activists also won greater respect from the press, which now referred to them as animal rights activists rather than animal lovers.

Spira and his group then sought to prohibit pound seizures. Many states in the postwar period had made it easier for researchers to acquire unclaimed animals at shelters. Collaborating with animal welfare groups, the animal rights activists succeeded in passing prohibitions in several states, including New York in 1979. Other groups in the 1970s exposed and condemned institutional cruelties and convinced major cosmetics companies to invest in nonanimal research for their products. These initial activities stimulated a much broader and effective animal rights movement in the 1980s.

CIVIL RIGHTS: FROM INTEGRATION TO CULTURAL NATIONALISM

Black Pride, the Politics of Identity, and New Forms of Civil Rights Protest

By 1970, despite legislation and court rulings that since the 1950s had attempted to advance civil rights, the racially polarized climate of the nation led many people of color to turn to their own communities for sustenance and to militant activity to change their relationship to U.S. society. Believing that the United States was incapable of shedding structural racism that penalized people of color in jobs, housing, public office, and prisons, many African Americans turned to their African roots, Chicanos to their Aztec/Mexican heritage, and Native Americans to more traditional ways of their forbearers to create alternative social structures and cultural traditions.

The Black Power movement, which emerged in the mid-1960s, attracted many young activists who were frustrated by the slow pace of change after a decade of nonviolent protest and continued police violence. Many were convinced that the civil rights movement's focus on integration and legislation had not obtained the dignity and opportunities that all citizens deserved, and they believed the movement needed to take a more aggressive direction. In addition, integration threatened to erase everything black, spurring cultural radicals to champion black pride and alternative institutions.

Even as the NAACP and the Congressional Black Caucus filed lawsuits and passed legislation to win and preserve civil rights, disillusionment with the courts and the political arena grew so that by the 1970s, both middle-class reformists and working-class activists demanded tangible social change rather than theoretical equality. By the early 1970s, the goals and ideologies of the NAACP and the Southern Christian Leadership Conference (SCLC) appealed to fewer young African Americans. The Student Nonviolent Coordinating Committee (SNCC) and the Congress of Racial Equality (CORE) adopted black nationalist agendas, rejected white members, and distanced themselves from white supporters.

At the National Black Political Assembly in Gary, Indiana, in 1972, a majority of the nearly 8.000 attendees acknowledged radical change as the only means of affecting mainstream politics on a fundamental level. This call to black nationalism drowned out moderate blacks' insistence that integration was the most effective means to make political change.

However, most white Americans and mainstream politicians during the 1970s were not as willing to negotiate with or lobby for radical African Americans as with those African Americans who had encouraged systematic, cooperative change from within the system years before. Black nationalism spawned a backlash from previously sympathetic politicians and white allies.

Activists gather on the steps of the Lincoln Memorial under a banner for the Revolutionary People's Constitutional Convention during the Black Panther Convention, June 19, 1970. (Library of Congress)

The Black Panther Party

When Black Panther Party (BPP) leader Huey Newton was released from prison in 1970, he found the party in disarray. Many chapters across the country were infiltrated by police and FBI. Newton sought to deemphasize confrontations with the police and moved the BPP to focus on survival programs that would educate and sustain African American communities, including a petition campaign for local control of police, free breakfasts for children, free health clinics, and liberation schools. These programs attracted new members and broadened the party's base in African American communities.

The media's focus on Eldridge Cleaver's radical rhetoric and exile, Bobby Seale's imprisonment, and the arrests of more than 300 other leaders hid the fact that the Panthers survived and flourished at the grassroots. The party had dozens of chapters in cities across the country and active political programs regarding police reform, prisoners' rights, and welfare issues. Its popular children's breakfast programs even won over white communities and business leaders.

Although Newton's leadership style was authoritarian, women in the BPP managed to lessen the group's paramilitary style of organization, and the BPP officially condemned male chauvinism. Elaine Brown became a powerful figure in the BPP. She moved from Los Angeles, where she had been a party activist, to Oakland in the early 1970s where she edited the Panther newspaper. She became chairperson of the BPP in 1974 and was able to merge radical and feminist strands in the city's progressive community to network among African American churches, the Democratic Party, and groups such as the Urban League. The party supported Brown's and Bobby Seale's runs in the 1973 Oakland city council elections against the conservative "establishment," which initiated a massive voter registration drive. Although neither candidate won a seat, as electoral novices they garnered a significant portion of the vote.

Angela Davis, a Communist Party member and another prominent female supporter of the Panthers, was arrested in 1970 for allegedly supplying arms to Jonathan Jackson, who was killed in a courtroom shootout. She was acquitted of charges in 1972. Jackson was the brother of George Jackson, the imprisoned Black Panther leader and author of the influential *Soledad Brother* (1970) who was killed by San Quentin prison guards in August 1971. After Jackson's death, protests erupted in other prisons including the uprising at Attica state prison in New York, where prisoners demanded improved living conditions.

By the mid-1970s the BPP could not withstand the hostile political climate and declined. Despite its weakened position due to FBI counterintelligence disruption and attacks, the BPP continued to inspire a host of other social movements. Many groups modeled themselves after the Black Panther Party, which advocated militant resistance, self-sufficiency, and identification with postcolonial revolutionary struggles. For example, the Young Lords Organization, which had begun as a Puerto Rican street gang, became a militant political organization following the model of the BPP.

Black power also emphasized positive aspects of African American culture and encouraged people of African descent to form a strong collective identity based on heritage and a common culture. Many of those who embraced black pride let their hair grow naturally into "naturals" or "afros," rebelling against the chemical and heated straightening to approximate "white" hair, and they wore *dashikis,* African-style dress in colorful prints. These expressions relayed the message that "black is beautiful," recognized African heritage, and communicated a demand for respect and rights in American society.

By 1970, protests on American campuses were just as often about minority concerns as about the war in Vietnam. The famous San Francisco State strike, in which militant African American students and their demands for an African American studies department resulted in a stand-off between students, the administration, and California legislature, helped trigger similar militant actions in several hundred colleges and universities. Students demanded changes to curricula that focused on middle-class whites and the creation of African American and ethnic studies programs.

Brown Power

By 1970, Mexican Americans were the second-largest minority in the United States, the largest in the Southwest, and the fastest growing ethnic group. Recognizing this rising demographic clout and the widespread discrimination that they experienced, and inspired by the successes of African American civil rights and black power movements, the Chicano movement burst on the scene in the mid-1960s. Latinos and Mexican Americans mobilized around "brown power" to address a wide range of issues, including land reparations, agricultural workers' rights, improved education, and political rights. Young activists self-identified as Chicano and Chicana to emphasize their militancy and pride associated with being Americans of Mexican descent. Mexican and Puerto Rican Americans were particularly active in the brown power struggle; the participants emphasized the importance of a collective history of domination and the power of political action, championing César Chávez and La Raza Unida Party.

The roots of brown power emerged in New Mexico's land grant movement of 1966 and 1967 in which Mexican Americans across the Southwest urged the federal government to honor the Treaty of Guadalupe Hidalgo, which ended the Mexican War in 1848 and promised to restore lands to Mexicans living in the region. From this action grew a concept of Chicano nationalism, which affirmed a cultural identity with Mexico. Rodolfo "Corky" Gonzales led efforts in Colorado to articulate this identity with the first national Chicano Youth Conference in 1969, which published "El Plan de Atzlan," a key document of the movement. It identified the Southwest or Atzlan as part of the Aztec empire, noting that Chicanos had never left the land and deserved a separate state because their labor

Two young Chicano men raise their fists during a National Chicano Moratorium Committee march in opposition to the Vietnam War, Los Angeles, California, February 28, 1970. (David Fenton/Getty Images)

had developed the region, and called for alternative education and legal reforms. The concept of a single Chicano identity proved particularly useful in uniting farmworkers to strike and boycott when labor concerns arose.

In late August 1970, Chicanos in East Los Angeles roused the nation to consider the plight of Mexican Americans, who represented a high proportion of deaths in the Vietnam War. Rosalio Muñoz, Brown Beret David Sanchez, Corky Gonzales, and César Chavez organized the National Chicano Moratorium and march to urge Chicanos to end the war and fight for social justice at home. But as more than 25,000 demonstrators gathered at Laguna Park, police ordered the park vacated after an altercation with a few protestors. Fighting broke out between police and some demonstrators, and dozens of fires were set. Police arrested hundreds, injured 70, and killed 2 Chicanos, including popular *Los Angeles Times* columnist Rubén Salazar, known for his reporting on civil rights and police brutality. Some believed that he had been targeted by police. While an inquest found that his death was a homicide, the deputy sheriff who fired the shell was not prosecuted. More demonstrations and more police violence emerged in East Los Angeles in subsequent months. LAPD agent provocateurs subsequently infiltrated the group and raided National Chicano Moratorium Committee offices. The organization dissolved by 1971.

Mexican American Education Council (MAEC) of Houston

When in May 1970 a federal district judge ordered Houston schools to desegregate through a pairing plan that would send Mexican American students as "white" to predominantly African American schools, Mexican Americans mobilized to protest what they viewed as discrimination. They pursued a legal strategy to argue that white students needed to be paired with black and brown schools to desegregate, and they worked to educate and involve parents in pressuring public officials. Houston Chicanos knew that the *Cisneros v. Corpus Christi Independent School District* case in 1970 had ruled that Mexican Americans were an identifiable ethnic minority group for desegregation purposes and sought to implement the ruling.

Activists formed the Mexican American Education Council (MAEC) to bring together different generations and barrios to plan how to respond to the Houston desegregation plan. MAEC staged school boycotts, organized *huelga* (or strike) schools to continue children's education during the boycotts, protested at school board meetings, and insisted on inclusion in a biracial committee to plan desegregation efforts. The high school and University of Houston Mexican American Youth Associations (MAYO) engaged in direct action protests. They occupied several churches, occupied a banquet attended by federal officials, interrupted a speech by the governor, and marched against the war in Vietnam. Other youth organizations formed, such as the Chicano Youth Council, to protest discrimination. Students came up with their own demands, which included establishing Chicano history courses and hiring more Mexican American teachers.

As the protests and intransigence of the school board dragged on, political divisions within the Chicano community emerged, especially among radicals. MAEC, as a liberal group with little opposition from conservatives, managed to survive and continue educational activities and litigation. According to Guadalupe San Miguel Jr., its persistence, effective leadership and resistance to fragmentation enabled the group to ultimately claim victory. By the fall of 1972, MAEC had won recognition for Chicanos as an identifiable minority group by the school board and federal courts. The schools issue encouraged Mexican American Houston residents to accept a nonwhite "brown" identity and the Chicano strategy of militancy.

High school students in Crystal City, Texas, galvanized the Chicano movement. Fed up with discrimination, a ban on speaking Spanish, and the lack of appropriate curricula, Mexican American students walked out of school, parents picketed, and federal officials investigated civil rights violations. By January 1970, the school board capitulated to student demands. Riding on the success of the walkout, activists formed La Raza Unida Party and won control of the school board in the 1970 elections. Chicanos elected one of the La Raza leaders, José Angel Gutiérrez, as board president and then as county judge in 1974.

Inspired by the Texas movement, many Chicanos believed that the third party La Raza would help assert brown power at local and state levels and formed chapters in Colorado and California. Some cities in Texas and California in which Mexican Americans made up the majority had no representatives of Mexican descent in political office. Frustrated with the Democratic Party for not adequately dealing with the nation's social problems, delegates from 18 states attended the first La Raza national convention in September 1972 in El Paso. But like other third parties in American history, the group was frustrated in efforts to obtain ballot status in key states such as California and Arizona. Unable to become a viable electoral force, La Raza's political action then focused primarily on workers' rights and voting inequality. Militants clashed with Mexican American moderates, especially those who believed that working within the system, often in the Democratic Party, would bring about positive change for Mexican Americans in employment, housing, education, and media perceptions of the culture. La Raza was unable to field candidates in any election after 1980, even in Texas where it met initial success.

The Chicano movement had made itself visible and achieved many goals, even as it diminished by mid-decade. The two main political parties sought to include more Mexican Americans, schools created more courses in Chicano history and culture and sought Chicano teachers and professors, and Chicanos gained greater representation in occupations and political office.

Red Power and the American Indian Movement

Formed in Minneapolis in 1968, the American Indian Movement (AIM) emulated the Black Panthers in seeking cultural autonomy, protection from police, and self-sufficiency for Native American people. As the federal government and the courts granted more autonomy to tribes in critical cases and legislation in the 1970s, the pan-Indian movement sought to assert sovereignty rights for Native Americans on reservations and in urban areas.

Public conceptions of Native Americans radically changed with the assertive actions of AIM, which drew attention to the broken promises and treaties of the U.S. government, and with new cultural representations of American Indians. No longer were Native Americans portrayed as savages deserving of conquest and assimilation. In 1970, the publication of Vine Deloria's *We Talk, You Listen,* Dee Brown's *Bury My Heart at Wounded Knee,* and the release of the film *Little Big Man,* starring Dustin Hoffman, all upturned previous interpretations of American history to reveal that Native Americans had been heroes and victims, and the U.S. government had violently subjugated the indigenous peoples of North America.

In the early 1970s, led by Dennis Banks and Russell Means, AIM carried out a series of flamboyant actions to draw public attention to the treatment of Native Americans. From November 1969 to June 1971, 100 Indians from several tribes joined AIM in occupying Alcatraz Island in San Francisco Bay, claiming it for all Native Americans and a site for an Indian university, museum, and cultural center. President Nixon refused to accommodate AIM's demands and ordered FBI agents and federal marshals to forcibly remove occupiers of the island. AIM also occupied Mount Rushmore and seized the *Mayflower* replica moored at Plymouth, Massachusetts, on Thanksgiving Day 1971.

AIM activists struggled for more than symbolic attention, however. They created a cultural center at an unused military facility in Seattle and improved health care access for Native Americans in Denver. AIM successfully pressured officials in Gordon, Nebraska, to bring charges against the whites who brutally murdered an Oglala Sioux, Raymond Yellow Thunder. These events drew thousands of young Native Americans into the AIM fold and inspired others, from Black Panthers and war resisters to countercultural hippies, to support their movement. By 1972, AIM had 43 chapters in the United States and was popular with both traditionalist elders and young people who began to wear braids, beads, and other regalia as symbols of cultural pride and political resistance.

In 1972, AIM sponsored the Trail of Broken Treaties march on Washington, occupied Bureau of Indian Affairs (BIA) offices, and sent a 20-point proposal to President Nixon to consider. The proposal called for renewal of historic contracts and treaties with Indian nations and "securing an Indian future in America," including a commission to review treaty commitments and violations; the creation of a congressional joint committee on reconstruction of Indian relations; restoration of a 110-million acre native land base; abolition of the BIA; protection of Indian religious freedom and cultural integrity; and assurances of health, housing, employment and education for Indian people, who suffered the highest rates of unemployment and poverty in the country.

Like many social movements from the period, AIM suffered from internal conflicts and disorganization. But its fluid structure allowed Native Americans from all parts of the country to participate in activities as they were able; the lack of membership lists also frustrated officials in the BIA and FBI who wanted to closely monitor and repress their activities. To many Native American people, AIM provided courageous role models and challenged racist stereotypes and institutions.

FBI harassment and infiltration, trials and convictions of key leaders, and violence damaged AIM's survival by the end of the decade. There was no general membership meeting after 1975, and after his family members were murdered on the Duck Valley reservation in Nevada in 1979, the last officer of AIM, poet John Trudell, resigned his position.

Although AIM's militant activities, especially the siege at Wounded Knee, dominated media coverage of Native American issues, other significant events

American Indian Movement (AIM) activists stand guard on March 7, 1973, during the occupation of Wounded Knee, South Dakota. The Oglala Sioux Civil Rights Organization on the Pine Ridge Reservation enlisted the aid of AIM to protest the abuses of elected council head of the reservation, Richard (Dick) Wilson. The Indian occupiers faced off with law enforcement officials for almost 70 days until a settlement was negotiated and both sides withdrew. (Bettmann/Corbis)

occurred during the 1970s to strengthen tribal sovereignty. In 1970, the Native American Rights Fund (NARF) was founded to provide legal services to Indian tribes on a national level. NARF grew out of legal services programs that had served the Native American poor near reservations. Attorneys recognized that to adequately handle these cases, they needed expertise in American Indian Law, a complex body of law composed of hundreds of treaties and court decisions, and thousands of federal statutes, regulations, and administrative rulings. It was clear to those working for Native American rights that cases involving major national issues of Indian law needed to be handled by legal experts who were sufficiently funded.

At the same time the Nixon administration was fighting AIM at Pine Ridge and in the courts, it also presided over the great expansion of tribal sovereignty. In 1975, Congress passed the Indian Self-Determination and Education Act, which directed the Interior secretary to contract directly with tribal organizations to plan and administer various programs, rather than working through the BIA. In 1978, Congress passed the Tribally Controlled Community College Assistance

Occupation of Wounded Knee (1973)

In February 1973 at the request of some Sioux tribal elders, about 150 AIM activists went to Wounded Knee, South Dakota—site of the last U.S. Army massacre of Native Americans in 1890—to help remove corrupt U.S.-approved tribal leaders and establish a more independent Oglala Sioux Nation on the Pine Ridge Reservation. The majority of the reservation's residents suffered poverty, unemployment, and substance abuse. The autocratic tribal president, Dick Wilson, provided with federal funds, created a paramilitary force called the Guardians of the Oglala Nation (or GOONs) that intimidated opponents. When opponents tried to impeach Wilson, he jailed those who might vote against him on the tribal council and banned all political meetings. AIM demanded improvement in conditions on reservations, investigations into the federal government's breaking of treaties with Indian nations, the end of strip mining on the reservation, and increased tribal sovereignty.

GOONs and FBI agents blocked off roads leaving the reservation, beginning a 71-day siege to remove AIM and its supporters. Federal marshals, BIA, and state police were activated to arrest anyone who tried to enter Wounded Knee. Over the next seven weeks, AIM militants and federal agents exchanged gunfire.

For a time, supporters smuggled weapons and food to the AIM activists, but as more police and marshals patrolled the area with sophisticated equipment and burned fields to eliminate cover, AIM was forced to negotiate. Agents' bullets had killed Buddy Lamont and wounded others, and AIM was almost out of food. Dennis Banks and six other leaders slipped out of Wounded Knee the night before arrests would be made and hid in Canada. The occupation ended on May 7 when federal officials agreed to investigate the Wilson regime and meet with traditional Oglala leaders. In exchange, 146 men and women surrendered. But little came of the meetings, and many AIM members drifted away from the Sioux reservation.

The government arrested 1,200 people involved in Wounded Knee, indicted 185 AIM leaders, and through the mid-1970s prosecuted many of the leaders in four major sensational trials. Dennis Banks was convicted and, facing a 15-year sentence, skipped bail and became a fugitive. William Kunstler, attorney for the Wounded Knee defendants, noted that the purpose of the prosecutions and trials was to break up AIM, much as the federal government had destroyed the Black Panthers.

Violence continued on Pine Ridge as Wilson's GOONs received weapons from the FBI. From March 1973 to March 1976, 69 AIM members and supporters were murdered, and at least 300 suffered serious physical assaults. During this period, Pine Ridge surpassed Detroit as the "murder capital" of the United States. Although Russell Means, a member of the Oglala tribe, beat Wilson in an electoral contest in 1974, the Justice Department would not assist him in taking office, and Wilson maintained control. In June 1975, two FBI men opened fire on an AIM encampment killing Joe Stuntz Kills Right and, receiving heavy return fire, were killed. The FBI then spent the next two months conducting military sweeps of the reservation, killing several people, and crushing AIM. In a controversial trial in the spring of 1977, Leonard Peltier was convicted of double homicide in the case of the FBI agents, although he and other AIM members claimed he was innocent.

Act, the American Indian Religious Freedom Act, and the Indian Child Welfare Act (ICWA), and the Supreme Court granted several land claims settlements to tribes. The ICWA was particularly significant in granting tribes control over placement of children, ending a century of efforts to remove children from their Native American homes and to assimilate them into white society, and led to the establishment of tribal courts.

The activism of the period inspired lawsuits and court cases that could remedy past abuses of Native American rights. Many tribes brought cases before the Indian Claims Commission to secure former lands. Through the 1970s, courts were generally sympathetic to Native American rights and land cases.

Yellow Power: Asian American Movements

Like the black, Chicano, and Native American liberation movements, Asian Americans also organized to combat discrimination, challenge oppression and power, and serve their communities. They, too, drew inspiration from and supported freedom movements of peoples in Africa, Asia, and Latin America, and they opposed the war in Vietnam. For example, the Philippine American Collegiate Endeavor (PACE), formed at San Francisco State College, acknowledged the racist society in which Asian Americans lived and identified more closely with Third World peoples.

It was this Third-World activism, the inspiration of the Black Panther Party, and the emergence of a generation of college-aged Japanese, Filipino, and Chinese American students that led to more formal and radical organization as Asian Americans. In late 1968, Asian American students at San Francisco State College and the University of California, Berkeley joined other students of color in leading Third-World strikes to protest racism and demand the establishment of ethnic studies programs. The five-month strike, which resulted in the country's first program in Ethnic Studies at San Francisco State, galvanized Asian American students across the country. By 1970, more than 60 college campuses had Asian American student groups. Asian Americans began linking their own struggles to a broader past heritage of exclusion and resistance. The Asian American Political Alliance (AAPA), which emerged from the strikes, promoted a pan-Asian membership and agenda to support civil rights efforts of all ethnic groups.

Asian American activists viewed intellectual and cultural work as important for asserting, establishing, and maintaining ethnic identity. Collective student, faculty, and community pressures led to the creation of academic centers, such as the UCLA Asian American Studies Center established in 1970, to foster research and teaching about Asian Americans and reach broad audiences. Journals such as *Bridge* (New York Chinatown, 1971–1985) and *Amerasia Journal* (Los Angeles, 1971–present) were created to foster historical, social science, cultural, and theoretical work about Asian America. In the early 1970s, the Yellow Pearl

Project at Basement Workshop in Chinatown in New York brought together dozens of Asian American artists and nonartists to work on collective projects, such as staging benefit concerts. In 1973, Chinese American playwright Frank Chin founded the Asian American Theater Company to develop and present original works of theater by and about Americans of Asian and Pacific Islander descent. The company was dedicated to producing groundbreaking, entertaining, and innovative art through video, film, or on stage that explored Asian American communities and identity.

Asian American groups on the east and west coasts sought assistance and reforms for their neighborhoods and Chinatowns, participated in anti-eviction campaigns, and established medical clinics, breakfast programs, and youth and senior programs. The Berkeley AAPA formed an Asian Community Center in 1970 to provide services to the larger pan-Asian community and to attract working people to their organization. In December 1972, activists in New York City established the United Asian Communities Center, which became a hub for political and social activities. Ray Tasaki and others started the Asian Involvement Office in Los Angeles's Little Tokyo in the early 1970s to provide senior lunches, legal aid, and a program to work with youth gangs. They also launched Asian American Hard Core to help young people escape drugs and work with the community to challenge and change the outcomes of capitalist society, including addiction, gangs, and alienation.

Focusing on community issues led many Asian Americans to embrace revolutionary ideas influenced by the Black Panthers and Brown Berets and the teachings of Marx, Lenin, and Mao. Chinese American students were particularly attracted to the teachings of Mao and the People's Republic of China. Community centers in New York and Berkeley showed films of life in mainland China that attracted huge crowds of older immigrants, curious about contemporary life in China.

Asian American groups in the Midwest had more difficulty organizing because they lacked the physical communities of Chinatowns, Little Tokyos, and Manilatowns of the east and west coasts. In 1974, Midwestern Asian American Conferences were held in Chicago and Madison, and campus groups at Oberlin, University of Illinois, University of Michigan, and elsewhere emerged, all focusing on issues of identity rather than the class and Third World–based emphases of coastal Asian American groups.

Asian American movements faced unique challenges that distinguished their experiences from African Americans, Latinos, and Native Americans, which had long been forced by slavery or conquest to recognize a pan-ethnic identity. Asian Americans came from numerous ethnic backgrounds, including some who had more recently immigrated, and pan-Asian coalitions became more difficult to organize and sustain. Despite a history of discrimination, too, Asian Americans had often been characterized as "model minorities," with access to financial and educational resources. Activists sought to balance the need to come strategically

Japanese American Redress Movement

The reaffirmation of ethnic identity in the early 1970s stimulated a redress movement among Japanese Americans to seek apologies and compensation from the federal government for the internment of more than 110,000 Japanese immigrants and their American-born children during World War II. Suffering from the psychological effects of internment and the racism that deterred reestablishment of ethnic communities, Nisei parents, the American-born children of immigrants, talked little about their internment to their Sansei children growing up in the 1950s and 1960s. The nationwide Asian American movement of the late 1960s and early 1970s stimulated the Sanseis' interest in their history and culture and a desire to uncover the hidden history of the internment. Jeanne Wakatsuki Houston's publication of her memoir of camp life, *Farewell to Manzanar* (1973) awakened many Japanese American college students to their parents' ordeal.

During the early 1970s, a few Japanese American Citizens League (JACL) chapters in San Francisco and Seattle began researching the possibility of reparations for Japanese Americans who lost income and property during their incarceration in the 1940s. Many Nisei, wishing not to reopen old wounds and a possible racial backlash, opposed these efforts. Concerned about the loss of this history, Sansei activists organized the first Day of Remembrance, held at the Puyallup fairgrounds near Seattle, where Japanese Americans from the Puget Sound area were first held before being sent to the Minidoka concentration camp in southern Idaho. The commemoration of the evacuation process was a big success, drawing over 2,000 Japanese American participants.

Similar events and the work of the Asian Law Caucus continued to draw attention to the issue of redress, and in 1981, the Commission on Wartime Relocation and Internment of Civilians heard testimony in major Japanese American communities across the nation. The Commission ultimately determined that internment had been based on "racial prejudice, wartime hysteria and a failure of political leadership" and recommended a formal government apology and individual payments of $20,000 to survivors. The redress movement represented a victory for Sansei and some Nisei activists, who saw it as a constitutional and civil liberties issue, and a matter that raised larger awareness of discrimination against Asian Americans.

together under one umbrella and to maintain their separate ethnicities. For example, they joined forces in the late 1970s to make certain that members of their group were adequately counted in the 1980 U.S. Census to secure government funding and political representation. Pan-Asian unity in various organizations declined with the end of U.S. intervention in Vietnam, and like many social movements that became energized at the outset of the decade, these groups struggled after the mid-1970s with membership, goals, and direction.

ENVIRONMENTALISMS

Recognizing Limits and Possibilities: New Environmental Movements

Before the 1970s, the American environmental movement had focused on conservation and preservation, seeking either to regulate use of or to protect the natural environment. By the 1970s, the environmental movement expanded in multiple directions, seeking preservation of species and habitats, opposing formerly promising technologies such as nuclear power for its life-threatening dangers, and demanding cleanup of workplace and urban as well as natural environments. The "new environmentalism" or "ecoactivism," as the press dubbed the modern movements that emerged in the 1970s, viewed the earth as a complex and delicate set of natural systems that needed greater appreciation and protection. The movements engaged science and the law as well as grassroots activism to preserve disappearing wilderness, protect threatened species, limit pollution from industry and autos, and clean up toxic neighborhoods.

In the post–World War II period, many Americans began to view the environment differently, as something to protect and preserve rather than simply utilize for economic growth. Postwar prosperity, improved highways, and tourism had led many more people to recreate in and appreciate the nation's rivers, forests, and parks, and to realize their endangerment from industries, pollution, clearcutting, and other development. Ecologists spoke about relating organisms to their environment; Rachel Carson's publication of *Silent Spring* in 1962 shocked many Americans into recognizing how postwar developments, such as widespread use of pesticides, accelerated dangers to the natural world. Well-publicized environmental horrors in the 1960s such as the chemical-laden Cuyahoga River in Cleveland bursting into flames, the contamination of fish in many rivers and bays, the smog enveloping many cities, and raw sewage damaging favorite beaches awakened many Americans to the need to take action.

The convergence of new public awareness about a threatened environment and the influence of 1960s protest movements created new enthusiasm for environmental movements. Opinion polls in 1970 revealed sharp increases in the number of Americans who were concerned about the degradation of the natural environment and who wanted government to do something about it.

Growing awareness and activism during the decade led President Nixon to declare the 1970s as "the environmental decade." Older established groups such as the Sierra Club and the Audubon Society grew rapidly. The Audubon Society increased its membership from 45,000 in 1966 to 321,000 six years later. During the same period, Sierra Club members increased from 35,000 to 147,000. After the first Earth Day in 1970, several hundred new national associations and several thousand local environmental groups emerged. Some of these organizations continued in the vein of older conservation groups to work within the political system to affect legislative, judicial, and regulatory changes to protect the environment; other groups adopted the protest strategies of other 1970s social movements to publicize environmental issues.

By the mid-1970s, frustrated with the narrow focus, bureaucratization, and racism and sexism of mainstream environmental organizations, new alternative and more radical groups formed. Many of these were often locally or regionally based; they were decentralized and emphasized direct action rather than working within the political system. Writer and naturalist Edward Abbey's popular novel, *The Monkey Wrench Gang* (1975), stimulated more militant forms of environmental protest. Abbey depicted a small gang of "monkey wrenchers," who, like the worker saboteurs who threw wooden shoes (*sabots*) into the gears of early industrial machinery, sabotaged road-building bulldozers that threatened the desert. Their commitment to the rights of nature brought the monkey wrenchers to consider blowing up Glen Canyon Dam to liberate the Colorado River, but declined in their resolve not to kill people by their actions.

In the early 1970s, Norwegian philosopher Arne Næss articulated the concept of deep ecology, which argued that all life, nonhuman as well as human, had value and should not be subordinated to economic needs and development. The ideas of deep ecology became popularized in the United States in the 1970s and became most known through the radical environmental group Earth First! This loosely organized direct action group emerged in the late 1970s when Dave Foreman and other Wilderness Society staff left that organization in frustration over compromises and bureaucratic wrangling with the Forest Service over roadless area reviews. Foreman and others sought to blend the tactics of civil disobedience with the "monkey-wrenching" advocated by Edward Abbey.

Some feminists, who had begun to explore the primeval connections between women and the Earth, believed that patriarchy had been responsible for dominating both nature and women. Influenced by the Gaia hypothesis that considered the Earth as a living organism, some feminist environmentalists created a new movement, first coined *ecofeminism* in the mid-1970s, which included alternative healing, Witchcraft covens, women's antinuclear camps, and other alternative activist communities. Susan Griffin published her book-length prose-poem *Women and Nature: The Roaring Inside Her* in 1978, which juxtaposed the voices of women, animals, and the natural world against the voices of patriarchy revealed in the texts of male scientists, philosophers, and theologians. In 1980, Carolyn Merchant published her scholarly and influential book, *The Death of Nature: Women, Ecology, and the Scientific Revolution,* which argued that scientists' conceptualization of the Earth as a machine rather than a living organism encouraged the domination of nature and women. Experiencing discrimination in mainstream environmental movements, many women gravitated toward ecofeminism and its gendered explanation of human relationships with the natural environment.

Working-class Americans and people of color also felt excluded from the mainstream environmental movement, which often did not consider factors of race, ethnicity, class, and power as contributors to disproportionate environmental degradation. A new environmental justice movement emerged in the 1970s that considered toxic waste, lead paint, and dumping and their effects on human health and neighborhoods as more important issues than wilderness and species preservation.

People of color also criticized the Zero Population Growth (ZPG) movement that by 1970 had over 30,000 members in 380 chapters around the country. Influenced by Paul Ehrlich's popular book *The Population Bomb* (1968), which warned that the world's population increases could not be sustained and that countries needed to restrict family size, some ZPG members became associated with advocating sterilization and restrictive immigration policies. Some members of ZPG and the Sierra Club helped form in 1978 the Federation of American Immigration Reform (FAIR), which sought to restrict immigration as a threat to environmental quality. These actions made many African Americans and Latinos wary of the environmental movement.

Other environmental groups formed in the 1970s to address concerns over the dangers and polluting effects of oil, coal, and nuclear sources of energy. Many citizens became involved in alternative energy movements, advocating development of small-scale hydropower, wind, and solar forms of energy.

Globally, environmental activism grew through the 1970s, spawning the Green or Ecology political parties throughout Europe and the Pacific. But American activists focused on pressuring the two main political parties to enact and enforce environmental protections. By the late 1970s, the environmental movement's popularity began to wane as conservatives protested against too many regulations, claiming that they cost the country needed jobs. They also portrayed environmentalists as fanatics and elitists who were out of touch with most Americans and their economic concerns.

Earth Day

The first Earth Day celebrated on April 22, 1970, symbolizes the emergence of modern environmentalism as a mass social and cultural movement. More than 20 million Americans participated in the event, gathering in streets, on campuses, in front of government buildings, in parks, and along riverbanks to draw attention to the dire state of the natural environment and to call for action to improve and protect it.

Democratic senator Gaylord Nelson of Wisconsin, longtime conservationist, conceived of a national teach-in on the environment that would bring together students, activists, and other citizens to discuss and debate the perils facing the environment. By late 1969, as the teach-in idea generated interest across the country, a new organization, which became Environmental Action, was created to handle calls to Nelson's office.

Some of President Nixon's aides saw the event as a golden opportunity to win support from the young who often protested against Nixon for war in Vietnam. Ultimately, the president decided to wait and see whether Earth Day events would be moderate before endorsing it, but he instructed staff to travel the country to emphasize the administration's support of a clean environment. Because of overwhelming public support for cleaning up the environment, in his 1970 state of the union address Nixon elevated environmental concerns as his administration's priority. But in a few months, Nixon's efforts to draw attention to the environment were overshadowed by his announcement of invading Cambodia.

Nelson enlisted Denis Hayes, a Harvard law student, to help organize Earth Day. Like other ecology activists, Hayes criticized existing governmental and industrial policies, but he also sought to distance the project from a New Left confrontational style to pull in diverse sectors from American society. He recruited volunteers from other universities to make Earth Day a more expansive event than a teach-in.

Both the New Left and older conservationist groups were wary of organizers' "moderate" approach to Earth Day. More radical environmentalists believed industry and government were responsible for the ecological crisis and wanted more dramatic and confrontational events. New Ecology Action groups sprang up, established centers, and held demonstrations, guerrilla theater actions, and their own teach-ins in advance of the national events planned for April 22. Older groups such as the Sierra Club, National Wildlife Federation, and Audubon Society were suspicious of the new activists and generally declined to participate in Earth Day. The established organizations also resented the media's "discovery" of an environmental crisis, when they had advocated for preservation of wild places and habitats for many years.

Despite organizers' efforts to present a moderate face to Earth Day, many Earth Day activities linked the environment to other issues. Students at the University of Oregon demonstrated in front of the campus ROTC building and occupied the administration building, forcing the university to suspend classes to hold several teach-ins about the war and the environment. Sen. Edmund Muskie, Nixon's Democratic rival, in an Earth Day speech linked environmental concerns to racial justice. The event mushroomed into small and large gatherings throughout the country due to grassroots organizing by activists well seasoned in civil rights and antiwar causes. Yet the range and diversity of Earth Day events, similar to street fairs, attracted a wide variety and ages of Americans, winning generally positive media coverage, unlike the equally large antiwar demonstrations of the period that had lost media attention.

Corporations sought to reposition themselves to change public perceptions of their responses to environmental concerns. Fearing new restrictive legislation and controls from environmental activism, they publicized efforts to control pollution with new technologies and stressed gradual, moderate improvements as the way to preserve both the industrial system and the environment.

Earth Day became an annual observation, albeit drained of the raw energy and critical edge of the first 1970 events. It triggered the formation of multiple new groups that advocated direct action as well as education and symbolized the decade's transition from New Left social movements of the 1960s into a new kind of social activism.

Pollution, Hazardous Waste, and the Environmental Justice Movement

Many low-income and minority Americans viewed the environmental movement as white and middle-class, and as focused on wilderness rather than the economic and social inequalities that affected urban America and the neighborhoods that disproportionately bore the effects of environmental pollution. The mainstream environmental movement was slow to recognize how Chicano and Mexican farmworkers, inner-city African Americans, and Native American uranium miners were affected by where they lived and worked because of race and income. The environmental justice movement emerged out of these communities to address both social and environmental concerns.

The first Earth Day celebration elicited dialogue among, and published articles about, African American and other communities of color and their responses to the new environmentalism. Many people articulated concerns about safe and sanitary housing and the dumping of garbage and hazardous materials in their neighborhoods. The Rev. Jesse Jackson, who founded Chicago's Operation PUSH in 1971, and several African American mayors, complained that the traditional environmental movement distracted attention from the civil rights movement and the environmental needs of poor urban Americans. On Earth Day 1970, African Americans in Chicago held their own separate environmental events. Through the decade, a multiracial coalition of urban activists, sociologists, public health officials, civil rights leaders, and others developed an environmental justice movement that focused on the class and race dimensions of environmental pollution.

Communities were finding themselves more widely exposed to pollution than they had first realized. Until the 1970s, hazardous wastes were treated as any other wastes and were typically dumped into landfills and waterways. As awareness of the harmful effects on human health grew, by the early 1970s environmental activists and residents often cooperated in seeking greater public control over the siting of waste dumps and disposal of hazardous materials.

In 1976, minority residents of Houston, Texas, who had opposed the locating of a hazardous waste site within 1,500 feet of a public school brought a lawsuit against Southwestern Waste Management Corporation for unfair discrimination

Rev. Jesse Jackson speaks on a radio broadcast from the Operation PUSH headquarters in Chicago, 1973. (National Archives)

against a neighborhood that had already been burdened by more than its share of waste. In 1979, a federal court judge ruled that the location of the site was unfortunate but not with racist intent. Still, the mobilization of citizens against unfair dumping continued. Also in 1979, the primarily African American North-wood Manor neighborhood of Houston challenged the Browning-Ferris Indus-tries' plans to locate a garbage dump nearby. Strong opposition convinced the Houston City Council to pass a resolution opposing the location of the sanitary landfill.

In 1976, the Urban Environment Conference brought together labor, religious, environmental, and minority activists to incorporate race and class issues in the environmental movement. Financed by the Sierra Club and labor unions, the conference generated a federal grant that funded eleven similar "City Care" con-ferences around the country. The conferences led to many states adopting Right-to-Know laws, which required new plants to notify communities of potential environmental risks.

The news of toxic waste in a white, working-class neighborhood in Buffalo, New York, and the response by residents, strengthened the environmental jus-tice movement. Residents of Love Canal discovered that their new homes were built along a toxic waste landfill. Children began suffering asthma and other respiratory problems from the school that had been built on top of the covered

Getting the Lead Out

Sometimes hazards were not as visible as neighborhood landfills or toxic industries. A major concern of low-income families was the presence of lead-based paint on the walls of older rental dwellings, and many urban communities organized to eliminate this health hazard. In the 1970s, a growing public health movement revealed the epidemic of childhood exposure to lead paint in poor neighborhoods. By 1970, dozens of community coalitions existed in older East Coast and Midwestern cities, which shared technical information and raised awareness about lead paint problems. Residents initiated screening and put pressure on Congress to prevent lead poisoning, resulting in the 1971 Lead-based Paint Poisoning Prevention Act, which limited lead content in paints and provided for lead-paint removal.

St. Louis community activist Ivory Perry found that slum property owners were often hard to identify and they often failed to fix collapsing stairs, backed-up sewage, and inadequate heating and water systems. In his visits to poor neighborhoods, he found a disproportionate number of children with skin and respiratory problems. Perry consulted with scientists at the Center for the Biology of Natural Systems at Washington University, who noted that children with nutritional deficiencies often ate sweet-tasting lead-based paint. In 1970, Perry organized a community campaign against lead poisoning and involved tenants, social workers, legislators, and the medical profession. The People's Coalition Against Lead Poisoning mobilized volunteers to establish a comprehensive lead-poisoning screening program and demanded that the city prosecute violators of the local lead control ordinance and detoxify dwellings. Education and agitation worked: after a June 1972 sit-in at city offices, the city attorney agreed to vigorously enforce the law and help eradicate lead poisoning.

Although the mainstream environmental movement failed to support low-income and urban efforts to deal with lead paint, it did rally around efforts to remove leaded gasoline from the environment. Studies in the 1970s revealed that 40 percent of blood lead came from the ambient environment, and environmental groups worked to pressure the EPA to eventually ban the sale of leaded gasoline.

dump of the Hooker Chemical Company. Toxic wastes drained into basements and backyards, where children burned their feet walking across lawns, and birth defects were reported. But residents could not get state officials to take action. Led by resident Lois Gibbs, whose own child had developed illnesses, in 1978 neighbors organized the Love Canal Homeowners' Association and collaborated with other environmental groups and scientists to force the state to identify the chemical hazards and provide a remedy. Investigations revealed over 400 chemicals, and evacuation became the solution. The state of New York purchased many of the homes and financed some relocation costs; by the late 1970s, President

Group Against Smog and Pollution (GASP)

Industrial Pittsburgh sought to improve area air quality by switching from coal to natural gas in the 1960s, although the local steel industry remained a major source of pollution. The Pittsburgh Chamber of Commerce opposed a local air-quality ordinance and the federal Clean Air Act of 1970. But local citizens formed the Group against Smog and Pollution (GASP) to pressure public and industry officials to reduce pollution for urban residents. Allied with the United Steelworkers of America (USWA), which was long concerned about industry air and its effects on worker health, GASP lobbied for stricter local and state air quality regulations. USWA had held the nation's first air pollution conference in Washington, D.C., in 1969 and had pressured Pennsylvania governor Raymond Schaeffer to enact more strict air quality standards. In 1970, Pennsylvania voters approved an "environmental rights" amendment to the state constitution, which granted citizens the right to clean air, water, and a natural environment. GASP persisted through the 1970s, determined to clean up the city's air by maintaining its independence and collecting technical information. It became the model for other citizen-based air quality advocacy groups in the nation.

But by the late 1970s, the relinquishment of environmental initiatives to policy makers and the decline of grassroots efforts weakened local progress on air quality. Pittsburgh's earlier strides were overcome by development interests and the rhetoric of jobs over environmental quality. The industrial city, fearing economic decline, denied the threats of pollution. Even the local American Lung Association, unlike its national parent that advocated improved air quality, refused to work with GASP and opposed efforts to enforce national pollution control measures. The Pennsylvania Environmental Council, representing industry, labor, and environmental professionals, established itself as the dominant environmental network in the early 1970s. Its professed tone of moderation and compromise with political and business leadership put it at odds with citizen advocacy groups like GASP.

Jimmy Carter had declared Love Canal a disaster area, entitling residents to federal aid for relocation.

The Ecumenical Task Force of the Niagara Frontier, Inc. (ETF) was founded on March 13, 1979, by the interfaith community of western New York in response to the Love Canal crisis. ETF worked with Love Canal residents to enlist the assistance of scientists to collect and interpret the information concerning the health risks in the community, and then, with state, federal, and local officials, to obtain relief for residents and remediation for the toxic waste problems at the Love Canal and other sites in Niagara County.

The Love Canal struggle emboldened many grassroots community groups across the country to take action against industrial pollution in their backyards.

It also pushed Congress to act in establishing cleanup procedures with the Comprehensive Emergency Response, Compensation, and Liability Act, better known as Superfund, in late 1980.

Environmental Legislation and Litigation

Many environmental groups sought to fundamentally change the practices of polluters and protect places and species through legislation and enforcement. The popularity of the environmental movement led to the passage of key legislation and regulatory policies in the 1970s. Combined with a sympathetic judiciary, environmentalists gained new clout and helped create a new field of law.

The comprehensive National Environmental Policy Act (NEPA), signed into law by President Nixon on the first day of 1970, provided the first important national policy to protect the environment. It established a Council on Environmental Quality (CEQ) to provide ecological research and required that environmental impact statements be prepared for major federal actions that would significantly affect the environment. It is a testament to the popularity of the environmental movement that Nixon, a conservative Republican, felt compelled to support strong legislation to outflank Democratic rivals, especially senators Gaylord Nelson and Edmund Muskie who supported protection of the environment, to appeal to voters. Washington senator Henry Jackson conceived of NEPA, and the legislation, which garnered little debate, became the cornerstone of modern U.S. environmental policy.

Nixon wanted to be viewed as a new Teddy Roosevelt, who employed efficiency and technology to encourage conservation. He also worried about the CEQ's potential to advocate "extreme" environmental positions and sought to counter it by reorganizing government environmental functions and enforcement into one body. With congressional support, Nixon merged federal environmental activities under one agency, the new Environmental Protection Agency (EPA). The EPA was charged with creating national pollution standards and enforcing them in cooperation with states.

In the years following NEPA, Congress passed a variety of laws protecting air, water, species, lands, and public health. Beginning with the Clean Air Act, passed in late 1970, which identified pollutants that caused smog and applied standards to regulate emissions, environmental legislation became increasingly prescriptive, detailed, and complex. During the early 1970s, CEQ developed a comprehensive environmental program that included amendments to the Federal Water Pollution Control Act, the Toxic Substances Control Act, the Resource Conservation and Recovery Act, Marine Mammal Protection Act, the Safe Drinking Water Act, and amendments to pesticides legislation. During its formative years, CEQ laid the groundwork for almost all current environmental legislation except for Superfund and asbestos control legislation. CEQ also developed guidelines for the environmental impact statement process. At the time they were developed, CEQ staffers had no idea how revolutionary the environmental impact statement process would become.

Leaders of key national environmental groups joined together in 1970 to form the bipartisan League of Conservation Voters (LCV) to track the voting records and policy decisions of Congress and the president, providing members the information necessary to persuade (or elect) officials to support more environmentally friendly legislation. Conceived by Marion Edey, who became the first unpaid staff person, the LCV, with support from David Brower and Friends of the Earth (FOE), decided it could be most effective by challenging vulnerable antienvironmental Democratic incumbents. Initially housed in the Washington, D.C., office of FOE, in 1972 philosophical differences split FOE, and most of the LCV staff left and created the Environmental Policy Center (later Environmental Policy Institute). Tensions within FOE during the 1970s reflected larger tensions in the environmental movement. Activists, including founder David Brower, sought to expand a more radical agenda and empower international and local chapters, but FOE professional staff insisted on utilizing resources for lobbying and policy functions.

Activists often used federal legislation to advance new efforts to protect the environment. The Clean Water Act was passed in 1972 and required industries to clean up their effluent and cities to treat sewage before releasing into waterways. As a result, fishermen and activists realized the possibility of returning formerly polluted streams and rivers into healthy ecosystems. The group American Rivers was founded in 1973 with the specific focus of increasing the number of rivers protected by the National Wild and Scenic Rivers System and preventing the construction of large new dams on the country's last wild rivers.

Activists helped pass the Resource Conservation and Recovery Act (RCRA) in 1975, which included provisions for waste recycling. Thousands of recycling centers were established around the country, and in the early 1970s, Oregon and Vermont successfully passed "bottle bills" to mandate that deposits be paid on glass containers and that businesses accept them for recycling. Two dozen additional states sought bottle bills, which pitted retail food businesses and labor groups that feared job loss against environmentalists.

Many environmental groups, while continuing educational and lobbying efforts through the 1970s, began to focus on litigation to enforce legislative gains made during the decade. Environmental groups used the environmental impact review process established by NEPA and turned to the courts to compel compliance. Relying on lawyers and scientists more than grassroots activists, the Environmental Defense Fund (EDF), Natural Resources Defense Council (NRDC), and the Sierra Club Legal Defense Fund developed campaigns to litigate to eliminate the use of lead, protect whales, and reduce pesticide hazards. Increasingly, during the 1970s, the environmental movement depended on the legal and scientific services offered by groups like the NRDC and EDF.

The expansion of national environmental groups and the increased funding and clout that they could muster reflected the general public acceptance and support of environmentalism. But because mainstream environmental organizations shifted their focus to litigation and policymaking, they became increasingly bureaucratic, with professional staff members moving between organizations and government positions, and relied on mail recruitment of members. Robert Gottlieb notes that the groups became "increasingly absorbed by the operation and maintenance of the policy system itself" and failed to create "a new kind of social movement," which might have mobilized the millions of Americans who were involved in local environmental groups through the 1970s (1993, 130–131). Many believe that this failure to develop and mobilize constituencies in support of environmental laws allowed business and ranching groups to represent themselves as "grass roots" to counter federally imposed environmental policies.

Increasingly, economic interests resisted implementation and enforcement of environmental legislation. The Endangered Species Act (ESA) of 1973 generated particular controversy. The act reflected Americans' growing concern about environmental imbalance and a willingness to limit human economic endeavors in the interests of the survival of other species. The act restricted the scale of development and resource extraction activities when the impacts of those activities threatened the survival of various species. In 1978, a citizens' group in Tennessee halted construction of a TVA dam because a rare fish, the snail darter, would lose critical habitat to be inundated by the Tellico dam. A coalition of farmers, whose lands were threatened by the dam, and environmentalists sued the TVA under the EPA. The Supreme Court ruled in favor of the fish and the ESA. But in 1979, Sen. Howard Baker of Tennessee worked tirelessly to amend the act to allow the dam project to be completed. Ultimately, by summer, the House and the Senate voted to amend the act to allow dam completion, and a reluctant President Carter, who needed Baker's support for the Panama Canal Treaty, signed the bill in September.

By 1974, the oil crisis, Nixon's resignation, and the linking of economic decline in forest products, mining, and manufacturing to stricter environmental regulations decreased public support for extensive environmental protection. Environmentalists found more support during the Carter administration of 1977–1980, but business groups, too, had mobilized by the late 1970s and put increasing pressure on Congress to limit environmental restrictions that might hurt the economy. Local governments and businesses often complained about new recordkeeping requirements and expensive adjustments to past polluting practices to comply with legislation such as the Occupational Safety and Health Administration (OSHA).

The Nuclear Threat

With a looming energy crisis by the 1970s, nuclear power was touted as a cheap, clean, and safe alternative source of power. But concerns for the environmental effects of nuclear power, whether for peaceful or military purposes, revived the antinuclear movement. People in western states, especially Native American miners in New Mexico, where almost half the nation's uranium was mined, became concerned about the health hazards from mining and the millions of tons of waste generated. Concerns also arose from the effects of the nuclear testing programs in Nevada, which particularly affected downwind Mormon communities in southwestern Utah. Eastern urban areas became concerned about technological flaws in reactors that could lead to serious accidents affecting workers and communities. As a result, communities mobilized to regulate and even halt nuclear production.

The Cold War expansion of nuclear weapons had earlier spawned an antinuclear movement in the 1950s, including nuclear physicists who helped create the atomic bomb and groups such as the National Committee for a Sane Nuclear Policy (SANE). SANE, Women Strike for Peace, and others pressured the U.S. government to halt weapons testing and reach nonproliferation agreements with the Soviet Union. In the early 1960s, David Brower resigned as president of the Sierra Club when the organization failed to criticize nuclear power, and he formed Friends of the Earth. But the antinuclear movement generally declined with advances the government made in regulation and in the preoccupation with other social and political issues, especially the Vietnam War.

In 1971, a small team of activists set off in an old fishing boat from Vancouver, British Columbia, to Amchitka, a tiny island off the West Coast of Alaska, to protest and block the United States from testing an underground nuclear bomb in this refuge for bald eagles, peregrine falcons, and endangered sea otters. The organizers of the voyage had quit the Sierra Club for its refusal to take a stand against nuclear weapons, and they inscribed the boat with the word "Greenpeace," to mark their concern for the planet and the nuclear arms race. The boat never made it to Amchitka, and the United States still detonated the bomb, but the journey sparked a flurry of public interest and support for what became an international environmental group. Nuclear testing on Amchitka ended that same year, and the island was later declared a bird sanctuary. Through the 1970s, Greenpeace expanded its visible protests against whaling, seal hunting, and nuclear testing.

National as well as local groups organized to oppose all nuclear materials, whether used in weapons or power plants. For example, the Prairie Alliance in Illinois mobilized to pressure Congress to ban all nuclear materials. The Union of Concerned Scientists, formed in 1971 at the Massachusetts Institute of Technology, added credibility to the movement as they questioned the safety of the nuclear power industry. Because of growing concerns over the possibilities of nuclear accidents, the Atomic Energy Commission in 1975 required new plants to provide emergency cooling systems to prevent meltdowns of the reactor core.

The mid-1970s energy crisis gave the nuclear industry more clout, but antinuclear groups also gained influence. The movement shifted from seeking regulation to direct action. In early 1974, the Ralph Nader network, Friends of the Earth, and the Union of Concerned Scientists helped create a new coalton of antinuclear groups called Critical Mass. In 1977, the Mobilization for Survival formed to bring together groups protesting nuclear power and an accelerating arms race dealing in nuclear weapons. But despite a growing antinuclear movement, between 1972 and 1976 almost all statewide antinuclear ballot measures were defeated.

The case of Karen Silkwood, employed by Kerr-McGee in an Oklahoma plant that made fuel rods for nuclear generators, mobilized many activists and labor unions to recognize threats of nuclear production. In 1974, she died in a mysterious auto accident, which many believed to be linked to her criticisms of the company's negligence in exposing employees to radioactive materials. Years of litigation forced the company to settle with the Silkwood estate for more than a million dollars, and the trials pushed companies to increase safety standards in the industry. The Mike Nichols film *Silkwood* (1983) starring Meryl Streep brought the story of Karen Silkwood's courageous efforts to tell the truth about nuclear contamination of workers to the American public.

Concerns over nuclear plant safety were heightened in 1979 by the accidental release of radiation at the Three Mile Island plant near Harrisburg, Pennsylvania. The plant suffered a near meltdown and contaminated the site, causing several billion dollars in damage, and forcing evacuation of the area. The event represented the worst commercial atomic power accident in U.S. history. The release of the film *The China Syndrome* about the same time, which portrayed a fictional nuclear plant disaster, convinced many Americans that stricter safeguards were needed for the nation's nuclear power plants.

Three Mile Island nuclear power facility near Harrisburg, Pennsylvania, site of the famous accident in 1979. (Greenpeace)

Just weeks after the Three Mile Island incident but receiving significantly less

Clamshell and Abalone Antinuclear Alliances

Many of those in the Left counterculture who had created communes in rural New England or northern California became part of a new nonviolent direct action movement against nuclear energy. Influenced by the successful German movement that blocked the construction of a nuclear power plant by sit-in protests, a group of New Englanders formed the Clamshell Alliance to halt construction of the Public Service Corporation's nuclear power plant in Seabrook, on the coast of New Hampshire. Adopting the principles of nonviolence and consensus decision making, in the summer of 1976, the Alliance organized a mass occupation, which was held the following April at the construction site and drew 24,000 people. Officials rounded up several thousand protestors and held them at seven armories in the state for two weeks, where the "leaderless" movement negotiated with state officials.

Women played a key role in the protest, and in sustaining the movement over the coming years. In addition to civil disobedience, activists sought to halt construction in the courts. Ultimately, the New Hampshire utility company with majority ownership of the Seabrook Station was bankrupted by the project, and the Three Mile Island accident led officials to add the requirement for an evacuation plan prior to commissioning. In the end, only one of the two planned reactors went on line.

The Clamshell Alliance inspired other antinuclear groups across the country and helped activate alliances between the counterculture, peace, and environmental movements to make their voices heard on this issue they believed threatened the planet. In 1976, the Abalone Alliance organized to protest the construction of the Diablo Canyon Power Plant on the central California coast. The Alliance joined with Mothers for Peace of San Luis Obispo to hold fundraisers and protests, such as one event at San Luis Obispo where 40,000 gathered to protest the nuclear plant, listen to rock music, and explore alternative energy sources. When Pacific Gas and Electric received the license to operate the Diablo nuclear plant in 1981, the Abalone Alliance called for a massive occupation of the site, and within two weeks, almost 2,000 protesters were arrested. When a PG&E engineer found a critical error in the construction blueprints, the plant was shut down for repairs. Alliance activists claimed that their nonviolent direct action had succeeded.

press coverage, radioactive tailings from mining operations in New Mexico spilled into the Rio Puerco, contaminating large portions of Navajo lands. But the antinuclear and environmental movements were slow to recognize Native Americans and other people of color as environmental victims.

That year the U.S. government tried to prevent *Progressive* magazine from publishing its expose, "The H-Bomb Secret—How We Got It, Why We're Telling It," even though the point of the November issue was to reveal how, through spreading atomic power throughout the world, the United States had made it easier for terrorists and others to acquire nuclear weapons. By the end of the decade, the Three Mile Island disaster, cost overruns and technical flaws in plant construction, and a persistent antinuclear movement dramatically slowed the expansion of the nuclear industry.

CONTESTING 1970S SOCIAL CHANGE

The Backlash to Protests and the Rise of Conservative Activism

By the mid-1970s, although liberal and leftist movements continued to organize and have an impact on American society, conservatives had also organized and began asserting greater political power to counter civil rights, antiwar, and environmental goals. Prompted by the rhetoric of President Nixon and Vice President Agnew that framed rising protests as "security threats" that could lead the nation to anarchy, the media, politicians, university administrators, and the general public began demanding harsher treatment of student radicals and their disruptive antics. The militant rhetoric of fringe sectarian groups garnered much media and political attention even though they never actually engaged in much violence, except when provoked by infiltrators or police. Nixon's earlier campaign appeal for "law and order" resonated among many Americans, who supported local police actions against demonstrators and radical groups as well as harsher penalties for drug use and other crimes.

Conservative think tanks such as the Heritage Foundation, founded in 1973, and the American Enterprise Institute provided the research and intellectual arguments to advance conservative issues. Conservatives wanted to limit the expansive government they believed had been achieved by decades of liberals in office. They were intent on rolling back what social movements of the 1960s and 1970s had created by reducing social welfare spending on programs for the aged, poor, students, and others.

The new conservative activists also intended to restrict what they viewed as an overly activist government in civil rights matters. The *Bakke* case reflected white resentments toward government programs such as affirmative action, which to them appeared to offer preferential benefits to minorities. Many whites in the 1970s had tired of hearing about race as an issue in American society and wanted to believe that civil rights gains of the 1960s had solved the country's racial problems and inequalities. President Nixon played a role in encouraging the racial backlash. On the one hand, his administration created the first important affirmative action programs for federally funded projects. But on the other hand, his 1968 campaign that stressed "law and order" not only took aim at youthful hippies, protestors, and militants but also so-called lawless urban minorities who threatened the safety of the "silent" (or white) majority. Nixon played on the public's fears of rioting African Americans in cities to cultivate an anti–civil rights constituency by appointing conservative judges and using the FBI and other federal agencies to curtail the activities of the Black Panther Party and other civil rights activists.

The backlash was expressed in increasingly threatening ways. Membership in the Ku Klux Klan tripled during the 1970s, and attacks on African American schoolchildren in South Boston and the killings of demonstrators in Greensboro revealed the extent of white rage at imagined inequities associated with civil rights demands. With a rising crime rate due to deindustrialization and decaying cities, and lurid media images of urban violence that associated African Americans with crime, whites increasingly saw themselves as victims and believed that minority groups had demanded too much.

Just as conservative activists attempted to beat back civil rights initiatives such as affirmative action, they asserted a rhetoric of "family values" to curtail feminist and gay rights agendas. Organized efforts to oppose gay rights measures began in earnest in 1977. In Miami-Dade County, the successful election of local candidates by a coalition of gay organizations, and their enactment of a county antidiscrimination law to include sexual preference, led conservative Christians to form the group Save Our Children (SOC) to oppose the law. SOC quickly acquired the necessary signatures to challenge the law, and with the support of the local media and singer Anita Bryant, repealed it with a large majority of voters. The SOC victory encouraged other antigay activists across the country to launch similar campaigns to repeal gay rights measures and to ban gay schoolteachers. Gay activists fought back and led a boycott of Florida orange juice, a product Bryant advertised. They also defeated repeal measures in Seattle and the statewide Briggs resolution in California in 1978. That same year, however, Oklahoma state senator Mary Helms led a successful effort to make it lawful for school districts to refuse employment to gays.

Even as they maligned 1970s social movements, conservative activists often borrowed their tactics to win widespread appeal and accomplish political change. The passage of the Federal Land Policy and Management Act in 1976 created a political movement in many western states during the late 1970s. Cattlemen, miners, loggers, developers, farmers, and others in states where the federal government owned a majority of the land argued that this "monopoly" had an adverse impact on the economy of their states. They also claimed that it violated the principle of states' rights. This "Sagebrush Rebellion" presaged privatization efforts of the late 20th century in demanding that the federal government transfer control over large amounts of public land to individual states, allowing private purchase or insisting that states control management of land and natural resources. After the election of Ronald Reagan in 1980 and his appointment of James Watt, who had been a leader of the movement in Wyoming, as secretary of the Interior, the rebellion was defused.

Ranchers and their supporters involved in the Sagebrush Rebellion were able to appear as victims of a faceless, elite bureaucracy, appealing to larger constituencies throughout the West. They helped portray in the public mind environmentalists as an elite movement based in Washington, D.C., "special interests" who sacrificed American jobs for their leisure-time pleasures. Despite continue public support for environmental protections, the conservative movement's effective actions made it harder for environmentalists to attract new supporters.

White Flight and Busing

By the 1970s, southern states had the nation's most integrated schools. In 1976, 45.1 percent of the South's African American students attended majority white schools, compared with 27.5 percent in the Northeast and 29.7 percent in the Midwest. The success of school integration depended on one of the most controversial federal decisions regarding civil rights—the decision to bus students.

In 1971, the U.S. Supreme Court ruled on *Swann v. Charlotte-Mecklenburg Board of Education,* a case that marked one of the first attempts to implement a broad-scale urban desegregation plan and also recognized busing as a means of achieving it. Discovering that the time and distances involved in the busing plan were no more inconvenient to Charlotte than the busing the city already participated in for nondesegregation purposes, the court ordered the school district to bus for the purpose of integrating its public schools.

Busing was immediately attacked by a large segment of the public as well as President Nixon's administration. Critics claimed busing undermined the sovereignty of communities and schools, constituted social engineering, and was impractical, intrusive, and a direct result of biased, liberal judicial activism. In 1972, President Nixon asked Congress to ban busing, and although his effort to stop busing failed, the public call for desegregation slowed. Nixon's new appointees to the Supreme Court would effectively limit busing in subsequent decisions.

As northern schools became increasingly segregated as whites left inner cities for suburbs, federal district courts sought to remedy this racial imbalance by busing white students across district boundaries to city schools. In 1974 in *Milliken v. Bradley,* the Supreme Court effectively halted busing within a Detroit suburb's borders. Justices cited "local control" as an important educational tradition that influenced the decision and emphasized that de facto segregation, or what occurs "naturally" because of residential patterns, could not be used in desegregation as in de jure segregation.

Three years later the Court decided another case in which it ordered Michigan and the Detroit school system to finance a plan to address educational deficits faced by its African American children. The deficits, the Court suspected, arose from enforced segregation and could not be cured by physical desegregation alone. In the late 1970s and early 1980s, private civil rights lawyers successfully

Busing Protests in Boston (1974)

Following desegregation orders in other communities, African American parents and community leaders, supported by the NAACP, accused the Boston public school system of unconstitutionally segregating the city's African American students. In the summer of 1974, U.S. District Court Judge W. Arthur Garrity Jr. issued the historic ruling that the Boston School Committee had "knowingly carried out a systematic program of segregation . . . and [had] intentionally brought about and maintained a dual school system" (Walsh, 2000, 3). Garrity relied on the plan of the director of the state education department's Bureau of Equal Educational Opportunity, Charles Glenn, a former Episcopal minister and civil rights activist, which divided the city into school districts that would ensure that each school have a more equal proportion of black and white children. But the plan called for busing children between neighborhoods that had become deeply segregated and distrustful of one another. When the plan was implemented in September, the white neighborhoods burst into violence.

Media images showed mobs of screaming, rock-hurling whites, mostly women, in South Boston attacking buses of African American schoolchildren. Rioting between white and black students at previously all-white South Boston High School brought the police to occupy the school. A small percentage of the 20,000 children designated to be bused actually rode the buses that September. The governor called up the National Guard, and President Ford considered sending U.S. troops to Boston. The city became emblematic of a growing white backlash against desegregation and signaled that it was just as difficult to break social patterns in the North as in the South. Also, in this battle between poor whites and poor African Americans, it represented the unraveling of the old New Deal, Democratic Party coalition.

South Boston women organized the group Restore Our Alienated Rights (ROAR) to protest the busing order. They fought for maintaining what they perceived as critical to their neighborhood integrity, including control of local schools and segregation in the city. They also emphasized their maternal roles in becoming so publicly active in the antibusing cause. Many had been active in their children's schools and the Home and School Association, and they supported the upwardly mobile Irish Catholic teachers, who were also opponents of desegregation. ROAR organized mass demonstrations, sent thousands to protest at the statehouse, and ran press conferences. They also had a publicly visible friend in the city council, Louise Day Hicks.

On the other side, despite the resistance, many civil rights leaders and educators believed that Boston's busing struggle was critical for the nation's promise of equitable educational opportunity for all, and many felt a sense of urgency in overcoming the civil disorder. African American parents campaigned against violence and sought to keep their children calm in the face of antagonism. The Freedom House became a place where African American parents from Roxbury could decompress and strategize with officials for greater security measures for their

Continued on next page

Busing Protests in Boston (1974), Continued

children, and where white and black student volunteers from area colleges and universities tutored children.

Yet the resistance to busing and desegregation in Boston, which many once saw as the center of American liberal tolerance, signaled a decline in public support for a race-blind society. Continued rigid segregated housing patterns and white flight to the suburbs helped institutionalize a segregated educational system, where poor African Americans were left inhabiting urban school districts. Boston's Roxbury and Dorchester neighborhoods had once been home to middle-class Jews, Irish, and African Americans, but by the early 1970s had became predominantly poor and black. South Boston and Charlestown had always been Irish enclaves, but as writer Catherine Walsh noted, "as the more well-to-do moved away, the poor Irish who were left behind clung to an often perverse territorial pride" (Walsh 2000). By the 1990s, just 15 percent of students in the Boston Public Schools were white. On the 25th anniversary of the desegregation decision, a group of white parents known as "Boston Children First" filed suit in federal court and charged that the use of race as a factor in assigning children to schools discriminated against white children. A few weeks later, the Boston School Committee decided to drop race as a consideration in student school assignments, beginning in the year 2000.

Black students are bused back to the Roxbury neighborhood from South Boston under heavy police guard on the third day of court-ordered busing as a means of public school integration, September 16, 1974. (Corbis)

pursued metropolitan school initiatives in such cities as Wilmington, Delaware, Indianapolis, Louisville, and St. Louis. However, the federal government did not assist in the cases and sometimes resisted the efforts.

Resistance to busing and to desegregation in general was expressed by white "flight," or the exodus of middle-class and working-class whites from city to suburbs through the 1970s. Continuing a process that had begun in the period following World War II, as whites and some middle-class African Americans moved to the suburbs, they helped change the landscape of the United States, the nature of metropolitan areas, and they increasingly left central cities poor and African American. In examin-

University of California v. Bakke (1978)

In 1974, Allen Bakke claimed that Affirmative Action policies prevented him from gaining admission to the University of California at Davis medical school. Affirmative action had been created to provide educational and job opportunities for historically disadvantaged groups, such as women and minorities. Bakke, who was white, insisted that because the medical school reserved sixteen slots for qualified minority applicants, his civil rights had been violated.

In ruling on *Regents of the University of California v. Bakke* in 1978, the Supreme Court sent mixed signals about the future of affirmative action. The justices voted 5–4 that quotas, or set-asides, such as those used by the University of California constituted reverse discrimination and were illegal. However, they also ruled 5–4 that recruitment or training programs for disadvantaged groups—the core idea of affirmative action—could be considered to help diversify the workplace and university.

The case symbolized how central understandings of race became in the 1970s. Frustrated by how little the liberal, integrationist model of civil rights had achieved, people of color asserted their racial and ethnic identities as a way to become recognized and respected. As Eric Porter notes, many activists believed that cultural pluralism, or accepting difference, "would provide a mechanism for achieving racial equity and a more equitable society" (2004, 56). But whites, too, capitalized on notions of difference and equality to maintain their position of privilege. Almost immediately, the concept of "reverse racism" gained credence and popularity among many whites, who could now blame any denial of positions to a supposed favoritism granted African Americans and other minorities under Affirmative Action. Many whites feared that in granting more equality to American minorities, they themselves would lose advantages, and they resented perceived benefits that government programs provided disproportionately to people of color.

ing the racial politics of Atlanta, a national center of the civil rights movement and black political power, Kevin Kruse concludes that segregationist resistance, which failed to stop the civil rights movement, nevertheless managed to preserve the world of segregation through suburbanization. Moreover, white flight transformed the political ideology of those involved, increased hostility to the federal government and the New Deal and Great Society support systems it provided, and gave birth to several new conservative causes, such as the tax revolt and privatization of public services.

Radical Threats: Weather Underground Organization

In addition to rising government repression, the conservative backlash and mobilization, and the exhaustion that affected 1970s social movements, the perceived radicalism of many movements doomed their potential popular appeal. Despite its small numbers, fewer than 500 after 1970, the Weather Underground Organization (WUO, its name changed from Weatherman in 1970 to reflect a new feminist consciousness) achieved notoriety for its embrace of violence as a means to end U.S. government oppression at home and abroad. As more young people became increasingly outraged by the war in Vietnam, the Weatherman's revolutionary rhetoric appealed to many in SDS, the major student-led organization of the 1960s, including National Committee members Mark Rudd, David Gilbert, and Bernadine Dohrn. Fractious divisions within SDS, and by 1969 its decline, essentially allowed the Weatherman to control the organization. Local SDS chapters soon disbanded, and by February 1970, the Weatherman decided to close the SDS National Office.

First used at the 1969 SDS national conference in Chicago, the name Weatherman was derived from the Bob Dylan song "Subterranean Homesick Blues," which included the lyrics "You don't need a weatherman to know which way the wind blows." The Weatherman pushed for more militancy in the antiwar movement, believing that only dramatic action could end racism, inequality, and the war. Made up primarily of white, middle-class youth, it was committed to the Black Panthers' perspective and emulated their rhetoric and tactics, although a split between the two groups arose at the 1969 SDS convention.

After the 1969 Chicago "Days of Rage," where street fighting with police resulted in many arrests, injuries, and damage to buildings, and the police shootings of Black Panther Party leader Fred Hampton, the Weatherman turned more violent, believing that only extremism could stop the U.S. military-police machine. Influenced by international revolutionary movements such as the 1968 student revolts in Paris, indigenous uprisings in Latin America, and Marxist-led independence movements in Africa, the Weatherman believed that urban guerilla actions in the United States could stimulate a similar revolution. In 1970, the group issued a "declaration of a state of war" against the United States government, using for the first time its new name, the Weather Underground Organization, adopting fake identities, halting contact with family and friends, and pursuing covert activities.

On March 6, 1970, as members of the group attempted to build a bomb at their Greenwich Village townhouse to detonate at a U.S. military officers' dance at Fort Dix, New Jersey, the device accidentally exploded. WUO members Theodore Gold, Diana Oughton, and Terry Robbins were killed by the blast. Although news of the bombing turned off many former student left supporters, the news media portrayed the WUO radicals as student protesters who had turned into serious revolutionaries. In the minds of many Americans, the Weather Underground represented what was wrong with the student and antiwar movements.

Despite their decline in popularity and increased surveillance and infiltration by the Nixon administration and FBI, the WUO persisted in attacking the United

Greensboro Massacre (1979)

Another setback to civil rights efforts occurred on November 3, 1979, as anti-Klan demonstrators gathered in an African American neighborhood of Greensboro, North Carolina, to begin a march for justice. About 35 Klansmen and Nazis descended on the public rally, opened fire on the unarmed demonstrators, and then drove away. The attackers killed dedicated activists Cesar Cauce, Dr. Mike Nathan, Bill Sampson, Sandi Smith, and Dr. Jim Waller, and wounded 11 others. The 5 killed had been organizing area hospital and textile workers.

The Communist Workers Party, which organized the demonstration, had obtained a parade permit and expected police protection. But instead of pursuing Klan attackers, police arrested activists, several of whom were seriously wounded from the shootings. There was also evidence indicating that law enforcement officials informed the Klan of the march location several days prior to their attack.

Rev. Nelson Johnson, one of the organizers of the protest, recalled in a 2004 interview the efforts of police to punish participants:

> They arrested me and held me, did not set a bond. As a matter of fact, I've had seven charges brought against me directly growing out of the incident of 1979. And I have been in jail under a bond twice that of any Klansperson. I was once in jail for under the $50,000, allegedly for using bad language. And the Klansmen were in for murder for $50,000, so if you work with that, it gives you a sense of the atmosphere, which was unbelievable, except for those of us who were in it. (Quoted in Goodman 2004)

Although televised videotaped recordings of the massacre indicated that the Klansmen and Nazis actually looked for particular individuals to kill, in the 1980 state trial, an all-white jury acquitted the six accused murderers. In the 1984 federal trial, the Klansmen and Nazis again claimed self-defense and pleaded successfully to another all-white jury that their motive was not racial but political. They only wanted to shoot communists that day—not African Americans—and therefore were not guilty of the charges. Finally, in 1985, after years of legal struggles, a successful civil suit was won by the victims and survivors of the massacre. Yet at the time, the Greensboro Massacre discouraged and intimidated many civil rights activists who saw the killings as a continuation of Klan and police complicity and a lack of national will to alter the balance of power between black and white, rich and poor.

States "from within." They took responsibility for the symbolic bombings of two dozen public buildings, including the Pentagon. But they notified officials of attacks in advance to avoid any loss of life—their message was to destroy the physical symbols of U.S. power, not the innocent workers who inhabited the buildings. WUO members remained largely successful at avoiding police and intelligence agencies.

Women, including Kathy Boudin, Bernardine Dohrn, and Cathy Wilkerson, played key leadership roles in the group, despite WUO's aggressive rhetoric and style and glamorization of violence. Like other revolutionary groups, WUO viewed imperialism as the source of all oppression, and believed that ending imperialism would liberate all peoples, men and women. Jane Alpert, as a member of the Weather Underground, increasingly criticized the male chauvinist basis of leftist politics. Her surrender in late 1974 polarized segments of the women's movement between those who saw her feminist commitment as a stand of courage and those who saw her conversion from radicalism to feminism as a betrayal.

Gradually, by the end of the 1970s, aware that the revolution they had all been working toward had failed to materialize, most remaining WUO members came aboveground and turned themselves in. After the group began dissolving, some members moved on to other armed revolutionary groups and were subsequently arrested and sentenced for long prison terms. Former WUO member Bill Ayers noted in a recent film interview that the goal of the group was to "bring the war home . . . that the best that we could do was to bring about a catastrophic series of actions that would get the attention of the world" (transcript of *The Weather Underground* in Goodman, 2003).

BIOGRAPHIES

Barry Commoner, 1917–

Biologist and Environmentalist

Born in Brooklyn, Barry Commoner attended Harvard University and received a doctorate in biology in 1941, focusing especially on ozone layer depletion. After the 1950s, he warned of the environmental threats posed by modern technology and became a leading environmental spokesman after the publication of his classic *Science and Survival* (1966). In February 1970, Commoner appeared on the cover of *Time* magazine, representing one of the "new jeremiads" warning of the earth's destruction if humankind did not alter its ways.

During the 1970s, he published several influential books outlining the problems of new technologies and calling for fundamental change in the postwar industrial system. In his popular book, *The Closing Circle,* published in 1971, he presented what he viewed as common-sense ecological laws: "Everything is Connected to Everything Else. Everything Must Go Somewhere. Nature Knows Best. There Is No Such Thing as a Free Lunch."

Moved by public expressions during the first Earth Day, Commoner felt he needed to provide an explanation of "the environmental crisis and its possible cures." His book described the planet's *ecosphere* as a set of interconnected parts, a delicate balance "so heavily strained that its continued stability is threatened." Although he did not outline solutions, Commoner laid out a coherent critique of how the dependence on technology and the wasteful byproducts of consumption had increased pollution and altered the planet's health. He expected that through understanding the social origins of the environmental crisis, the country could begin "to manage the huge undertaking of surviving it" (Commoner 1971, 109).

Commoner's subsequent work and writings in the decade focused on energy problems. Relying on research from scientists associated with his Center for the Biology of Natural Systems, Commoner found postwar energy choices as inefficient and contributing to the environmental crisis. In his books *Energy and Human Welfare* (1975), *The Poverty of Power* (1976), and *The Politics of Energy* (1979), he linked his advocacy of renewable energy to the need for a different economic system.

Commoner was a visible public speaker and commentator through the 1970s, making frequent appearances on college campuses. The mainstream environmental movement considered many of Commoner's solutions as too radical, especially when he combined his socialist and environmental beliefs in a brief Citizen's Party presidential campaign in 1979–1980. For the next 20 years, he directed the Center for the Biology of Natural Systems at Queens College in New York City.

Maggie Kuhn, 1905–1995

Leader of the Gray Panthers

The fastest-growing segment of the American population, the elderly, found its radical voice in the Gray Panthers. Formed by Margaret "Maggie" Kuhn and other retirees in 1970 as the Consultation of Older and Younger Adults for Social Change, the group became known as the Gray Panthers in 1972. An active antiwar protestor, Kuhn was forced to retire from her job because of her age. In sharing her story with friends, she learned her plight was not unusual and became determined to restore dignity to the elderly. Ageism, Kuhn claimed, was just as much an oppressive force as racism, sexism, and militarism. The Panthers called for a "New Deal" for seniors, including a national health service to improve Medicare, and public housing and food assistance.

Born into a conservative Buffalo, New York, household, Kuhn attended Western Reserve University's College for Women in Cleveland, where a sociology course introduced her to the horrors of jails, sweatshops, and slums, and she began to think about a life of activism. Her first job was with the YWCA where she worked with working women.

Later Kuhn was critical of the leading senior groups AARP and the National Council of Senior Citizens (NCSC) for not addressing race, class, and gender inequities. Outraged that the president's 1971 White House Conference on Aging ignored the special needs of African American elderly, who with a lower life expectancy than whites did not live long enough to receive benefits and suffered greater poverty and health problems, the Gray Panthers and the National Caucus on the Black Aged held an alternative conference drawing attention to these issues. The "Black House Conference" garnered publicity for the Panthers and Kuhn. In 1972, Kuhn spoke at a press conference at the United Presbyterian Church general assembly and caught the attention of reporters because of her frank and knowledgeable comments about retirement, nursing homes, and sex.

The public attention helped pressure President Nixon to propose expanding Medicare, increasing Social Security benefits, and establishing a nutrition program for the elderly. But poverty and health care issues were not the only concern of the Gray Panthers. They also called for the elimination of child poverty, the end to war, and the preservation of the environment.

Visible protests, such as the guerrilla theater action in front of the AMA annual convention in Chicago in 1973, which raised concerns about physician fees and lack of medical research on the elderly, attracted national headlines. By 1979, the Gray Panthers had 30,000 members across the country. The national Gray Panthers was run out of Kuhn's West Philadelphia home, which she shared with some young people, but local chapters across the country acted autonomously, engaging in local projects of interest and concern.

Jane Fonda, 1937–

Actress and Activist

One of the more celebrated and reviled antiwar activists, Jane Fonda came to her activism fairly late. Coming from a family of actors, including noteworthy father, Henry Fonda, in 1970 Jane Fonda became a passionate supporter of militant Native Americans who had taken over the Alcatraz Island site to draw attention to grievances. That year, after meeting several influential activists at Hollywood parties, including Fred Gardner who had launched the GI coffeehouse movement, Fonda began protesting the war and supporting other causes, including demonstrating in front of stores selling nonunion lettuce. She was instrumental in raising funds for the Winter Soldier investigations.

Fonda's antiwar politics, however, made it difficult for her to land significant roles in Hollywood. Even after winning the Oscar for her role in *Klute,* she worked in minor films until in 1977, when she appeared with George Segal in *Fun with Dick and Jane,* a satire of unemployment, corporate corruption, and suburbia. Her films underscored her political values, including *Coming Home* (1978), which critiqued the Vietnam War, and *China Syndrome* (1979), which exposed the danger of nuclear power. Believing in the educational value of films, she formed the company IPC (Indochina Peace Campaign) Films, Inc.

Many Americans felt that Fonda destroyed her credibility when she visited North Vietnam in 1972 and claimed that U.S. POWs were treated well. Called

"Hanoi Jane," the label stuck through the decades and elicited lasting hostile feelings, more than directed at male antiwar personalities, which suggested that her role as an outspoken female contributed to that public hostility.

Retiring from Hollywood in the early 1980s, Fonda developed a successful fitness program and home workout tapes to encourage women to keep fit. After 16 years of marriage to 1960s activist Tom Hayden, she divorced in 1989 and married media mogul Ted Turner in 1991. Despite her retirement from the celebrity limelight, through the decades she retained her controversial status among Vietnam War supporters as "Hanoi Jane."

Lois Gibbs, 1951–

Environmental Justice Activist

In the late 1970s, Lois Gibbs came to represent the thousands of ordinary activists around the United States who saw a community environmental problem and labored tirelessly to try to fix it. Gibbs had moved to Love Canal, New York, with her husband and two young children in the mid-1970s to what they thought was a picturesque, working-class neighborhood near the Niagara River. A few years later, Gibbs became alarmed by the numerous illnesses such as epilepsy, asthma, and urinary tract infections that frequently hospitalized her children. When in April 1978 *Niagara Falls Gazette* reporter Michael Brown published a series of articles about the 20,000-ton chemical waste dump in town, Gibbs learned that her son's elementary school was located directly above large amounts of toxic waste.

Gibbs canvassed the neighborhood to petition the closure of the 99th Street School. As she went door to door, she discovered many children born with birth defects and women who had suffered miscarriages. Although she lacked formal education or knowledge of environmental issues, she began to ask the government to clean up or relocate residents. When officials refused to help, she organized her neighbors into the Love Canal Homeowners Association.

At the same time, the New York State Department of Health began conducting health studies of the 239 families near

Lois Gibbs, neighborhood activist who brought national attention to the Love Canal toxic waste disaster in the late 1970s, helped launch the environmental justice movement. (April Waters: aprilwaters.com)

the canal. On April 25, 1978, the New York State commissioner of Health, Dr. Robert Whalen, declared a public health hazard existing in the community. He ordered the Niagara County Health Department to remove exposed chemicals from the site and install a protective fence around the area. When the county refused to close the school, Whalen declared a medical state of emergency at Love Canal on August 2, 1978, and ordered the immediate closure of the 99th Street School. The state recommended that pregnant women and children under two who lived in the immediate area of the Love Canal move. On August 7, President Jimmy Carter declared the Love Canal area a federal emergency and provided funds to relocate permanently the 239 families living in the first two rows of homes encircling the landfill.

But families outside the evacuation zone, including Gibbs, were outraged. Angry residents held two federal experts hostage in their Home Owners Association headquarters until the FBI came and negotiated their release. The EPA agreed to provide "temporary permanent" relocation to remaining residents.

In 1980, Gibbs established the Citizens Clearinghouse for Hazardous Wastes (later the Center for Health, Environment and Justice) to help other communities with toxic waste problems and fight for greater toxin controls. Gibbs also brought a no-compromise approach to establishing safe and clean environments for all. Her efforts also led to the creation of the EPA's "Superfund," which is used to identify and clean up toxic sites throughout the United States, and infused the environmental justice movement with new energy and media attention.

John Lennon, 1940–1980

Musician and Activist

Lennon's break with the Beatles and move to New York in 1971 represented his creative and political rebirth. Relocating for personal reasons to assist wife Yoko Ono regain custody of her daughter, the couple embraced New York as home and used their celebrity status to advocate social and political causes. Although British, Lennon represents an iconic American figure in his embrace of U.S. diversity and creative energies, his commitment to American ideals of democracy and freedom, and the transatlantic nature of 1970s rock music. Together with artist Ono, Lennon released numerous hit records as he increasingly attacked the war in Vietnam, racism, and sexism. He wrote "front-page songs" to spread the word, and he and Ono staged pop events with a political edge to attract media attention.

Just as another rock icon, Bob Dylan, had seemingly abandoned social commentary in the early 1970s, Lennon became more focused on social justice in his music. He became involved in what remained of the American political New Left to offer his music in organizing youth. He and Yoko played at the "Free John Sinclair" rally in Ann Arbor in late 1971, Lennon's first U.S. concert in five years, to help release the radical activist imprisoned for selling two joints to an undercover agent. The Left described the concert as its version of Woodstock, without the mud and drugs and with clear success in convincing officials to release Sinclair. In late 1971 John and Yoko played a benefit concert in Harlem for families of prisoners shot in the Attica prison uprising. That year Lennon's utopian *Imagine* became the biggest selling album internationally. Yoko influenced Lennon to embrace feminism, another important movement of the 1970s, and to recognize that political and social revolution required women's liberation.

Lennon's political activities and commitment to mixing art with activism concerned the Nixon administration, and the FBI began surveillance of him after the "clever Beatle" moved to the United States in 1971. Nixon's targeting Lennon reflected the potency of rock and roll as well as his own paranoia. Lennon and his radical friends were planning a concert tour to coincide with the 1972 elec-

British singer-songwriter and former member of The Beatles, John Lennon. Lennon and his wife Yoko Ono moved to the United States in 1971 and advocated for various social and political causes until his death in 1980. (Library of Congress)

tion campaign to urge young people to vote and mobilize against the war. The FBI tried a number of dirty tricks, including attempting to set Lennon up for a drug bust so they could deport him before the election. In March 1972, the INS moved to revoke Lennon's visa and to deport him.

Lennon's biographer Jon Wiener, after spending 14 years making FOIA requests and suing government agencies in court to release Lennon's FBI files, concludes that Lennon's three-year legal battle to prevent his deportation sapped his radical and creative energies. In October 1975, the U.S. Court of Appeals overturned the deportation order, and Yoko gave birth to their son Sean. John declared that he would withdraw from the music business to focus on fatherhood and then became less engaged politically. On December 8, 1980, a deluded former Beatle fan shot and killed Lennon outside his New York City residence, the Dakota.

Tom McCall, 1913–1983

Governor of Oregon

During the 1970s, many states and communities took the lead in practicing a new environmentalism that initiated new methods of protecting the environment.

The state of Oregon became known as "ecotopia" for its environmentally friendly legislation. Tom McCall, Republican governor from 1967 to 1974, responded to Oregonians' concerns for environmental quality and spearheaded important initiatives, such as creating the Oregon Department of Environmental Quality and using highway revenues to build bicycle paths. Perhaps his most noteworthy act was to create the Land Conservation and Development Commission in 1973, which set limits on urban sprawl by establishing growth boundaries and preserving farmland.

Born into a wealthy Massachusetts family, McCall studied journalism at the University of Oregon and became a newscaster and commentator at KPTV, Oregon's first TV station, in 1955, and soon joined the news team at the new station KGW-TV. In 1962, McCall produced and hosted an award-winning documentary, "Pollution in Paradise," about the poor condition of the Willamette River and of air quality throughout Oregon. He left KGW in 1964 to run for Secretary of State, and was elected governor in 1966 and reelected in 1970.

McCall led Oregon to pass important new environmental legislation, including cleanup of the Willamette River, maintaining public ownership of the state's beaches, requiring deposits on beverage bottles, and the first statewide land-use planning system, all of which became models for state initiatives in the rest of the country. McCall's interest in protecting Oregon's environment was perhaps best reflected in his well-known comment made to CBS News' Terry Drinkwater in January 1971: "Come visit us again and again. This is a state of excitement. But for heaven's sake, don't move here to live."

McCall was prevented by the state constitution from running for a third term, and late in the decade his most lasting legacy, the state's land-use planning system that established urban growth boundaries around the state's cities, came under attack. A private-property rights group launched an initiative to repeal the system. Although McCall was dying of cancer, he led the successful public campaign to defeat Measure 6 in the 1982 election. Yet, as Ellen Stroud points out in her article about North Portland, these land-use regulations adversely affected working-class and minority residents. Planners sought to concentrate industries and dumps along the Columbia Slough that bordered low-income neighborhoods in the north of the city. Despite residents mobilizing in 1974 to demand that the Department of Environmental Quality enforce air quality standards, it continued to issue permits to polluting industries, and the City of Portland continued to ignore citizen requests and zoned the slough area for heavy industry and kept open a landfill.

Ralph Nader, 1934–

Consumer Advocate and Activist
Born of Lebanese immigrant parents in Connecticut, Ralph Nader first emerged as a public figure in the mid-1960s with the publication of *Unsafe at Any Speed,*

a critique of General Motors. "Naderism" soon became a credo for consumer rights, but his tireless activism in the 1970s linked Nader to many movements for change, all initiated to protect ordinary Americans from the excesses of corporations.

In 1970, more than 30,000 students applied for 200 summer jobs that Nader created to investigate corporate misdeeds and advocate greater public regulation. In subsequent summers, "Nader's Raiders," as they were called, researched and published reports and launched campaigns on water pollution and air quality, the concentration of power at First National City Bank (now Citibank), the crashworthiness of cars, the tar and nicotine levels of cigarettes, nursing home fraud, the use of pesticides on agricultural crops, and the legal profession's price fixing.

In 1972, Nader created Public Citizen, a membership organization that eventually consisted of the semi-autonomous groups Congress Watch, a nationwide network of Public Interest Research Groups, the Center for Auto Safety, the National Insurance Consumer Organization, the Health Research Group, the Litigation Group, Critical Mass Energy Project, and Buyers Up, a fuel-buying cooperative. His 1974 and 1975 "Critical Mass" conferences on atomic power, which he labeled a "technological Vietnam," helped launch a movement that helped to reshape global energy policy.

In crusading for American consumers, Nader sought to stimulate competition in the marketplace and to generate greater quantities of reliable consumer information about products and services to induce new, more socially beneficial forms of competition. To that end, in the 1970s Nader was one of the leading champions of consumer cooperatives and "group buying" experiments, such as Buyers Up, a purchasing organization for home heating oil that served consumers in several East Coast cities. Also to help consumers, Nader forces helped win passage of the landmark 1974 amendments to the Freedom of Information Act, which activists used to obtain government documents that often exposed abuses by government and industry. Nader tried to obtain more consumer influence in corporate governance by agitating for three seats for public representatives on the General Motors board of directors. Although the effort failed, it demonstrated a tactic that would be embraced by future dissident shareholder campaigns on behalf of citizen groups. His book *Taming the Giant Corporation* (1976) advocated greater public accountability in corporate governance through federal chartering of corporations.

Nader and the thousands of volunteers that aided him through the decade were directly or indirectly responsible for significant reforms and innovations, including the formation of the Occupational Safety and Health Administration, the Consumer Product Safety Commission, and the Capitol Hill News Service, which in the early 1970s pioneered investigative reporting about Congress. Nader also tried to educate journalists about how they could obtain government documents through the Freedom of Information Clearinghouse.

REFERENCES AND FURTHER READINGS

Abbey, Edward. 1975. *The Monkey Wrench Gang*. New York: Harper Collins.

Anderson, Terry H. 1995. *The Movement and the Sixties: Protest in America from Greensboro to Wounded Knee*. New York: Oxford University Press.

Banks, Dennis, with Richard Erdoes. 2004. *Ojibwa Warrior: Dennis Banks and the Rise of the American Indian Movement*. Norman: University of Oklahoma Press.

Bateson, Stephanie. 2004. "Weatherman Underground Organization." In *Encyclopedia of American Social Movements,* vol. 4, edited by Immanuel Ness, 1196–1200. Armonk, NY: M. E. Sharpe.

Bermanzohn, Sally Avery. 2003. *Through Survivor's Eyes: From the Sixties to the Greensboro Massacre*. Nashville: Vanderbilt University Press.

Brown, Dee. 1970. *Bury My Heart At Wounded Knee: An Indian History of the American West*. New York: Holt, Rinehart & Winston.

Bruchey, Eleanor. 1999. "The Rights of the Elderly as a Social Movement in the United States." In *Ideas, Ideologies, and Social Movements: The U.S. Experience since 1800,* edited by Peter A. Coclanis and Stuart Bruchey, 102–111. Columbia: University of South Carolina Press.

Commoner, Barry. 1971. *The Closing Circle: Nature, Man and Technology*. New York: Alfred Knopf.

Corpus, Martha Monaghan. 2004. "Gray Panthers Movement." In *Encyclopedia of American Social Movements,* vol. 4, edited by Immanuel Ness, 1230–1235. Armonk, NY: M. E. Sharpe.

Cruikshank, Margaret. 1992. *The Gay and Lesbian Liberation Movement*. New York: Routledge.

DeLeon, David. 1988. *Everything Is Changing: Contemporary U.S. Movements in Historical Perspective*. New York: Praeger.

Deloria, Vine. 1970. *We Talk, You Listen; New Tribes, New Turf*. New York: Macmillan.

Dunlap, Riley E., and Angela G. Mertig, eds. 1992. *American Environmentalism: The U.S. Environmental Movement, 1970–1990*. New York: Taylor & Francis.

Ehrlich, Paul R. 1968. *The Population Bomb*. New York: Ballantine Books.

Epstein, Barbara. 1991. *Political Protest and Cultural Revolution: Nonviolent Direct Action in the 1970s and 1980s*. Berkeley: University of California Press.

Espiritu, Yen Le. 1992. *Asian American Panethnicity: Bridging Institutions and Identities*. Philadelphia: Temple University Press.

Finsen, Lawrence, and Susan Finsen. 1994. *The Animal Rights Movement in America: From Compassion to Respect*. New York: Twayne.

Flippen, J. Brooks. 2000. *Nixon and the Environment*. Albuquerque: University of New Mexico Press.

Formisano, Ronald P. 1991. *Boston Against Busing: Race, Class, and Ethnicity in the 1960s and 1970s*. Chapel Hill: University of North Carolina Press.

Goodman, Amy. Interview segment on "Ex-Weather Underground Member Kathy Boudin Granted Parole." *Democracy Now,* August 21, 2003. http://www.democracynow.org/article.pl?sid=03/08/21/1441247. Accessed July 20, 2006.

Goodman, Amy. Interview Transcript: "Remembering the 1979 Greensboro Massacre: 25 Years Later Survivors Form Country's First Truth and Reconciliation Commission." *Democracy Now* November 18, 2004. http://www.democracynow.org/2004/11/18/remembering_the_1979_greensboro_massacre_25. Accessed July 21, 2006.

Gottlieb, Robert. 1993. *Forcing the Spring: The Transformation of the American Environmental Movement*. Washington, DC: Island Press.

Griffin, Susan. 1978. *Woman and Nature: The Roaring Inside Her*. New York: Harper & Row.

Hammerback, John C., Richard J. Jensen, and José Angel Gutiérrez. 1985. *A War of Words: Chicano Protest in the 1960s and 1970s*. Westport, CT: Greenwood Press.

Hays, Samuel P. 2003. "Beyond Celebration: Pittsburgh and Its Region in the Environmental Era—Notes by a Participant Observer." In *Devastation and Renewal: An Environmental History of Pittsburgh and Its Region,* edited by Joel A. Tarr, 193–215. Pittsburgh: University of Pittsburgh Press.

Heineman, Kenneth J. 1993. *Campus Wars: The Peace Movement at American State Universities in the Vietnam Era*. New York: New York University Press.

Holt Labor Library. "Greensboro Massacre." http://www.holtlaborlibrary.org/greensboro.html. Accessed July 21, 2006.

Hunt, Andrew E. 1999. *The Turning: A History of Vietnam Veterans against the War*. New York: New York University Press.

Jacobs, Ron. 1997. *The Way the Wind Blew: A History of the Weather Underground*. New York: Verson.

Jay, Karla, and Allen Young, eds. 1972. Reprint 1992. *Out of the Closets: Voices of Gay Liberation*. New York: New York University Press.

Jones, Charles E., ed. 1998. *The Black Panther Party (Reconsidered)*. Baltimore: Black Classic Press.

"The H-Bomb Secret—How We Got It, Why We're Telling It." *The Progressive* 43, no. 11 (November 1979): 1–39.

Holleran, Andrew. 1978. *Dancer from the Dance*. New York: Morrow.

Houston, Jeanne Wakatsuki, and James D. Houston. 1973. *Farewell to Manzanar: A True Story of Japanese American Experience during and after the World War II Internment*. Boston: Houghton Mifflin.

Kerry, John. "Statement before the Senate Foreign Relations Committee on April 23, 1971." History News Network. http://hnn.us/articles/3631.html Accessed May 14, 2008.

Klarman, Michael J. 2004. *Jim Crow to Civil Rights: The Supreme Court and the Struggle for Racial Equality*. New York: Oxford University Press.

Kline, Benjamin. 2000. *First Along the River: A Brief History of the U.S. Environmental Movement*. San Francisco: Acada Books.

Kruse, Kevin M. 2005. *White Flight: Atlanta and the Making of Modern Conservatism*. Princeton, NJ: Princeton University Press.

Louie, Steve, and Glenn K. Omatsu, eds. 2001. *Asian Americans: The Movement and the Moment*. Los Angeles: UCLA Asian American Studies Center Press.

Merchant, Carolyn. 1980. *The Death of Nature: Women, Ecology, and the Scientific Revolution*. San Francisco: Harper & Row.

Ogbar, Jeffrey O. G. 2004. *Black Power: Radical Politics and African American Identity*. Baltimore: Johns Hopkins University Press.

Omatsu, Glenn. 2000. "The 'Four Prisons' and the Movements of Liberation: Asian American Activism from the 1960s to the 1990s." In *Contemporary Asian America: A Multidisciplinary Reader,* edited by Min Zhou and James V. Gatewood, 80–112. New York: New York University Press.

Porter, Eric. 2004. "Affirming and Disaffirming Actions: Remaking Race in the 1970s." *America in the 70s,* edited by Beth Bailey and David Farber, 50–74. Lawrence: University Press of Kansas.

Reich, Charles A. 1970. *The Greening of America: How the Youth Revolution Is Trying to Make America Livable*. New York: Random House.

San Miguel Jr., Guadalupe. 2001. *Brown, Not White: School Integration and the Chicano Movement in Houston*. College Station: Texas A&M University Press.

Shabecoff, Philip. 2003. *A Fierce Green Fire: The American Environmental Movement*. Washington DC: Island Press.

Singer, Peter. 1975. *Animal Liberation: A New Ethics for Our Treatment of Animals*. New York: Random House.

Sir! No Sir! GI Movement Archives. "Resistance Chronology." http://www.sirnosir.com/index.html Accessed May 14, 2008.

Small, Melvin. 2002. *Antiwarriors: The Vietnam War and the Battle for America's Hearts and Minds*. Lanham, MD: Scholarly Resources.

State University of New York at Buffalo. "Love Canal Collection." Ecumenical Task Force of the Niagara Frontier. http://ublib.buffalo.edu/libraries/projects/lovecanal/index.html Accessed June 15, 2006.

Stroud, Ellen. 1999. "Troubled Waters in Ecotopia: Environmental Racism in Portland, Oregon." *Radical History Review* 74 (1999): 65–95.

Takezawa, Yasuko I. 2000. "Children of Inmates: The Effects of the Redress Movement among Third-Generation Japanese Americans." In *Contemporary Asian America: A Multidisiplinary Reader,* edited by Min Zhou and James V. Gatewood, 299–314. New York: New York University Press.

Walsh, Catherine. 2000. "Busing in Boston: Looking Back at the History and Legacy." *Ed. Magazine.* Harvard Graduate School of Education, September 1. http://www.gse.harvard.edu/news/features/busing09012000_page1.html Accessed July 22, 2006.

Wei, William. 1993. *The Asian American Movement.* Philadelphia: Temple University Press.

Wrigley, Julia. 1998. "From Housewives to Activists: Women and the Division of Political Labor in the Boston Antibusing Movement." In *No Middle Ground: Women and Radical Protest,* edited by Kathleen M. Blee, 251–288. New York University Press.

Feminisms and
Changing Gender Roles

OVERVIEW

On August 26, 1970, in honor of the 50th anniversary of the passage of the women's suffrage amendment, tens of thousands of women across the country marched in demonstrations, blocked rush hour traffic, held rallies and teach-ins, and generated considerable media attention for their demands for abortion, education, employment, and child care rights. Women's Strike for Equality Day was initially conceived by Betty Friedan, a feminist icon of the 1960s, as she stepped down from her post as National Organization for Women (NOW) president in March. NOW called for a national women's strike with the slogan "Don't Iron While the Strike Is Hot." The exuberance of the day became a symbol for how millions of women and men over the course of the decade would transform gender roles and relations. Although the "second-wave" feminist movement mobilized in the 1960s, it expanded in the 1970s, when other 1960s-era social movements had weakened or expired. These were the "golden years" of feminist achievement, when an almost dizzying array of legislative and court victories expanded women's rights and opportunities, and gender roles changed dramatically.

Historians have frequently employed a water metaphor to describe the sudden growth and momentum of feminism in the United States. The "first wave" began in the mid-19th century and culminated in the passage of the 19th Amendment to the U.S. Constitution in 1920, which granted women the right to vote. The "second wave" of feminism began in the 1960s and created a "tidal wave," as Sara Evans describes, that by the end of the century had changed the country forever (Evans 2003, 1). Others have noted how such periodization neglects a host of other resistance movements by working-class women and women of color. In the mid-20th century, for example, women active in the civil rights movement and in labor unions had been among the first to embrace the idea of equality under the law in the pre–second wave era.

Nonetheless, in the early 1960s, women's options in education, careers, health care, and politics were limited. By the 1970s, women's groups had not only knocked down many legal barricades but had also challenged assumptions about gender roles between the sexes in the culture at large. Through the 1970s, feminists discussed their concerns in consciousness-raising groups, lobbied for legislation, protested discrimination, established rape crisis centers and women's shelters, and laid the foundation for what they believed would be a radical transformation of society and the ways in which women and men related to each other. Reflecting this energy, over 500 feminist publications appeared in the United States between 1968 and 1973. Moreover, the feminist movement galvanized women into action because it not only identified problems that connected to their personal lives but it also offered inspiring notions about equality, dignity, and social change.

Feminists recognized gender inequalities in American society and determined to change conditions for women. Yet there were so many different ideological and strategic approaches to challenging gender restrictions, roles, and relations that we must examine the multiplicity of "feminisms" rather than one social movement. There were many strands of feminisms that appeared, separated, and were reshaped in the 1970s.

Scholars often divide feminist movements of the 1970s into liberal and radical camps although recent studies have demonstrated that there was much more overlap than these distinctions imply. The first second-wave feminists, spurred by Betty Friedan and NOW, identified the problem of sex oppression and advocated equality. Then younger feminists, involved in the social activism of the 1960s, particularly in the black freedom struggle and the New Left, charged that equality in the public sphere could never be attained unless the private sphere was transformed. The women's liberation movement introduced one of the distinctive features of second-wave feminism with its phrase "the personal is political" that linked the everyday concerns of women about family life, sexuality, and domestic violence to the public concerns of "politics."

Liberal feminist organizations sought to operate within the existing political system to effect change and often had a more bureaucratic approach through local, state, regional, and national chapters. Radical groups, on the other hand, embraced a grassroots and nonhierarchical style and rejected formal politics in favor of more spontaneous, militant tactics to bring attention to their issues and undermine the system itself. But women's liberationists divided over whether patriarchy was the primary oppression in women's lives; other feminists emphasized the intersections of race and class with gender in creating identities and subjugation; still others believed that only class struggle and revolution would bring about gender equality.

Women of color, working-class, and lesbian feminists criticized liberal and radical feminism for privileging gender and not adequately considering other forms of discrimination based on sexual orientation, race, and class. The ideal of "sisterhood" was often challenged by the realities of conflict and by women who felt that their interests were not necessarily represented by white middle-class women. Despite the presence of women's caucuses, newsletters, and organizations within every racial and ethnic group, the feminist movement was often associated as primarily a white women's movement. This assumption, the insensitivity of many white activists, and different issues and approaches made it difficult for white women and women of color to cross divides in common struggle. Feminists of color, labor feminists, and lesbians defined themselves as feminist but often created their own organizations to pursue their interests and concerns.

Ideological struggles, divisions between leftists and more mainstream feminists, and differences between lesbian, Chicana, disabled, and African American feminists represented one set of tensions; the other involved questions of style and process. Jo Freeman pointed out in her influential article "The Tyranny of Structurelessness" (1970) that the movement's tendency to shun structure and hierarchy had actually allowed self-appointed "leaders" to speak for groups of women without any accountability and crippled the possibilities for political action. Resentments, self-righteousness, and attacks drove many talented feminist leaders and writers from various groups.

Government and conservative attacks also challenged feminist movements through the 1970s. Many feminists came to believe that FBI infiltration damaged the women's movement by the early 1970s. Betty Friedan, for example, blamed the failure of ERA passage on infiltration; younger feminists believed undercover dissenters pushed many groups to the radical fringe. A growing conservative movement, which targeted feminism's undermining of the traditional family and gender roles, created effective countermovements that halted the ERA, limited abortion rights, and threatened to stall feminist progress on employment and cultural issues.

Factions, schisms, and concern about infiltrators and the right wing wore down the vitality of the feminist movement, and forced many feminist groups to take more defensive positions and actions. Nonetheless, feminism continued to attract new adherents through the 1970s. Groups grew in numbers by becoming more inclusive and matured in sophistication by analyzing differences and breaking down assumptions about "sisterhood." By the end of the decade, the dynamic and radical women's liberation movements had subsided, and the feminist movement took new turns, focusing on specific issues, cultural feminism, and multicultural feminism. As in other social movements, divisions may have appeared to weaken efforts but they also expanded understandings of gender inequality, sexuality, family, politics, and culture. Many have attributed the dynamism that sustained the movement through the 1970s and beyond to the tensions within various feminisms.

The 1970s witnessed remarkable changes in the ways Americans viewed women's potential, roles, and rights. One of the century's most significant social movements had transformed American society in fundamental ways. By the 1980s, although sex discrimination and inequities persisted, women could enter professional schools, become construction workers or CEOs, live alone and remain single, take out loans and start businesses, seek contraceptives or an abortion—and their radically altered roles were largely accepted by the public. Women not only gained entry to various educational and professional institutions but they also changed what was taught. The entire vocabulary changed— women were introduced as marriage status-neutral Ms. rather than Miss or Mrs., and other gendered terms such as "chairman" or "chairwoman" became "chairs" or "chairpersons." Feminism changed the way men and women viewed the world and their place in it.

TIMELINE

1970   The nationwide Women's Strike for Equality takes place.

Shulamith Firestone publishes *The Dialectic of Sex*.

Kate Millett publishes *Sexual Politics*.

Rock singer Janis Joplin dies of overdose.

North American Indian Women's Association is founded.

Comisión Femenil Mexicana is founded to give voice to Chicana concerns.

Feminist Bella Abzug is elected to Congress.

Robin Morgan publishes *Sisterhood Is Powerful*.

Toni Cade publishes *The Black Woman: An Anthology*.

The Feminist Press begins recovering and promoting women writers.

The Catholic Church establishes the National Right to Life Committee.

The Third World Women's Alliance forms.

1971   The National Women's Political Caucus forms.

The first feminist health clinic is started in Los Angeles.

The National Press Club admits women members.

First National Conference of Chicanas is held in Houston.

President Nixon vetoes the Comprehensive Child Development Act that would provide federally funded child care.

The Women's Caucus organizes within the American Academy of Religion.

1972   The Equal Rights Amendment passes both houses of Congress.

Congress passes Title IX of the Educational Amendments to the Civil Rights Act mandating sex equity in education.

The Equal Employment Opportunity Act is passed.

Ms. magazine is launched.

Phyllis Schlafly creates the "StopERA" organization.

The first Lesbian Feminist Conference is held in Los Angeles.

Black Sisters United forms.

The founding meeting of the National Conference of Puerto Rican Women takes place.

Stewardesses for Women's Rights forms.

1973   Boston Women's Health Collective publishes *Our Bodies, Ourselves*.

The Supreme Court decides on *Roe v. Wade*.

Helen Reddy's song "I Am Woman" wins a Grammy Award.

The National Black Feminist Organization forms.

The International Feminist Planning Conference meets in Cambridge, Massachusetts.

The U.S. Tennis Association grants equal prizes to men and women in the U.S. Open.

The women's record company Olivia Records is established.

The first battered women's shelters open.

AT&T agrees to the largest sex discrimination settlement in history.

The American Psychiatric Association removes homosexuality from list of disorders.

Black Women Organized for Action forms.

The Supreme Court decides in *New Jersey Welfare Rights Organization v. Cahill* that states cannot deny welfare assistance to children whose parents are not legally married.

Marian Wright Edelman establishes the Children's Defense Fund (CDF).

1974   The Coalition of Labor Union Women is founded.

More than 1,000 colleges and universities offer women's studies courses.

Congress passes the Equal Credit Opportunity Act.

The National Coalition for Women and Girls in Education (NCWGE) forms.

The Mexican American Women's National Association (MANA) is founded.

The first National Women's Music Festival is held at the University of Illinois.

1975   Susan Brownmiller publishes *Against Our Will: Men, Women and Rape.*

The National Women's Health Network is formed.

The United Nations first international women's conference is held in Mexico City.

1976   The National Alliance of Black Feminists forms in Chicago.

Congress passes the Hyde Amendment, which limits the expenditure of federal funds on abortion services.

West Point military academy begins accepting women.

1977   The first National Women's Conference is held in Houston.

The National Women's Studies Association is founded.

"Take Back the Night" marches are organized by feminist groups to protest rape.

Janelle Commissiong of Trinidad & Tobago becomes the first black woman to be crowned Miss Universe.

1978   Congress passes the Pregnancy Discrimination Act.

Women Against Pornography (WAP) forms in New York City.

The Equal Rights Amendment demonstration in Washington, D.C., draws 100,000.

The National Coalition Against Domestic Violence forms.

The Women's Educational Equity Act is reauthorized to enforce Title IX.

The Displaced Homemakers Network forms.

1979	The National March for lesbians and gays is held in Washington, D.C.
	Judy Chicago's piece *The Dinner Party* startles the art world.
	Sonia Johnson is excommunicated from the Mormon Church for her support of the ERA.
	Catharine MacKinnon publishes *The Sexual Harassment of Working Women.*
	More than 5,000 supporters join WAP in march on Times Square.

THE STRUGGLE FOR EQUAL RIGHTS

National Organization for Women (NOW)

Beginning in the mid-1960s, women articulated an "equal rights" feminism that advocated equal treatment of women under the law and in society. Initiated by professional women involved in state and federal commissions on women, and from politically active women in groups such as Business and Professional Women, the Democratic Party, and the League of Women Voters, these feminists sought policy and legal changes that would grant equal status to women in the workplace, in education, and in the polity. Women held conferences and established membership and lobbying organizations to raise awareness and pursue equal opportunity through legislation and the courts. They were optimistic about how existing American institutions could assist in their goals to obtain equal treatment for women.

By far the largest feminist organization through the 1970s, NOW represented the enthusiasm and tensions of the decade's women's movement. Formed in 1966 in Washington, D.C., by women attending the Third National Conference of the

National Organization for Women president Betty Friedan and feminists march in New York City on August 26, 1970. The march commemorated the 50th anniversary of the passage of the Nineteenth Amendment, which granted American women full suffrage. (JP Laffont/Sygma/Corbis)

Commission on the Status of Women, the group acknowledged and vowed to change the fact that women in the United States still were discriminated against in virtually every aspect of life. Among NOW's 28 founders was its first president, Betty Friedan, author of the influential book that exposed women's unequal condition, *The Feminine Mystique* (1963).

NOW expanded its political direction with lobbying and passage of legislation such as the ERA and Equal Employment Opportunity Act. By 1970, the organization had adopted a number of positions and goals that advocated for women in addition to supporting equal rights. It tried to balance its need for grassroots membership support with a hierarchical structure needed to advance political reforms. By late 1973, NOW had more than 600 chapters and 27 national task forces.

The organization formed coalitions with groups such as Women's Equity Action League (WEAL), Business and Professional Women, the League of Women Voters, and the American Association of University Women (AAUW) to support legislation that advanced women's rights. NOW also provided the initial staging ground for new groups that went on to tackle specific feminist issues. NOW created a Legal Defense and Education Fund (LDEF) to initiate and support critical sex discrimination legal cases.

By the early 1970s, several schisms had developed in the organization. Some members felt NOW had become too conservative, and others believed its positions too radical. Women's liberationists often characterized NOW as too reformist and middle class because it sought equality within the system rather than its alteration. Robin Morgan's 1970 bestseller *Sisterhood Is Powerful* challenged NOW as merely seeking political reforms instead of women's true liberation. NOW activists such as Betty Friedan equally challenged women's liberationists' attacks on the family as diverting attention from political struggles.

Women who disagreed with NOW's stance on abortion rights left to create WEAL, women from the United Auto Workers (UAW) withdrew over the Equal Rights Amendment, and a number of lesbians quit over the failure to recognize sexual identity as a feminist issue. Yet this dissension led to new debates and discussions both inside and outside NOW. The UAW ultimately came to support the ERA, WEAL eventually backed a woman's right to choose abortion, and NOW soon formally endorsed lesbian rights. Despite tensions over the gay-straight issue and disagreement over how acknowledgement of lesbian rights might hurt or help the feminist cause, when *Time* magazine criticized Kate Millett in 1970 for her bisexualism, gay and straight feminists united to condemn this unfair attack. In 1971, the national NOW convention passed a resolution recognizing the right of women to express their own sexuality and acknowledging the oppression of lesbians as a legitimate feminist concern.

Although criticized for being too white and middle class, NOW sought to elevate women of color in leadership positions and to support antiracist and low-income issues. In 1970, Aileen Hernandez, an African American who was the

Ms. Magazine

In 1971, journalist and feminist Gloria Steinem began to conceive a mainstream publication that would reach a larger female audience not directly involved in the feminist movement. The December 1971 preview issue of *Ms.* featured stories about housewives, abortion, and welfare. Despite discouragement by other publishers, Steinem clearly found an audience. The preview and subsequent July 1972 premier issues quickly sold out after hitting the newsstands. The network news anchor Harry Reasoner challenged, "I'll give it six months before they run out of things to say." But the magazine had plenty to say about women's issues over the next three decades and reached about three million readers. In 1978, *Ms.* became a nonprofit magazine published by the Ms. Foundation for Education and Communication. After several ownership shifts in subsequent decades, *Ms.* was acquired in 2001 by the Feminist Majority Foundation.

Ms. was the first national magazine to make feminist voices available to the public. It demonstrated that women had interests other than recipes and cosmetics; the magazine listed prominent American women who demanded the repeal of laws that criminalized abortion, advocated for the ERA, rated presidential candidates on women's issues, featured serious topics on the cover such as domestic violence and sexual harassment, and included articles that covered a range of issues from the feminist protest of pornography, to date rape, to the "de-sexing" of the English language. *Ms.* also criticized the undue influence of advertising on magazine journalism and featured the *Ms.* Women of the Year Awards, to counter *Time* magazine's traditional practice of honoring "man of the year."

Ms. became an important source of consciousness-raising among young and middle-aged (mostly middle-class white) women. It generated an astonishing number of letters each week. Housewives reported new self-confidence and the steps they were taking to change their lives and resist subordination. With its glossy cover that mimicked other women's magazines, *Ms.* was strikingly different for advocating independence rather than how to keep a man. The April 1973 issue that featured singer Judy Collins without makeup excited readers to write to the magazine in appreciation for the natural rather than cover-girl photo. The title *Ms.* itself marked a radical change in the way many women now preferred to be addressed. Like *Mr.,* the title included all women regardless of marital status.

In addition to its mainstream detractors, the magazine was criticized by many radical feminists. For some, the magazine represented the strength and popularity of feminism; for others, it signaled the crass commercialization of the movement. Despite Steinem's profound contribution to the women's movement through her mainstream publication, many feminists, including those who had worked behind the scenes for many years, resented her glamour and domination of the media spotlight.

first woman on the Equal Employment Opportunity Commission, was elected president of NOW.

The influence of the women's liberation movement appeared in the fractious 1974 election of Karen DeCrow as president of NOW. Winning by a narrow margin over long-time NOW activist Jean Collins-Robson, DeCrow had used radical rhetoric and emphasized lesbian and minority rights. A dozen board members later joined DeCrow in forming a "Majority Caucus" to work for structural changes within NOW, leading to bitter divisions at the 1975 national conference. The conference theme, "Out of the Mainstream, Into the Revolution," suggested a more radical direction for the organization, and sessions focused on a range of issues from pay equity to rape and wife abuse.

By 1977, under the leadership of Eleanor Smeal, NOW focused on the ERA as a mobilizing issue for women. The feminist organization grew from 35,000 members in 1975 to a quarter of a million by the early 1980s. It organized public demonstrations and marches, which expanded the strength of local and national chapters. In 1978, a NOW-organized march in support of the Equal Rights Amendment drew more than 100,000 people to Washington, D.C.

Yet the national goal to pass the ERA was often not emphasized in local chapters, which as recent scholarship has revealed, were often simultaneously liberal and radical, both working within the system and adopting confrontational tactics when necessary. Memphis NOW members focused on the problem of rape, feminists in Chicago urged members to work on behalf of all parents and children to establish affordable child care, and NOW members in San Francisco and New York chapters developed cooperative child care programs, promoted women's caucuses in unions and professions, and protested insulting images of women in the media. Boston NOW members created a task force that increased awareness of gender discrimination at area universities and colleges.

Equal Rights Amendment

The Equal Rights Amendment, passed by Congress in 1972, came to represent for many Americans what was right and wrong about feminism, and it consumed the energies and passions of many feminists and their opponents through the decade. For almost 50 years, women's rights advocates had lobbied Congress to introduce the amendment that would guarantee that "rights under the law shall not be abridged on account of sex," but the amendment rarely came forward for a vote. Recognizing increasing support for the amendment, NOW had put the ERA high on its agenda after its formation in 1966. The Task Force on Women's Rights and Responsibilities, appointed by President Nixon, released a report in 1970, *A Matter of Simple Justice,* which endorsed the ERA. NOW demonstrators convinced the U.S. House Judiciary Committee to review the ERA, and soon Rep. Martha Griffiths filed a petition to release the bill onto the floor of the House.

Text of ERA

Section 1. Equality of rights under the law shall not be denied or abridged by the United States or by any state on account of sex.

Section 2. The Congress shall have the power to enforce, by appropriate legislation, the provisions of this article.

Section 3. This amendment shall take effect two years after the date of ratification.

That year the House passed the amendment by a two-thirds majority. But some politicians and major national newspapers voiced their opposition, and the Senate pressed for amendments that would exclude women from the draft and retain protective labor laws. Many feminist groups believed equality mandated equal responsibilities along with equal rights and opposed the weakening of the legislation. Flora Crater and her group known as "Crater's Raiders" joined together with the newly formed Women United to mobilize the nation's women's groups to lobby for the ERA without proposed exemptions that may have weakened the amendment's blanket guarantees.

In 1971, the House again passed the ERA without amendments by a 354 to 23 margin. By February 1972, the Senate Judiciary Committee still had not reported on the amendment for a floor vote, so the network of women's lobbyists stepped up efforts to pressure senators through a massive mail campaign and personal lobbying. Their efforts succeeded, and within a month, the Judiciary Committee approved the ERA. Sen. Sam Ervin was one of the most vociferous opponents, raising objections about the draft, divorce, child support, and unisex bathrooms that would jeopardize the ERA in years to come. Nonetheless, the Senate ultimately voted to pass the ERA by an 84 to 8 margin.

Within a year, 30 states had endorsed the ERA and no significant opposition appeared on the horizon. Support for equal rights was high among most Americans in the early 1970s, and ratification of the 1972 amendment seemed assured. Yet in the next six years, despite feminist lobbying, only five more states approved and five other states rescinded their earlier approval of the amendment, preventing ratification by the 1982 deadline.

How did an opposition mobilize to defeat the ERA, given its initial widespread support? Just as in the 1920s, many women opposed the legislation fearing it would erase protective legislation that acknowledged women's greater vulnerability in the workplace. But by the early 1970s, the labor movement generally supported the ERA, recognizing that equality would enhance working women's position more than protective legislation.

Women protest the Equal Rights Amendment outside the White House, February 1977.
(Library of Congress)

Many have credited one woman, Phyllis Schlafly, for the ERA reversal, although her success was aided by a changing political climate. Schlafly developed a persuasive anti-ERA platform that mobilized thousands of women and men around the country. A conservative activist, Schlafly tapped into the unease among many Americans about changing gender roles. Conservative sentiments in general were on the rise by the mid-1970s and ERA opponents claimed equality would damage family life. George Wallace's American Party and the John Birch Society claimed the ERA was "communist" and dedicated to "destroy the home."

Pro-ERA strategists failed to acknowledge the real concerns of many women about the "full equality" consequences of the ERA, especially regarding divorce and possible combat roles for women in the military. The military issue became one of the most emotionally charged arguments against the ERA, and feminists' arguments deconstructing claims of unisex bathrooms lacked the power to allay fears generated by ERA opponents. Race, too, played a role in the defeat of the ERA, as Donald Mathews and Jane DeHart concluded in their study of the ERA in North Carolina. Nine of the states that refused to ratify the amendment were Southern. In the minds of opponents, civil rights and feminism were linked, representing a federal "intrusion" into the Southern "way of life," or racial and gender hierarchy.

Montana ERA Ratification Council

After Congress passed the ERA in 1972, the amendment went to the states for rat-ification. Many state ERA organizations formed to convince state legislatures to sup-port the amendment. The Montana ERA Ratification Council, organized in 1973, brought together into a working coalition representatives from some 35 Montana organizations that supported the ERA. These included the American Association of University Women, League of Women Voters, Federation of Business and Profes-sional Women, AFL-CIO, Women's Law Association, American Federation of Teach-ers, Montana Education Association, Montana Democratic Party, Montana Nurses Association, National Organization of Women (NOW), Common Cause, State Bar, Soroptimist International Association, Press Women, and Church Women United.

The Montana House of Representatives passed the ERA in 1973 by a vote of 72–23. The resolution failed to get out of the Montana Senate that year but was ratified the following year by a vote of 29–21. Montana became the 32nd state to ratify the ERA. After the 1974 Montana ratification, the Council changed its name to the Montana Equal Rights Council to help the national effort to extend the seven-year ratification period, to protect Montana's ratification and block rescis-sion efforts, and to prepare strategies to reintroduce the ERA following the fail-ure of ratification in the next Congress.

Opponents of the ERA attempted to rescind Montana's ratification in every leg-islative session between 1974 and June 30, 1982. National "Stop-ERA," led by Phyllis Schlafly, campaigned vigorously through Montana branches of organizations opposing the ERA, including the Daughters of the American Revolution, Eagle Fo-rum, John Birch Society, Knights of Columbus, Liberty Lobby, National Council of Catholic Women, Veterans of Foreign Wars, and Rabbinical Alliance of America. In Montana, the Church of Jesus Christ of Latter Day Saints was a particularly strong and well-organized opponent. The rescission movement was stopped in 1975, 1977, and again in 1979 by effective lobbying from the Equal Rights Council.

With the failure of the ERA in 1982, the Montana Equal Rights Council phased out its work with a final public program in Helena with a promise to have the ERA arise "from the ashes like the Phoenix bird." As directed by the bylaws, remain-ing funds left in the treasury were distributed to organizations working on behalf of women's issues including the Women's Lobby Fund, National Organization for Women, and the League of Women Voters of Montana.

As opponents successfully built support through passionate rhetoric, the is-sue became more divisive, and male state legislators grew more reluctant to defend the ERA. ERA supporters did mobilize massive support, however, as rep-resented by the large march on the nation's capital in 1978. The major feminist organizations made the ERA a prominent issue in political campaigns of 1978 and worked to elect sympathizers who would extend the Congressional deadline until 1982. Opponents of ERA hoped to defeat the extension. In 1978, the new

Congress voted to extend the deadline to June 30, 1982. Because more Americans feared the defeat of the ERA, membership in groups such as NOW, which was focusing on the ERA, grew tremendously. Although the ERA ultimately fell three states short of ratification, the struggle for the amendment mobilized and educated many Americans about women's issues and facilitated a national conversation (or battle) about gender roles in American society.

During the 1970s and 1980s, women won many of the equal rights protections through the courts that the ERA would have mandated. The issue galvanized a new conservative movement that challenged feminism's principles and goals, and rallied feminists to defend those goals.

Legislative and Legal Changes

Many feminists recognized that political power was central to realizing feminist goals, and increasing numbers of women ran for public office in the early 1970s. Yet despite increasing their numbers in political office, by the end of the decade, the percentage of women in elected positions in Congress, as governors, and even in state legislatures was only slightly higher than at the beginning of the decade. Just as women gained more possibilities for political office, they faced greater obstacles from the high costs of elections and the presence of powerful political action committees (PACs) that favored incumbents.

Women countered these obstacles through the election of highly visible and articulate feminists such as Bella Abzug and Shirley Chisholm who could advocate forcefully for women' issues, through the formation of state and national lobbying groups, and in the creation of organizations such as the National Women's Political Caucus that focused on electing women to office.

If women did not dramatically increase their numbers in electoral positions, they did reshape the major political parties through greater representation and, especially in the Democratic Party, gaining a more prominent voice. Through the 1970s, Democratic women pushed for equal representation and by 1980 had almost 50 percent of voting delegates at the party convention. Most of these delegates supported resolutions on the ERA and abortion that Jimmy Carter's campaign opposed but were adopted by the convention.

Feminists also were successful in lobbying for key equal rights legislation. By the end of 1972, the 92nd Congress had passed a record number of bills supporting women's rights. Much of this legislation was passed through the efforts of new task forces and research centers that focused on specific issues by collecting data and launching investigations.

When investigations revealed that the credit industry discriminated against women, NOW worked with the ACLU and others to demand hearings. In 1972, NOW members Jane Roberts Chapman and Margaret Gates obtained grants from Ralph Nader's group and the Ford Foundation to establish the Center for Women Policy Studies to investigate the issue of consumer credit for women and de-

The National Women's Political Caucus

In July 1971, a group of 300 women politicians and feminist activists gathered in Washington, D.C., to form the National Women's Political Caucus (NWPC). Along with a raucous group of younger activists were the iconic Fannie Lou Hamer, Bella Abzug, Gloria Steinem, and Shirley Chisholm, who came together to find ways to increase women's representation in electoral politics, which they believed would best advance women's issues and interests. The group approved a statement of purpose to oppose sexism, racism, institutional violence, and poverty through the election and appointment of women to political office; to reform party structures to give women an equal voice in decision making; to select candidates who would increase the numbers of registered women voters; and to support women's issues and feminist candidates across party lines.

From the outset, the NWPC demonstrated its position of inclusiveness by featuring in its leadership women of color, labor union women, civil rights activists, and Republicans and media celebrities such as Steinem and Abzug. State chapters of NWPC concentrated on gaining access to the major party presidential conventions in 1972. The women's efforts had astounding results, doubling the percentage of women delegates at the Republican convention and tripling the percentage of women Democrat delegates. Shirley Chisholm ran for president that year, hoping to push the Democratic Party to consider more seriously concerns of feminists and African Americans. But NWPC activists were divided on whether to support her; many recognized the realities of party politics and supported instead Sen. George McGovern, who opposed the war and had a chance of winning the party's nomination.

velop data for use by organizations in hearings. All of this activity resulted in the 1974 passage of the Equal Credit Opportunity Act (ECOA), with near unanimous votes in House and Senate, and enforcement measures to ensure compliance. Passage of the ECOA dramatically changed women's access to credit, and by the end of the decade, single women owned 10 percent of home mortgages.

Feminist legal efforts, too, were successful in overturning a host of state and federal laws that were discriminatory, including revising rape statutes, and in enforcing civil rights protections. Title VII lawsuits helped to end widespread discriminatory practices against pregnant women and mothers in the workforce. By the early 1970s, bans on the hiring of unwed mothers and firing of pregnant or married workers, had largely disappeared. Unions turned to the courts to force employers to provide pregnancy benefits, claiming that pregnancy had to be treated as any disability.

Enforcement of Title IX, an amendment to the 1964 Civil Rights Act that forbade discrimination based on sex in education, generated much opposition

National Women's Conference, Houston (1977)

The United Nations declared the 1970s as the "Women's Decade" and launched international meetings and programs. When it declared 1975 International Women's Year, congresswomen Bella Abzug, Patsy Mink, and Margaret Heckler won support in Congress to fund a conference in Houston in 1977 to promote women's equality with men. The preceding state conferences, which would choose delegates and shape issues to be deliberated, were broadly inclusive and provided funding for low-income women to attend. More than 2,000 women, elected by various constituencies in their states, including a number of antifeminists, attended the conference in Houston. Planners included dramatic symbolism to convey the significance of the gathering to the American public. Relay runners carried torches from Seneca Falls, New York, the birthplace of the mid-19th century women's movement, to Houston, where presidents' wives Rosalyn Carter, Betty Ford, and Lady Bird Johnson opened the conference.

The conference offered substantive recommendations, forged through extensive dialogue and compromise. In a lengthy platform, delegates endorsed the ERA, lesbian rights, and the needs of battered, older, poor, and minority women. Behind the scenes, Gloria Steinem and Charlotte Bunch brought together the goals of various minority caucuses and the convention leadership to build a unique unity. But the thousands of right-wing women meeting across town to counter the conference signaled a new and formidable challenge for the feminist movement in the late 1970s. Phyllis Schlafly, in fact, credited the Houston conference's support for equal rights, regardless of sexual orientation, as aiding her antifeminist efforts.

from the male sports establishment, especially the National Collegiate Athletic Association (NCAA). By designating equal athletic opportunities for girls' and boys' sports, many feared that funding for male sports would be cut. In 1974, a coalition of some 60 women's and girls' organizations formed a task force, the National Coalition for Women and Girls in Education, to enforce Title IX. Funding for women's sports rose slowly in the 1970s. Title IX forced educational institutions to make other changes that provided girls and women equal access to admissions, scholarships, courses, facilities, and employment.

THE STRUGGLE FOR WOMEN'S LIBERATION

The Personal Is Political

Women's liberation movements energized the feminist movements of the 1970s by attracting activists and intellectuals, stimulating important theoretical debates,

Women march for equal rights in Washington, D.C., on August 26, 1970. (Library of Congress)

and grabbing media attention that spread feminist ideas to a wider public. Building on their effective public protests of 1968 and 1969, which targeted beauty pageants, Wall Street, men's gyms, bridal fairs, and newspaper offices, feminists in the 1970s continued to protest, rally, and march on American streets to call attention to unequal and degrading treatment of women.

The women's liberation movement had its roots in civil rights and student movements of the 1960s. As many scholars characterize it, whereas the New Left was self-destructing, the women's movement was dynamically expanding. Disillusioned by the sexism in the New Left and with the middle-class, liberal focus of the mainstream women's movement, young women began articulating a new feminism that advocated liberation, not equality. Blasting the sexism and hypocrisy of male radicals, Robin Morgan wrote in her influential polemic of 1970, "Goodbye to All That," claiming "women are the real Left." Women's liberationists brought to their new movement skills, political tactics, intellectual sophistication, and irreverence, learned from their involvement in other social movements.

Rather than organized under associations such as NOW, with its formal political structure and branches in all 50 states, women's liberation groups sprang up informally across the country and developed different strategies to challenge sexism. Women's liberationists believed revolutionary change could only occur when family roles were transformed, and they shunned formal politics. They saw patriarchy and male chauvinism as the main causes of women's oppression, and until these social relations could be changed, women could not obtain equality.

Yet the women's liberation movement itself was not unified but was divided over critiques of patriarchy, sexuality, race, capitalism, and what constituted "revolutionary." By 1970, dozens of manifestos, mimeographed articles, and newsletters, and splintered groups forming new groups revealed the multiplicity of ideologies and affinities.

Although radical feminist groups were modeled on the separatism advocated by black and brown power movements, they often could not overcome a racial divide. Many white feminists could not understand African American women's interests and needs, and many women of color saw their main issues with their particular communities, not separated from men. Although many women's liberation groups sought dialogue with and inclusion of women of color, their meeting styles and focus on particular issues such as abortion rights alienated many women of color.

Despite these divisions, the conflicts within women's liberation movements generated much vitality, self-reflection, and theoretical advances in understanding women's oppression and how a utopian society might be achieved. Although most of the original women's liberation groups had disintegrated by 1975, the movement itself took different forms as women often abandoned utopian yet divisive radical movements for more pragmatic and local efforts to improve life for women, such as establishing rape crisis centers and women's health clinics.

Radical Feminists

Radical feminism included a variety of activists who may not have shared a precise orientation but identified themselves as distinct from "liberal" feminists and operated outside of mainstream politics. Radical feminists believed that women constituted a distinct "class," and that other forms of racial and economic subordination could not be overcome until gender oppression was eliminated. Sexism and gender oppression were not "natural" states but part of a social system embedded in institutions that could be transformed. Initially a minority in most women's liberation groups, radical feminists came to dominate the groups through their cutting-edge theories, recruitment of young women, and media attention.

One example of this media attention came with radical feminists organizing a sit-in at the *Ladies Home Journal* offices in New York City in 1970. Several hundred women, including those involved in Redstockings, The Feminists, and New York Radical Feminists, presented the editor-in-chief with a list of demands that included hiring more women and African American staff, establishing a day care center for working mothers, eliminating advertising degrading to women, and publishing a special issue focusing on women's liberation. Frustrated by slow negotiations, Shulamith Firestone climbed atop chief editor John M. Carter's desk and began shredding copies of the *Journal*. The editor then agreed to negotiate, but radicals were ultimately disappointed in achieving only one of their goals, a special issue of the magazine.

Radical feminists saw the patriarchal family as a chief form of oppression and sought to change its character or abolish it altogether. Many radical feminists shunned the institution of marriage and even criticized women who decided to bear children. They also intended to alter America's sexual culture and reinterpreted sexual pleasure from a woman's perspective. But many cautioned that male-defined sexual liberation did not necessarily equate women's liberation. Kate Millett's influential *Sexual Politics,* published in 1970, questioned just how "liberatory" was the sexual revolution and pointed to the misogyny in much literature that celebrated sex. Millett blamed women's oppression on the sex role system, not men per se, arguing that men, too, were trapped by societal expectations and assumptions.

Socialist feminism represented another strand of radical feminism and flourished from the early to mid-1970s. Initially radical feminists considered socialist feminists or "politicos" as privileging class over gender, but socialist feminists viewed both male supremacy and capitalism as responsible for women's oppression. Feminist groups such as Bread and Roses in Boston and the Chicago Women's Liberation Union articulated the need to consider economic inequalities along with gender to create a more humane society. They criticized separatist movements and sought to build a broader movement that included working-class and poor women. Yet socialist feminism experienced the same kinds of challenges as other women's movements from the sectarian Left as well as charges of racism and antilesbianism. Feminists' interest in socialist feminism persisted, however, and by the late 1970s, it became a serious point of engagement for the burgeoning women's studies movement. It became a way, too, for women of color to find a useful theory to explain class, gender, and race oppression.

By the mid-70s, many radical feminist groups had split over ideological arguments, and the sectarianism that diffused the strength of the New Left also infected women's movements. In most cities, groups formed, grew larger, divided over politics, strategy, and leadership, and created new groups. These splits prevented any broad-based movement from developing or sustaining itself.

Divisions also emerged over leaders. The women's liberation movement was so concerned about equity and hierarchy that radical feminists often criticized those women who gained media or literary attention. Susan Brownmiller noted that the antileader stance often undermined programs, involved hurtful "trashing" of talented people, and consumed so much energy that authoritarian practices often emerged. While alternating leaders and sharing tasks was admirable in theory, it often meant that work did not get done. Yet the ideal of nonhierarchical organization remained central to feminist organizing through the next decade, and this style of sharing power often was effectively carried out in many successful cooperatives.

Antiporn Movement

Beginning in the mid-1970s, many feminists began organizing against pornography as the symbol of men's oppression and commodification of women. Many activists came to link pornography with violence against women. Catharine MacKinnon and Andrea Dworkin were two influential writers who claimed that pornographic films such as *Deep Throat* (1972) and *Snuff* (1976) encouraged brutal sex acts or rape. By the late 1970s, antipornography became a more important issue for many feminists. In 1978, some feminists sponsored a conference on violence, pornography, and media and a year later formed the group Women Against Pornography (WAP). But many feminists insisted that the focus on pornography could hurt women's efforts at sexual liberation, reinforcing conventional ideas about sexuality, and that censorship could only hurt the feminist project to transform American society and culture.

The demise of radical feminism was not entirely internal. Kathie Sarachild, Carol Hanisch, and some others from Redstockings published the book *Feminist Revolution* in 1978 which criticized liberal feminists for co-opting much from the radical movement and cultural feminists for retreating into a feminist counterculture. Alice Echols argues that liberal feminism's move toward radical feminism accounted for its success in the 1970s. The media, too, began focusing more on the mainstream movement as some radical ideas were adopted and became "mainstream."

Yet these divisions did not mark all women's liberation groups around the country. In fact, because of its decentralization, radical feminism developed differently and pursued separate agendas in different parts of the country. Many radical feminists cooperated with other groups in their communities to advance women's status and conditions. For example, in Columbus, Ohio, women activists at Ohio State University struggled for day care, birth control services at the student health clinic, and equal athletic facilities. In smaller cities such as Columbus, Nancy Whittier found, activists at the university and in the community often combined efforts as part of the umbrella group Women's Action Collective. Their efforts led to an impressive array of support groups for lesbians and single mothers, media and garage cooperatives, book and health collectives, and legal action and publishing groups.

After the mid-1970s, influenced by many lesbian activists, radical feminists increasingly saw separatism as a central goal and strategy for achieving social change. Many argued that women needed separate spaces to develop leadership skills and political critiques without the potential domination of men who, even if unconsciously, were acculturated to dominate women. This revealed the

Bread and Roses

Named for the famous 1912 strike of women textile workers in Lawrence, Massachusetts, Bread and Roses was founded in Boston in 1969 as a loose network of small collectives that were part of the larger umbrella organization. It reflected the broader radical feminist project to establish democratic, nonhierarchical movements that pursued local projects while maintaining an international critique of capitalism. The group saw itself as feminist and socialist and believed that capitalism had generated inequalities of class and race as well as sex. They insisted on changing the entire social fabric of society through public action. As a 1970 outreach leaflet stated, "DO WE WANT EQUALITY IN THE MAN'S WORLD, OR DO WE WANT TO MAKE IT A NEW WORLD?" Bread and Roses advocated that women talk with friends to bring about change rather than participate in formal associations.

The group tackled projects as varied as teaching courses on auto mechanics, agitating for child care for working women, and participating in antiwar marches and abortion rights campaigns. Bread and Roses feminists also created a number of women's unions around the country, but the unions disintegrated after sectarian leftists alienated members.

tensions or contradictions within radical feminism, for, on one hand, it sought to deconstruct the notion of gender difference as an historical and social creation, on the other hand, it accentuated gender difference to create a separate "women's" culture. Cultural feminism distanced itself from the Left and embraced many conventional ideas about gender, arguing that women could best flourish in a counterculture by and for women.

The fragmentation that occurred mid-decade should be understood in the context of the decade, when the shocks to the American economy of inflation and unemployment, the end of the Vietnam War, the new backlash from the right and the divisions and exhaustion facing many social movements also affected women's liberation. The sectarianism and counterculturalism that influenced the New Left by the mid-1970s also diluted the former energy of the women's movement. Yet the debates, theoretical advances, and new models for women's sexuality and liberation promoted by radical feminists dramatically changed American culture and society.

Lesbian Separatism

Initially, lesbians saw feminist struggles as their own. But the gay liberation movement heightened differences over sexuality, and lesbians demanded recognition and attention to different issues. Debates became bitter within NOW over lesbian concerns and demands for recognition. Betty Friedan famously opposed special recognition of lesbians because she feared the move would alienate many American women. Many heterosexual activists feared that feminism would become marked as lesbian. Lesbians resented the conservatism of NOW and its early refusal to champion gay rights, and as a result, Rita Mae Brown and two others resigned from the Executive Board. Brown became associated with Redstockings, a more radical women's liberation group that supported the Gay Liberation Front. In 1971, NOW reversed itself and affirmed the right to sexual choice.

Lesbians within other women's groups began challenging resistance to their recognition and issues. In May 1970, activists at the second annual Congress to Unite Women dramatically turned out the lights in an auditorium with several hundred women. When they turned the lights back on, they stood on stage with "Lavender Menace" T-shirts and posters proclaiming "take a lesbian to lunch" to compel the audience to discuss issues of sexual identity and discrimination.

Many lesbians insisted that lesbianism and feminism were the same, that to overcome male supremacy women had to remove themselves from the company of men. They concluded that lesbianism was more than a sexual preference but a political choice in which a woman proclaimed her commitment to other women. Yet many straight women perceived this claim as a threat or as an ideologically rigid stance that would alienate, rather than broaden, feminism's appeal to other women.

In 1970, New York City's Radicalesbians asserted lesbianism as a political choice and denounced heterosexuality as betraying the women's movement. This "lavender" movement to put lesbians in the vanguard met a mixture of fear and delight from other feminists, either concerned about the political and theoretical impacts or relieved to "come out" and declare their gay sexual identity. Not feeling completely connected to either the gay liberation or feminist movements, lesbian feminists carved out a separate movement that combined a politics of gender and sexual identity. Lesbian separatist groups formed in cities across the country in the early 1970s. But the gay-straight split in many radical women's groups diffused their strength, and as the Wash-

Flyer advertising the second Congress To Unite Women, a gathering of women's groups held in New York City in 1970. (Library of Congress)

Furies Collective

One of the more well-known lesbian separatist groups, the Furies, formed in 1971 in Washington, D.C., and included leading theorists Rita Mae Brown and Charlotte Bunch. The Furies contended that heterosexism was a form of domination that assumed that heterosexual sex was the only "natural" relationship, and that women were bound to men in all social and economic institutions.

The Furies established a residential collective and became one of the city's best-known communal living groups in the early 1970s. The 12 women living on 11th Street SE constituted an important experiment in lesbians of diverse social and economic backgrounds living together and working to make their political and social beliefs a day-to-day reality. Known first as Those Women, they changed the group's name when the collective began publishing a newspaper called The Furies.

From January 1972 until mid-1973, the collective's groundbreaking newspaper featured some of the most insightful lesbian-feminist writing, including contributions by Brown and Bunch. In its premier issue, the newspaper emphasized its philosophy by calling on feminists to come out: "Lesbianism is not a matter of sexual preference, but rather one of political choice which every woman must make if she is to . . . end male supremacy" (Rainbow History Project). The small group of women involved in the Furies had influence far beyond their numbers through the national distribution of the newspaper.

But the Furies' hard line about lesbian separatism, its estrangement from the larger feminist community, and its own intolerance of dissent within the collective, led to its rapid demise. When the collective disbanded in late spring 1972, the core newspaper staff decided to continue the paper.

ington, D.C., Furies discovered, radical separatism did not usher in the "revolution" that they desired.

While debates among lesbian and straight feminists sometimes divided the movement, they also stimulated new ideas and theories about sex and gender. Writers such as Adrienne Rich boldly theorized how society enforced heterosexuality through methods ranging from romantic idealism to rape and discouraged the fundamental attachments between women. Lesbian activists also sustained the women's movement by "working in the trenches," running shelters, hot lines, and clinics for women. Their experiments with women-run institutions and enterprises paved the way for cultural feminism.

Consciousness Raising

Consciousness raising, or CR, as it became known, was a central feature and activity of women's liberation groups. Across the United States, women came

From the Ground Up,
Seattle Feminist Publication

In an era before the Internet, radical feminists depended on circulating ideas and news, and generating members and support for their groups through printed publications. Many of these publications were simply mimeographed and distributed at meetings, campuses, and coffeehouses; others were professionally printed and more widely circulated. Many of these were short-lived, but by the mid-1970s, more than 500 feminist publications were reaching women on a local, regional, and national basis.

In June 1974, in response to what feminists in Seattle viewed as a fragmented Women's Liberation movement, a group of women published the first issue of the feminist newspaper *From the Ground Up.* The founders bemoaned the fact that Seattle's movement had fractured, dispersing to focus on specific needs such as rape relief, abortion rights, health care, and women's studies. The monthly paper promised to provide a feminist perspective on Seattle events, attempt to "build again from the ground up a sisterhood based on shared experiences," and work toward radical social and political change. The Seattle women saw a need to start a feminist paper because of the "cute" and "safe" coverage of women's issues by the mass media and the lack of analysis or deeper reporting by Seattle area women's publications.

The first issue of *From the Ground Up* included articles about local hospital and clerical workers, the Coalition of Labor Union Women, Group Health's failure to cover birth control pills, and letters from a lesbian about police raiding a gay bar and another denouncing the treatment of women prisoners at the Purdy Treatment Center for Women.

together in small groups to discuss family life, work, sex, and education. Through the process of sharing their life stories and observations, collectively women made new discoveries about their and other women's lives, came to question the inequality that pervaded home and society, and found meaning in the expression "the personal is political." Women discovered that even what seemed most mundane and private, such as childrearing and housework, could be political issues subject to collective change. One of the architects of CR, Kathie Sarachild of Redstockings, believed it was critical for developing class solidarity or "sisterhood" among women.

Thousands of CR groups organized around the country, informally and formally, reflecting the significant impact of the 1970s feminist movement on women's lives. Although many feminists, such as those in NOW, feared that CR was a form of therapy rather than political change, the reflective activities often led to action and drew thousands of women into the movement. Through their discussions, CR groups often took action in the public sphere, advocating abortion rights, establishing battered women's shelters, or challenging male insults. Many accounts by women reveal the euphoria, intellectual stimulation, and energy associated with these self-organized efforts.

Some criticized this method of relying on personal experience to acknowledge and solve problems. Betty Friedan referred to CR as "naval gazing," not leading to constructive political change. And because CR groups usually consisted of women who came from the same socioeconomic backgrounds, they tended to see their problems as universal and often did not recognize other issues of significance to women of color and third world women.

MOVEMENT CHALLENGED

African American Feminisms

Feminists of color often joined with white feminists in common struggle and projects, but they for the most part created their own associations that tackled issues of greater concern. The black, brown, red, and yellow power movements had spawned an identity politics that focused on solidarity within racial/ethnic groups, and women of color often felt compelled to work with their communities against racism and in political struggles. Unlike their white counterparts who openly criticized the male New Left, women of color were more reluctant to break with men in their communities. Yet they also experienced gender oppression and created numerous women-only caucuses and organizations to deal with specific feminist concerns.

Despite optimistic pronouncements of "sisterhood," the predominately white feminist movements neglected to acknowledge racial privilege, and African American women, for the most part, chose not to participate. At the heart of this reluctance, Kimberly Springer argues, were relations between black men and women and cultural pressures to resist exacerbating those tensions by asserting a feminist agenda. African American women also feared diluting their energies in the black freedom struggle.

Yet through the 1970s, polls indicated that African American women in general supported the women's liberation movement to a greater degree than white women. African American women also participated in both mainstream and radical feminist organizations, and they asserted feminist principles in their communities, in high profile positions in government and nonprofit organizations, and in literary and creative works.

African American feminists had to navigate the margins of both the women's and black liberation movements. Francis Beale noted the dilemma in her widely read essay, "Double Jeopardy: Black and Female," in which she noted that the advent of black power had led many men to diminish the potential of African

Civil rights activist Angela Davis addresses a rally in Raleigh, North Carolina, on July 4, 1974. (Bettmann/Corbis)

American women leaders. On the other hand, Beale pointed out to white feminists that African American women did not view sexism as severe a problem as economic inequalities and racism. In the 1970s, a number of leading African American female artists, writers, and scholars, including Nikki Giovanni, Eleanor Holmes Norton, Toni Morrison, and Angela Davis concurred that racism persisted as the leading problem for African American women. Other critics claimed that feminism would represent another effort by whites to divide black men and women, and noted that goals such as abortion rights represented traditional white efforts to limit the growth of the African American population. In addition to civil rights and black power struggles, African American women often took an active part in welfare rights movements and efforts to improve local child care, education, medical care, and police treatment. They practiced their politics "in the cracks," or as Kimberly Springer describes, "interstitial politics," where they recognized and acted upon their intersecting identities. They also walked a tightrope in fending off criticism from many African American men (and women) who viewed feminism as a diversion from the "real" struggles against racism and class oppression.

Although African American women were as likely to be engaged with these multiple issues, they did form a number of organizations that explicitly advocated feminist goals within race, class, and sexual orientation identities. In 1973,

The Combahee River Collective Statement (1977)

In 1974, a group of African American feminist lesbians in Boston started the Combahee River Collective, named after the 1863 guerrilla action led by Harriet Tubman that freed more than 750 slaves. Collective members had left NBFO because of its middle-class orientation and lack of political action. Committed to struggling against racial, sexual, heterosexual, and class oppression, members called for recognizing the "interlocking" nature of these systems of oppression, thus heralding an important new way of recognizing multiple identities, which would later become a hallmark of feminist theory.

The collective counted hundreds of women as members in the mid-1970s. Among its activities, it defended an African American doctor who performed abortions, sponsored a series of retreats that brought together black feminists from East Coast cities, organized workshops on college campuses, and mobilized groups in Boston to prosecute the murders of 12 African American women. Divisions in the group after 1976 led it to become primarily a study group that focused on collecting and supporting African American feminist writing.

In 1977, Barbara Smith, Beverly Smith, and Demita Frazier created the *Collective Statement* to contribute to an anthology on socialist feminism. The *Statement* noted African American feminism's origins in the historic struggles of ordinary women and its presence in the second wave of the women's movement since the late 1960s. But it was critical of the racism and elitism of the larger women's movement and the sexism of the black liberation movements. The *Statement* outlined the difficulties impeding African American women's mobilization behind feminism. Proclaiming their socialism, the women also argued that a socialist revolution "that is not also a feminist and anti-racist revolution will not guarantee our liberation." In consciousness-raising sessions, African American women created a multilayered form of "talking/testifying" that articulated the difficulties intellectual women faced in their communities, and rejected lesbian separatism as an unviable political strategy within these communities.

Like most political writing by African American and other feminists of color in the 1970s, the *Statement* found its widest audience through more informal means of distribution as collective members made copies and distributed by hand at various events. In the 1980s, it was reprinted in a number of feminist anthologies, including *This Bridge Called My Back: Writings by Radical Women of Color,* and became a classic in feminist theory.

Aileen Hernandez, a former president of NOW, co-founded Black Women Organized for Action (BWOA) to stimulate African American women's leadership development and participation in politics. Margaret Sloan, a founding editor of *Ms.* magazine, spent two years on a speaking tour with Gloria Steinem and became convinced that African American women wanted a feminist organization.

In 1973, she helped establish the National Black Feminist Organization (NBFO). NBFO founders believed that predominantly white organizations had failed to adequately address African American women's concerns and wanted to attract more African American women to the feminist movement. NBFO held a national conference and generated local chapters. Just as the NBFO emerged from the civil rights and women's movements, it spawned new groups that differed in ideological and strategic orientation. The National Alliance of Black Feminists began as a NBFO chapter in Chicago but separated to launch more political organizing and activities in the city. The Combahee River Collective also split from NBFO to pursue a more class-based lesbian feminism.

Many women in black nationalist groups, like other Marxist feminists, believed sexism would disappear with the destruction of the capitalist economic system. Despite the hypermasculinity of such groups, women played critical leadership roles. By the mid-1970s, a number of African American women began to articulate more forcefully an opposition to male oppression. Elaine Brown, who became head of the Black Panther Party in 1975, and dozens of radical African American women artists and scholars, began embracing a feminist sensibility, albeit closely connected to the intersection with class and race.

Chicana Feminism and La Raza

Mexican American women, too, struggled with how to support La Raza, "the race," or Mexican American people, without remaining subservient to male leaders of the Chicano movement. Chicanas did not want to reject men in the movement who were seeking cultural and political power, nor did they want to reject family, community, and tradition, so critical to their struggles and survival.

Still, Chicanas wanted to pursue women's concerns, even as they rejected much of the middle-class orientation of Euro-American feminism and the antimale rhetoric of radicals. They remained active in major movement organizations such as La Raza Unida and CASA as well as created their own organizations. For example, in 1970, women created the Comisión Feminil Mexicana (Mexican Women's Commission) to work on such issues as child care, abortion, and leadership training for Chicanas. A group of Chicanas living in Washington, D.C., formed the Mexican American Women's National Association in 1974. Finding the city's feminist movement dominated by Anglos and African Americans, and Latino organizations dominated by men, the women sought to provide leadership opportunities for Chicanas, serve as a communications network for others around the country, and raise issues of particular concern to Chicanas/Latinas. Despite the fact that most members had grown up as Catholics, they were explicitly pro-choice. They also spoke out against sterilization abuse.

Young Chicanas organized feminist groups on college campuses. Jennie Chavez organized a women's group, Las Chicanas, on the University of New Mexico campus that grew strong despite criticism from males and females in the Chicano movement. Tensions over loyalties remained, however, as reflected in the first national conference of Chicana activists that met in Houston in 1971. Nearly half of the 600 delegates walked out over resolutions that called for free birth control and abortions, acknowledged the oppressive nature of the Catholic Church, and declared traditional roles for Chicanas unacceptable. Although the Houston conference confronted the movement with feminist issues, many Chicano leaders reacted defensively, arguing that the power of the movement depended on women's traditional supportive roles.

Other Chicana activists sought to serve their communities in fighting against sterilization, improving barrio schools, helping poor women, working for political change, and protesting the Vietnam War. The Chicana Action Service Center in East Los Angeles offered job training and placement for single mothers. In the early 1970s, Chicana activists in south Texas created a caucus within the third party, La Raza Unida, which sought to change Texas (and later the Southwest) through the ballot box.

Chicana writers and artists articulated a radical feminism in the context of culture and community. Chicana lesbian feminists, including Gloria Anzaldúa, Emma Pérez, and Cherríe Moraga, wrote about the alienation they felt as they navigated Chicano and feminist movements in the context of American imperialism. Feminists sought to insert women in their reconstruction of symbols of the Chicano struggle. Artists portrayed La Virgen de Guadalupe, the ubiquitous Mexican religious symbol, as feminist, organizer, and worker. Feminists reinterpreted the image of La Malinche, the Aztec woman who translated for the Spanish conqueror Hernán Cortes, from a cursed traitor to her people to someone who was a leader and made decisions within the confines of her society. Chicana writers such as Cordelia Candelaria considered Malinche a feminist and role model.

Native American, Asian Pacific Islander and Other Women of Color Critiques

Other women of color asserted their needs and concerns as women in the context of larger cultural, economic, and political struggles. Native American women fought for tribal recognition, cultural preservation, and health and social services for their communities. LaDonna Harris, an Indian activist with national visibility, became the founder and president of Americans for Indian Opportunity (AIO) in the early 1970s. AIO sought to press for reforms in Washington's handling of Indian affairs but also developed strategies for grassroots groups to improve Native Americans' lives.

American women of Asian and Pacific Islands descent also viewed much Asian American activism of the 1970s as focused primarily on race without considering other social categories such as gender, sexuality, and nationality. Asian

LaDonna Harris, founder of Americans for Indian Opportunity, speaks with a young Native American girl, 1973. (Bettmann/Corbis)

American feminists organized across ethnic lines as well as within ethnic groups. The Organization of Pan Asian American Women was founded in 1976 to have an impact on public policy. Pan Asia concerned itself with feminist priorities as well as the problems of recent immigrants. Since its membership was largely professional, the group faced the same obstacles as white feminist groups that had difficulty reaching low-income and working-class women. Other groups such as Asian Women United and the Organization of Asian Women also had a middle-class orientation, partly because immigrants who participated in such groups came to the United States after 1965 and were anxious to advance in the economy and use their professional training to obtain better jobs.

Asian American women struggled with issues of filial piety and obedience, valued in their cultures though at odds with radical sentiments about liberation. Often, these feminists were stymied in their quest to make their roles as women count in various struggles because they were accused of being "divisive" or adopting bourgeois white feminist goals. Women in Yellow Power and other groups often felt excluded from decision-making roles and relegated to auxiliary or supportive status.

There were also efforts among women of color to create pan–racial/ethnic alliances, especially in opposition to U.S. imperialism and in support of Third World struggles. In 1970, the Black Women's Alliance changed its name to Third World Women's Alliance to reflect its new multicultural solidarity among African American, Asian American, Chicana, Native American, and Puerto Rican women. It expanded to establish chapters on the West Coast.

These challenges to white feminism in the 1970s became core expressions of feminism by the late 1970s and early 1980s. Minority women's voices, expressed by writers such as Toni Morrison, Maxine Hong Kingston, Audre Lorde, Gloria Anzaldúa, Paula Gunn Allen, and Cherríe Moraga, and theoretical works by Bell Hooks and Barbara Smith were widely read and considered by a large general public and students. They clearly moved feminists of color from margin to center.

Media Portrayals

The feminist movement broke into the media in September 1968, when a few hundred activists from New York Radical Women flamboyantly protested women's objectification at the Miss America pageant in Atlantic City by, among other symbolic acts, crowning a live sheep Miss America. But like other social movements, feminist movements struggled to have their goals, views, and activities honestly represented and reported. The media either affirmed negative stereotypes about bra-burning extremists or trivialized feminists by ridiculing their protests. They often focused on a more palatable feminism that celebrated individual female success, such as that of television stars Marlo Thomas and Mary Tyler Moore, who portrayed single, independent, career women in the city. At the same time, such media coverage, as inaccurate as it might be in portraying feminism's aims, inadvertently helped boost membership in feminist groups by drawing attention to women's concerns and lifestyles. For example, membership in NOW jumped from 3,000 in 1970 to more than 50,000 in 1974.

Beginning in the 1970s, women working for the nation's media began protesting both the content of stories about women and their own treatment as journalists. In March 1970, *Newsweek* featured a cover story on feminism while its own female professional staff filed sex-discrimination charges with EEOC against the magazine. The women protested the fact that 34 of 35 researchers for *Newsweek* were female while only 1 of 52 writers was a woman. The magazine soon worked out a settlement with its female staff.

As feminism gained in popularity and began having real impacts on women's lives in American society, advertisers sought to capitalize on new roles and images. Philip Morris introduced Virginia Slims cigarettes and linked smoking to freedom and glamour. The cigarettes were marketed with the slogan, "You've Come a Long Way Baby," which became universally recognized through the decade as a mark of female independence. As women increasingly shunned makeup and other commercial trappings of beauty, cosmetics and clothing manufacturers promised the "natural look" embraced by the young. New magazines that target working and urban women exploited the commercial advertising potential of such a large demographic group.

By the mid-1970s, words such as "feminism" and "sexism" had entered the lexicon, publications sought to eliminate gendered language, and women and their movements were more regularly featured in media, revealing the influence of the past half dozen years of the feminist movement. Yet the media continued to define feminism in ways that reflected a conservative trend. As antiabortion and anti-ERA movements grew in strength, media sources repeatedly focused on the lack of public appeal and decline of feminism.

By the late 1970s, two images of "feminists" came to dominate the American consciousness, thanks to popular media. One portrayed the man-hating unattractive complainer, the other the "superwoman" who tried to do and have it all. Both of these symbols appeared unhappy and came to represent much that was wrong with America. These portrayals often blamed feminism for the competition for jobs and dramatic changes in the family affecting the late 20th century. This is why hundreds of feminist publications appeared and *Ms.* magazine had such startling success—women were unsatisfied with mass media's portrayals of their lives and concerns, and they turned to their own publications to counter these stereotypes.

Backlash from the Right

As feminisms were reconceptualized by theoretical and activist considerations of race, ethnicity, class, and sexual orientation, and as the women's movement was embraced by popular culture and a growing number of American women, a reinvigorated conservative movement targeted feminism as a peril to the nation. Believing that women's demands for equality threatened family stability and traditional patriarchal values, in the 1970s conservatives mobilized to create new religious, political, and intellectual associations to halt feminism's momentum. The many successes of the feminist movement made during the decade came under increasing assault, as conservatives often mobilized around defeating feminist initiatives. Right-wing activists lobbied President Nixon to veto the Comprehensive Child Development Act of 1971, which would have provided universal child care. In 1972, Phyllis Schlafly began her campaign to halt passage of the ERA. In 1979, television evangelist Jerry Falwell founded the Moral Majority, which made abortion one of its primary concerns. Conservative activists were successful in reshaping the Republican Party to promote a "family values" agenda that opposed divorce, federally funded child care, abortion, and other feminist goals. In 1980, the party—for the first time in the 20th century—dropped the ERA from its political platform.

The Right also targeted popular culture, attempting to halt what it considered promiscuous images and ideas that threatened the traditional family and to celebrate customary gender roles. One of the most popular antifeminist books of the decade was Marabel Morgan's *Total Woman*. Published in 1973, the book echoed many women's magazines in prescribing solutions to "save your marriage." Morgan advocated reading the Bible and giving a man "everything he wants," including power to make all decisions. Yet Morgan's advice also revealed the influence of the sexual revolution by telling women to greet husbands in the nude or in sexy lingerie.

The Right was successful in offering competing cultural ideals although they were not embraced by a majority of Americans who had come to accept women's demands for less restrictive roles in society. Conservatives were more successful in defeating some principal legal goals of feminists, such as the ERA and weakening abortion access by states.

REPRODUCTIVE RIGHTS, WORK, AND FAMILY

Roe v. Wade

On January 22, 1973, the Supreme Court issued its decision that struck down state laws preventing or restricting abortion and affirmed a woman's right to privacy. The landmark decision was heralded as one of the great achievements of the feminist movement. *Roe v. Wade* affirmed women's rights to abortions but also ushered in a powerful movement that sought to limit and end legal abortions.

Many feminists believed that central to their movement was the right for women to control their own reproduction. The use of contraceptives and abortion had been increasing since the 1930s, and physicians were increasingly called upon by patients to perform therapeutic abortions through the 1960s. Although the greater availability of birth control and the sexual revolution expanded women's reproductive choices, many women still sought to terminate unwanted pregnancies. It is estimated that close to one million illegal abortions were performed each year in the United States. In the late 1960s and early 1970s, feminists created abortion referral services and health clinics, and they sought to reform state laws. The Chicago women's liberation collective Jane arranged and performed thousands of safe illegal abortions between 1969 and 1973. By the early 1970s, a number of states had liberalized abortion laws, but access remained limited and costs high. The growing women's movement demanded abolition of all laws that restricted a woman's right to abortion, and feminists publicized personal stories about illegal abortions in "speak-outs," teach-ins, and publications. By the time of the *Roe v. Wade* decision, 17 states had decriminalized or legalized abortion. But many feminists believed that a single judicial decision would be more effective than changing laws state-by-state.

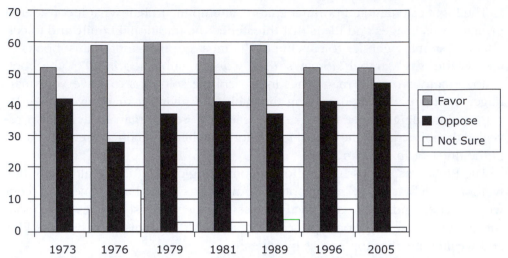

Figure 2.1 *American Attitudes toward* Roe v Wade. Source: *Based on Harris Interactive, The Harris Poll, 2006.*

The case that led to the Supreme Court decision began with the young Texas attorneys Linda Coffee and Sarah Weddington, who sympathized with the plight of women unable to obtain abortions in their state. They searched for the right plaintiff to challenge the law; Norma McCorvey, a pregnant, low-income single mother, became that plaintiff.

In developing the case, Coffee and Weddington decided to emphasize that legal rights for individuals begin at birth, avoiding the fetal rights ethical arguments. They also decided to make an argument based on privacy rights because there were precedents that seemed promising. McCorvey became Jane Roe, to protect her identity.

Coffee filed the original pleadings in Dallas on March 3, 1970, asking for a judgment stating that the Texas abortion statutes were unconstitutional under the First, Fourth, Fifth, Eighth, Ninth, and Fourteenth amendments, and that chief law enforcement officer Henry Wade should be restrained from enforcing the law. In June, a panel of judges declared the Texas law illegal.

In January 1973, the Supreme Court announced its decision; by a vote of 7 to 2, it struck down almost all state laws restricting abortion. In the majority opinion, Justice Harry Blackmun rejected the argument that a woman's right to abortion was absolute and wrote that after the first trimester of pregnancy the State could regulate, and in the third trimester could even prohibit, the procedure. The decision ruled that abortion was a medical decision.

In the following years, the issue of abortion would divide the nation and contribute to a growing conservative backlash against the women's movement. Once legal, the abortion struggle was represented, on one hand, by feminists who saw birth control, including abortion, as an individual right and an expres-

sion of society's commitment to equality, and on the other hand, by conservatives who believed that birth control
should be restricted to prevent it from
eroding morality and families.

Before the Supreme Court decision,
there was little visible sign of polarization over the issue of abortion. As Linda
Gordon argues, abortion became controversial only when it became associated
with feminists' goals for self-determination. And only with the birth of the Right
to Life movement did issues of morality
become associated with what had historically been a common—if since the
mid-19th century illegal—procedure.

Many states were reluctant to lift their
antiabortion laws, and by July 1973,
NARAL and the ACLU had filed lawsuits
in a number of states to compel public
hospitals to provide abortion services.
Meanwhile, antiabortion advocates mobilized to fight for the decision's removal
and weaken its legality. Congressional
sympathizers to the antiabortion posi-

*Demonstrators protest antiabortion
candidate Ellen McCormack at the
Democratic National Convention in
New York City, July 1976. (Library of
Congress)*

tion were successful in passing various amendments to budget authorization
bills from 1976 on, which limited federal funds used for the procedure and limited poor women's access to legal abortion.

As groups opposing abortion became more politically powerful—represented
by the Right-to-Life coalition, the Catholic Church, and fundamentalist Protestant denominations—defenders of abortion adopted what they viewed the
more politically expedient term "pro-choice" to underscore their defense of
women's rights to make their own decisions about pregnancies. Radical feminists criticized this change in language that avoided claiming women's rights
to abortion.

Not all feminists placed contraception and abortion rights at the center of
their agenda. Although polls showed that women of color were more pro-choice
than white women, feminists of color often saw antiracist and antipoverty goals
as more critical. Women of color were also often suspicious of the emphasis on
abortion given the history of discrimination and feared genocidal motives. Feminists within the Young Lords, a Puerto Rican civil rights group in New York
City, challenged the high rates of government-sponsored sterilization campaigns
among Puerto Ricans. Because of lawsuits brought by activists against doctors

National Abortion Rights Action League (NARAL)

In 1969, abortion rights activists met in Chicago and formed the National Association for the Repeal of Abortion Laws. They realized that reforms had made little difference in making it easier for women to obtain abortions and came to advocate repeal of restrictive laws. The organization sought to consolidate and strengthen the efforts of state abortion–rights groups under the umbrella of the first national organization.

NARAL first worked to change state laws, coordinate lobbying efforts in states, and organize grassroots demonstrations, but it soon focused primarily on lobbying for federal legislation to guarantee abortion rights. In 1970, NARAL and other organizations succeeded in backing a bill to repeal abortion restrictions in heavily Catholic New York state. In 1972, the new law was nearly revoked, but Gov. Nelson Rockefeller vetoed a bill to rescind it. After the *Roe v. Wade* decision, NARAL changed its name to the National Abortion Rights Action League and moved its offices to Washington, D.C., to emphasize federal lobbying and policy.

NARAL became a well-funded and effective organization, despite challenges to abortion rights beginning in the 1970s. It created a tax-exempt educational operation called the NARAL Foundation and an electoral arm called the NARAL Political Action Committee to finance and elect Republican and Democrat pro-choice candidates at all levels of government. It expanded its membership base and supported 36 state affiliates.

who had performed coercive sterilizations, in 1974 the Department of Health, Education and Welfare required informed consent for sterilization procedures paid for by federal money. Yet abuses continued, and women's coalitions lobbied through the decade for more stringent regulations. In 1977, activists in New York City established the Committee for Abortion Rights and Against Sterilization Abuse (CARASA) that, with other groups, convinced the city to adopt more stringent sterilization guidelines.

Working Women

The ability to control reproduction, care for children, and find adequate work to sustain families had been central concerns for women for centuries. The 1970s feminist movement opened new possibilities for women because they no longer needed to confine themselves to domestic roles of mother, wife, and homemaker. Surveys through the decade revealed that the majority of women graduating from college believed that a career was as important as a good marriage.

The Hyde Amendment (1977)

The *Roe v. Wade* decision provoked an almost immediate countermovement to repeal abortion rights legislation. By 1977, the antiabortion movement had lobbied Congress successfully to pass an amendment that disallowed federal funding of abortions except in the case of extreme danger to a woman's life. Introduced by congressman Henry J. Hyde (R-Ill.), the Hyde Amendment barred the use of federal Medicaid funds for abortion except when the life of the woman would be endangered by carrying the pregnancy to term.

A coalition of pro-choice groups, including the Reproductive Freedom Project, the Center for Constitutional Rights, and Planned Parenthood, blocked the implementation of the Hyde Amendment for nearly a year by an injunction representing a pregnant Medicaid recipient and health care providers who challenged the amendment in *McRae v. Mathews.* The Supreme Court vacated the injunction in August 1977. With the Hyde Amendment in effect, abortions financed by federal Medicaid funds dropped from about 300,000 per year to a few thousand. Since most poor women relied on Medicaid, they either had to scrape together personal funds at great cost to their families, give birth, or resort to unsafe, nonmedical abortions.

Although the Hyde Amendment has been reenacted every year since 1977, the exceptions to the funding ban have varied. After hard-fought battles in Congress, the fiscal 1978 Hyde Amendment contained—in addition to the exception for life endangerment—new exceptions for rape and incest victims and women whose health would be severely damaged by carrying a pregnancy to term. However, in 1980 the Supreme Court upheld the constitutionality of the original Hyde Amendment language that contained a single exception for life endangerment.

Beginning in the mid-1970s, most state legislatures also imposed restrictions on public funding for abortion, which limited the use of state Medicaid funds to pay for abortions. By the early 1980s, Congress had added restrictions similar to the Hyde Amendment to other federal programs in addition to Medicaid, affecting Native American women, federal employees and their dependents, Peace Corps volunteers, low-income residents of Washington, D.C., military personnel and their dependents, and federal prisoners.

By 1970, half of all American women were in the workforce, and predictions were that their employment numbers would continue to grow. A drop in the fertility rate, a changing and deindustrializing economy that demanded multiple family breadwinners, and new job opportunities for women drew them outside the home into the wage economy. The dramatic increase of women in the formal economy did not just represent college-educated women who desired careers; 42 percent of women in the workforce were single, widowed, divorced, or separated and had to work to survive.

Table 2.1. American Women's Labor Force Participation, 1970 and 1980

Occupations providing the largest number of new jobs for women	Percentage female	
	1970	1980
Secretaries	97.8	98.8
Managers and administrators	15.6	26.9
General office clerks	75.3	82.1
Cashiers	84.2	83.5
Registered nurses	97.3	95.9
Teachers, elementary school	83.9	75.4
Assemblers	45.7	49.5
Child care workers, except private household	92.5	93.2
Nursing aides	87.0	87.8
Machine operators	35.6	33.5

Source: U.S. Department of Commerce, Bureau of the Census (1984).

Ideas about equality had long attracted working women. Labor union women had played a critical role in founding NOW and in pursuing antidiscrimination in the workforce through enforcement of Title VII in the late 1960s. Working women who had the protection of unions freely filed EEOC complaints about wage and job discrimination. Historian Dorothy Sue Cobble has referred to women labor activists as "labor feminists" for their recognition of sex-based disadvantages in the workplace and because they championed labor unions as the best way to improve the lives of working-class women.

But working women were divided over the ERA. Some, especially those in female-dominated occupations, wanted to maintain hard-won wage and hour protections for women, something that would be abolished by an ERA. The AFL-CIO and many labor women remained adamantly opposed to the ERA, portraying its adherents as reflecting business and professional rather than worker interests. But in 1970, women in the United Auto Workers secured an ERA endorsement from their union. The American Federation of Teachers and the Teamsters soon followed suit. The AFL-CIO finally changed its position at its 1973 convention. Many unions became core defenders of the ERA through the 1970s and began to move toward eliminating remaining discriminatory legislation and replacing it with adequate labor standards to protect both men and women.

In addition to breaking down barriers in unions to women's membership and leadership, many labor feminists sought to organize the vast numbers of new women workers, often in the service sector. In 1971, San Francisco–area feminists and trade unionists created Union WAGE (Women's Alliance to Gain Equality) to organize women into unions and to emphasize women workers' issues—primarily health and child care—to employers and unions. WAGE sought a Labor

Engineer Delores Brown tests satellite circuits, 1973. Women joined the workforce in increasing numbers during the 1970s as job opportunities multiplied and economic need increased. (National Archives)

ERA that would extend beneficial labor standard legislation that had protected women to all workers.

In 1972, influenced by César Chávez's United Farm Workers, which combined civil rights issues with union organizing, Day Piercy and Heather Booth founded Women Employed to organize Chicago Loop workers. Women Employed filed suits against major corporations for violations of Title VII and carried out media-savvy protests. When legal secretary Iris Rivera was fired from her job for refusing to make coffee, Women Employed protestors turned up at her Chicago law firm employer to present attorneys with some used coffee grounds and instructions on how to make coffee.

Ellen Cassedy spent a few months working with Women Employed and returned to Boston and the group of Harvard office workers organized by Karen Nussbaum to create a larger network of clerical workers, 9 to 5. These groups sought not only to boost the abysmal pay of office workers but also to work against sexual harassment and other daily humiliations facing all-female workforces.

Trans World Airlines (TWA) flight attendants give the "V for victory" sign shortly after launching a strike against the carrier at midnight on October 20, 1970. The Transport Workers Union called the strike when contract negotiations failed, shutting down TWA's domestic operations. (Bettmann/Corbis)

WAGE, Women Employed, and 9 to 5 inspired similar groups in other cities, and their struggles for a more equitable and respectful workplace inspired the Hollywood film *9 to 5* (1980) about women office workers who endure, and ultimately triumph over, a sexist boss. The film helped popularize the issues pursued by women's unions, including gender inequality and sexism in the workplace, the desire for recognition as women workers, and dignified treatment on the job.

Through the 1970s, working women began demanding recognition of their merits as workers rather than appearances. The case of women flight attendants best illustrates this movement. In the late 1960s, stewardesses could not marry, had to fit the airlines' definition of glamour, and were forced to leave their jobs once in their early 30s. Two American Airline flight attendants, Nancy Collins and Dusty Roads, their union, and NOW, lobbied the EEOC to remove these gender-based limits on employment. By the early 1970s, flight attendants could be any race or sex, could marry, and could work past age 30. Still, the airlines increasingly expected their employees to adopt a sexualized image. In response, flight attendants created a national organization, Stewardesses for Women's Rights, to end their objectification. They filed lawsuits claiming a hostile work environment and distributed buttons that read "Go Fly Yourself" to counter National

Sexual Harassment

Just as women had argued that rape and battering were unacceptable assertions of male power and control, so too did women identify male harassment in the workplace as criminal. But feminists had to educate their employers, the courts, and the public about the seriousness of sexual harassment. In the early 1970s, several women challenged sexual coercion in the workplace under Title VII of the Civil Rights Act. Judges dismissed these early cases as "a personal matter." In 1975, a group of Cornell University women indicted the behavior of a male professor and used the phrase "sexual harassment." Early media coverage often trivialized the issue of sexual harassment, and many men reacted in anger, claiming that feminists were expecting unnatural shifts in men's roles in the workplace and the classroom.

Feminists created new organizations and strategies for reshaping popular understandings of the issue. In the spring of 1975, women in Ithaca, New York, staged the first speak-out and formed the first organization to address harassment, Working Women United. Other groups, such as the Alliance Against Sexual Coercion, which formed in Boston in 1976, grew out of the rape crisis movement. In 1977, *Ms.* magazine and the Working Women's Institute organized a well-attended and well-covered speak-out in New York City, where journalists were prohibited from photographing or naming speakers. Because of the media coverage, sexual harassment became a well-known issue. By the late 1970s, many groups were dealing with sexual harassment, including those with particular concerns for women breaking into nontraditional and male-dominated occupations like mining and construction. These efforts were successful in convincing the Equal Employment Opportunity Commission to add unwelcome sexual advances as a violation of a woman's rights.

Airlines' slogan, "Fly Me." Although the association folded in 1976, by then flight attendants had won more dignified treatment and uniforms.

Working-class women often felt that the predominately white, middle-class feminist movements often excluded them and ignored their issues. Many issues of importance to college-educated women, such as job opportunity and reproductive freedom, were not as important to working women who recognized the divide of class. But in the early 1970s, many feminist groups sought alliances with and advocated for working women. NOW, for example, worked against job discrimination, passage of legislation that discriminated against poor women, and cuts in welfare benefits. It and other women's organizations advocated for more health and child support services for the working poor.

Labor unions and feminists joined women of color who led the fight for fair labor standards to extend to domestic workers. Finally, in 1974 after decades of struggle, domestic workers were added to the Fair Labor Standards Act. States

COYOTE

Many feminists viewed the world's "oldest profession" as another form of gender exploitation and sought its regulation. Unlike their European feminist counterparts who collaborated with prostitutes to improve their working conditions, American feminists were ambivalent at best toward sex workers. But at the first feminist conference on prostitution held in New York, a group of prostitutes disrupted the meeting, claiming that their work was no more exploitative than most women's work.

On Mother's Day in 1973, Margo St. James, who had been an occasional sex worker and feminist activist, organized a union of prostitutes in San Francisco. Called COYOTE (Call Off Your Old Tired Ethics), the group advocated decriminalization of prostitution and assistance for prostitutes, and worked to end the stigma associated with sex work. St. James believed that many feminists were making judgments about prostitution without considering the perspective of prostitutes themselves.

St. James and COYOTE sought to recast prostitution as a labor rather than sexual issue, and claimed one of the fundamental principles of feminism: women have the right to control their own bodies. The group advocated replacing antiprostitution laws with labor laws that deal with working conditions in third-party owned and managed prostitution businesses. They called for the establishment of local commissions, a majority of whose members should be prostitutes or ex-prostitutes, to develop guidelines for the operation of these businesses, including health and safety issues and employer/employee relations.

COYOTE held its first prostitutes convention in 1974, and membership grew to 20,000 by the end of the decade. COYOTE members testified at government hearings, served as expert witnesses in trials, helped police with investigations of crimes against prostitutes, and provided sensitivity training to government and private nonprofit agencies that provided services to prostitutes. COYOTE stimulated the formation of similar groups around the country, including the Sex Workers' Action Coalition (SWAC), the North American Task Force on Prostitution (NTFP) in New York, Hooking Is Real Employment (HIRE) in Atlanta, and Prostitutes of New York (PONY).

Despite the success of COYOTE in reframing discussions and understanding of prostitution and empowering sex workers to voice their own concerns, feminists remained divided over the issue of sex work. Many, including some former prostitutes, saw sex work as a class issue and coercive since few economic options remained open to women. Believing that women were largely forced into prostitution because of a need to survive, they organized to punish pimps and clients, not sex workers.

Child Care

Greater access to birth control information and the availability of the Pill after 1960 made women's efforts to control reproduction easier than in the past. The disappearance of legal barriers to women working outside the home, and access to credit, and divorces made independent lives more possible. Yet women faced other challenges as they struggled simultaneously for greater control over their lives and for assistance from the state in caring for families.

As more women entered the workforce, demands for adequate child care increased. In 1971, Congress introduced a comprehensive child care bill to help poor families. But conservative groups mobilized against the bill and claimed that such a plan was socialistic and would undermine the family structure. Although the bill passed Congress, President Nixon vetoed it and Congress was unable to override. Feminist groups, busy with lobbying for the ERA, failed to organize sufficiently to support the bill. Subsequent attempts through the 1970s to pass child care legislation failed.

Feminists were more successful in obtaining child-care tax deductions, but these primarily benefited the middle class. The Revenue Act of 1971 increased the deductable for child care expenses. After 1974, under Title XX, federal block grants could be used by states to support child care for the working poor, but not all states used the funds for this purpose. The Tax Reform Act of 1976 and Revenue Act of 1978 established tax credits for child care.

began adding household employees to their minimum wage and workers' compensation coverage, benefits that had previously been denied these female low-wage workers.

In 1974, 3,000 union women met in Chicago to form the Coalition of Labor Union Women (CLUW). The recent labor consensus around the ERA and the rising militancy and separatism of African American trade unionists had stimulated women to consider a national association. Women of color were well represented in the first CLUW gathering, including Addie Wyatt, director of Women's Affairs for the Amalgamated Butcher Workmen, who was elected CLUW vice-president. The group pledged to end sex discrimination and harassment in the workplace, provide leadership roles in their unions, improve job training, and create child care and flexible schedules for women workers. Yet many younger, more militant women workers saw CLUW as a continuation of rather than a break from, the stodgy and bureaucratic labor movement. Other women felt they could be more effective working for women's representation in their own unions rather than in a national women's group. Nonetheless, CLUW grew through the 1970s, and its 1979 president, Joyce Miller, became the first woman to serve on the AFL-CIO executive council in 1980.

Women also successfully campaigned to end the mystique and limitations of pregnancy by achieving the passage of the Pregnancy Discrimination Act in 1978. The act prohibited discrimination against pregnant workers and required employers with health insurance to provide coverage for childbirth and related conditions. Although changing gender roles created new possibilities for motherhood and fatherhood, the realities of the "double day" for women who juggled wage work and family care, sexual harassment, the unequal economic consequences of divorce, and the lack of affordable child care continued to plague working women and mothers through the 1970s.

Campaign for Comparable Worth

Despite greater employment opportunities, in the mid-1970s women still earned only 60 cents for every dollar earned by men. Feminists became convinced that women's wages were lower than men's because they were segregated in occupations that were lower paid precisely because the work was done by women, not because of skills or education required. By the mid-1970s, feminists adopted comparable worth, or pay equity, as a strategy to boost women's incomes. The principle was that if an employer had two people employed in different job classifications but essentially doing comparable work, their pay should be similar.

As the percentage and position of women in labor unions grew in the 1970s, pay equity became a goal of the labor movement. In 1973, the American Federation of State, County, and Municipal Employees (AFSCME) persuaded Washington governor Dan Evans to compare state jobs where men and women were concentrated. Researchers discovered that women's jobs were paid about 20 percent less than men's. Efforts to institute raises for women stalled although the Washington case stimulated actions in other states. AFSCME finally won its Title VII lawsuit in Washington State in 1983. As EEOC chair from 1977 to 1981, Eleanor Holmes Norton, in support of comparable worth, encouraged the agency to initiate lawsuits regarding wage discrimination in women's jobs.

Conservatives objected to comparable worth much as they had other feminist legislative initiatives. Although fiscal concerns were primary, conservatives argued that pay changes would diminish the male breadwinner role. Working-class men worried that their jobs would be devalued in the process of raising women's pay. Greater resistance to comparable worth in the 1980s convinced many activists that the issue was too complex to win over immediate wide support.

New Representations of Masculinity, Fatherhood, and Family Roles

The 1960s and 1970s counterculture helped challenge notions of masculinity and gender boundaries. Women and men in the counterculture literally let their hair down and created what they believed was a more "natural" and uninhibited state,

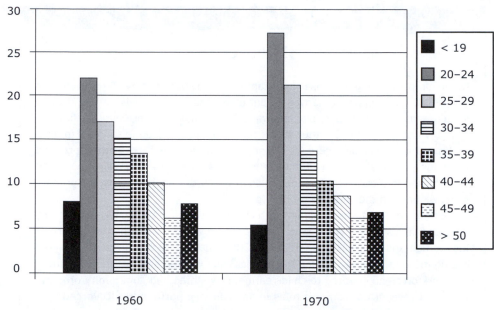

Figure 2.2 *Divorce Rates in 1960 and 1970.* Source: *Adapted from Robert T. Michael,* *"The Rise of Divorce Rates, 1960–1974: Age-Specific Components,"* Demography, *15, 2 (1978): 180.*

rejecting mass gendered standards of beauty and propriety. Women dispensed with curlers and chemicals, abandoned makeup, and allowed hair under arms and on legs to grow. Men and women often adopted the same dress—jeans, T-shirts, and dashikis. This androgyny or abandonment of traditional gendered appearances and behavior was further complicated by feminists' deconstruction of gender roles and gay and lesbian challenges to sexual identities.

All manner of traditional views of "femininity" and "masculinity" came under attack. Women's liberationists ridiculed beauty pageants and cheerleading, which they viewed as objectifying women and supporting commercial notions of beauty. They also demanded equality in relationships with men—in the kitchen and the bedroom and with child care. Many men sought out their feminine side and eschewed traditional notions of "toughness" by learning to cook, parent, and play as a partner rather than a dominator in relationships.

Women's liberation, divorce, communal living, and postponement of marriage challenged traditional ideas about family. More and more women and men lived as single people or in unmarried relationships. More women headed households of children. Yet despite changing gender roles and definitions of the family, women still performed 75 percent of household work in 1975, whether or not they were employed outside the home.

The men's liberation movement sought to analyze these and other disparities that victimized men as much as women, and sought to reconnect men to

Divorce

Divorce rates had begun to rise significantly in the 1960s, and by 1975, there was one divorce for every two marriages. But many had come to believe that divorce should be as painless as possible, and when California passed the country's first no-fault divorce law in 1970, other states followed suit. Although feminists initially embraced more lax divorce laws for providing women escape from oppressive marriages, divorce often hurt the dependent partner, almost always women, who were locked into traditional gender roles in which the husband was the primary breadwinner and the wife the primary parent.

During the 1970s, more women with children fell below the poverty line. Many blamed feminists for divorce laws that penalized women with children. In treating women and men alike in settlements that equally divided property acquired during marriage, the laws failed to consider what women had lost in years out of the workforce and devoted to child-rearing. Few states had community property laws that recognized women's roles in an economic partnership. Divorced men saw their standard of living increase while women's declined by 73 percent. Feminists lobbied for changes in laws to acknowledge the unequal impact of divorce to protect women's economic and family interests. Yet for many working-class and poor women, the rise in female-headed households paralleled the decline in wages and employment for men in the 1970s.

domestic life. Fathers' rights groups began demanding that men be considered as primary parents in custody battles and lobbied hard for gender-blind laws that would award custody based on the best interests of the child. The 1979 academy-award winning film *Kramer vs. Kramer,* starring Dustin Hoffman and Meryl Streep, provided a sympathetic portrayal of these custody struggles. Streep plays a frustrated woman who leaves her workaholic husband and first-grade son to find self-fulfillment, forcing the father to discover the demands of parenting. She returns to claim custody of the son a year later, and the parents battle in court the dilemma of families breaking apart. The film sympathetically portrays the father who is unfairly denied custody by the traditional court system that favored mothers.

Cultural Feminism

Roots of Cultural Feminism

By the late 1970s, radical feminism had all but disappeared, and cultural feminism and its espousal of a separate women's counterculture came to dominate the movement. Moving away from its roots of radical feminism that criticized society's conflation of women's roles with nurturing, cultural feminists came to embrace women's "special" characteristics as a model for a new society and appeared to celebrate rather than challenge gender difference.

Many radical feminists gave up on the idea of immediate transformation of society and sought to provide critical services to women, such as domestic violence counseling and shelters, self-defense training, and cultural programs and centers. Historian Alice Echols explains that cultural feminism sought to bind all women together, just as the feminist movement divided in the 1970s, challenged by lesbians, women of color, and leftists.

Despite continued strains between feminists who designated themselves as liberal, radical, or lesbian, many often worked together on common political and cultural projects. And as efforts to influence policy, such as the ERA, began to founder, many mainstream feminists began to put more effort behind services and projects for women. Funding sources also stimulated this activity as money became available to research rape prevention and improve women's health.

Cultural feminists created woman-centered and woman-generated institutions, art, and businesses. Many of these groups and enterprises popped up around the country through the 1970s, and many had disappeared by the early 1980s. The women's centers established in many American cities often provided important coordination and networking for these various women's enterprises and activities. These centers were distinguished by their autonomy and local, rather than national, orientations. They often depended on a participatory operating style and excluded men.

Lesbian feminism influenced the shaping of cultural feminism with its articulation and practice of separatism and the idea that women could find the most support and room for expression in the company of other women. Lesbian groups were at the forefront of celebrating women's culture and establishing women-operated businesses and cultural institutions. Active women's communities formed in most cities across the country, where many women spent much of their time in the company of other women, in discussion groups, listening to concerts, and viewing art exhibits.

Often to the dismay of radical and socialist feminists, many cultural feminists embraced capitalism as a way to counter patriarchal control of enterprise and gain some power in the economy. By the mid-1970s, women had created hundreds of businesses across the country to primarily serve women, in bookstores, credit unions, co-op garages, publishing, and music enterprises.

Women's Health Movement

In the early 1970s, the feminist movement's emphasis on reproductive rights and the community health movement's work with low-income communities

The original manual of Our Bodies, Ourselves, *assembled by a group of Boston women, which advocated self-help health care and inspired the women's health movement. (Courtesy Boston Women's Health Book Collective)*

inspired the women's health movement. Feminists' dissatisfaction with the medical profession and its lack of attention to women's concerns led many to seek ways of providing alternative health care and easier access to health information. In 1971, about 800 women attended the first feminist health conference. By 1973, more than 1,000 groups addressed a wide range of health issues affecting women.

The Boston Women's Health Collective and its publication of the popular *Our Bodies, Ourselves* helped the women's health movement gain national and international visibility and influence. Women advocated taking control of their health and providing information about their bodies, even providing tools, in particular the plastic speculum, for self-exams.

Efforts to establish women's health clinics across the country led to a coalition of primarily white health providers and feminists who worked with poor women of color to focus on reproductive rights, rather than abortion, to end the practice of sterilization of women who sought government assistance. The National Women's Health Network (NWHN) formed in 1975 to promote the health of all women, regardless of race and class, and to monitor government and medical health practices.

Feminists generally sought an expansion of women's reproductive choices but did not want women's health endangered as corporations pursued profits to meet that demand. In 1970, the Dalkon Shield IUD (intrauterine birth control device) was introduced by the firm A. H. Robins, and millions of American women used it before reports in 1974 revealed that it had led to widespread uterine infections and several deaths. Over the next decade, the NWHN campaigned for its recall.

Women's concerns led to heightened investigations of the health effects of the Pill, diethylstilbestrol (DES), and the frequency of cesarean deliveries and hysterectomies. Research that demonstrated possible long-term health effects of the Pill and women's own discomfort from the side effects led to decreased use of the contraceptive by the end of the decade. Women tried to reframe pregnancy as a natural process rather than a disease and helped develop birthing

The Boston Women's Health Book Collective and *Our Bodies, Ourselves*

The Boston Women's Health Book collective formed in 1970 and published at its expense the newsprint booklet that would become the best-selling *Our Bodies, Ourselves.* Women in the collective had earlier met to share experiences about abortion and childbirth, and continued to meet to research and write about various aspects of health care central to their experiences. The women held informal evening courses, and participants added to the collection of health information. The group believed in advocating for women's health on a strong foundation of accurate information. This collection of information and notes became the health booklet.

The success of the 1970 manual convinced the collective to allow New York publisher Simon and Schuster to publish the book in 1973 with the condition that royalties would support women's health education and discounts would be offered to nonprofits and clinics. The popularity of *Our Bodies, Ourselves* revealed a new women's health movement and brought it national and international visibility and influence. The authors of *Our Bodies, Ourselves,* through affirming women's bodies and celebrating difference, including pregnancy, contributed to cultural feminism's dual approach of advocating power and equality while affirming women's difference from men.

In 1971, the original group members formed a legal corporation and decided not to take in new members, a step that some deemed exclusionary but that group members claimed helped the collective's longevity. The Boston group represented one of the most successful women's collectives formed in the 1970s.

classes and pressured hospitals to allow midwives, husbands, and partners into the delivery room. Yet the numbers of cesarean sections continued to rise, which revealed obstacles to challenging medical practices.

Although the women's health movement was at times insensitive to poor women's needs and their desires for more formal medical care and too dismissive of the medical establishment, it did bring about changes in how women were provided health care. Doctors and hospitals began offering nontraditional "natural" childbirth, more sensitivity to reproductive needs, and special women's clinics.

Women's Centers, Rape Crisis Centers, and Battered Women's Shelters

The feminist movements of the 1970s reconceptualized rape and domestic violence in the context of male domination and power, and initiated new laws to protect and new shelters to assist women victims of violence. In the early 1970s, police and courts still favored the accused in rape cases, and it was difficult for women to prove they had been raped. Susan Griffin's article, "Rape: The All-American Crime," published in *Ramparts* magazine in 1971 argued that rape was not about sex but about power and the system of male dominance. A few years later, Susan Brownmiller's influential book *Against Our Will: Men, Women, and Rape* revealed the ubiquity of rape in American society. Feminists staged speak-outs that criticized the system's treatment of victims as perpetrators, urged women to break the silence about rape, and brought public attention to this crime.

Feminists felt a sense of urgency to establish immediate contact with rape victims and offer them assistance through volunteer-staffed telephone crisis lines, and to pressure local police forces and state legislatures to protect women and prosecute perpetrators. In 1972, the first rape crisis hotline was started in Washington, D.C., and rape crisis centers and hot lines sprang up in communities across the country. Most provided trained volunteers who could offer advice to a victim or accompany her to a hospital or police station. By the mid-1970s, NOW chapters had formed hundreds of rape task forces, and groups sought to change state laws to prosecute rapists more forcefully. Because of this pressure, hospitals and police began treating rape victims more sensitively, and many states altered courts' abilities to consider a victim's past sexual history in rape trials.

The celebrated cases of Inez Garcia and Joanne Little, who had each killed their assailants in 1974 and 1975, respectively, symbolized women's assertions of their rights to defend themselves. After national campaigns to defend them, both women were acquitted.

"Take Back the Night" marches, begun in 1977, represented another dramatic effort to draw attention to the problems of rape and violence against women. The marches became annual events on college campuses and in communities across the country as thousands of women demonstrated and demanded their right to walk their city streets without fear of attack.

Attention to rape and the prevalence of marital rape and incest led feminists to attend to the plight of battered women. Long the chief source of violence in American communities, domestic violence nonetheless received little attention, except in police reports. Rape crisis hotlines and centers exposed the ubiquity of violence against women, and feminists searched for housing alternatives for women fleeing abusive men. Feminist activists purchased houses or rented storefronts to establish hundreds of battered women's shelters through the 1970s, raised local and national attention to the problem, and helped redefine "wife-beating" as a crime rather than custom.

Shelters were initially created and run by volunteers, but during the late 1970s, shelters began to request and receive state and federal funds for operation, and feminists divided over the trend toward institutionalization. Many of the shelters were rooted in feminist collective efforts that stressed the relationship of battering to male domination, but as the shelters became the domain of professionals, they emphasized the plague of "family violence" instead of male privilege.

Women's centers also met challenges in continuing their mission through the decade. Established by collectives and groups of feminists in cities across the country through the 1970s, women's centers sought to provide a central clearinghouse for information and meeting place for women's activities. They offered workshops and classes, and they mobilized women behind political actions. Almost immediately, many women's centers felt compelled to offer rape crisis and domestic violence counseling, which often became the central activities of the centers. Then, as social service agencies and nonprofits began offering these services, women's centers sometimes lost their sense of purpose and volunteer energy. The Helena (Montana) Woman's Center was a case in point. Incorporated in May 1975, it initally provided a place for women to develop job skills; receive information, referral services, and a monthly newsletter; and attend consciousness-raising groups. In August the Center began its Rape Awareness Program (RAP), which operated a 24-hour crisis line, a referral service, and a speaker's bureau. Extensive training and education were provided to volunteers and to the public on the incidence of rape, on self-defense, and on rape counseling. The Center also initiated a Battered Woman Task Force, which later merged with the Rape Awareness Program to form the Violence Against Women Program. In April 1983, faced with loss of funding and difficulty in recruiting volunteers to run its programs, the Helena Woman's Center formally dissolved.

Feminist Scholarship

The feminist movement, along with other social movements of the 1960s and 1970s, dramatically altered academic scholarship. No discipline was left untouched by new theories and research that challenged biological assumptions about gender, placed women at the center of study, and re-examined gender inequalities in a historical, social, and economic context. Feminist scholars asked new questions about their fields, which led to new discoveries, interpretations, and ways of understanding science, medicine, the humanities, and social sciences. In 1969, there were few courses in American universities that focused on women; by the early 1970s, there were thousands. Women's studies courses began cropping up on college campuses throughout the country in the early 1970s. Feminist scholar and activist Sheila Tobias counted 4,000 courses and 600 women's studies programs by the end of the decade.

Feminist scholars, noting the absence of women as subjects, began uncovering their work and lives and inserting their stories and contributions into traditional narratives about science, literature, and history. These studies laid the groundwork for completely reconceptualizing disciplines. For example, historian

Joan Kelly, encouraged by Gerda Lerner who was exploring the historical contributions of women, began to rethink the Renaissance from the perspective of women. Her research revealed that the so-called Dark Ages actually offered more freedom for women than the later period.

Women also challenged the structures of the academy that limited both the number of women scholars and the content of the disciplines. In 1970, WEAL spearheaded an effort to convince the U.S. Department of Labor to review the hiring practices of colleges and universities that held federal contracts. Universities began to pay closer attention to antidiscrimination requirements both in hiring and in the enrollment of women students. As the barriers dropped, women flocked to schools with law, medicine, architecture, divinity, and doctoral programs. The few scholars who had already been studying women soon found eager audiences and, together with graduate students, led the explosion of new scholarship and theory that forged the field of women's studies in the 1970s.

Through the 1970s, feminist students and academics pressured their colleges and universities to establish women's studies courses and programs on college campuses. Women's studies centers and programs often organized feminist activities as well as academic programs. Women's resource centers organized speakers, political action, concerts, and consciousness-raising groups, and offered information and referrals regarding health care, abortion, and rape counseling. Many of these centers were more successful than their community counterparts and remained fixtures of the university for the next decades. The National Women's Studies Association, founded in 1977, brought together academics, students, and activists in pursuing women's studies. But women's studies often reflected the splits in the larger feminist movement, including tensions over leadership, power, sexual identity, class, and race.

Feeling excluded from the main professional associations, feminist scholars established their own conferences and associations. The first Berkshire Conference on the History of Women was organized in 1972 and drew close to a thousand participants, revealing the passion for uncovering women's history and the extent of new scholarship in the field. The 1975 conference drew thousands to Radcliffe College and generated enthusiasm for conferences that focused on and were largely attended by women.

New publishing houses and scholarly journals were critical to the expansion of feminist theory and scholarship in the 1970s. The Feminist Press, established by Florence Howe and Paul Lauter in 1970, uncovered and reprinted forgotten works by women writers. A hallmark of feminist studies was its interdisciplinarity, the breaking down of barriers between disciplines to pursue more holistic approaches to understanding women and gender. The journals *Women's Studies* and *Feminist Studies,* both established in 1972, and *Signs: A Journal of Women in Culture and Society,* begun in 1975, demonstrated how the scholarly profession could feature work from a variety of disciplines that analyzed women's history and culture from many angles. The journals received hundreds of sub-

Historians' Debate: What Happened to the Women's Liberation Movement?

Historians still grapple with the question of whether and why the second-wave feminist movement declined by the 1980s. They have often focused on the divisions within feminism, categorizing different "types" of feminism as liberal, radical, socialist, or cultural. Sara Evans, Linda Gordon, Rosalyn Baxandall, and other scholars divide the 1970s movements into those who advocated equality and those who wanted liberation. Jo Freeman and other activists from the period observe that the movements were more complex than often described, and that feminists of various political stripes often collaborated on common goals and particular projects.

Scholars have also recently questioned the liberal–radical dichotomy among feminisms of the 1970s. Sociologist Barbara Ryan notes that differences have been emphasized instead of examining how different groups of feminists often worked together. She also argues that these divisions are inaccurate because all of the emerging feminist groups of the 1970s represented radical departures. Ryan claims that although "liberal" feminism was often branded ineffective for demanding inclusion in the existing political, social, and economic systems rather than radically transforming them, "liberal" feminism attracted the most followers and largely did the work of pushing legislation forward and organizing assistance that improved women's lives. Barbara Epstein claims that women's liberation may have inspired the movement, but liberal feminists actually achieved concrete, albeit much less ambitious, political and economic victories. Critics of liberal feminism claim it was primarily concerned with individual rights, but the movement also championed broader notions of justice and drew activists to work within civil rights, antiwar, welfare, and other social justice movements. Although the women's liberation movement challenged equal rights feminism for not being bold enough, NOW and other mainstream feminist groups continued to grow through the 1970s even as women's liberation groups declined after mid-decade.

Within women's liberation groups other differences emerged about ideology, theory, sexual orientation, race, class, leadership, and strategy. Linda Gordon and Rosalyn Baxandall argue that ideological divisions that appeared significant between feminists in the 1970s do not loom as large in hindsight because feminists at the time were crafting new political theories that appeared to emphasize differences. Socialist feminists considered issues of race and class equally with those of gender, and although radical feminists prioritized sexual oppression, they did not ignore other forms of oppression. Baxandall and Gordon argue that the gay-straight conflict has also been exaggerated, and while feminists of color may have objected to racism and priorities of the white feminist movements, they themselves created a variety of movements that in turn divided over class and sexual identity. Sara Evans argues that these very tensions energized the movement

Continued on next page

Historians' Debate: What Happened to the Women's Liberation Movement?, Continued

rather than killed it. According to Jane Mansbridge, preserving a particular group or organization was not so important for many radicals of the period; it was natural to move on to other activities and groups.

Alice Echols' influential work, *Daring to Be Bad,* which focuses on radical feminism in the two leading urban centers of New York and Chicago, argues that radical feminism had been replaced by cultural feminism by the mid-1970s (Echols 1989). The internal struggles, the lure of cultural feminism that created women-only spaces and institutions, and, as Barbara Epstein notes, the end of the Vietnam War that marginalized all radical groups, tore apart radical feminism (Epstein 2002). Flora Davis describes the internal conflicts—the gay-straight split, trashing, and Socialist Workers' Party disruption—that created dissension in many groups. She also emphasizes the wearing effect of FBI informers and provocateurs and member burnout. But as Nancy Whittier concludes in her study of Columbus, Ohio, radical and cultural feminists created separate institutions but maintained their commitment to challenge the political system. It was not until the 1980s that feminist organizations began to decline from a more conservative political climate and fewer resources.

Local studies may change the way we understand the evolution of the women's movement in the 1970s. Focusing on Dayton, Ohio, Judith Ezekiel finds that radical feminism, with its focus on liberation, thrived in the city through the 1970s and actually predated liberal feminism, which did not take root until the end of the decade. Dayton Women's Liberation spawned 40 CR groups, established a Women's Center and clinic, and offered classes and referral services. Ezekiel argues that when equal rights concerns began to dominate the movement, it lost its vision and commitment to long-term change (Ezekiel 2002).

---

missions each year and had large circulations. Feminist scholarship was also openly political, which often came under scrutiny and criticism within and outside the academy.

Women's Art

During the 1970s, women's art—created by and for women—flourished. Women's poetry readings, art shows, and concerts targeted growing feminist audiences. Artists sought ways to explore feminist subject matter and alternative ways of producing their work as well as finding all-women audiences.

In the early 1970s, women's art was practically invisible. Feminist artists concentrated on getting women's art shown in galleries and museums and reviewed in art magazines. In September 1971, feminist art critic Lucy Lippard revealed

Members of the all-female vocal group Sweet Honey in the Rock, founded in 1973 at the Washington, D.C., Black Repertory Theater Company, 1994. (Left to right: Ysaye Maria Barnwell, Nitanju Bolade-Casel, Shirley Childress Johnson, Carol Lynn Maillard, Aisha Kahlil, and Bernice Johnson Reagon in foreground). (Michael A. Smith/Time Life Pictures/Getty Images)

the discrimination against women in the art world in the magazine *Art in America*. She explained the difficulty women had in finding venues to exhibit their work and obtaining serious attention and reviews because the power and resources of the art world rested with men. To alter this balance of power, Lippard began focusing her own reviews on women's art and in 1977 cofounded with other women in the visual art community the feminist journal *Heresies*.

Women's art was intensely political and personal and often focused on the importance of women's understanding of their sexuality. Women's exploration of patriarchal subordination through domestic roles is another prominent theme. For example, in their New York show in 1971, Emily and Vivian Kline featured domestic objects, such as a mop and a Tampax, exaggerated in gigantic proportions, to suggest women's oppression.

Women formed the Women's Art Registry (WAR) and opened all-women cooperative galleries such as A.I.R. and Soho 20 in New York City, but they remained excluded from commercial galleries and financial success. Few museum shows in the 1970s organized around feminist themes or prominently displayed feminist art.

Women's fiction with feminist themes met greater commercial and popular success in the 1970s than visual art. In *Fear of Flying* (1973), Erica Jong put a married woman at the center of her sexual odyssey. Marge Piercy's *Small Changes* (1972), Rita Mae Brown's *Rubyfruit Jungle* (1973), Lisa Althere's *Kinflicks* (1975), Alice Walker's *Meridian* (1976), and Marilyn French's *The Women's Room* (1977) also dealt boldly with themes of sex, lesbianism, motherhood, divorce, sexism, racism, and struggles for identity. Feminist publishing houses, such as Shameless Hussy Press, also emerged in the 1970s to publish feminist writers and distribute works to women readers.

Women's music, which featured women musicians and feminist themes marketed to women audiences, also expanded in the 1970s. Artists such as the Women's Liberation Rock and Roll Band and Holly Near frequented campuses, rock festivals, and women's clubs and coffeehouses. One of the most popular women's groups was the Washington, D.C.–based Sweet Honey in the Rock. Founded in 1973 by Dr. Bernice Johnson Reagon, the Grammy Award–winning African American female a cappella ensemble revived traditional sacred music of the black church—spirituals, hymns, gospel—as well as jazz and blues. Sweet Honey also incorporated songs with feminist and other political themes that addressed oppression and exploitation. Under Reagon's direction, the six women singers joined their powerful voices with hand percussion instruments and narrative to relate history, condemn injustice, and encourage activism.

BIOGRAPHIES

Judy Chicago, 1939–

Feminist Artist

Born in the city she later used as her last name, Judy Cohen attended the Art Institute of Chicago and later earned art degrees at UCLA. In 1966, she had her first exhibition in Los Angeles. She began the nation's first feminist art education program in Fresno and in 1971 started the Feminist Art Program in the California Institute of the Arts in Valencia. Judy Chicago was a leader in the feminist art movement of the 1970s; she encouraged students to draw on their experiences and read feminist literature for inspiration for their work. She helped develop the cooperative Womanspace Gallery and the Woman's Building, which served as an important art center and political space, in Los Angeles.

In the mid-1970s, Chicago created her most well-known work, "The Dinner Party," which honored women throughout history. Each of the historic "guests" was represented by handmade porcelain plates sitting on an embroidered runner featuring the needlework style of the historic period. The dinner table rested on a floor painted with 999 names of significant women in history. The exhibit not only publicized forgotten women scientists, writers, artists, and activists but it also represented women's forgotten contributions in cooking and caretaking, and it employed women's traditional arts in its composition. Executed between 1974 and 1979 with the participation of hundreds of volunteers, this monumental multimedia project opened in 1979 at the Museum of Modern Art in San Francisco. It drew more than one million viewers during its 16 exhibitions held at venues spanning six countries. Although general viewers loved it, art critics found "The Dinner Party" unworthy of exhibition, and many museums refused to show it until women's groups pressured them to install it. Nonetheless, the exhibition had an enduring impact and has been the subject of countless publications in diverse fields.

American artist Judy Chicago, about 1975. Her work focused on feminist themes, often celebrating women's sexuality. Her ambitious 1979 work The Dinner Party *gained notoriety for representing women who were ignored by history. (Alex Gotfryd/Corbis)*

Mary Daly, 1928–

Theologian and Feminist Theorist

Growing up in a working-class neighborhood in Schenectady, New York, Mary Daly attended Catholic educational institutions from early childhood through completion of three doctorate degrees. Influenced by the Second Vatican Council and its reforms and the feminist movement, Mary Daly reread Scriptures with women at the center of her analysis to develop a feminist theology. Boston College tried to terminate her contract in 1969, but students protested and she retained her teaching job. In early 1971, she published an article in *Commonweal,* "After the Death of God the Father: Women's Liberation and the Transformation of Christian Consciousness," which argued that the core symbolism of Christianity had been misrepresented by a patriarchal perspective and women should challenge and transform traditional religion.

Daly transformed religious philosophy in the United States. In her influential book *Beyond God the Father* (1973) Daly articulated a more radical vision of a new religious tradition initiated and within a women's community that could completely sweep away old values and beliefs. In her new introduction to the reissued *The Church and the Second Sex* (1975), Daly denounced the possibility of working with men or reforming the church and advocated a separatist solution. By 1979, in her book *Gyn/Ecology,* she outlined how patriarchy had dominated the world beyond the Judeo-Christian West and how women would need to re-create spirituality in their own world removed from men and patriarchal institutions.

Daly's work influenced the growth of feminist spirituality in the 1970s, which featured new magazines, workshops, books, and sects that focused on the search for a Goddess, meanings in women's rituals, expanding personal growth and power, and new forms of healing.

Shulamith Firestone, 1945–

Feminist Activist, Theorist, and Author

Shulamith Firestone helped to form one of the earliest women's liberation groups, the Chicago Westside Group, in 1967. She later joined New York Radical Women and became increasingly disillusioned with the New Left and its insensitivity toward women. Firestone helped form Redstockings and then New York Radical Feminists, both of which identified men as a class of oppressors of women. In her path-breaking 1970 book *The Dialectic of Sex: The Case for Feminist Revolution,* which both borrowed from and rejected Engels, Marx, and Freud to explain the historical dominance of men over women, she advocated "not just the elimination of male *privilege* but of the sex *distinction* itself" (Firestone 1970, 11). She argued that the only way to end the sex class system and women's subordination was to remove sex/gender difference by eliminating the family, replacing biological with artificial reproduction, and emphasizing bisexual relations.

While many feminists embraced Firestone's provocative solution to women's repression, others, such as Sherry Ortner, criticized Firestone's reduction of domination to biology, insisting that ideas about gender and nurturing were cultural and could be changed. Mainstream feminists such as Betty Friedan criticized Firestone for linking the family with oppression. But Firestone argued that rather than plugging women into a male world, social relations needed to be reorganized to eliminate "the sex class distinction altogether," and she believed technology could relieve women of the burden of reproductive labor as well as undermine capitalism.

Nonetheless, by the mid-1970s, as radical feminism increasingly celebrated female uniqueness, Firestone's ideas became too "male." And although an antiracist, she was criticized by women of color along with other white feminists for ignoring race and elevating sexism as the supreme hierarchy.

Myra Wolfgang, 1914–1976

Labor Union Activist

Influenced by leftist politics and her Jewish-Lithuanian immigrant background, Myra Wolfgang became a union activist in the 1930s and was nicknamed the "battling belle of Detroit" by the local media for her role in leading sit-down strikes of salesclerks and counter waitresses in the city's 40 Woolworth's five-and-dime stores. During the 1940s and 1950s, she served as a leader in Detroit's Hotel Employees and Restaurant Employees Union (HERE) and eventually became an international vice president. Wolfgang famously pushed Hugh Hefner and the Playboy Clubs to the bargaining table in the late 1960s, and HERE won a national contract covering all the Playboy Clubs by 1969.

Although she considered herself a feminist and vocally called for an end to gender discrimination, she headed the national committee against the repeal of women's protective legislation, such as maximum hour laws, and opposed the ERA until 1972. Her hostility to the ERA sprang from her own class resentments about perceived privileges of middle-class women and a belief that the legislation would hurt working women. In a debate with Betty Friedan at Wayne State University in 1970, she accused the well-known feminist of demeaning household work, romanticizing wage labor, and ignoring working women's concerns. Friedan labeled Wolfgang an "Aunt Tom" for being subservient to the "labor bosses," and Wolfgang called Friedan "the Chamber of Commerce's Aunt Tom." Wolfgang died from cancer in 1976 at age 61.

REFERENCES AND FURTHER READINGS

Baker, Carrie N. 2003. "'He Said, She Said': Popular Representations of Sexual Harrassment and Second-Wave Feminism." In *Disco Divas: Women and Popular Culture in the 1970s,* edited by Sherrie A. Inness, 39–53. Philadelphia: University of Pennsylvania Press.

Baxandall, Rosalyn, and Linda Gordon. 2000. *Dear Sisters: Dispatches from the Women's Liberation Movement*. New York: Basic Books.

Beale, Francis. 1970. "Double Jeopardy: To Be Black and Female." In *Sisterhood Is Powerful,* edited by Robin Morgan, 344.

Boston Women's Health Book Collective. 1973. *Our Bodies, Ourselves; a Book by and for Women*. New York: Simon and Schuster.

Breines, Wini. 2002. "What's Love Got to Do with It? White Women, Black Women, and Feminism in the Movement Years." *Signs: A Journal of Women in Culture and Society* 27(4): 1095–1133.

Brownmiller, Susan. 1975. *Against Our Will: Men, Women, and Rape.* New York: Simon and Schuster.

Cobble, Dorothy Sue. 2004. *The Others Women's Movement: Workplace Justice and Social Rights in Modern America*. Princeton, N.J.: Princeton University Press.

Collins, Patricia Hill. 2000. *Black Feminist Thought: Knowledge, Consciousness, and the Politics of Empowerment,* 2nd ed. New York: Routledge.

Combahee River Collective Staff. 1986. *The Combahee River Collective Statement: Black Feminist Organizing in the Seventies and Eighties.* New York: Kitchen Table: Women of Color Press.

Conover, Pamela Johnston. 1983. *Feminism and the New Right: Conflict over the American Family.* New York: Praeger.

Cottingham, Laura. 2000. *Seeing through the Seventies: Essays on Feminism and Art.* London: G&B Arts International.

Craig, Steve. 2003. "Madison Avenue Versus *The Feminine Mystique:* The Advertising Industry's Response to the Women's Movement." In *Disco Divas: Women and Popular Culture in the 1970s,* ed. Sherrie A. Inness, 13–23. Philadelphia: University of Pennsylvania Press.

Daly, Mary. 1973. *Beyond God the Father: Toward a Philosophy Of Women's Liberation.* Boston: Beacon Press.

Daly, Mary. 1978. *Gyn/Ecology: The Metaethics of Radical Feminism.* Boston: Beacon Press.

Davis, Flora. 1991. *Moving the Mountain: The Women's Movement in America Since 1960.* New York: Touchstone.

Echols, Alice. 1989. *Daring to Be Bad: Radical Feminism in America 1967–1975.* Minneapolis: University of Minnesota Press.

Echols, Alice. 2002. *Shaky Ground: The '60s and Its Aftershocks.* New York: Columbia University Press.

Epstein, Barbara. 2002. "The Successes and Failures of Feminism." *Journal of Women's History* 14 (2): 118–125.

Evans, Sara M. 1980. *Personal Politics: The Roots of Women's Liberation in the Civil Rights Movement and the New Left.* New York: Knopf.

Evans, Sara M. 2003. *Tidal Wave: How Women Changed America at Century's End.* New York: The Free Press.

Ezekiel, Judith. 2002. *Feminism in the Heartland.* Columbus: Ohio State University Press.

Farrell, Amy Erdman. 1998. *Yours in Sisterhood:* Ms. *Magazine and the Promise of Popular Sisterhood.* Chapel Hill: University of North Carolina Press.

Faux, Marian. 1988. *Roe v. Wade: The Untold Story of the Landmark Supreme Court Decision that Made Abortion Legal.* New York: Macmillan.

Firestone, Shulamith. 1970. *The Dialectic of Sex: The Case for Feminist Revolution.* New York: William Morrow.

Freeman, Jo. 1975. *The Politics of Women's Liberation: A Case Study of an Emerging Social Movement and Its Relation to the Policy Process*. New York: McKay.

Freeman, Jo. 1972. "The Tyranny of Structurelessness." *Berkeley Journal of Sociology* 17: 151–165.

Friedan, Betty. 1963. *The Feminine Mystique*. New York: Norton.

Gilmore, Stephanie. 2003. "The Dynamics of Second-Wave Feminist Activism in Memphis, 1971–1982: Rethinking the Liberal/Radical Divide." *NWSA Journal* 15 (1): 94–117.

Gordon, Linda. 2002. *The Moral Property of Women: A History of Birth Control Politics in America*. Urbana: University of Illinois Press.

Griffin, Susan. 1971. "Rape: The All-American Crime." *Ramparts* 10 (September 1971), 26–35.

Harris, Duchess. "All of Who I am in the Same Place": The Combahee River Collective, http://www.uga.edu/~womanist/harris3.1.htm. Accessed December 20, 2005.

HistoryLink.org: The Online Encyclopedia of Washington State History. "Seattle feminists publish first issue of *From the Ground Up* in June 1974." http://www.historylink.org/essays/output.cfm?file_id=2319. Accessed January 14, 2006.

Jay, Karla, and Allen Young, eds. 1972. *Out of the Closets: Voices of Gay Liberation*. New York: New York University Press. Reprint 1992.

Lippard, Lucy. 1971. "Sexual Politics, Art Style." *Art in America* 59, no. 5 (September–October 1971), 19–20.

Mansbridge, Jane. 1986. *Why We Lost the ER*. Chicago: University of Chicago Press.

Mathews, Donald G., and Jane Sherron De Hart. 1990. *Sex, Gender, and the Politics of ERA. A State and the Nation*. New York: Oxford University Press.

Montana Historical Society Research Center Archives. "Guide to the Montana ERA Ratification Council / Montana Equal Rights Council records, 1972–1987." http://nwda-db.wsulibs.wsu.edu/print/ark:/80444/xv50620. Accessed January 15, 2006.

Moraga, Cherríe; and Gloria Anzaldúa, eds. 1981. *This Bridge Called My Back: Writings by Radical Women of Color*. Watertown, MA: Persephone Press.

Morgan, Marabel. *The Total Woman*. Old Tappan, NJ: F. H. Revell.

Morgan, Robin, ed. 1970. *Sisterhood Is Powerful; An Anthology of Writings from the Women's Liberation Movement*. New York: Random House.

The Rainbow History Project. "The Furies Collective." http://www.rainbowhistory.org/furies.htm. Accessed January 2, 2006.

Rosen, Ruth. 2000. *The World Split Open: How the Modern Women's Movement Changed America*. New York: Viking Penguin.

Roth, Benita. 2004. *Separate Roads to Feminism: Black, Chicana, and White Feminist Movements in America's Second Wave*. New York: Cambridge University Press.

Ruiz, Vicki L. 1998. *From out of the Shadows: Mexican Women in Twentieth-Century America*. New York: Oxford University Press.

Ryan, Barbara. 1992. *Feminism and the Women's Movement: Dynamics of Change in Social Movement, Ideology and Activism*. New York: Routledge.

Sarachild, Kathie, ed. 1978. *Feminist Revolution*. New York: Random House.

Scanlon, Jennifer, ed. 1999. *Significant Contemporary American Feminists: A Biographical Sourcebook*. Westport, CT: Greenwood Press.

Shah, Sonia, ed. 1997. *Dragon Ladies: Asian American Feminists Breathe Fire*. Boston: South End Press.

Smith, Barbara, ed. 1983. *Home Girls: A Black Feminist Anthology*. New York: Kitchen Table–Women of Color Press.

Springer, Kimberly. 2005. *Living for the Revolution: Black Feminist Organizations, 1968–1980*. Durham: Duke University Press.

Sweet Honey in the Rock, http://www.sweethoney.com/. Accessed February 2, 2006.

Tobias, Sheila. 1997. *Faces of Feminism: An Activist's Reflections on the Women's Movement*. Boulder, CO: Westview Press.

Wandersee, Winifred D. 1988. *On the Move: American Women in the 1970s*. Boston: Twayne Publishers.

Whittier, Nancy. 1995. *Feminist Generations: The Persistence of the Radical Women's Movement*. Philadelphia: Temple University Press.

Transforming Place, Self, and Spirit

OVERVIEW

The profusion of 1970s social movements concerned with war, the environment, civil rights, and identities changed American society. Americans also altered the face of the country through their individual choices to migrate or create new ways of living. They sought self-improvement or new spiritual beliefs and practices. They embraced new choices in family and sexual life. And many Americans hoped to continue the legacy of 1960s and 1970s social movements through utopian experiments and cooperative enterprises that provided new models for social change.

One of these movements was quite literally physical. Americans continued to migrate from North to South and West, and from city to suburb, following desirable jobs and housing and creating new social and political arrangements. These physical realignments were not without ironies. The United States became more racially segregated as it championed new methods of integration such as school busing. As the population sprawled beyond city cores into new suburbs and exurbs, and depended more than ever on the automobile, the country faced an oil crisis and deteriorating metropolitan infrastructures. As cities were drained of white middle-class families, they were re-energized by black political power, new immigrants, and youthful singles. New immigrants from Asia and Latin America created new communities and helped make the late 20th century one of the largest and most important periods of immigration in U.S. history.

In the 1970s the counterculture turned to new ways of living and relating to one another outside traditional structures of society. Some people experimented with creating alternative kinds of communities; others joined more disciplined communities that stressed spiritual growth or inner development. Young people developed communes, cooperatives, and collectives in rural areas and in cities, believing that society and self could be changed only by turning away from the old and developing model institutions based on equality, freedom, and respect for the environment.

Americans searched for spiritual meaning in the 1970s. Evangelical Christianity became attractive to many; others flocked to new Eastern religions and New Age philosophies. Young people dissatisfied with Judeo-Christian religious traditions and the industrial capitalist system that their parents supported turned to alternative religions and communities. A plethora of new methods for handling modern life emerged, including yoga, meditation, and vegetarian diets. Consciousness-raising as a practice of the feminist movement influenced greater personal self-reflection in the 1970s. The "human potential" movement generated interest in new forms of therapeutic practices to "feel good" at work and home. Others attempted to find themselves through mind-altering drugs, sexual experimentation, and other earthly pleasures.

The era reflected a contradictory mix of fear and optimism. Some turned to various experiments as part of millennial expectations; others believed they could create utopia in the present. Still others recognized the world's problems and worked to create technological and practical solutions for the future. Although many have characterized the post-Vietnam period as turning away from utopian idealism to "pragmatic activism," the 1970s experiments explored in this chapter reveal a certain expectation that life could be made better and that anything was possible.

TIMELINE

1970   *East West Journal* becomes the first periodical devoted to the New Age Movement.

Jane Roberts publishes the *Seth Materials*.

Shunryu Suzuki releases *Zen Mind, Beginner's Mind*.

National Organization for the Reform of Marijuana Laws (NORML) is established.

Mother Earth News begins publication.

1971   *Diet for a Small Planet* by Francis Moore Lappé encourages vegetarian cooking.

Hunter S. Thompson's *Fear and Loathing in Las Vegas* celebrates the drug culture.

Charles Manson is convicted and sentenced to life on conspiracy to commit murder.

Ram Dass (Richard Albert) publishes *Be Here Now*.

Jesus Christ Superstar has its first showing on Broadway.

Ted Patrick establishes the first anticult movement, the Parents Committee to Free Our Sons and Daughters from the Children of God (FREECOG).

Divine Light Mission establishes its headquarters in Denver, Colorado.

Stephen Gaskin and others establish the Farm intentional community in Summertown, Tennessee.

1972   Nixon's trip to China normalizes relations and allows an exchange of information that includes traditional Chinese medicine.

The Joy of Sex is published.

World Plan Executive Council (WPEC) is formed and takes steps in propagating Transcendental Meditation across the world.

Jesus People USA establishes its ministry in Milwaukee.

Explo '72, a religious version of Woodstock, brings together 80,000 young people in Dallas, Texas.

Whole Earth Catalog wins the National Book Award.

Molly Katzen and friends open the cooperative Moosewood Restaurant in Ithaca, New York.

Hippie love-rock musical HAIR closes on Broadway and tours other U.S. cities.

1973   *Fear of Flying* is published by Erica Jong.

Elizabeth Clair Prophet assumes control over the Church Universal and Triumphant.

Playgirl magazine hits the newsstands.

Oregon becomes first state to decriminalize marijuana use.

1974   Cult Awareness Network is formed.

Naropa Institute is founded in Boulder, Colorado.

Hanuman Foundation is established in Santa Fe, New Mexico.

1975   Kirkpatrick Sale's *Power Shift* describes new economic and
                 political power of Sunbelt region.

                 The largest Wiccan coven in America, the Church of Circle
                 Wicca, is established in Madison, Wisconsin, by Selena Fox
                 and Jim Alan.

                 Fritjof Capra's *Tao of Physics* is published.

                 Media Burn is performed at the Cow Palace by the Ant Farm,
                 an artistic collective based in San Francisco.

                 Congress passes the Refugee Assistance Act encouraging
                 the relocation and resettlement of those fleeing violence
                 or intimidation in Southeast Asian countries.

1976   David Spangler's *Revelation, the Birth of a New Age* is
                 published as a manifesto for the New Age Movement.

                 The vegetarian cookbook *Laurel's Kitchen* is published.

                 Helen Schucman introduces her *A Course in Miracles*.

                 The Hite Report about sexuality becomes a bestseller.

1977   J. Z. Knight has her first encounter with a spiritual being
                 named Ramtha and eventually becomes regarded as a popular
                 channeler, opening Ramtha's School of Enlightenment.

1978   A mass suicide takes place by the Peoples Temple in
                 Jonestown, Guyana.

                 American Holistic Medical Association is founded.

                 First Ben and Jerry's Homemade Ice Cream Parlor opens in
                 Burlington, Vermont.

                 Calvin Klein jeans commercials featuring Brooke Shields create
                 controversy.

1979   *Hinduism Today* monthly magazine on Indian spirituality
                 begins publication.

                 The Moral Majority is founded.

DEMOGRAPHIC SHIFTS: RISE OF THE SUNBELT, DECLINE OF THE RUSTBELT

Immigration and Migration

At the beginning of the 1970s, the U.S. population climbed past the 200 million mark for the first time. There were also changes in the makeup of the American population. Baby boomers, reaching adulthood, had fewer children than their parents, so the population was aging, with the median age increasing to 30 by 1980. In 1970, 88 percent of Americans categorized themselves as "white," but by the end of the decade, this figure decreased by five percent, mostly due to new immigration. The historic 1965 immigration legislation that abandoned the restrictive national-origins quota system established in the 1920s allowed approximately 7 million immigrants to enter the United States during the 1970s. Most came from Latin America and Asia. By the 1980s, only 11 percent of immigrants came from Europe, the source of most immigrants in the previous century. The 1980 census revealed that about half of foreign-born residents arrived before 1965, but nearly half of all Asian immigrants had entered the United States between 1975 and 1980.

The destinations of these immigrants were also different than for previous generations. Economic opportunities, proximity to their homelands, and traditional migration patterns compelled many from various Latin American, Pacific, and Asian countries to settle in the southern rim of the United States. The foreign-born population in both West and South doubled during the 1970s, compared with a much smaller 9 percent increase in the Northeast. During this period, more than 20 percent of immigrants landed in Pacific Rim ports, and 40 percent through the Miami-Honolulu axis. Miami and Honolulu alternated as the second busiest ports of entry through the 1970s, next to New York City. Two-fifths of the newcomers to Honolulu, most of whom were Filipino and Korean, identified California as their destination. California became the lead destination point for immigrants beginning in the 1970s, hosting 25 percent of the nation's newcomers. Mexican, Vietnamese, Chinese, Cuban, Filipino, and Salvadoran immigrants landed in Los Angeles during the decade, making almost a third of that city's population foreign born by 1980.

More than half of immigrants in the 1970s settled in eight gateway cities—New York, Los Angeles, San Francisco, Chicago, Miami, Houston, San Diego, and Washington, D.C.—where there were more economic opportunities and where family members had earlier settled Before the 1940s, Mexicans primarily migrated to rural agricultural areas, but by 1970, they had become the most urbanized immigrant group. In 1970, Los Angeles had the largest Mexican population in the world behind Mexico City and Guadalajara.

Table 3.1. Population of the 10 Largest Cities in the United States, 1970

Place	Population (rounded)	Density (average population per square mile)
New York City, NY	7,900,000	26,343
Chicago, IL	3,400,000	15,126
Los Angeles, CA	2,900,000	6,073
Philadelphia, PA	2,000,000	15,164
Detroit, MI	1,500,000	10,953
Houston, TX	1,300,000	2,841
Baltimore, MD	905,000	11,568
Dallas, TX	844,000	3,179
Washington, DC	757,000	12,321
Cleveland, OH	751,000	9,893

Source: U.S. Bureau of the Census.

The class dimensions of immigration changed in the 1970s, too. More immigrants, almost 40 percent of the total, were educated and professional workers, especially from the Philippines and India, but a larger portion were poor and unskilled, especially from Mexico, and migrated to low-paid, labor-intensive jobs. Those immigrants who came to the United States with skills for professional jobs or capital to start small businesses were more quickly able to ascend the economic ladder.

The 1970s became the first decade in U.S. history to admit significant numbers of refugees because of policies that favored political and religious refugees from Cuba, Southeast Asia, and Eastern Europe. After 1975, when South Vietnam fell to the communist forces, many Vietnamese who had supported the American military or South Vietnamese government emigrated to the United States and other countries, creating sizable expatriate communities. As a token of appreciation to the Mien and Hmong people who served in the CIA secret army of northern Laos, the United States accepted many of the refugees as naturalized citizens. Many more Hmong continued to seek asylum in neighboring Thailand. In 1975, after Congress passed a Refugee Assistance Act to administer resettlement programs, 200,000 Southeast Asians arrived in the United States. The Refugee Act of 1980 raised the number of annual immigrants permitted from 290,000 to 320,000, of which 50,000 could be refugees. By 1985, nearly 400,000 refugees settled in the United States. Throughout this period, Jewish refugees from Russia continued to be admitted.

Legislative changes that made special provisions for Cubans increased Caribbean immigration to nearly 18 percent of total immigration in the 1970s. Since the Cuban revolution in 1959, anti-Castro exiles crowded Miami, making the city majority immigrant by 1980. Such a concentration of Cubans allowed for cultural adaptation to life in the United States without complete assimilation. Most Miami Cubans continued to speak Spanish at home, aided by multiple Spanish-language radio and television stations, residential patterns, and the Catholic Church. Dade County surrounding Miami became officially bilingual in 1973.

The Immigration and Nationality Act Amendments of 1976, which imposed annual ceilings and quotas for Western Hemisphere countries, sharply increased the number of illegal Mexican immigrants entering the United States. For a half century, Mexican workers had been encouraged to cross the border, and they had built extensive migration and family connections in major U.S. cities and throughout the Southwest. The end of the *bracero,* or guest worker, program, and the 1965 and 1976 immigration acts did not shut off these networks. The Immigration and Naturalization Service (INS) arrested and deported a half million illegal migrants each year after 1975.

Vietnamese refugee with his belongings secured between his teeth climbs a cargo net to the deck of the USS White Plains *in the South China Sea, July 1979. After the fall of Saigon in 1975, thousands fled the political persecution and economic hardship of Vietnam and immigrated to the United States. (National Archives)*

The New South and New West

In the period after World War II, the nation's population and wealth began shifting south and west, and this internal movement accelerated during the 1970s. Republican strategist Kevin Phillips, in his influential 1969 book *The Emerging Republican Majority,* called that section of the country stretching from Florida to California the "Sunbelt." He predicted that the demographic shift would strengthen the Republican Party and the conservative movement, which proved correct. Presidents elected during the 1970s and after hailed from the South and California, and the region accumulated more political and economic power. In fact, the Sunbelt concept was seized by journalists in the mid-1970s to explain larger national economic and political shifts. Nonetheless, the term gained popular currency.

Fueling this demographic shift was a changing economy. Deindustrialization, or the decline or relocation of U.S. manufacturing, eliminated the economic base

Haitian Immigrants

Despite its proximity to the United States, few immigrants from Haiti came to the United States in the years before the 1965 Immigration Act because of racial exclusions and historic migration patterns that favored France. But during the late 1970s, crude sailboats, often nearly overflowing with Haitian refugees, began to arrive regularly onto South Florida's shores. Dictator François Duvalier's death in 1971 brought no appreciable change in Haiti's repressive political climate; his son, Jean-Claude (nicknamed "Baby Doc"), became president-for-life and continued his father's reign of terror, forcing many Haitians to flee.

Although Haitian advocates argued that they were escaping legitimate political persecution and at least deserved a chance to make their case, the INS used its resources to turn Haitians back. In contrast to the way their predominantly white Cuban counterparts were accepted as refugees once reaching U.S. shores, the Coast Guard attempted to intercept boats before they left Haitian waters. A disproportionate number of undocumented Haitians who made it to the United States were incarcerated, and requests for political asylum were met with the highest rejection rate of any national group. Cuban Americans in Miami continued to pressure the INS to reject Haitian arrivals, claiming they were economic rather than political refugees. African Americans were the only ethnic group to consistently support the rights of Haitians coming to Miami-Dade County in the 1970s, perhaps because over 20 percent of the area's blacks were Caribbean born, including Afro-Cubans, Haitians, and Jamaicans.

Haitian immigrants in Miami clustered in the Edison–Little River area, north of the central city and with old housing stock that saw an increasing exodus by 1980 of white elderly and working-class residents. Like other immigrants, Haitians joined settled kin and neighbors in chain migration patterns. They found work in nearby garment, hotel, and warehouse districts although they suffered high rates of unemployment because of discrimination. Nonetheless, Miami's Haitians built a vibrant "Little Haiti" with scores of small businesses and featuring the bright colors, cuisine, and music of the Caribbean.

of Northern industrial cities, and the shift to a post-industrial service economy favored newer suburbs and cities of the South and West. U.S. corporations had long pursued a "Southern strategy" of escaping labor unions and obtaining cheaper wages by moving production south. The oil crisis of 1973 and the mid-1970s recession exacerbated problems in the industrial North. In spite of the larger economic crisis, massive federal redistribution of wealth through investment in military facilities pumped up the Sunbelt economy. Kirkpatrick Sale, in his 1975 book, *Power Shift,* described the new "financial colossus" of the region from North Carolina to southern California. Once maligned as a region of rednecks, the South gained more respect in the national press, and by 1976 the

Sunbelt City: Houston

As Robert Fisher argues, no city better represented the Sunbelt than Houston, Texas, which was positioned in the center, or the "buckle," of this region. Houston boomed in the 1970s as capital shifted from North to South. It grew faster than any other American city and during the decade constructed more than 200 large office buildings, which represented most of the large office buildings in the entire city. Despite its economic prosperity, the city had large impoverished areas and segregated African American and Mexican American neighborhoods. And for all its championing of "free enterprise," like other Sunbelt cities, Houston depended on federal largesse for much of its economic growth—for dredging the ship channel, granting oil pipeline and military contracts, and NASA development.

Like other Sunbelt cities, a local business elite dominated "nonpartisan" at-large city elections, which resulted in continuing low taxes that benefited business but few social services to provide residents. For example, Houston had a police force half the size of other large cities and one of the highest murder rates in the country. The city's African American and Mexican American populations made up about 35 percent of the registered voters but exercised little electoral clout, except in mayoral elections, because of this at-large system. When the city annexed six mostly white areas in 1977, the Justice Department pressured the city to adopt a new plan to elect the council. The business elite were willing to allow some additional power to minorities to avoid potential conflict. Houston switched to a mixed election system and granted 9 of 14 council seats to be elected on a single district basis and just 5 remaining at-large.

term "Sunbelt" was used routinely and favorably, framed in opposition to the "Frostbelt"—an uninviting term to describe the North and Northeast.

By 1980, 54 percent of the nation's population lived in the South and West. In Florida, more than half of the population had been born outside the South. Once a rural state with little ethnic diversity, Florida became one of the most urban and heterogeneous places in the nation. During the 1970s, the decades-long outmigration of African Americans from the South reversed; however, their percentage of the population in the North increased. At the start of the 20th century, about 90 percent of African Americans lived in the South, but by the 1970s, more than half lived outside the region.

In 1980, half of the nation's 10 largest cities—Los Angeles, Houston, Dallas, Phoenix, and San Diego—were in the Sunbelt, which had not had large metropolitan areas a half century earlier. Along with this shift came the decline in old national centers in the Midwest and Northeast. Unlike older urban American cities, Sunbelt cities were not built next to industries but around the mid-20th century highway system and the automobile. They had small downtown areas, and as they sprawled outward, the Sunbelt cities annexed new suburban developments and older small communities, connecting them by freeways; residents worked in industrial "parks" and spent time and money in malls. Sunbelt cities grew in conjunction with the new service economy and attracted corporate headquarters and technology firms and more than 5 million Americans from the Midwest and Northeast during the 1970s.

From City to Suburbs

Americans had been moving to the suburbs in large numbers since the end of World War II, but it was during the 1970s that the United States became a markedly suburban society. By 1980, more than three-fourths of all Americans lived in metropolitan areas, a majority of these in the suburbs. Metropolitan areas spread for hundreds or thousands of square miles, and the interstate highway system linked sprawling suburban neighborhoods and industrial or office "parks" to the central city. But the city core became less important to many Americans, no longer holding together the metropolis in common social, cultural, political, and economic bonds. While metropolitan areas grew, between 1970 and 1977 the nation's central cities lost 4.6 percent of their population.

Even more than suburbs, "exurbia," or rural or nonmetropolitan areas, grew rapidly during the 1970s. Much of this growth was due to manufacturing plants relocating from Northern cities to the rural South. Between 1970 and 1978, about 700,000 new manufacturing jobs were created in southern small towns to take advantage of nonunion workforces and low taxes.

The movement from city to suburbs also became explicitly racially defined, and urban-suburban politics mirrored the fault lines of race. Many white families wanted to preserve segregation, despite the courts' efforts to desegregate schools, and relocated to wealthier and whiter suburbs. To mitigate the effects of this increasing racial polarization in the schools, some federal judges attempted to mandate busing between cities and suburbs to cross these racial boundaries. But in 1974, the Supreme Court ruled in *Milliken v. Bradley* that efforts to desegregate could not overrule "local control" of schools and cross district lines.

As urban whites moved to the suburbs, central cities became more represented by low-income African Americans, Latinos, and new immigrants. During the 1970s the numbers of white residents in cities declined by 8.1 percent while the numbers of poor minority residents increased. As tax revenues and populations in former industrial cities like Detroit, St. Louis, Pittsburgh, and Cleveland declined, many parts of major American cities began to literally crumble. In the early 1970s, many feared that older central cities were on the verge of collapse. Books and articles warned of the urban crisis, and most commentators blamed the growth of the suburbs for this demise.

Latino children play amid graffiti-covered walls in a park in Brooklyn, New York, 1974. (Danny Lyon/EPA/National Archives)

For example, New York City's South Bronx population dropped 50 percent between 1970 and 1980, leaving tens of thousands of apartment buildings abandoned and leading to increasing social problems and crime. Owners sometimes sought insurance compensation and hired arsonists to set buildings ablaze, which made the area seem like a war zone. Rising crime and deterioration only accelerated the flight to the suburbs. The urban core lost businesses, and lowered property values attracted pornography, prostitution, drug, and other illicit activities.

The fiscal crisis of the 1970s only heightened the problems of cities. New York and Cleveland faced bankruptcy, unable to borrow against declining revenues to pay operating expenses. And where some cities such as New York were able to adjust to deindustrialization because of their more diverse economies and internationally linked service and information sectors, manufacturing cities like Detroit rapidly lost thousands of well-paying blue-collar jobs, a process that had begun in the 1950s but accelerated in the 1970s. Detroit deteriorated and became more intensely segregated by race and class in the 1970s, even with open housing laws, affirmative action, and other measures to remedy past discrimination.

The loss of manufacturing jobs had drained the city of resources to grapple with postwar economic change.

Although African Americans—the most urbanized ethnic group in the United States—were most deeply affected by white flight and urban decay, they were "the group in national life most deeply engaged in challenging urban decline and imagining remedies to the urban crisis" (Self 2003, 1). African Americans became the majority in many major cities such as Detroit; Baltimore; Washington, D.C.; Chicago; Newark, New Jersey; New Orleans; Atlanta; and Gary, Indiana, and they elected African Americans to public office to advocate for urban issues and attempt to resolve the crisis.

Although more Americans were heading to the suburbs and exurbs, this development was not without costs and critics. Urban planners were particularly critical of the larger, hidden costs in serving metropolitan residents without benefiting from tax revenues, which drained cities of resources. The three-volume government report *The Costs of Sprawl* (1974) noted that low-density developments added expensive infrastructure and damaged air and water quality. But Robert Bruegmann argues that the much-touted costs of sprawl, claimed by antisuburban environmental and urban advocates in the 1970s, were exaggerated. Much of the inner-city infrastructure was outdated and, for example, would cost more to update schools than build new ones.

Opposition to Urban Renewal

By the 1970s many city activists began to question the efficacy of federal urban renewal programs that had promised to revitalize cities in the 1960s. Efforts to "clean up" slums and rebuild urban cores often meant poorer residents lost their homes, the loss of residents hurt retail businesses, and the replacement of historic albeit dilapidated buildings with new concrete and steel diminished the charm and organic economies of cities. For example, between 1956 and 1966, more than 12 percent of the people in Atlanta lost their homes to urban renewal, expressways, and a downtown building boom.

Coalitions of neighborhood groups launched "freeway revolts" to prevent development from destroying businesses and neighborhoods; their grassroots efforts led to political changes that stopped wholesale destruction and included residents in the planning process. In Boston, community activists halted construction of the proposed Southwest Expressway, although a three-mile long stretch of land had been cleared. Mayor Joseph Alioto of San Francisco publicly renounced the policy of urban renewal, and with the backing of community groups, forced the state to end construction of highways through the central city. In 1973 in Atlanta, a coalition of white, middle-class antifreeway residents and African American community leaders paved the way for the election of Maynard Jackson, who pledged to increase involvement of neighborhoods in planning to counter business leader's development interests.

As activists successfully blocked urban renewal demolition and freeway plans, they pressured city governments to include neighborhood groups in planning. In 1970, residents of the older, inner-city neighborhood of Lair Hill in Portland, Oregon, formed the Hill Park Association to block the Portland Development Commission's plans to level their neighborhood for housing for Portland State University and Oregon Health Sciences Center and to include them in planning for the area. Other neighborhood groups emerged in the 1970s to play a role in city planning and helped to elect Neil Goldschmidt as mayor in 1972 for his efforts to preserve and diversify city neighborhoods. In 1976, the Lair Hill area became one of the first historic conservation districts in Portland. In other cities, low- and moderate-income groups often organized to lobby for government Community Development Block Grant program (CDBG) funds, which were distributed by local governments and housing authorities.

During the 1970s, President Richard Nixon shifted money away from urban renewal projects to rehabilitation and restoration, and turned authority back to local entities. At the same time, a preservation movement made popular the styles and practice of rehabilitating historic places and buildings. With tax incentives, more Americans purchased and began fixing up the historic houses and buildings in urban neighborhoods.

But historic preservation, too, was often contested as urban residents debated the function of city spaces. Unlike the planned, exclusive central markets of Boston and Baltimore, Seattle preservationists carefully renewed their historic waterfront market so that it retained its grubby and vital character. Saved from destruction in 1971 when Seattle voters rejected an urban renewal project that would have eliminated the revered market, Pike Place maintained its fishmongers, hardscrabble farmers, hippie craftspeople, and immigrant entrepreneurs. But like other urban markets that attempted to preserve a working character, Seattle's Pike Place often became overcrowded with tourists and gawkers as much as daily shoppers.

Urban Revitalization

The urban America of the 1970s was "definitely on the skids," as described by historian Jon Teaford. But not all cities were in crisis mode, as witnessed by booming Sunbelt cities and signs of urban revival, stimulated by new youthful residents and foreign-born immigrants. Between 1975 and 1982, the numbers of young adults between the ages of 25 to 44 represented almost 75 percent of the nation's population growth. They were attracted to growing white-collar jobs, cultural diversity, and entertainment in the central cities.

The tax act of 1976, which allowed attractive tax credits for rehabilitating historic buildings, helped in this urban revitalization effort. Rehabilitated urban markets or downtown "malls" also attracted young whites to the city. The architectural team of James Rouse and Benjamin Thompson brought life back to

Boston's Faneuil Hall Marketplace in 1978, remaking the 19th-century market to fit the city's new slick corporate image, offering stalls of fresh foods and retail shops. Rouse-Thompson created other successful urban marketplaces, such as Baltimore's Harborplace and the Gallery, which opened in 1980.

Race again shaped the contours of city residential patterns and revitalization. The 1970s gentrification of some city neighborhoods, such as Georgetown in Washington, D.C., Lincoln Park in Chicago, Capitol Hill in Seattle, and Queen Village in Philadelphia, also decreased the proportion of African American residents. Often there was a transition period in the early 1970s in which white artists, radicals, and gays claimed urban neighborhoods for cheap rents and bohemian lifestyles before the neighborhoods gradually became more upscale. Attracted to an active cultural and nightlife scene and the tolerance of a larger community, they often became the "shock troops" of gentrification. For example, Haight-Ashbury, once a hippie magnet, by 1978 had become one of San Francisco's more expensive neighborhoods.

Just as young people began to move to some older urban sections, new immigrants to the nation also made cities their home. Like their late 19th-century industrial counterparts, cities in the 1970s became a powerful magnet for new immigrants searching for work and ethnic communities. For example, Latinos made up at least 20 percent of the populations of Miami, New York City, Los Angeles, and Houston by the end of the 1970s.

Not all service-sector employment headed for the suburbs. New office buildings in city centers such as the twin-tower World Trade Center, built in New York City in the early 1970s; San Francisco's Transamerica Pyramid, opened in 1972; and the 1,450-foot-high Sears Tower, completed in Chicago in 1974, carved optimistic skylines and futures.

Planned Communities

Some Americans concerned with the fate of their cities in the 1970s thought that new towns, much like those conceived in Europe, might solve social problems by including a mix of housing for all incomes and races. Title VII of the Housing and Urban Development Act of 1970 authorized the government to guarantee bonds to developers who financed new towns with these innovative goals in mind. A wealthy Minnesota businessman founded the town of Jonathan 25 miles southwest of Minneapolis to preserve the site's wetlands and other natural features while experimenting in innovative house designs. But by the mid-1970s, Jonathan and other new towns faced serious financial trouble. The recession, record high interest rates, double-digit inflation that made building costs soar, and government red tape and reluctance to fund the program at levels to make it sustainable were to blame. But Americans' hesitation to embrace experimental housing that was environmentally sound and included racial and economic diversity also indicated that many stubbornly clung to what traditional suburbs had to offer.

Malls

The shopping center changed the face of American communities and accompanied the growth of suburbs. By 1971, shopping centers captured half of all retail trade in the country and, five years later, close to 80 percent of department store receipts. By the end of the decade, more than 20,000 suburban centers had been built. Often one large supermarket or department store anchored an array of other stores, usually enclosed, surrounded by huge parking lots to serve mostly single-passenger vehicles. Competition from shopping malls devastated older downtown businesses, which could not compete in price or parking. In the 1970s, super regional malls, like Houston's Galleria and Atlanta's Cumberland/Galleria complex, often overshadowed 1960s-era malls with new features such as ice rinks and multiple levels of stores and restaurants, and they attracted shoppers from 100 miles away.

Suburban shopping centers also altered the ways in which Americans could interact with one another. They provided new social gathering places for teenagers, but they also restricted opportunities for free speech and free assembly. In *Lloyd v. Tanner* (1972) the Supreme Court, reflecting a growing conservatism with new Nixon appointees, ruled that the First Amendment did not guarantee access to shopping malls. In the case of antiwar advocates passing out leaflets at the Lloyd Center in Portland, Oregon, Justice Lewis Powell wrote for the majority in stating that the action infringed on property rights and leaflets could be distributed elsewhere. In his dissent, Justice Marshall noted that with private businesses taking over more of the public square, "it becomes harder and harder for citizens to communicate with other citizens."

More successful planned communities emphasized segregation. Sun City, Arizona, a massive subdivision outside Phoenix, built itself as a retirement haven for the elderly. The community emphasized leisure for retirees, such as golf and supper clubs, and provided all business and cultural amenities within its borders, reducing interactions with other generations. Sun City changed its character in the 1970s as it moved from affordable haven for the elderly to affluent resort. Phase II, which opened in 1970, offered more expensive housing and features such as a manufactured lake, and increased the stratification of the village. The average annual income of residents, along with housing prices, increased through the decade. By 1980, Sun City had 45,000 residents, making it Arizona's eighth-largest city, and it became a model for similar retirement developments across the country. John Findlay observed that planning was not based on residents' desires or social ideals but on buyers' preferences.

Although neighborhood groups struggled against top-down authority in city governments when it came to planning developments, many local governments adopted citywide plans in the 1970s to deal with economic change, mounting traffic congestion, and efforts to make cities more attractive alternatives to suburbs. For greater efficiency in an era of declining revenues, many cities reached out to suburban neighbors to create metro governing bodies to invest in mass transit and coordinate transportation and other metro services.

Many antisprawl activists believed that they had won more public support for planning in the early and mid-1970s with the energy crisis, new popular environmental legislation, and antigrowth successes in several cities. The trend-setting state of Oregon passed a Land Conservation and Development Act in 1973 to establish urban growth boundaries to protect farmland and forests that were quickly gobbled up by suburban expansion. Led by the state's popular governor Tom McCall, who warned in 1972 about the "ravenous rampage of suburbia," the slow-growth attitude became popular in a state that feared becoming like Los Angeles.

Divided Communities: Greater Oakland and Prop 13

Oakland represented typical suburban expansion, absorbing many new migrants who came to California following World War II, and doubling its population between 1950 and 1970. Industries, subdivisions, shopping malls, and businesses sprawled into new spaces away from the center city, aided by the Nimitz Interstate Highway, which for 40 miles stitched together greater Oakland, including large suburbs of San Lorenzo, Fremont, and Hayward. The suburbs provided new homes for most of the migrants from other states, Mexico, and Asia but excluded African Americans from homes and jobs through the mid-1970s.

As Robert Self describes, greater Oakland reflected the divisions emerging between urban and suburban American goals. By 1970, many African Americans had become attracted to many of the precepts of black power and self-determination as they saw the promises of 1960s antipoverty programs fail them. Local and federal governments shifted resources away from these programs just as capital and tax revenue were siphoned off to the suburbs. The Black Panther Party, which began in Oakland in 1966, played an important role in shaping African American politics in the city through the 1970s. Community activists coming out of the War on Poverty also continued to keep problems of racism and poverty before the public.

African American leaders in Oakland called for the same kind of social democratic city that white labor leaders had demanded in the 1940s. But deindustrialization, growing poverty, a weak tax base, and racism stymied African American goals and power. In the 1970s, cities across America were confronting the legacy of segregation and disparate metropolitan development at the same time its resources for urban problems were shrinking.

Suburbs drew more middle-class and working-class whites anxious to be relieved of tax burdens and social responsibilities of the urban core. Yet property taxes increased for California homeowners as the real estate boom increased

Historians' Debate:
Is the Sunbelt a Distinct Region?

Ever since Kevin Phillips' description of the "sunbelt" as a separate region, historians have debated its boundaries and meaning. What, if anything, connects disparate states like Alabama and California? Did the belt begin in Virginia or Florida? Carl Abbott claims the region was more discontiguous and includes places like Oregon, Denver, and Seattle, clearly north of Sunbelt symbols California and Arizona and without the sunny, warm climate the region touts. Others noted that the region could just as likely be called a "sweatbelt" for its lower wages, or a Latino belt for hosting much of the growing Spanish-speaking population of the nation. Noted for its prosperity, the region also had stark disparities in wealth, including many poor and underemployed residents. The recessions of the 1980s eliminated the "boom" reputation of many Sunbelt places, and observers referred to the remaining areas of economic vitality as "sunspots."

Many scholars contend that the West and the South had little in common with one another, other than population growth, and even that was concentrated in particular areas within each region. The two regions had different ethnic assimilation patterns, religious traditions, and political values. During the 1970s, the West was the most urbanized region in the nation, with often half of state populations living in one city such as Phoenix or Portland while the South retained its rural character. Still, generalizations could be contested. A Southern city like Memphis was more likely to vote Democratic and suburban California to vote Republican.

Urban historians highlighted the differences between Sunbelt cities. Richard M. Bernard and Bradley R. Rice gathered new research about the region in their seminal anthology, *Sunbelt Cities* (1983), which warned about generalizations about urbanization. For example, ethnic and racial mixes varied tremendously in cities like Atlanta, Miami, and Phoenix. Some historians question whether there were developments in the urban South that distinguished it from what was similarly happening in the urban North of the 1970s—suburbanization, deindustrialization, and new migrations. Randall M. Miller and George E. Pozzetta find parallels in broker politics and ethnic diversity between ethnic communities in Canada and the northern United States and Southern cities. Ronald H. Bayor found that in many cities of the Sunbelt South, a "Northern model" of ethnic and race relations, which included federal intervention and minority organization, emerged to dramatically change urban politics. Blaine Brownell observed that Southern cities shared more with their Northern urban counterparts than with the larger Southern rural region. As in Northern cities, white residents left the central cities for the suburbs. For example, downtown Atlanta lost residents and office space while its suburbs doubled in size in the 1970s. Conversely, David Goldfield has argued that a history of segregation, resistance to public services, and inertia have helped southern cities retain their peculiarity.

Continued on next page

Historians' Debate:
Is the Sunbelt a Distinct Region?, Continued

In making distinctions between the North and Sunbelt, most writers have emphasized economic developments. But here Roger Lotchin notes that the Sunbelt "boom" was not due to the mechanisms of the market and industrial flight south but to federal military spending in the region. Lotchin probes how the "second war between the states" emerged in the early 1970s, and what enabled the Sunbelt to secure the nation's largest proportion of defense contracts and military bases. Sectional struggles in Congress in the 1950s reveal that the defense budget was as "much a matter of welfare as warfare" as the North even then began to lose its industrial hegemony (Lotchin 1990).

Despite problems with definitions and generalizations about the Sunbelt, the category remained useful to historians in exploring demographic, political, and economic change in the United States in the post–World War II period. Scholars could agree on the significance of general migration patterns and the rise of new centers of production and political power.

property values, and as an unprecedented number of children entered schools. Encouraged by California realtors, homeowners resisted taxation and desegregation. Moreover, homeowners were as much preoccupied with class as race, and worked to keep low-income renters, whether Mexican American, African American, or white, from their neighborhoods. Yet despite this opposition, through the 1970s, developers interested in profits from new housing needs constructed more multifamily rental units in area suburbs.

It was from these suburbs, where homeowners increasingly saw themselves as victims from unfair taxation and mandates to desegregate, that the 1970s tax revolt and suburban break from liberalism emerged. Just as African Americans in Oakland were seeking to save the city from further deindustrialization and unemployment, in 1978 suburban whites revived the cause of tax reform, leading what Robert Self has called "one of the most far-reaching conservative political movements of the twentieth century": the passage of Proposition 13 (Self 2003, 291)

ALTERNATIVE COMMUNITIES, INSTITUTIONS, AND CONSUMPTION

Creating Utopia: Back-to-the-Land Movement and Communes

In the late 1960s and through the 1970s many young people began creating new intentional communities of like-minded peers in the countryside and city. Building on 19th-century utopian experiments and the more contemporary counterculture, the communes of the 1970s maintained that a more humane and ecologically balanced world could be created through a more intimate, egalitarian, and collective life. Either disillusioned with American military-industrial society or optimistic about building model utopias, these urban and rural "pioneers" believed they were creating new pathways toward a better society. Although many have characterized this movement in the 1970s as a retreat from political activism, many communes embraced social justice and social responsibility, or they saw themselves as participating in a new movement that could transform the world.

Most communards shared a rejection of capitalism, a "return to the basics," and an effort to make human relationships and cooperation central to life. As social scientists have noted, they were mostly white, middle-class, college-educated, and involved in protest politics of the era. The prosperity of the period had allowed many young people the privilege of rejecting the grind of careers for an antimaterialist experiment. Despite the relative homogeneity of participants, communes were diverse in their organizational purpose. They brought people together in Asian religious ashrams, "Jesus Freak" houses, rock bands, protest politics, and back-to-the-land efforts.

A number of communes established in the 1960s provided the cornerstones for later 1970s developments. In 1963, Huw "Piper" Williams, a veteran peace activist, established Tolstoy Farm on some of his family's land near Davenport, Washington. Tolstoy attracted about 50 members, and its only rule was that no one would be asked to leave. It avoided the money economy through self-sufficient agriculture and barter and survived through the 20th century. Drop City, near Trinidad, Colorado, founded in 1965, embraced anarchy and voluntary poverty to achieve freedom. But the experiment disintegrated in 1973. The Walden Two experiments, inspired by B. F. Skinner's 1948 novel, spawned the Twin Oaks commune, planned in 1967 in Ann Arbor. The Walden group purchased an old tobacco farm in Virginia and created a form of government modeled on Skinner's book. The 50-member commune was committed to egalitarianism in sharing a common purse, workloads, and gender roles. Its only prohibitions were drugs and television. These early models inspired many to seek communal heaven.

Journalists writing in 1970 and 1971 estimated the number of communes in the United States to be in the thousands and the number of participants in the hundreds of thousands. Reporters in Philadelphia, Boston, and Berkeley counted hundreds of communes in each of their cities; in 1975 scholar Patrick Conover calculated about 50,000 communes in the nation. So confident in their vision were they that in the early 1970s a network of communities created the Federation of Egalitarian Communities. The tremendous number of consciously organized communal living arrangements constituted a significant social trend in 1970s America. Although communes had formed throughout U.S. history, there was never a period when they were so prevalent.

An extensive literature of communal experiences inspired many to want to join or at least visit these idealized ventures. Raymond Mungo's *Total Loss Farm* (1971) told his romantic version of his experiences at Packer Corner Farm in southern Vermont. Richard Fairfield toured the country's communes and published his findings in *Communes USA: A Personal Tour* (1972), which revealed the wide diversity within the communal movement.

The success of various communes had much to do with their organizational structure. Some were anarchistic and rejected any form of organization or rules. Members could come and go and contributed to the commune as they could. Others had clearer expectations about work roles. Communes were typically small, with a dozen or few dozen people, to better manage the experiment. They were self-sufficient, often growing their own food, building their own shelter, and developing ecologically friendly enterprises. Though many outsiders exaggerated the sex and drugs they imagined to dominate, many communes shared a toleration for nonmarital and rotating sexual relationships, nudity, marijuana often grown on site, and LSD use, which many in the counterculture saw as enhancing one's spiritual and mental state.

Most communes were urban rather than rural. They were easier to organize, facilitating an old practice of groups of people coming together to rent a house or building to share expenses, and cities offered jobs to help make ends meet. Some urban communes were based around common interests in political change or spirituality; others tried to reinvent the family by sharing intimate daily life with others. Urban communes were for the most part, as Rosabeth Moss Kanter observed, "laboratories for new kinds of family relationships" (Kanter 1979, 113). Although they might attract countercultural hippies and contribute to household food through backyard or front porch gardens, they had little in common with their rural counterparts.

Although they were more difficult to organize because they required land purchases and were located distances from urban sources of income, rural communes had better survival rates. They also captured the 1970s imagination, as many young people romanticized what rural life might offer. As Hugh Gardner found, in 1970 most rural communes were concentrated in three regions of the country: northern California/southern Oregon; southern Colorado/northern

Residents relax at the Manera Nueva (New Way) commune in Placitas, New Mexico, 1969. (Bettmann/Corbis)

New Mexico; and rural New England. These were relatively isolated places where there was little commercial agriculture, so land could be obtained cheaply, and there was not significant local and police opposition to their presence. Many communes depended on wealthy hippie benefactors to pay rent or purchase property. Others could make cheap payments on available land in the wake of rural depopulation and farm failures.

Most communes were male-founded and male-dominated, and feminist struggles emerged in these as in other communities, especially after 1970. Although gender roles might not be clearly dictated, familiar patterns emerged, with men doing fieldwork and women cooking and cleaning. But the shared social space also allowed women to collectively discuss frustrations and challenge these roles, and some left to establish women's communes, many of them lesbian. The Oregon Farm was a short-lived rural commune where women rebelled against men's assumptions that they would handle house and child care. In 1974, WomanShare was founded by three lesbian friends as a feminist retreat center and self-sufficient women-only community in rural southern Oregon. The periodical *Country Women,* begun in 1973, was explicitly devoted to helping women interested in rural communes, as Warren Belasco describes, "go back to the land without surrendering to the earth mother model" (Belasco 1989, 83).

The commune movement waned by the mid-1970s. External pressures from local officials and neighbors' harassment, the lack of personal privacy, and economic problems ended many communal efforts. Also, egalitarian principles sometimes did not work in reality, with some communards feeling resentful of others if the workload was not shared. Communes often attracted too many visitors and hangers-on, damaging the collective vision of the original experiments. Though they might grow their own food and believe they lived a healthy life, rural communards often faced illness and hepatitis outbreaks from poor water and sanitation. Initial optimism in the possibilities of organic farming were also dashed by 1973, when inflation and stagnant markets hurt the enterprise.

The failure of many communes, and the onset of the economic recession in the mid-1970s discouraged others from embarking on communal experiments. The collapse of the student protest movement and the rise of radical feminism also lessened interest in the familial experiments. Still, as the mid-1990s Communes Oral History Project revealed, the communal experience had a profound effect on participants' lives. Even after leaving communes, most former participants had continued lives that rejected acquisitive values and worked for social change either in their jobs or as citizens.

Urban Communes: Terrasquirma in Portland, Oregon (1972–1979)

A group of Portland antiwar activists influenced by the Quaker Movement for a New Society (MNS) created in 1972 a new household called "Terrasquirma," or earthworm, named for the group's commitment to ecological principles. Like other communes, residents shared chores, bills, earnings, scavenged food from dumpsters and area fruit trees, and a commitment to harmonious living.

MSN's vision for radical democratic organizations that would use communal living collectives as a base for community organizing began in Philadelphia and spread to other cities. By 1975, 14 MNS-affiliated households were established in Portland.

Terrasquirma residents pooled their earnings and resources to support household expenses and robust political activities. With the signing of the Paris Peace accords in 1973 and an end to U.S. combat forces in Vietnam, residents turned their attention to assisting the American Indian Movement (AIM) besieged at Wounded Knee. They organized demonstrations and a support group that filled a U-Haul truck with supplies to deliver to Pine Ridge. The FBI halted the truck en route; the Oregon ACLU filed civil charges against the FBI, and once the support group retrieved the goods, donated them to the Portland Urban Indian Center. Terrasquirma created the Sunflower Recycling Collective, which operated for 20 years and helped to establish the infrastructure for the city's recycling system. Several members established a Rape Relief Hotline in 1974 and set up discussion groups for women to share their experiences with domestic violence. Terrasquirma protested the construction of the Trojan Nuclear Plant 40 miles west of Portland on the Columbia River, failing to halt the construction but helping to form a movement that would ultimately lead to the plant's closure in 1993. The commune also led an effort to organize the People's Bicentennial Commission to celebrate the nation's more noble revolutionary traditions, for example engaging in civil disobedience at the Lloyd Center mall, which had banned petitioning.

Like many other communes, Terrasquirma disintegrated in the late 1970s as founders aged and began to focus on relationships rather than protests. Children also disrupted the commune's harmony and ability to sustain member financial needs. But former commune members sustained Portland's long-lasting counterculture and alternative radical institutions and continued to work for social change.

Rural Communes: The Farm in Tennessee (1971–)

Of all the many communes established in the United States in the 1970s, the Farm, near Summertown, Tennessee, was perhaps the best known and most successful. Stephen Gaskin, a popular professor at San Francisco State College in the late 1960s, attracted thousands to his Monday Night Class about meditation and the world's religious traditions. In 1970, Gaskin announced an extended speaking tour; a caravan of fans followed, and the group decided to settle in rural Tennessee in 1971. The population of the Farm grew from a few hundred to a peak of 1,500 in the early 1980s, and it acquired several thousand acres. It retained its spiritual core and commitment to voluntary poverty, with Gaskin providing leadership.

Respect for the environment and life shaped the Farm's economy, daily life, and gender roles. Farm residents were vegan and early on learned how to plant and use soybeans creatively and developed commercial soy ice cream. They also developed environmentally friendly technology, including passive solar and wind-power systems. In its early years, the Farm shunned artificial contraceptives and abortion and, under the leadership of Ina May Gaskin, developed extensive prenatal and child care, delivering hundreds of babies a year for Farm and area women, and caring for those children if mothers chose not to accept parenthood.

In 1974, the Farm created the hippie version of the Peace Corps in an organization called Plenty. The group helped neighbors in need, sent busloads of Farmers to help repair tornado-damaged homes in nearby Alabama, created the Plenty Ambulance service in the South Bronx, and sent carpenters to Guatemala following a 1976 earthquake. The Farm continued its Latin American connections and to this day offers products produced by worker collectives in Central America.

The national farm crisis and health care costs hit the Farm hard in the late 1970s, and the community found itself deep in debt. To survive, members voted to decollectivize and charge dues, which meant that all residents would have to contribute some kind of income from a Farm business or an outside job. Jobs were hard to come by in rural Tennessee, and by the late 1980s, the commune's population dropped to a few hundred. In subsequent years, members revived the commune with several small businesses, and Gaskin created a new elder commune, Rocinante, where old hippies might live their final years in a collective setting.

The Sunrise Communal Farm, Michigan (1971–1978)

In May 1971, a group of Michigan State University students quit school, disappointing their parents, and pooled their savings to purchase a farm near Evart, Michigan. The students had been radicalized in the late 1960s as Students for a Democratic Society (SDS) members, but some had become disillusioned with the efficacy of political action after witnessing police violence; others wanted to escape the "authoritarian power structure" and change the world by providing an appealing and successful commune alternative.

The students voted to call their new home Sunrise Communal Farm, and they established that decisions would be made democratically, with all residents having an equal voice, and formulated a plan of economic self-sufficiency. Members decided to create and contribute their labors to an arts-and-crafts business that would sustain the farm. For its first five years, Sunrise maintained a core membership of 12 people. But like other communes, the population grew dramatically during summers, when friends and others who had heard about the experiment visited and pitched tents in nearby fields.

Fortunately, several Sunrise members had expertise in business management, which helped the commune survive when others failed. In 1973, so they could secure business loans, the communal members voted to incorporate to maintain equal control. This work ethic and relative success made the commune more acceptable in the eyes of rural neighbors and the local sheriff. Townspeople in Evart realized that the Sunrisers spent money locally, and the commune tried to regulate behavior of visitors that might be offensive, such as nude bathing at a local beach. In 1974, Sunriser Aimee Colmery began contributing a local column, which often portrayed an idealized image of farming, to the *Evart Review,* which gained the commune even more legitimacy in the community.

Children often presented communes with dilemmas. Most communes shunned traditional family arrangements, and most found it difficult to balance the need for adult labor with child care expenses. The Sunrisers who developed monogamous relationships and had children desired private space, although the commune agreed that mothers needed child care in order to complete their work obligations. Resentments between parents and nonparents grew, and after 1974, many of the nonparents who believed that Sunrise was becoming too much like mainstream society in its tolerance of the nuclear family, moved away.

Although Sunrise encountered many of the problems facing other communes that ultimately led to their demise, it survived through the 1970s because of its flexibility and adherence to democratic principles. It rotated leadership roles and shunned hierarchy. Members enforced conflict resolution when personal clashes arose between members. Sunrise was initially vegetarian, but as more non-vegetarians joined, it allowed more meat products. Sunrise evolved from having a communal work ideal to developing a cooperative with specific work arrangements. And it moved from its original anarchistic, collective vision to allow incorporation and more traditional family arrangements. This reflected the growing conservatism of American society as well as the aging of the commune participants. Membership at Sunrise dwindled, and in 1978, the only two remaining Sunrisers, Patti and Phillip Anderson, sold the property to run the commune's business and store.

Urban Collectives and Cooperatives

The collective—a work group in which all members share power and decisions—became a popular form of organization for the many stores, communes, underground newspapers, free schools and universities, child care centers, clinics, legal services, and cooperatives established by radicals, feminists, young professionals, and the counterculture during the 1970s. Many were attracted to the unbureaucratic and democratic model that had been used for centuries by indigenous groups, Quakers, anarchists, and others. In its 1970s form, the collective movement adopted the feminist insight "the personal is political," believing that changing daily lives and practices was as important as political revolution.

Collectives thrived in some cities in particular, including Boston and the San Francisco Bay area. By the late 1970s, there were more than 50 worker collectives in and around Boston, including the New England Free Press, Newsreel Films, Walrus Woodworking, and Cambridge Auto Co-op. In the San Francisco area, more than 150 collectives and collective-cooperatives organized. The Bay Warehouse Collective, founded in Berkeley in 1972, operated auto repair, print, electronics, pottery, and wood shops. About 40 members made decisions about how to run each shop, and all income went to the central collective to pay members based on need. Unable to generate enough income to pay warehouse rent, after 18 months the group split into smaller collectives in smaller spaces, continuing Inkworks, CarWorld, Nexus, and Heartwood for several decades.

Many collectives began as efforts to provide needed services to a community, rather than accumulate profits, and often the perceived need was healthy, inexpensive food. In 1972, Mollie Katzen and 20 friends established Moosewood Restaurant in Ithaca, New York, as a "community project." Workers participated in all aspects of running the restaurant, from planning menus to changing light bulbs, and profits were distributed to them or back into the restaurant. Some restaurant collectives sought to educate patrons about simplicity as well as healthy eating. The Communion Restaurant collective in San Francisco, founded in 1973, offered 60-cent vegetarian meals and expected customers to eat only what they needed and make their own change at the open cash register. The restaurant encouraged silence to enable customers to focus on food and eating.

In the early 1970s, some graduates of Harvard and Boston University law schools formed several radical law collectives in order to accomplish political goals and engage in egalitarian and satisfying work with friends. The Boston Law Commune, the Law Collective, and the Women's Law Collective all shared the same floor of a run-down building in Central Square, and all sought to combine activism with low-cost legal aid. The Commune provided legal services to antiwar and community activists, the Collective sought to assist black and white working-class and poor people, and the Women's Collective assisted women's organizations and handled women's issues. The lawyers rotated secretarial and cleaning duties. Each group collectively decided on which cases to handle and salaries were based on need. Although the collectives successfully represented Puerto Rican parents in a school desegregation case, politically active prisoners, an independent labor union, tenants, and blocked a commercial high-rise in a residential neighborhood; they also executed more mundane real-estate transactions, tax filings, and child custody cases. Within a few years, many of the founders left the collectives to take better-paying jobs or raise children. The elimination of the draft in 1972 ended an important income-generating practice. By 1976, income problems and the realization that they were servicing grassroots groups and low-income people in conventional rather than radical ways led to the groups' dissolution. Only the Law Collective continued to practice.

Ant Farm was a collective of architects and artists that lasted from 1968 to 1978 in San Francisco and Houston. Founded by Doug Michels and Chip Lord,

Cadillac Ranch *in 2006. The art collective Ant Farm advocated and experimented with new art forms and created one of the iconic works of the 1970s: a public art installation of ten Cadillacs partially buried along Route 66 near Amarillo, Texas, symbolizing the limits of progress. (Marshall Astor)*

Food Co-ops

People in cities might not be able to go "back to the land" to raise their own food, but they developed food cooperatives across the country in the 1970s to supply organic and anticorporate alternatives to chain grocery stores. Often begun as buying clubs or "food conspiracies" in the late 1960s, by the early 1970s a "new wave" of co-ops appeared in major cities and college towns catering to the counterculture and a more food-conscious society. Co-op members decided what food to sell and how to purchase and distribute it. Like their 1930s forbearers, these cooperatives were often worker- or producer-run, organized democratically, and represented another way to create fundamental institutions outside capitalist society. Small-scale and neighborhood-based, co-ops involved many more people than communes and may have represented the most successful alternative institution developed in the 1970s. Between 1969 and 1979, close to 10,000 new wave food co-ops were established, serving not only university and hip communities but also many working-class neighborhoods.

As organic foods became more popular, commercial markets began stocking them, and small cooperatives began organizing wholesale and trucking collectives to compete. From the Southern California Cooperating Communities to the New England People's Cooperatives, by the mid-1970s an alternative food system stretched across the country.

By the mid-1970s, the food system movement faced an economic crisis and ideological divisions. Some members believed the co-ops should serve working people as a nonprofit; others thought co-op workers and consumers should decide the question of profits. Some people argued for a more centralized system; others fought to retain a decentralized, consensus model. Political, health, and economic goals often clashed. Co-ops tried to buy local, organic, and bulk foods and assiduously avoided boycotted foods, such as nonunion table grapes, but sometimes decisions were hotly debated. Should the co-op buy only organic, even if expensive and out of range of low-income shoppers?

The recession, inflation, and competition from commercial grocers also threatened cooperatives, which, in trying to expand to remain viable, often had to become more bureaucratic. And expansion did not necessarily save the enterprise. The Austin (Texas) Community Project, for example, began in 1972 to develop methods of distributing natural foods. Within a few years, it included co-op stores, buying clubs, four organic farms, and a variety of baking, canning, and restaurant collectives, with more than a thousand members. In 1976, most of the project collapsed from over-extension, although some of the groups continued.

Ideological differences, tensions between workers and volunteers, and the strains in trying to stay afloat while retaining countercultural and political aims also weakened the promising cooperative movement. The People's Warehouse, which emerged from the successful food co-op movement in Minneapolis, exploded in conflict in 1975. The warehouse provided a central location for food distribution

Continued on next page

Food Co-ops, Continued

and relationship-building among co-op volunteers, who optimistically believed they might provide for all the food needs of the city someday. But co-op members became increasingly estranged from the warehouse workers' collective, which they believed unfairly profited from wages and illegal sales of goods that were destined for the co-ops. Some co-op members criticized the co-ops for becoming too white and middle class, not reaching out to the working class, and neglecting important political work, and they argued for introducing some canned and processed foods. When warehouse workers incorporated the business, co-ops were outraged that they chose not to create a cooperative form of governance. A "democratic-centralist" faction used force to take over the warehouse, and many co-ops left and formed a new competing warehouse. Food systems around the country took "radical" or "liberal" sides, boycotting either warehouse, and both warehouses met near extinction, shaking the cooperative movement.

the collective sought to create a more revolutionary architectural and artistic style that was playful, pointed, and nomadic. Touring colleges and universities in their "Media Van," they staged architectural happenings and how-to workshops. Ant Farm experimented with new art forms such as performance and video, and created two iconic works of the 1970s: *Media Burn,* with Michels and Curtis Schreier dressed as space cowboys driving a 1959 Cadillac through a pyramid of flaming televisions; and *Cadillac Ranch,* a public art design of ten Cadillacs, dating from 1948 to 1964, partially buried along Route 66 near Amarillo, Texas, with tailfins up, a "dual symbol of progress and obsolescence."

New Markets and Enterprises

As collectives and co-ops struggled with how to combine political missions with economic survival, new businesses emerged in the 1970s that sought to embrace profits while maintaining a social conscience. In keeping with the late-1960s rejection of excess for simplicity, the most popular and successful new enterprises provided for the basics desired by the counterculture: food, clothing, shelter, and health services. So popular were these new enterprises in the 1970s that Raymond Mungo surveyed and described "hip" businesses in his 1980 book, *Cosmic Profit.* These businesses sold a particular product as well as a set of social values that many Americans wanted to support.

In the 1970s, many Americans began to reject the frozen, canned, and dehydrated food options of the post–World War II period to embrace what was perceived as "natural" and unprocessed. While many attempted to grow their own food, witnessed by the expansion of the publication *Organic Gardening and Farming,* which reached close to a million readers by 1971, most people sought to purchase farm fresh foods. The growth of food cooperatives and natural food stores provided markets for herbal teas, soy products, whole grains, organic vegetables, and granola and presented opportunities for countercultural entrepreneurs. For example, the Farm commune produced a variety of soy-based foods, including milk, ice cream, and burgers that it sold commercially, as well as providing for its own protein needs.

Part of the New Age movement included efforts to transform Far East practices into credible enterprises, and new shops, clinics, and books on holistic health proliferated in the 1970s. Encouraged by the success of Paavo Airola's *How to Get Well* (1974), other authors produced books on natural healing that also analyzed the western medical establishment and emphasized the body, mind, and spirit as an integrative system. In 1978, Dr. Clyde Norman Shealy founded the American Holistic Medical Association. Soon after, the book *Wholistic Dimensions in Healing,* edited by Leslie Kaslof, listed 80 holistic health organizations in North America. Chiropractic, herbal medicine, naturopathy, meditation, and acupuncture clinics opened in most major cities and college towns, and competed with traditional physician care.

Many new entrepreneurs, even if success enabled them to expand beyond their original community roots, retained commitments to social justice. Long-time friends Jerry Greenfield and Ben Cohen decided to start a food business together and settled on ice cream because its start-up costs were small. In 1978, they located their first Ben & Jerry's Homemade Ice Cream Parlor in Burlington, Vermont, because the college town lacked an ice cream store. Ben & Jerry's became as well known for its rich, unusual flavors as it was for its activities reflected in the slogan "Business has a responsibility to give back to the community."

But some alternative enterprises lost their original social goals as they achieved success. In 1970, Mo Siegel began a company in Boulder, Colorado, to provide organically grown and multiple varieties of herbal tea. By 1978, Celestial Seasonings was a multimillion dollar business that employed 200 people, who received free daily lunches, T-shirts, and shareholding plans. But Siegel's style was autocratic, and workers earned less than the average Boulder wage. By the late 1970s, the company began selling to supermarkets rather than exclusively to co-ops and health food stores, and in 1984 Siegel sold the company to the large Dart & Kraft, Inc.

Larger commercial enterprises took advantage of the popularity of the "countercuisine" and notions of living lightly to create new profitable products, often at the expense of alternative products. Miller Beer first marketed its "Lite" beer in 1974, and other products appealed to a health-conscious society. Lite foods were especially profitable to processors such as General Mills, Pillsbury, and Campbell's, much to the disappointment of whole foods advocates who supported raw, bulk foods. At the same time that larger corporations were incorporating rhetoric about health to advertise "natural" products, as Warren Belasco argues, the countercuisine "got mugged and subdued" (Belasco 1984, 260). In addition to corporations infringing on its markets, media accounts emphasized the dangers of contamination from organic foods, the Nixon administration and state politicians defended agribusinesses, and local health authorities harassed communes, co-ops, and whole food restaurants.

By the late 1970s, it was difficult for small co-ops and health food stores to survive, and many folded or consolidated with larger stores. The Whole Foods Market, a natural food chain, opened in 1980 in Austin, Texas, and it merged with or acquired a variety of stores across the country, including Whole Food Company, which opened in New Orleans in 1974; Bread & Circus, founded in Brookline, Massachusetts, in 1975; Mrs. Gooch's Natural Foods Market of West Los Angeles, which opened its doors in 1977; and Allegro Coffee Company, started by brothers Jeff and Roger Cohn in 1977 in Boulder.

Vegetarianism

Growing numbers of books and restaurants appeared in the 1970s that responded to the new popularity of vegetarianism. The choice of a vegetarian lifestyle was sometimes inspired by encounters with Eastern religions, most notably Hindu yogis who spread the influence of ahimsa, which called for the rejection of harming and killing other living beings, especially animals, for food. Ashrams served strict vegetarian meals and sometimes compiled their recipes. Several spiritual communities catered to vegetarians by opening restaurants. ISKCON (Hare Krishnas) opened a chain of vegetarian restaurants that operated throughout the world. Vegetarianism became a common enough lifestyle in the mid-1970s for periodicals like the *Vegetarian Times* to attract a steady circulation.

The appeal of natural and organic foods inspired many entrepreneurs to open their own restaurants, and women in particular found success with these enterprises, seeing their efforts as community service in promoting wholesome foods. Alice Waters began Chez Panisse in 1971 as an extension of the meals she had long prepared for Berkeley radicals. Alice May Brock, of "Alice's Restaurant" fame, wrote in her book *My Life as a Restaurant* (1975) that she saw herself as a hip therapist who provided a communal atmosphere to help diners battle "alienation." Feminists Jill Ward and Dolores Alexander opened New York's Mother Courage Restaurant in 1972 to help create a social milieu where women could meet over good food. The Moosewood Restaurant of Ithaca, New York, began in 1973 as a collective and community project that served vegetarian dishes. Cofounder Mollie Katzen and co-workers published the *Moosewood Cookbook* (1977) and several subsequent vegetarian cookbooks.

Best-selling cookbooks revealed the popularity of whole foods cooking. Frances Moore Lappé's *Diet for a Small Planet* (1971) provided compelling evidence for a vegetarian diet as well as tasty recipes. Lappé argued that animals required many more pounds of vegetable protein that could more efficiently be used to feed humans. She demonstrated how foods in combination, such as beans, nuts, and grains, could provide more than enough protein without relying on meat. Her book sold almost 2 million copies in several languages over the next decade. Edward Espe Brown's *Tassajara Bread Book* (1970) and *Tassajara Cooking Book* (1973) extolled the virtues of thoughtful cooking, emphasizing bread-making, for example, as a "process." The "countercuisine" advocated slowing down. One of the many popular vegetarian cookbooks, *Laurel's Kitchen* (1976), written by disciples of Eknath Easwaran, warned against "speedy refueling."

SOCIAL LIBERATION AND CHALLENGING TRADITIONAL LIFEWAYS

Sexual Liberation

By the 1970s, the "sexual revolution" had come to describe a variety of more liberal attitudes toward sex. The availability of the birth control pill, the Supreme Court overturning many censorship laws, the rise in premarital sex, the counterculture's public displays of bodies and lovemaking, the proliferation of gay and straight bathhouses and clubs, and an expanding hard-core porn film industry were part of this revolution. The feminist movement and greater access to birth control gave women in particular more sexual freedom. By 1970, 60 percent of all adult women were using either the Pill, an intrauterine device, or sterilization to control reproduction. The 1973 *Roe v. Wade* decision assured women greater access to abortion. Birth rates fell dramatically during the decade.

Historians have found different periods of sexual experimentation in the 18th through the 20th centuries, making the 1960s and 1970s sexual revolution less revolutionary than its proponents and detractors claimed. Nonetheless, as Stephen Garton notes, the period stands out as unprecedented because of "new sexual scripts" created by feminism, gay liberation, and a new permissiveness. Sex was part of the era's radical struggles that opposed sexism, capitalism, and homophobia and, many claimed, provided another route to liberation. Moreover, because of new methods of controlling reproduction and drugs to cure sexually transmitted diseases, this was the first decade in American history where sex seemed to have few negative consequences.

Popular culture helped introduce and reinforce these trends. Best-selling books such as Alex Comfort's *The Joy of Sex* (1972) revealed Americans' fascination with sex and desire to learn about formerly taboo methods of lovemaking. Erica Jong's *Fear of Flying* (1973) was the first best-selling novel to deal with women's sexual expression; the novel featured the character Isadora Wing, who leaves her husband to travel and search for the perfect orgasm. The book challenged literary taboos and the double standard to assert that women, too, saw the world in sexual terms and could achieve sexual satisfaction. Popular women's magazines discussed the options of "swinging" and spouse swapping, which caught on with many young bored couples in the suburbs. Group sex became popular with the urban upper-middle-class as well as hippies. The popular 1969 film *Bob & Carol & Ted & Alice* addressed changing cultural mores about free love within marriage. Later in the age of AIDS, the promiscuous trends of the early 1970s seemed shocking, but as David Allyn notes, experimentation with group sex and mate swapping were considered "relatively innocent." Stephanie Coontz argues that much of the sexual radicalism of the 1970s was exaggerated in order to break with past practices. Nena and George McNeil, whose 1972 bestseller *Open Marriage* (1972) advocated experimentation with multiple partners, later noted that their recommendations were unwise but deliberately extreme to rupture traditional notions of marriage.

Perhaps the revolution in sexual mores was expressed most on college campuses. Chaperones, curfews, and sex-segregated dorms disappeared in the 1970s, and more college students experimented with sex and cohabitated temporarily with partners. Ira Robinson and Davor Jedlicka found in their 1982 survey of college males and females looser attitudes toward premarital sex, reflected in increased rates of sexual intercourse through the 1970s.

But not all Americans embraced the sexual revolution, and historians have demonstrated that it represented not a uniform revolt but rather competing struggles. Although feminists recognized that women had just as much right to sexual pleasure as men and valued sexual experimentation that liberated women from purely reproductive roles, many feminists saw much sexual "liberation" as yet another objectification of women. The radical women in the Weatherman Underground may have initiated an antimonogamy campaign in an effort to integrate politics and pleasure, but other radical critics saw this revolution as a largely apolitical celebration of a larger sex, drugs, and rock and roll culture, often appropriated by commercial interests.

Although many believed a more permissive culture regarding sex could only enhance individual pleasure, there were public health consequences. Sexually transmitted diseases increased dramatically. Herpes Simplex II, or genital herpes, was discovered in 1979 as resistant to antibiotics. The frequency of antibiotics use, especially among gay men, may have weakened their immune systems. And the bathhouses that had become popular symbols in the 1970s as places for gay men to meet and have casual sex, by the 1980s, were largely shut down as purveyors of AIDS. Sexual exploration exacted a heavy price for many.

Although those advocating sexual freedom were never organized as an interest group, their opponents were. A strong backlash emerged in the late 1970s

The Commercialization of Sex

Sex became a booming business in the 1970s, as publications, films, and clubs were launched by entrepreneurs seeking to satisfy a growing number of consumers. Bob Guccione recognized the financial success of Hugh Hefner's *Playboy* and launched *Penthouse* in April 1970. The magazine pledged to push the boundaries of what was printable, keeping its middle-class readers on the front lines of the sexual revolution. Helen Gurley Brown also took her women's magazine *Cosmopolitan* in new directions in the 1970s, challenging the double standard by featuring a nude Burt Reynolds in its new centerfold feature in April 1972.

Proving that porn was profitable, X-rated films grew in popularity in the early 1970s. Sex films were decriminalized in San Francisco, and one of the city's porn cinema operators, Arlene Elster, helped organize the First International Erotic Film Festival in late 1970. Gerald Damiano's film *Deep Throat* (1972) brought hardcore porn to a large audience. Critics praised the film for acknowledging female sexual needs, although many feminists objected to its portrayal of female sexuality through a male lens. The film's star, Linda Lovelace, became a celebrity. Attempts to ban the film were overturned on First Amendment protection principles, and by the end of 1972, it had become one of the nation's most popular films.

Porn motivated entrepreneur Steve Ostrow to provide consumers the real thing in a commercial sex club. He opened the Continental Baths in the basement of New York's elegant Ansonia Hotel, and the combination of public sex with cabaret-style entertainment created a public sensation. Initially a gay club, as it became more popular with heterosexuals the bathhouse was bought and became Plato's Retreat in 1977. Bathhouses spread for a gay clientele in New York and across the country. By 1977, there were about 130 gay bathhouses in the United States, celebrated in Charles Silverstein and Edmund White's book *The Joy of Gay Sex* (1977).

Many feminists saw the sex industry as misogynist and commodifying women's bodies and began fighting commercial pornography in the 1970s. Some feminists in Seattle attacked adult bookstores with stinkbombs, and in New York firebombed three porn theaters. Feminists were also alarmed by the rise of sadomasochism or s/m "chic," as expressed by department store mannequins and the controversial 1976 billboard advertising the most popular rock band's recent album, which depicted a bruised, bound woman under the phrase "I'm Black and Blue from the Rolling Stones—and I love it!" The billboard was removed after mass protests, although it earned the band widespread press coverage. Feminists Andrea Dworkin and Catherine MacKinnon formed Women Against Pornography (WAP), which held a major national conference, protested excesses such as *Hustler's* June 1978 cover of a nude woman being ground into meat, and in 1979 led demonstrations in Times Square in New York to protest porn. However, many feminists were uncomfortable with WAP's alliance with the religious right to combat porn.

as social conservatives were aided by conservative fundraiser Richard Viguerie and Paul Weyrich of the National Committee for the Survival of a Free Congress. They created the Moral Majority in 1979 with minister Jerry Falwell at the head. Conservatives fought against sex education, condom distribution, abortion, pornography, and other elements of the sexual revolution that they believed were corrupting American morals. Groups across the country, such as the Concerned Community Citizens of Mason City, Iowa, organized to pass zoning regulations and to restrict the availability of sexual material. President Nixon's new conservative chief justice, Warren Burger, helped move the Supreme Court in *Miller v. California* (1973) to allow "local community standards" to decide what might be obscene. Federal prosecutors pursued porn actors, such as *Deep Throat*'s Harry Reems, and publishers, including *Hustler's* Larry Flynt, who in several publicized trials in 1977 and 1978 condemned censorship and in one trial was shot, leaving him paralyzed from the waist down.

Other signs of the backlash appeared in popular culture. For instance, the 1977 film *Looking for Mr. Goodbar* featured Diane Keaton as a young woman who frequented singles bars and was gruesomely murdered by one of her pickups, which underscored the supposed dangers of single life and sexual liberation.

Changes in Family Life

Family life underwent profound changes in the 1970s. Divorce rates increased dramatically, rising from 2.2 per 1,000 in 1960 to 4.6 per 1,000 in 1974. Women and men were waiting later to marry and were having fewer children. By 1975, the "traditional" nuclear family with a breadwinning father and homemaker mother represented a small 7 percent of the population. Fewer families were headed by two parents, and the baby boom generation embraced the single life. By the end of the decade, almost 25 percent of Americans lived alone. Women especially experimented with new roles, pursuing careers, sexual relations outside marriage, and relationships with women instead of men. Many women who divorced chose not to remarry.

The numbers of unmarried men and women living together doubled in the 1970s, reflecting a rising acceptance of cohabitation in American society. In 1972 in *Eisenstadt v. Baird,* the Supreme Court guaranteed the right to unmarried men and women to purchase contraceptives. Other legal changes forbad discrimination in consumer credit or home loans on the basis of marital status, and most states abolished laws preventing unmarried couples from renting property together.

The institution of marriage itself changed as women demanded more equality in relationships. The revolution in birth control that allowed women to control childbirth, feminist critiques of marriage, and the 1970s enforcement of civil rights laws for women that allowed greater access to jobs and education made many couples rethink how marriages should function. Polls indicated that the numbers of Americans who believed that men and women had equal responsibility to care for children doubled from 33 percent in 1970 to 60 percent by 1980. Couples often created their own wedding ceremonies, held in parks or other places outside churches. Because women often decided to retain their maiden names, hyphenated surnames for children became more common.

Although many blamed rising divorce rates on new no-fault divorce laws that made it easy for men to exit marital responsibilities, "fault" divorce rates were rising in the 1950s and 1960s and, combined with women's growing expectations for relationships and economic independence, accelerated divorce rates in the 1970s. No-fault laws made it easier to dissolve relationships in trouble, but states without no-fault laws also saw increases in divorce rates. Popular culture helped normalize divorce. Films such as *Kramer vs. Kramer* and *An Unmarried Woman* (1978), demonstrated that women could find more satisfying lives outside marriage. In a prelude to reality TV, millions of Americans watched a marriage dissolve over the course of 1973 in the PBS series *An American Family*. But although divorce rates rose, women and men still supported the institution of marriage. Almost a third of women who married in 1978 had previously been divorced, suggesting they had not given up on the institution but on a particular mate.

Many Americans believed that feminism, gay rights, and sexual permissiveness had eroded the basic foundation of American family life, and they sought to halt this decline through political action. Both statistical realities and perceived breakdowns in traditional family roles as represented in popular culture fueled an organized campaign against those changes by the mid-1970s. The Moral Majority, created in 1979 by minister Jerry Falwell, campaigned on issues it believed central to upholding its conception of Christian moral law, including efforts to bolster traditional marriage, restore school prayer, and fight against gay rights, abortion, and the Equal Rights Amendment.

Informality as a Way of Life: Fashion

New attitudes about sex and relationships were part of how individuals transformed themselves during the 1970s. Appearances also changed as youthful experiments infiltrated the larger cultural scene. The counterculture's embrace of informality and androgyny—both men and women sporting long hair or natural afros and wearing the ubiquitous bell-bottomed jeans and unisex tie-died T-shirts—influenced the fashion choices of other men and women and the commercial fashion world.

Women and men also celebrated spontaneity and the freedom to wear what they chose, grabbing an array of styles and clothing to fit moods and celebrate individuality, whether it be a miniskirt one day or a long high-necked Granny

Men wearing the signature bell-bottom pants and platform shoes of the 1970s. (National Archives)

dress the next. Hippies borrowed ethnic styles from around the world, such as caftans, kimonos, muumuus, djellaba robes, Spanish shawls, Greek macramé bags, Mexican ponchos, and Indian silk scarves.

This casual and eclectic style was reflected in the album jackets of the decade, such as braless Carly Simon with floppy hat on her 1972 *No Secrets* album, and in men's denim business suits and women's pantsuits. The extreme casual style could be found on many communes, where residents often chose to work and play in the nude.

By the late 1960s, jeans and informal wear were the uniform of the young and the counterculture. Just as entrepreneurs seized upon other aspects of 1970s culture as a way of making a quick buck, Calvin Klein recognized the profit potential of blue jeans. Using young teen model Brooke Shields in provocative poses, Klein hoisted the price of his low-cut workaday jeans to $50 a pair, making jeans fashionable and sexy as well as practical. By 1978, millions of people were clamoring for jeans with the Calvin Klein label, although many feminists protested Klein's advertisements as demeaning toward women.

Men and women also adopted bolder fashions in the 1970s to assert their individuality. The commercial fashion industry embraced the opposition to conformity to promote any number of new lines and bright colors. Men's fashions in particular—traditionally conservative and undistinguished for decades with uniform dark suits and hats—reflected a startling brashness. The "Peacock Revolution," ushered in by hippie experimentation, African American styles, and youthful revolts, featured flamboyant garments and accessories, from leisure suits to wide ties and bellbottom plaid slacks to beads and medallions.

Although much ethnic clothing required natural fibers, polyester and other synthetic fabrics became popular for their wrinkle-free ease of care and bright colors. They were also comfortable and reflected disco lights for dancing. Urban youth carefully created more sexualized fashions with unbuttoned shirts revealing a medallion, crotch-hugging double-knit pants, and platform shoes for height, a look popularized by John Travolta in *Saturday Night Fever* (1977).

Hair on Broadway (1968–1972)

The hit musical *Hair* embodied the values of the counterculture in espousing a new society, an "Age of Aquarius," and peace, love, freedom, and casual fashion and sex. The "American tribal love-rock musical" helped revive Broadway in New York City when it premiered in the late 1960s. It was a hit, too, in Chicago, Los Angeles, and San Francisco, but it met more hostility when it traveled to other American cities. The on-stage criticisms of the Vietnam War, nudity, and desecration of the American flag angered many who sought to ban the show and made *Hair* a battle cry for proponents of the First Amendment.

In 1970, Boston district attorney Garret Byrne tried to shut down the production of *Hair* for questionable content, claiming it was "lewd and lascivious." The case went to the Supreme Judicial Court of Massachusetts, which ruled that the Boston performances should be allowed to continue if each member of the cast remained clothed and if the show eliminated any "simulation of sexual intercourse or deviation." Unwilling to alter the content of the show, the cast of *Hair* closed down the show on April 10, 1970, in protest of the ruling. The Actors' Equity Association and other groups protested the censorship, and the case became a centerpiece for advocates of freedom of expression, speech, and the arts. The Massachusetts State Supreme Court's decision was appealed to the U.S. Supreme Court. Justices ruled to reopen *Hair* with a 4–4 vote, but the court did not enable it to reopen until May 22, 1970. *Hair*'s long run on Broadway, its successful and controversial tours, and its radical content had a lasting impact on American musical theatre, influencing later rock operas such as *Godspell* and *Jesus Christ, Superstar*.

Escape into the Drug Culture

The 1970s perpetuated two opposing images of drugs, aided by popular culture. The mystique of the peaceful, drug-infused countercultural rock festival Woodstock, held in 1969 in Bethel, New York, was countered by the drug-induced violence at the Rolling Stones concert at Altamont and the Manson murders in Los Angeles that same year. The tragic drug-related deaths in 1971 of the brilliant rock stars Jimi Hendrix, Janis Joplin, and Jim Morrison further stained the breakthrough possibilities of drugs and accentuated their dangers. Yet drug jokes were routinely told on *Saturday Night Live,* mass-circulation magazines such as *Playboy* featured Timothy Leary advocating LSD, and the old antidrug film *Reefer Madness* became a college cult comedy. Throughout popular culture, drugs gained a public acceptance heretofore unknown in American history.

Thomas King Forcade, known as the "Hugh Hefner of Dope," launched the magazine *High Times* in 1974, which symbolized the boldness of the drug culture during the decade. A former marijuana smuggler and son of a retired U.S. Army officer, Forcade founded in 1969 the Alternative Press Syndicate, which provided material for underground newspapers across the country. He intended *High Times* to parody *Playboy* by glamorizing drugs and featuring botanical and medical information, history and folklore, interviews with outspoken drug-taking celebrities, and adventure stories of smugglers who traveled to exotic places. *High Times,* one of the fastest-growing publications in the nation, also revealed the broad commercial success of drugs in its Dow Jones–like price indexes and advertisements for paraphernalia.

Although LSD had been the counterculture's signal drug in the 1960s because it promised a mystical and intellectual awakening or escape from the mundane realities of daily life, the psychedelic high became less a sign of expanded awareness in the 1970s. By the early 1970s, studies indicated that LSD use had declined. Instead, many in the psychedelic culture turned to nondrug alternatives for transcending reality. Ram Dass noted in 1970 that he thought LSD was becoming "obsolete" because people realized that "if you want to stay high, you have to work on yourself." New movements for human potential and spiritual awakening without drugs grew through the decade.

Other drugs appeared that sharpened the edges of life in the 1970s. Hunter S. Thompson's gonzo epic *Fear and Loathing in Las Vegas* (1971) itemizes sheer quantities of drugs consumed, including methamphetamine, barbiturates, cocaine, and LSD. This was in opposition to Timothy Leary's self-conscious approach to psychedelics—they were used not for enlightenment but for getting "ripped." Others in the counterculture lamented cocaine's ascent. Poet Allen Ginsberg noted the drug's "aggression," distinct from pot and acid, and writer Tom Robbins saw its "darkness."

Despite its expense and increased prison sentences for possession, cocaine use increased sevenfold in the 1970s, far outpacing heroin use for the first time. Cocaine became the drug of the elite, used by athletes, musicians, and Hollywood stars as much for its perceived status as for the subtle high it offered. Oliver Stone, who won an Academy Award in 1979 for his screenplay for *Midnight Express,* which depicted the nightmare of Billy Hayes' imprisonment in Turkey for attempting to smuggle hashish, described cocaine use in Hollywood as "a fever." Woody Allen's famous sneeze in his 1977 film *Annie Hall,* which unwittingly destroyed his friend's expensive cocaine stash, signaled the drug's arrival in the living rooms of hip Americans. The songs of the Grateful Dead, Eric Clapton, and the Rolling Stones referenced the drug, and the black urban culture of the film *Super Fly* glamorized it. Bob Sabbag's book *Snowblind: A Brief Career in the Cocaine Trade* (1977) became one of the first best sellers about drugs. Coke spoons openly decorated necklines and club ceilings. The message in popular culture was that cocaine was nonaddictive and fashionable, and by the end of the decade, it had become a nationwide problem.

Marijuana Use and NORML

Marijuana remained the most accessible and popular drug, and in the early 1970s polls indicated that 60 percent of college students had smoked pot. The 1970s became known as the "Golden Age" of marijuana, and multiple varieties were grown on communes and farms throughout the United States and imported from Mexico, Jamaica, and Southeast Asia. Northern California became a haven for pot farmers, who raised the prized sensimilla plants in fields tucked between forests and ranches.

The ubiquity of marijuana use in all sectors of American society, not just among the young and the counterculture, led many to believe that it could become a legal drug much like alcohol and tobacco. Yet despite its popularity, thousands of pot smokers were arrested each year. Keith Stroup, a young attorney who saw many of his friends busted, decided to try to change the laws. He formed the National Organization for the Reform of Marijuana Laws (NORML) in 1970 to educate Americans about the myths associated with the drug and to urge consumers to demand decriminalization. Aided by a hefty grant from Hugh Hefner, who believed that marijuana enhanced the sexual revolution he promoted in *Playboy,* Stroup was able to make NORML a national movement.

Despite his antidrug rhetoric, President Nixon revamped drug laws in the Controlled Dangerous Substances Act of 1970 to ease federal penalties for marijuana. Clearly, marijuana was a relatively harmless recreational drug compared to the serious heroin epidemic in many cities and among returning veterans. A Republican commission appointed by President Nixon had recommended decriminalization, and when President Carter, who had earlier advocated decriminalization, assumed office, NORML supporters recognized an unprecedented opportunity to reform the law. Carter still supported prosecution of drug dealers but supported legislation that would remove criminal penalties for possession of up to an ounce of marijuana. Nonetheless, to NORML's dismay, the Carter administration continued to supply Mexico with the poison paraquat to spray marijuana fields, which harmed the health of those smoking the imported weed.

Following the federal example, many states made marijuana use a minor offense. Oregon ended criminal penalties for marijuana use in 1973, making possession of up to an ounce punishable by a maximum civil fine of $100. The state provided a proving ground for NORML and other decriminalization advocates because Oregon did not go to "pot" as opponents predicted. Ohio, Colorado, Maine, California, Alaska, Minnesota, Mississippi, New York, and North Carolina also revamped state laws in the next few years.

Support for marijuana reform began to fall apart in 1978, when Dr. Peter Bourne, Carter's White House drug czar, attended a NORML Christmas party where cocaine was snorted. The subsequent publicity chilled White House reform efforts and generated more enthusiasm for a growing antidrug parents' movement, which

Continued on next page

Marijuana Use and NORML, Continued

feared the impact of legalization on school-age children. The popularity of the 1978 Cheech and Chong comedy *Up In Smoke,* which celebrated pot smoking, further alarmed parents who saw the acceptance of marijuana tied to the decline in parental authority, the abolition of school prayer, and the overall loosening of morals. By 1978, parent groups sprang up in suburban communities across the country to insist on "zero tolerance" for all drugs, although public health experts tried to separate marijuana from more addictive and harmful drugs and to point out the alarming increase of alcohol among high-school students in the late 1970s.

Presidential candidate Ronald Reagan successfully tapped into this concern, calling the Democrats the "party of pot." As president, he launched a new war on drugs in the 1980s, which stifled efforts to legalize marijuana.

If illicit drugs became popular in many circles, more Americans became addicted to legal drugs during the decade, especially alcohol and Valium. Valium became the most prescribed drug in the 1970s, and its abuse was exposed in popular magazines, television programs, and the widely publicized admission by former First Lady Betty Ford that she was hooked on it and alcohol in 1978. The Valium epidemic challenged national stereotypes about drugs involving hippies, black and Latino urban youth, and Hollywood celebrities to reveal that "respectable" physicians, pharmaceutical companies, and white middle-class housewives were also responsible for pushing drugs. In 1975, the government's Drug Abuse Warning Network identified Valium as the drug most frequently found in overdose victims. The women's health movement of the early 1970s, followed by women's popular magazines, turned blame away from female users to link the prescription of psychotropics to women's social control and stifling real political grievances about housewifery.

As with many trends during the 1970s, there were countertrends, or efforts to halt the spread of drugs in American society. In 1969, President Richard Nixon announced a "national attack" on drug abuse and, in 1971, became the first president to declare an official war on drugs, pumping $155 million into the new Special Action Office for Drug Abuse Prevention and additional monies into drug enforcement and interdiction.

Although Nixon had said that heroin traffickers deserved death and pot-smoking symbolized all that was wrong in America, he was pragmatic about what could actually reduce drug use, and experts recommended treatment. Moreover, Nixon realized that drugs were flowing to American GIs in Southeast Asia, and up to 25 percent in many units were addicted to heroin, creating problems not only for prosecution of the war but in the domestic adjustments of returning

servicemen. Despite the president's de-
nouncements, the new drug czar, Dr.
Jerome Jaffe, knew that although marijuana was the most widely used illegal
drug, it was relatively harmless; on the
other hand, heroin was much more addictive and generated much crime. Treating addicts became Jaffe's priority.

The Nixon White House launched
new treatment programs that appeared
to reduce street crime, and then pursued
a methadone program to further reduce
crime. Nixon's aides even hoped to enlist Elvis Presley, who visited the White
House in late 1970, to publicly speak
out against drugs. The singer expressed
his patriotism and opposition to drugs,
but his offer was largely hollow because
his own abuse of prescription drugs is
believed to be responsible for his death
in 1977.

*President Richard Nixon shakes hands
with Elvis Presley on December 21,
1970. The unlikely meeting, in which
Presley suggested he become a federal
drug enforcement agent, became even
more notorious following his death,
when the extent of his drug abuse was
revealed. (National Archives)*

Politics interfered with the success of
the drug program as Nixon geared up
for the 1972 election and promised more
crackdowns on drug dealers. During the Carter administration, spending on
drug treatment remained flat, which in terms of inflationary dollars meant decline, and the administration stepped up poppy and marijuana eradication programs in Mexico.

THE SPIRITUAL IMPULSE

New Age Movement

The New Age movement of the 1970s revived attempts to merge Eastern and
Western spiritual practices that had begun as early as the 19th century in the
United States. Transcendentalism was among the first American philosophical
movements to incorporate Asian wisdom to advance an alternative religious
tradition to Christianity.

In the 1970s, the "New Age," or "Age of Aquarius," became recognized as
a symbol of hope among students, the counterculture, and practitioners of the
occult for a coming new era of abundance, peace, and brotherly love during a
time of poverty, war, and racism. Largely popularized by the theosophist and

Channeling

The New Age Movement was an eclectic assemblage of beliefs and practices, but channeling, neopaganism, and alternative healing had an undeniable impact on some of its fundamental ideas. Channeling attracted a growing group of followers during the 1970s who hoped to bring divine messengers and spiritual teachers to guide humanity into a new age of consciousness. It built on the earlier theosophical movement of Madame Helen Petrovna Blavatsky (1831–1891), who claimed to have encounters with highly evolved beings known as the Mahatmas or ascended masters, and her later disciples.

A number of books and "schools" helped popularize channeling. Jane Roberts introduced many to channeling through the *Seth Materials* (1970). Helen Schucman's *A Course in Miracles* (1976) inspired hundreds of "A Course in Miracles" (ACIM) study groups and renewed popular interest in channeling across North America. Notable New Age figures such as J. Z. Knight established the Ramtha's School of Enlightenment following her spiritual encounter with the entity Ramtha in 1977.

Most of these teachers offered personal sessions and workshops that detailed the teachings of ascended masters, and they encouraged individuals to foster their own spiritual encounters. But others limited the direction and purpose of their channeling as a function of their unique authority alone. Elizabeth Clair Prophet assumed control of the Church Universal and Triumphant (CUT) following her husband's death in 1973. Prophet's claims of channeling Jesus, Buddha, and Saint Germain, among others, gradually boosted membership in CUT into the 1980s. She imposed strict guidelines upon her followers, and her authoritarianism led to media reports of the group as a cult.

By the late 1970s, skepticism of channeling grew as it became viewed as a spiritual practice for the well-to-do, and the outrageous sums commanded by some channelers brought charges of fraud.

medium Alice Bailey (1880–1949), who claimed that an influx of cosmic energy caused by the changing stellar configuration at the century's end would bring a new society dominated by occult wisdom, the movement was characterized by the possibility of personal and cultural transformation, new spiritual practices, and the belief that the self is divine. The popular New Age Movement capitalized on what has been described as a general spiritual hunger and dissatisfaction with Judeo-Christian traditions during the 1970s.

The demographics of the nation also contributed to the rise of various spiritual movements. People from all walks of life and generations sought spiritual fulfillment in the New Age Movement, but the bulk of its followers were white, middle-class baby boomers with leisure time and disposable income to explore new beliefs and ways of living. The appeal of alternative religions among the

Neopaganism

Neopaganism emerged in the United States during the 1970s as an effort to revive ancient spirituality by reconnecting with indigenous practices, feminine spirituality, and the veneration of natural, earthly forces. Great Britain's Gerald B. Gardner (1884–1964), who had reestablished knowledge of witchcraft after the repeal of England's witchcraft laws in 1951, influenced the establishment of dozens of Wiccan covens across the United States. Selena Fox and Jim Alan established the largest of these, the Church of Circle Wicca, in Madison, Wisconsin, in 1975. The same year the Covenant of the Goddess was formed as an organization on the West Coast that linked together autonomous groups based upon Wiccan traditions.

Neopagan groups, particularly Wicca, attracted many feminists. Some, such as feminist Zsuzsanna Budapest, advocated the formation of all-female covens. Although most organizations did not restrict membership based on gender, the desire for equality and to elevate femininity became part of revitalizing the pre-Christian nature religions. During the 1970s, archaeologists and historians drew the interests of neopagans in their attempts to reconstruct a woman-centered past and explain the demonization of feminine deities within the Christian tradition.

Emphasis on feminine deities was connected to the deep ecology of neopaganism. James Lovelock's Gaia (the Greek goddess of Earth) hypothesis reintroduced an ancient concept to the scientific community in 1975 that theorized that the whole planet is a single living organism. The notion was popular among neopagans who already accepted "Mother Earth" and "Mother Nature."

Rituals typically followed Celtic Druidism, Norse, or Egyptian traditions, but some neopagans and others in the New Age Movement also began incorporating the sacred sites and rituals of Native Americans. Locations like Mt. Shasta, California, that had been deemed sacred by the Wintu people for thousands of years gradually attracted groups such as CUT and I AM Religious Activity as a spiritual place of healing. The neopagan adoption of shamanic roles, drum circles, healing ceremonies, and Indian dress generated much controversy among American Indians and heightened distrust of New Age groups. Many Native peoples criticized New Age groups for their superficial understanding of Native ways and their willingness to sell spirituality as a commodity.

young also became part of a more general rebellion against traditional structures and beliefs that were unable to respond to the dramatic changes of the time. Although New Age communities were established throughout the United States, they became most prevalent in California and the Mountain States of the West and Southwest, especially in San Francisco; Boulder, Colorado; Santa Fe, New Mexico; and Sedona, Arizona.

The passage of the 1965 Immigration Act, which repealed the restrictive quotas of non-Europeans, prompted a steady increase in immigrants from Asia, who helped spur the New Age movement. By the early 1970s, a number of Hindu and Buddhist spiritual teachers either moved to the United States or acquired visas with the intention of establishing missions to spread Eastern wisdom. During the decade, 216 new religious communities had formed, many of which were a direct consequence of influences from the new Asian immigrants.

Spiritual centers, books, and journals helped articulate the eclectic nature of the New Age philosophy. *East West Journal* was introduced in 1970 as the first periodical devoted to the New Age Movement, which was shortly followed by other titles and newsletters promoting yoga, alternative medicine, occult studies, and other spiritual practices. Baba Ram Dass introduced New Age thought to a large audience in *Be Here Now* (1971), which sold over half a million copies and became the counterculture's spiritual guidebook. Other popular works included Fritjof Capra's *Tao of Physics* (1975), which demonstrated parallels between modern Western science and Eastern philosophy, and David Spangler's *Revelation, the Birth of a New Age* (1976), which identified the essential ideas that formed the New Age movement. Additionally, fictional works like Richard Bach's *Jonathan Livingston Seagull* (1970) and Robert Persig's *Zen and the Art of Motorcycle Maintenance* (1974) helped to popularize the movement. The demand for New Age classes and products were served by new ashrams and spiritual centers, specialty bookstores, health food stores, and alternative health clinics that sprouted in major cities across the country. The San Francisco publication *Common Ground* served as just one of the many guides to local New Age centers and activities.

Many adherents of the New Age Movement were women. Allowed more positions of spiritual authority than mainstream religions, women could be mediators and leaders for their communities as channelers or priestesses. New Age religions further appealed to women because of their affirmation of goddess and nature worship, recognizing the feminine form as a relevant and essential part of religion.

Eastern Philosophy and Religions

Exposure to Japanese culture following World War II, changes in American immigration policies, new relationships with China, and the general rebellion by the counterculture contributed to the growth and appeal of Buddhist and Hindu teachings during the 1970s. Numerous gurus from India tapped into Americans' spiritual hunger with writings and teachings that offered new perspectives on life, health, and well-being. Unlike the New Age movement, these teachers sought to preserve their respective traditions rather than dilute or intermingle them. Zen Buddhists, Tibetan Buddhists, Hindu gurus, and Sikhs were encouraged by American devotees to establish missions and spiritual centers in the United States, which flourished in the decade.

Zen Buddhism was established in the United States during the 1950s as part of the San Francisco Renaissance. D. T. Suzuki influenced the Beat Generation writers Jack Kerouac, Allen Ginsberg, and Gary Snyder. The English-born Zen Buddhist philosopher Alan Watts interested the 1960s and 1970s counterculture with his popular introductory material. Japanese-born Taizan Maezumi Roshi founded the Zen Center of Los Angeles in 1967 and later established the Kuroda Institute for the Study of Buddhism and Human Values in 1976. The San Francisco Zen Center acquired several properties and buildings and became the largest communal center in America by 1972. Its farm and monastery north of San Francisco attempted to resemble the isolated Zen training facilities of Japan.

Whereas Buddhist traditions of Asia were overwhelmingly male, the women in American Zen communities numbered at least half of all practitioners. Many women became teachers and leaders of Zen communities. Jiyu Kennett, a Soto Zen master, founded Mt. Shasta Abbey in 1970. In 1972, Gesshin Myoko Prabhasa Dharma, a recognized Zen priest and teacher, became the acting director and vice-abbot of the Mt. Baldy and Comarron Zen Centers in Los Angeles. Jan Chozen Bays became an ordained Zen priest in 1977 and later assumed the position of resident teacher at the Zen Community of Oregon.

Zen communities also had to become more flexible to retain American participants. The high turnover was partly attributed to the long sitting and rigorous meditation practice, and some Zen masters and centers accommodated the American lifestyle by providing drop-in instructional sessions, less rigorous meditation sessions, and accessible books for the layperson, including the popular *Zen Mind, Beginner's Mind* (1970), written by Shunryu Suzuki, a founder of the San Francisco Zen Center.

Other Buddhist traditions that had a significant influence on the decade emerged from Tibet. Vajrayana or Tantrism was celebrated by the counterculture and the New Age movement for its sexual freedom and tolerance of materialism and became the means through which many experienced Eastern philosophy for the first time. Its basic tenet in rejecting life-denying habits and practices that prevent the experience of spiritual ecstasy was welcomed by those

Buddhist nuns at Mt. Shasta Abbey in California, 1973. At least as many women as men lived and practiced in America's Zen communities during the 1970s. (Ted Streshinsky/Corbis)

Transcendental Meditation

Transcendental meditation (TM), which taught the restful alertness of mind and body and a pure consciousness, grew in popularity in the late 1960s, especially after the Beatles encountered Maharishi Mahesh Yogi in 1967. Over the next several years, TM became fashionable and attracted celebrities like Joe Namath and Mia Farrow.

As popularity in the course grew, Maharishi announced his plan to use TM as a vehicle for global transformation. In 1972, the World Plan Executive Council (WPEC) was formed with the lofty goal of providing 3,600 centers across the world and with 1,000 teachers at each facility. Although nearly a million people had taken TM courses, the movement did not retain the number of students it had anticipated. By 1976, interest in TM had declined, and a further setback occurred in 1978 when a New Jersey court deemed TM a religious practice and not a science. The decision prohibited TM from being taught in public schools and institutes with public funding. The case had been pursued by a large Christian evangelical opposition that included the Spiritual Counterfeits Project. By the end of the 1970s, the WPEC had fallen short of its goal to expand operations globally. But hundreds of centers were established in the United States and Europe with tens of thousands of students.

who sought to revolt against repressive Judeo-Christian values. Tantra became something of a pop religion, drawing rock stars like Mike Jagger and Jimi Hendrix.

The Hindu and Sikh traditions were by far the largest of the Eastern philosophies that influenced the 1970s. Although many spiritualists had become familiar with Hinduism prior to the 1960s, it was not until changes in immigration laws in 1965 that a substantial number of gurus moved to the United States to teach. The spiritual desires of American devotees in India and the Beatles' encounters with Maharishi Mahesh Yogi in 1967 furthered curiosity in alternative traditions.

During the 1970s, gurus from Hindu and Sikh traditions established thousands of centers and ashrams (religious communities) as places for self-realization, enlightenment, and worship. Among the most popular in the 1970s was the Ananda Church of Self Realization of Nevada City, California, founded in 1968 by J. Donald Waters, Swami Kriyananda (1926–), in dedication to the vision of Paramhansa Yogananda (1893–1952). Yogi Bhajan (1929–2004) inaugurated the Sikh mission Healthy, Happy, Holy Organization (3HO) in 1969 after traveling to the United States and seeing a need for yoga to meet the challenges of the modern world. He reached out to young people, recognizing that their experimentation with drugs expressed a need for liberation and wholeness, and introduced many to kundalini yoga, meditation, a healthy diet, and a compassionate philosophy as a natural and healthy alternative. As word of his teachings spread, the organization grew, and centers were established throughout the United States. Another popular yogi, Swami Rama (1925–1996) established the Himalayan International Institute of Yoga Science and Philosophy in 1971. The institute was originally established in Illinois and then relocated in 1977 to northeastern Pennsylvania near Honesdale.

The Christian Evangelical Revival and the Jesus People Movement

In addition to the popularity of new Eastern religions in the 1970s, old-fashioned Christian evangelism experienced a revival. Many Americans who felt repulsed by trends of the times, from the feminist and gay rights movements to sexual liberation and the secular New Age movement, turned to a more literal interpretation of the Bible and to charismatic ministers who offered strong moral guideposts in navigating a changing world. The Christian evangelical movement grew rapidly in the 1970s and became a foundation for a new conservative politics that linked social conservatism to economic and foreign policy goals of the New Right. The influential Moral Majority was one outgrowth of this newfound Christian fundamentalist visibility, self-confidence, and political activism that aimed to halt what it viewed as corroding morals and to restore Christian values to American society.

It was not just the counterculture and the young who became disillusioned with mainline Christian denominations. Influenced by the antiauthoritarianism of the era, many Americans rejected the hierarchy of many traditional churches and sought more personal, immediate connections to God. Protestant sects that had been on the margins in American society grew in numbers during the 1970s. Pentecostalism, founded by African American preacher William J. Seymour in 1906, attracted many to its Spirit baptism and the manifestation of glossolalia, or speaking in tongues, believed to be a miraculous act in which a believer, with the aid of the Holy Spirit, speaks in a language without having knowledge of it.

Other Americans found God in their living rooms as Assemblies of God televangelists Jim Bakker and Jimmy Swaggart employed the flair of celebrity talk-show hosts and built media empires intent on conversions and fund-raising. Jim Bakker and wife, Tammy Faye, began their emotional television ministry in 1978 on Pat Robertson's *The 700 Club*. Bakker left the Christian Broadcasting Network to join Paul Croach in launching the Trinity Broadcasting Company, and then returned to the East Coast where they built the PTL Television Network and Heritage USA. Bakker and Swaggart are perhaps best remembered for their sexual scandals, exploitations, and fraud convictions in the 1980s, but they helped launch religious broadcasting that changed the spiritual and political landscapes of America during the 1970s.

As much as many fundamentalist Christians might condemn the excesses of the era, another significant Christian revival known as the Jesus People Movement emerged that embraced the counterculture to communicate religious messages to youth. The movement's identification with Jesus as a longhaired, informally dressed wayfarer brought its members the label "Jesus Freaks." The Jesus People were able to convey an alternative for those disillusioned with the secular left and New Age spirituality as well as mainstream Christianity. The movement started as urban Christian missions offering stable places for the countless numbers of street people who had experienced the harsher realities of hippie life following the "summer of love." The Living Room coffeehouse in Haight-Ashbury, opened by Ted and Liz Wise in 1967, served sandwiches and sermons to thousands of homeless, hungry, and drug-addicted runaway teens and young adults. It became a template for other street ministries in California and eventually across North America.

The ministries of the Jesus People sometimes were affiliated with established churches, but more often than not, they were independently run. Many youths in the movement felt that Christianity had become too complacent amidst an age of revolutionary change and sought to reawaken the faith through experimentation. Heavily influenced by Pentecostalism, Jesus People leaned toward a literal or fundamental interpretation of the Bible but emphasized the primacy of experience and advocated spiritual ecstasy, speaking in tongues, and visions as well as traditional prayer.

The June 1971 *Time* magazine cover story "The Jesus Revolution" began a steady stream of press attention that increased the popularity of the religious awakening. Underground Jesus People newspapers like the *Hollywood Free Paper* increased its street-corner circulation and ministries grew. As many as 3 million people were involved in the Jesus People movement at its peak in the early 1970s. Some mainstream ministries reconsidered the way young people stimulated a Christian revival within the counterculture. Thousands of youth gesturing upward with their index finger and shouting "One Way!" inspired evangelist Billy Graham to embrace the "Jesus Revolution" during his 1971 and 1972 crusades.

Ministers of many mainline denominations often adorned hippie fashion to promote the Christian message and appeal to youth. Richard York, an Episcopal priest of Berkeley, once celebrated the Feast of the Blessed Virgin Mary as a Christian Hippie Happening that brought a thousand hippies together for a day of food and rock music. The happening also observed Episcopal rituals, foot washings, and a volley of balloons marked "love," "peace," and "Mary." Other ministries such as the Calvary Chapel in Costa Mesa, California, featured mass baptisms in the Pacific Ocean. Under the guidance of the hippie evangelical Lonnie Frisbee (also known as the "John the Baptist" of Southern California) thousands of hippies converted to Christianity and were baptized in the early 1970s.

On college campuses ministries emerged to counter left-leaning groups. The Christian World Liberation Front (CWLF) begun by Dr. Jack Sparks on the University of California, Berkeley campus in 1969 and affiliated with Campus Crusade for Christ, aggressively evangelized and drew accusations of right-wing infiltration. The CWLF published its own newspaper, *Right On!,* which publicized communal housing and was successful in attracting many students to its ministry.

Other Jesus People rejected right-wing politics and advocated a strong social ethic that they adopted from the New Left and that differed dramatically from other evangelicals like Billy Graham. Whereas many fundamentalist Christians embraced the values of private ownership and supported the Vietnam War, the Jesus people were antimaterialistic and antiwar. Most lived communally, selling their property, sharing possessions, and trusting in God to fulfill their needs. The Jesus People marched in protest to end the Vietnam War and were against the draft.

But despite their countercultural convictions, many Jesus People remained politically indifferent, choosing instead to concentrate on spreading the message of Jesus. They were first a movement directed toward the institutional change of Christianity and individual transformation. Their views were generally fatalistic, acknowledging social injustices but insisting that the increase of sin was evident in Biblical prophecy.

Because of its literalistic, Messianic, and emotional religious fervor, the Jesus People Movement was sometimes criticized by Christians and non-Christians as anti-intellectual or not operating within a theological system. One popular figure who drew this particular criticism was Hal Lindsey, author of *The Late Great Planet Earth,* which became the most widely read book of the decade. In 1970, Lindsey left the Campus Crusade for Christ organization to begin the Jesus Christ Light and Power Company, a youth-oriented ministry at the University of California, Los Angeles, and published his book, which capitalized on a sense of apocalyptic expectancy that Jesus' return was imminent.

The Jesus People Movement also developed a new form of popular Christian rock music. The 1971 musical show *Jesus Christ Superstar* featured a Jesus whose fashion and mannerisms resembled that of a street hippie. The show was a huge success with mainstream audiences and aided in presenting the story of Jesus through a hip musical genre. In 1972, Campus Crusade for Christ International sponsored a huge music festival in Dallas, Texas, called Explo '72. Dubbed "Godstock," a religious version of Woodstock, the festival brought together 80,000 young followers from across the world for a week of music, prayer, and fellowship.

By the mid- to late-1970s, the end of the Vietnam War, the decline of the counterculture, and the realization that the "Jesus Revolution" was not likely to

Congregants raise their arms for Jesus at Explo '72. The evangelical conference and rock festival took place in Dallas, Texas, over five days in June 1972. (JP Laffont/ Sygma/Corbis)

usher in the second coming of Christ gradually diminished the popularity of the Jesus People Movement. Many of the ministries began shifting their Messianic messages to a more traditional focus concerning family values and financial responsibility. Some former followers joined established churches or concentrated on theological training. Communes started to break apart as financial strains and authoritarian leadership discouraged many. Hippie street ministers became a rare sight in American cities. Perhaps the most lasting development of the Jesus People Movement is the popularity of Christian rock music, which has continued to be a means of expression and conversion for many young evangelicals.

Cults

Suspicions toward alternative religions were raised in the early 1970s as organizations began to actively recruit street youths and students from college campuses, worrying many parents. The success of Campus Crusade for Christ encouraged recruitment efforts of groups such as the International Society for Krishna Consciousness (ISKCON or Hare Krishna), the Unification Church, and the Divine Light Mission, among others. Many young people were attracted to

Jesus People Communes

As with secular communes, Jesus People communes provided an intimate setting in which participants could live cheaply and simply with others who shared their beliefs. They became both support centers and places that inspired values of racial equality, peace, love, and togetherness.

Urban communes were the most prevalent. Unlike other communes, they banned drugs, alcohol, and nonmarital sex. Benefactors, including Christian businessmen who saw the Jesus People as a healthy alternative to the indulgences of the counterculture, sometimes supported the communes. Established churches maintained others or they remained independent. As with the street missions and coffeehouses, many communes assisted homeless and drug addicted youths. Jesus People USA became the largest single-site commune with 450 members and service to drug addicts and runaways. Established around 1972 by Jim and Sue Palosaari in Milwaukee, in 1974 Jesus People USA permanently settled in Chicago. By the late 1970s, the commune, which purchased an old hotel to house its activities, provided a soup kitchen, homeless shelter, job training, a crisis pregnancy center, and transitional housing.

Most residents of communes declined paid jobs in favor of mission work. Nevertheless, some communes also operated their own businesses and industries. In the early 1970s, John Higgins of the House of Miracles moved to Eugene, Oregon, along with 30 other Christians and established the largest network of communes to emerge out of the Jesus People Movement. Known as the Shiloh Youth Revival Centers Organization, Higgins established 178 communes across the country with central operations assembled on a 90-acre plot of land in Oregon. Between 1968 and 1978, the commune operated farms, a credit union, canneries, and auto-repair shops. Other communes were not as ambitious but operated modest enterprises that sustained them. The Vine Street Church Community in Chattanooga, Tennessee, operated a health-food deli that helped to support its five communal houses.

Some observers were concerned about the Jesus Movement's separatism as well as their tactics in luring vulnerable youths into communal life. Many communes were established around authoritarian and charismatic figures that appeared to control the behavior of members and were accused of being cults. They drew further suspicion because of their Messianic teachings as well as their enthusiastic and emotional tendencies toward worship. Some communes endured harassment from their surrounding communities. In 1978, the Vine Street Church Community relocated to Vermont after experiencing discrimination from Chattanooga neighbors for its racially integrated housing.

Member of the Hare Krishna chants and plays a drum. During the 1970s, the Hare Krishnas were one of many religious sects that became popular among young people who were able to combine their countercultural values with a quest for spiritual growth. (Corel)

new religions because they embodied values similar to the general counter-culture. But the insidious hold of some groups earned them the more pejorative label of "cults."

ISKCON was one of the most widely criticized cults of the 1970s. Although a garden-variety sect from India, its capacity to convert young Americans to embrace a monastic life of poverty alarmed parents and critics of the religion. Chanting Hare Krishna devotees wearing robes and with shaved heads were visible in cities such as San Francisco and in airport terminals where their aggressive panhandling and peddling of books was regarded as a public nuisance. The discovery by authorities of a cache of weapons located on the group's communal farms, reportedly acquired for self-defense after suffering harassment, contradicted the group's stated beliefs in pacifism. Occurring on the heels of the Jonestown suicides and murders, the weapons discovery damaged the credibility of the movement.

The millennialist anticipation of the arrival of a messiah by both the Jesus People movement and New Age spiritualists increased the membership of cults. Some gurus successfully dissuaded followers from embracing a messiah to instead focus on self-realization, but others in their enthusiasm to establish a vital

Anticult Movement

As converts became more involved with their new religions, they sometimes dropped out of school, severed ties to family, and immersed themselves into their beliefs and communal associations. Parents became alarmed and claimed that their children were subjected to mental manipulation and brainwashing. The media attention surrounding Charles Manson's ability to turn intelligent middle-class youths into violent killers and later the mass suicide of the Peoples Temple gave credence to concerns about cult activities. The anticult movement emerged in this context and identified suspicious groups, published cult awareness materials, and employed controversial tactics to rescue the children of worried family members.

In 1971, William Rambur and Ted Patrick, with parents whose children were involved with the Children of God, formed the first anticult organization in California. The organization was initially called the "Parents Committee to Free our Sons and Daughters from the Children of God" or FREECOG. The group was transformed into a national movement when families with children involved in other cults requested help. In response to the growing need, Patrick helped to establish the Citizens Freedom Foundation (CFF), later called the Cult Awareness Network (CAN).

Anticult activists believed that cult followers did not join or remain voluntarily but were deprived of their free will and coerced into a kind of group think that prevented them from thinking independently or clearly. In 1976, Patrick and Tom Dulack published the book *Let Our Children Go,* which documents instances of "mind control" and "brainwashing" used by cult leaders. Patrick and others relied on deprogramming to break the grip of mind control. The technique required forcibly removing the member from the cult, isolating them in a secluded place for several days, and subjecting them to intense questioning and interrogation until they renounced their affiliation with the cult. Deprogramming was controversial and expensive but had the support of some psychologists as well as parents.

At times critics accused anticultists of illegally intruding on the freedom of individuals, arguing that the abandonment of middle-class aspirations in favor of an alternative life choice did not amount to brainwashing. Patrick and anticult organizations became the target of lawsuits filed by individuals who cited incidents of abuse and violence following their captivity at the hands of deprogrammers. In such cases deprogramming often lead to the further alienation between children and their parents. Although deprogrammers were often exonerated from charges, the credibility of anticult organizations was damaged by the use of the technique, and CFF eventually abandoned deprogramming.

In 1978, the anticult movement became reenergized with the attention given to the mass suicide/murder of members from the Peoples Temple in Jonestown, Guyana. Hearings conducted by Sen. Robert Dole on the Guyana tragedy gave the anticult movement an opportunity to shed light on other potentially dangerous cults. Government agencies like the Internal Revenue Service began to scrutinize the finances of several alternative religious groups during the 1970s. Perhaps the best-known case resulted in the 1982 arrest of the founder of the Unification Church, Rev. Sun Myung Moon, who was charged with tax evasion for undisclosed funds during the early 1970s.

mission in the United States were swept into this role. The arrival of the 13-year-old Prem Rawat, also known as Guru Maharaj Ji, in 1971 attracted many disciples who believed him to be the messiah. The boy guru became recognized as the "Perfect Master," as a representation of God on Earth and the primary authority of sacred knowledge. In 1971, he established the Divine Light Mission in Denver, Colorado, which grew rapidly and established ashrams, schools, and centers in major cities along with a medical clinic in New York. Hundreds of thousands of Americans joined the guru's movement, and it appeared that the Divine Light Mission was on course to become one of the most successful new religions.

In 1973, convinced that the mission would transform the world, Maharaj Ji rented the Houston Astrodome for an event called Millenium '73, which would celebrate Shri Hans Maharaj Ji's birthday and usher in a thousand years of peace. The event failed to attract a sizable attendance and was protested by members of the Spiritual Counterfeits Project. The mission was left with a $600,000 debt and was forced to close many of its operations. With his marriage to an American-born woman in 1974, internal conflicts erupted within his family, and followers began to question his divinity. As Maharaj Ji gathered the attention of anticult organizations and the media, ex-members began accusing him of brainwashing and luring in members for financial gain. In an effort to lessen its appearance as a cult, the Divine Light Mission began to favor western attire, discouraged communal living, and requested followers to no longer view Maharaj Ji as a god. The westernization of the mission caused many members to leave and resulted in a permanent separation between family members who returned to India. By 1979, the mission had lost half of its membership and closed its headquarters in Denver.

The most controversial cults were those that emerged from the Jesus People movement. The radicalization of the Christian message by groups seeking revolutionary change unsettled many mainstream Christian denominations. Leaders of Christian cults often assumed the role of prophet and initiated new revelations that altered and sometimes deviated from Christian teachings. In some cases, the utopian aspirations of groups yielded to authoritarian hierarchies that required obedience from followers.

The Children of God, later called the Family of Love, formed in Huntington Beach, California, in 1969 under the leadership of David Berg, an ex-minister from the Christian and Missionary Alliance Church. The Children of God recruited among street youth. Followers travelled and lived together communally and organized as a family with Berg at the head and referred to as "Dad." It began as a unit of 50 but quickly grew and divided into several subgroups for purposes of covering more territory and converting people. By the mid-1970s, between 7,000 and 10,000 people had joined the group throughout the world. Berg became controversial because he encouraged his followers to engage in free love and embraced practices like adultery, incest, and communal sex, and urged female members to engage in "flirty fishing," a practice of prostitution to lure men

Jim Jones, Jonestown, and the Peoples Temple

The Jonestown communal settlement in Guyana was the utopian vision of the Peoples Temple, a religious group founded by Jim Jones in the early 1960s. Affiliated with the Disciples of Christ in Indianapolis, the Temple initially began as a Christian church with a Pentecostal influence. In later years, the church subscribed to a religiously based social and political activism that was critical of the United States and aimed to build a new society based on racial equality. The Temple was one of the few racially integrated churches in Indiana and continued to attract a large African American audience with its relocation to San Francisco in 1972. In California, the Peoples Temple provided social services to the poor and recruited a large number of elderly apostates.

Members of the Peoples Temple were captivated by Jones's charisma as well as his theatrics as a faith healer and prophet. Jones asserted that he was the incarnation of God and was the vehicle for the Second Coming. Temple members, children and adults alike, referred to Jones as "Dad" and considered themselves as part of one big family. Jones gradually asserted a greater authority over his followers and frequently practiced a form of communal confession and punishment known as catharsis to control behavior.

Jones and over a thousand members of the Peoples Temple moved from California to Guyana in 1977 to escape mounting controversies. Impending investigations by the IRS threatened to revoke the church's tax-exempt status, and an onslaught of negative press initiated by ex-members called the "Concerned Relatives" also drew the attention of public authorities. Jones convinced members to relocate to Guyana to escape nuclear annihilation from an inevitable confrontation between the United States and USSR.

At Jonestown, residents lived together in cramped quarters in the middle of a jungle. Children were usually separated from their parents, and most able-bodied adults were required to work long hours in sweltering heat either on the commune's farm or in some administrative capacity. Members were fed only meager portions of beans and rice, and outbreaks of fever and other illnesses were common. Armed guards prevented residents from leaving Jonestown. Those who attempted to escape were severely beaten or ridiculed by Jones in front of the whole community. Jones became addicted to phenobarbital and other prescription drugs, which made him delusional. His descent into irrationality accelerated when members began to defect.

Concerned Relatives convinced U.S. congressman Jim Ryan from California to investigate Jonestown abuses. Ryan and several journalists arrived in Guyana on November 14, 1978. Despite protests from Jones, Ryan negotiated a visit to Jonestown to interview members and to see whether anyone was being held against their will. Ryan was initially convinced of no wrongdoing. However, on November 18, a Jonestown resident secretly passed a note to one of the reporters requesting help in leaving the commune. Before his party's departure, Ryan asked whether

Continued on next page

Jim Jones, Jonestown, and the Peoples Temple, Continued

any one wished to leave with him. To the surprise of Jones over a dozen people requested to leave. As the party assembled, a Temple member attempted to murder Ryan. The group left hastily to an airstrip in Port Kaituma. There, as they began to board, a group of armed guards from Jonestown ambushed the party and killed five people, including Ryan.

Anticipating an armed retaliation against the commune for Ryan's death, Jones prepared members of the Temple for a "revolutionary suicide" and distributed cups of Flav-R-Aid mixed with drugs and cyanide. Residents who resisted the poison were forced to drink or injected with a lethal dose. Those who attempted to hide or escape were shot. Jonestown became the scene of the largest murder/suicide in American history. In total, 913 people lost their lives including 276 children. Jones was found sitting in a chair dead with a bullet wound to the head.

Publication of the Children of God, a controversial new religion of the 1970s. The Children of God was structured like a family under the patriarchal leadership of its founder, David Berg. (Davidson Library, University of California, Santa Barbara)

into the cult. Anticult organizations used the testimonies of ex-members to expose the sexual excesses of Berg. As pressures mounted around the cult's practices, particularly following the Peoples Temple suicides, Berg changed the name to the Family of Love and moved most of its operations to Europe and Latin America.

BIOGRAPHIES

Stewart Brand, 1938–

Innovator and Producer of the *Whole Earth Catalog*

With degrees in biology and art, and experience in the military, Stewart Brand became associated with the creative edge of the counterculture in the mid-1960s in San Francisco. He associated with author Ken Kesey and the "Merry Pranksters" and produced the Trips Festival, a pioneering effort involving rock music and light shows. Brand became best known for founding the *Whole Earth Catalog,* which became the chief reference tool for the appropriate-technology radicals, environmentalists, hippies, back-to-the-land communal residents, computer techies, and others of the 1970s who might seek a range of information about everything from building solar collectors to modifying toilets to reduce water waste.

Brand had observed that many of his friends from Haight-Ashbury had left the city for communes in New Mexico and northern California, and after he received an inheritance, he intended to help them create a new kind of civilization. Brand created "a survival manual for citizens of planet Earth," and believed that providing tools for ordinary citizens could change the culture that was destroying the environment.

First published in 1968, the *Whole Earth Catalog* espoused three fundamental laws that revealed the influence of the environmental, alternative technology, and eastern spirituality movements: "Everything's connected to everything; Everything's got to go somewhere; There's no such thing as a free lunch." Brand articulated countercultural principles on the inside cover of each edition: "We are as gods and might as well get good at it. . . . Tools that aid this process are sought and promoted by the *Whole Earth* Catalog." In the early 1970s, the catalog mushroomed to more than 400 pages in large-size format, sold millions, and convinced many, especially after the early 1970s energy crisis, that alternative energy solutions had to be—and could be—created.

Stewart Brand, founder of the Whole Earth Catalog. *The catalog became a staple among its countercultural readers for its tools and products that advocated self-sufficiency. (Tom Graves)*

Unlike most catalogs that attempted to lure consumers to purchase its products, *Whole Earth* made no profits on any sales. The catalog was a network and forum for sharing information about appropriate products. *Whole Earth* included descriptions of useful items, from books to a one-person sawmill, and reviews by Brand or a reader, with information about how to locate and purchase the items. The catalog had a homespun look and feel, and celebrated do-it-yourself technological possibilities, including geodesic domes and the latest telecommunications hardware. As Fred Turner observed, it "established a relationship between information technology, economic activity, and alternative forms of community that would outlast the counterculture itself and become a key feature of the digital world" (Turner 2005, 488).

Brand thought he would publish the last catalog in 1971, but the publication's popularity continued to grow, and he soon started the *Co-Evolution Quarterly* (which later became the *Whole Earth Review*) and supplements to the catalog through the 1970s and 1980s. Brand later regretted the catalog's uncritical enthusiasm for dropout politics and self-sufficiency, writing in his co-edited anthology *Soft Tech* (1978) that the effort to be self-sufficient could be mind numbing and lonely. But the vast majority of *Whole Earth* readers never left the city and found the manual appealing for its optimism in innovation that could solve society's worst environmental and political problems. The catalog helped inspire new work in alternative technologies and convinced a generation that solutions to daunting problems were possible.

Ram Dass, 1931–

Spiritual Leader

Among the most prominent figures to promote the New Age movement was Baba Ram Dass. Born Richard Albert, in Boston, Massachusetts, to a wealthy family, Alpert received a degree from Tufts College in 1952, followed by a Master's degree in psychology from Wesleyan University in 1953 and a Ph.D. from Stanford University in 1957. Alpert gained notoriety for his research and experiments with LSD at Harvard University, which he conducted with Timothy Leary, Aldous Huxley, Allen Ginsberg, and others. In 1963, he and Leary were dismissed from the university due to the growing controversy surrounding psychedelic drug use. Alpert continued his research through a private university until 1967.

Discouraged with the use of drugs as a conduit to reach a higher state of consciousness, Alpert turned to Eastern spirituality. In 1967, he traveled to India and became a faithful student of Neem Karoli Baba, who gave Alpert the name Ram Dass, "servant of God." Over the following years, Ram Dass studied a variety of spiritual practices including Buddhism, Sufism, and Judaism and developed a devotional practice to the Hindu deity Hanuman.

Returning to the United States, Ram Dass settled in New Hampshire and wrote the book *Be Here Now* in 1971, which sold over one million copies in 34 printings. To expedite the journey to enlightenment, Ram Dass recommended that each individual follow a different exercise, which might include yoga, sex, renunciation, drug use, meditation, or mantras.

Ram Dass traveled and lectured and formed a network of organizations to promote his teachings. In 1974, he established the Hanuman foundation in Santa Fe to consolidate efforts to provide education, service, and spiritual training. It included the Prison-Ashram Project to provide prison libraries with spiritual literature and introduce meditation to interested inmates.

In 1978, Ram Dass became a co-founder of an international organization called the Seva Foundation, devoted to the relief of suffering around the world. Programs focus on curable blindness in India, health care for Native Americans, the restoration of impoverished agricultural areas in Guatemala, and homelessness in the United States.

Eknath Easwaran, 1910–1999

Meditation Leader and Author

Easwaran was a well-known professor, writer, and lecturer in India who had been influenced by Mahatma Gandhi. Easwaran came to the University of California, Berkeley in 1959 on the Fulbright exchange program and lectured on India's spiritual heritage. He soon attracted a dedicated group of people who studied his teachings. In 1968, he inaugurated a course on meditation, believed to be the first of its kind offered at any major American university. In 1970, Easwaran and his wife, Christine, established the Blue Mountain Center of Meditation in Marin County. He published the *Bhagavad Gita for Daily Living* in 1975, and *Meditation* in 1978, which became best sellers. His Nilgiri Press and teachings also became well known through *Laurel's Kitchen* (1976), the best-selling vegetarian cookbook written by several of his students.

Buckminster Fuller, 1895–1983

Inventor, Architect, Engineer, Philosopher

Born in New England and influenced by the Transcendentalists, Fuller was a celebrated 1970s figure popular with younger generations for his creative designs that used the environment more efficiently. Emerging from a suicidal depression in 1927, Fuller dedicated his life to improving humanity and became an adherent of well-designed technology to achieve that goal. He developed what he called "Comprehensive Anticipatory Design Science," which, through higher technology, would provide "more and more life support for everybody, with less and less resources" (Buckminster Fuller Institute).

His geodesic dome became an alternative technology symbol of the 1970s and popped up in cities and the countryside with its igloolike or space-age rounded walls, a series of interconnected triangles and spheres instead of straight lines and boxes. It was the preferred design for commune homes because it was cheap, easy to construct, and had less impact on the environment. His concept of "dymaxion" held that the best design did "the most with the least."

Fuller authored many books, including the classic *Operating Manual for Spaceship Earth* (1969), *Utopia or Oblivion* (1970), *Earth, Inc.* (1973), *Synergetics* (1975), *Synergetics 2* (1979), and *Critical Path* (1981). Fuller had faith in the young to eventually come to grips with their situation aboard "Spaceship Earth" and saw his role as one of exploring big picture or "comprehensivist" viewpoints in light of what he saw as a dangerously overspecializing curriculum.

Fuller retired in 1975 from Southern Illinois University at Carbondale, where he had taught since 1959, but continued his active speaking schedule throughout the country and world. In addition to many honorary academic awards, he was the recipient of many architectural and design awards including the Gold Medal of the American Institute of Architects (1970).

Shere Hite, 1943–

Sexuality Researcher

Shere Hite moved from Florida to New York in the mid-1960s to work toward a Ph.D. in social history at Columbia University. She did not complete the degree and instead became a fashion model and then an active feminist. Director of the National Organization for Women's feminist sexuality project from 1972 to 1978, Hite sent out questionnaires for her research study on female sexuality. Most of her respondents were from feminist circles or readers of church newsletters and women's magazines.

The result of the study, despite its sampling flaws, became the first *Hite Report: A Nationwide Study of Female Sexuality,* published in 1976. The best-selling book became a focus of world attention because it was the first research by women for women. It presented the voices of 3,000 women, ages 14 to 78, who provided confessional accounts of their sexual activities, desires, and dissatisfactions. Hite criticized other researchers who had "wound up *telling* women how they should feel rather than *asking* them how they do feel"(Hite Research International).

Hite's research followed on the heels of earlier comprehensive studies on American sexuality by Alfred Kinsey and Masters and Johnson, but her research reached different conclusions. Hite's major groundbreaking conclusion was that women can orgasm easily during self-stimulation and that it was not women but society that had a problem with the way women reached orgasm. Hite claimed that this was a human rights issue that had not yet been recognized because other sexologists, popular culture, and pornography maintained that it was normal for a woman to reach orgasm during coitus. In fact, the second half of the book analyzed the way society defined sex and sexual pleasure. Since 1978, Hite has directed Hite Research International.

Chögyam Trungpa Rinpoche, 1939–1987

Leader of Tibetan Buddhism

Chögyam Trungpa Rinpoche became one of the better-known teachers of Tantric Buddhism during the 1970s. Like the Dalai Lama, Trungpa became an exile from his home in Tibet following its invasion by the Chinese in 1959. After spending some years in England and studying at Oxford University, he moved to the United States to teach. Trungpa settled in Boulder, Colorado, in 1970 and established the Rocky Mountain Dharma Center the same year. In 1974, he founded the Naropa Institute (now Naropa University), the only Buddhist-inspired four-year institute in North America. Naropa became a premier center for studying the Tibetan Buddhist tradition in the West and featured the Jack Kerouac School for Disembodied Poets with courses taught by Allen Ginsberg and Anne Waldman. Such programs attracted people from the counterculture. In 1977, Trungpa also established Shambhala Training, an international network of centers with programs for secular meditation for the public.

Trungpa was a controversial figure, known for his eccentric behavior that was often juxtaposed to the countercultural, idealistic, and antimaterialistic character of some of his students. Trungpa seemed far from most Americans' ideas of ascetic yogis meditating on snowy mountaintops. He ate rich foods, drank alcohol, smoked, and freely joined in ingesting psychedelics. Despite his carefree behavior, Trungpa demanded intensive study and a rigorous meditation practice.

Hunter S. Thompson, 1937–2005

Writer

The "gonzo" journalism of Hunter S. Thompson, which celebrated the subjective observations of the reporter, symbolized the celebrity writer of the 1970s, who blended a new writing style with contemporary culture and politics. Thompson first appeared in *Rolling Stone* with an article, "The Battle of Aspen," describing his 1970 bid for sheriff of Pitkin County, Colorado, on the "Freak Power" ticket. Thompson narrowly lost the election to the incumbent Republican, having run on a platform promoting drug decriminalization and bike paths. Thompson then adopted the alter ego "Raoul Duke" in his reporting to blur fact, fiction, and fantasy and released a series of *Rolling Stone* articles in 1971 titled "Fear and Loathing in Las Vegas" about Duke and his 300 pound Samoan attorney, Dr. Gonzo (inspired by Thompson's friend, Chicano lawyer Oscar Zeta Acosta), who go to the gambling city to cover a motorcycle race and then a convention of narcotics officers. The two become sidetracked by a search for the American dream with the assistance of copious amounts of alcohol, acid, mescaline, cocaine, marijuana, and other drugs. Thompson published these accounts into a book later that year, which became a canonical text for the drug culture and rebel youth of the 1970s, much like Kerouac's *On the Road* had for the 1950s generation.

Thompson's next big assignment for *Rolling Stone* was covering the Democratic Party and the 1972 election, which he collected into one of the most preeminent works on a presidential election, *Fear and Loathing: On the Campaign Trail '72.* The book focuses largely on the Democratic primaries and splits between the different candidates, McGovern, Muskie, and Humphrey. Thompson became a fierce critic of President Nixon, both during and after his presidency, and became more involved in national politics, supporting and advising Jimmy Carter before and during his run for the presidency in 1976.

While to the public Thompson was often viewed as a subversive, drug-addled novelist, he viewed himself as a serious sports and political writer. His literary success, however, was due not so much to his subject matter but to the wild and breathless way he wrote, catching action as it was happening and fictionalizing occasionally to make clearer sense of the heart of the matter. Thompson became more disillusioned by the growing greed and emptiness of American politics and culture in the 1980s and remained more on his Colorado ranch where he followed the political scene on cable TV. He committed suicide at his ranch in 2005.

REFERENCES AND FURTHER READINGS

Abbott, Carl. 1990. "Southwestern Cityscapes: Approaches to an American Urban Environment." In *Searching for the Sunbelt: Historical Perspectives on a Region,* edited by Raymond A. Mohl, 59–86. Knoxville: University of Tennessee Press.

Allit, Patrick. 2003. *Religion in America since 1945.* New York: Columbia University.

Allyn, David. 2000. *Make Love, Not War: The Sexual Revolution, An Unfettered History.* Boston: Little, Brown.

Anderson, Terry H. 1995. *The Movement and the Sixties: Protest in America from Greensboro to Wounded Knee.* New York: Oxford University Press.

Barkan, Elliott. 1990. "New Origins, New Homeland, New Region: American Immigration and the Emergence of the Sunbelt, 1955–1985." In *Searching for the Sunbelt: Historical Perspectives on a Region,* edited by Raymond A. Mohl, 124–148. Knoxville: University of Tennessee Press.

Bayor, Ronald H. 1990. "Models of Ethnic and Racial Politics in the Sunbelt South." In *Searching for the Sunbelt: Historical Perspectives on a Region,* edited by Raymond A. Mohl, 105–123. Knoxville: University of Tennessee Press.

Belasco, Warren J. 1989. *Appetite for Change: How the Counterculture Took On the Food Industry, 1966–1988.* New York: Pantheon Books.

Belasco, Warren J. 1984. "Lite Economics: Less Food, More Profit." *Radical History Review* 28:254–278.

Bernard, Richard M., and Bradley R. Rice, eds. 1983. *Sunbelt Cities: Politics and Growth since World War II.* Austin: University of Texas Press.

Bouvard, Marguerite. 1975. *The Intentional Community Movement: Building a New Moral World.* Port Washington, NY: Kennikat Press.

Braunstein, Peter, and Michael William Doyle. 2002. *Imagine Nation: The Counterculture of the 1960s and 70s.* New York: Routledge.

Brownell, Blaine A., and David R. Goldfield, eds. 1977. *The City in Southern History: The Growth of Urban Civilization in the South.* Port Washington, NY: Kennikat Press.

Bruegmann, Robert. 2005. *Sprawl: A Compact History.* Chicago: University of Chicago Press.

Buckminster Fuller Institute. "Introduction to Buckminster Fuller." http://www .bfi.org/node/15. Accessed August 6, 2006.

Case, John, and Rosemary C. R. Taylor, eds. 1979. *Co-ops, Communes and Collectives: Experiments in Social Change in the 1960s and 1970s.* New York: Pantheon Books.

Cohen, Lizabeth. 2003. *A Consumers' Republic: The Politics of Mass Consumption in Postwar America.* New York: Knopf.

Coontz, Stephanie. 2005. *Marriage, a History.* New York: Viking.

Cox, Craig. 1994. *Storefront Revolution: Food Co-ops and the Counterculture.* New Brunswick, NJ: Rutgers University Press.

Cravens, Hamilton. 1997. "Postmodern Psychobabble: The Recovery Movement for Individual Self-Esteem in Mental Health Since World War II." *Journal of Policy History* 9 (1): 141–154.

Curl, John. 1980. *History of Work Cooperation in America.* Berkeley, CA: Homeward Press.

Di Sabatino, David. 1999. *The Jesus People Movement: An Annotated Bibliography and General Resource.* Westport, CT: Greenwood Press.

Ellwood, Robert S. 1979. *Alternative Alters: Unconventional and Eastern Spirituality in America*. Chicago: University of Chicago Press.

Eskridge, Larry. 1998. "One Way: Billy Graham, the Jesus Generation, and the Idea of an Evangelical Youth Culture," *Church History* 67 (1): 83–107.

Fairfield, Richard. 1972. *Communes USA: A Personal Tour*. Baltimore: Penguin.

Farrell, Amy Erdman. 1998. *Yours in Sisterhood: Ms. Magazine and the Promise of Popular Feminism*. Chapel Hill: University of North Carolina Press.

Findlay, John M. 1992. *Magic Lands: Western Cityscapes and American Culture after 1940*. Berkeley: University of California Press.

Fisher, Robert. 1990. "The Urban Sunbelt in Comparative Perspective: Houston in Context." In *Essays on Sunbelt Cities and Recent Urban America,* edited by Robert B. Fairbanks and Kathleen Underwood, 33–58. College Station: Texas A&M University Press.

Frederickson, George, ed. *Neighborhood Control in the 1970s: Politics, Administration, and Citizen Participation*. San Francisco: The Chandler Press, 1973.

Frum, David. 2000. *How We Got Here: The 70s, the Decade that Brought You Modern Life (For Better or Worse)*. New York: Basic Books.

Gardner, Hugh. 1978. *The Children of Prosperity: Thirteen Modern American Communes*. New York: St. Martin's Press.

Garton, Stephen. 2004. *Histories of Sexuality: From Antiquity to Sexual Revolution*. New York: Routledge.

Grinspoon, Lester, and James B. Bakalar. 1979. *Psychedelic Drugs Reconsidered*. New York: Basic Books.

Herzberg, David. 2006. "The Pill You Love Can Turn on You: Feminism, Tranquilizers, and the Valium Panic of the 1970s." *American Quarterly* 58 (1): 79–103.

Hite Research International. 2005. "Shere Hite and the Hite Reports." http://www.hite-research.com/. Accessed August 8, 2006.

Hoefferie, Caroline. 1997. "Just at Sunrise: The Sunrise Communal Farm in Rural Mid-Michigan, 1971–1978." *Michigan Historical Review* 23 (1): 71–104.

Hogeland, Lisa Maria. 1995. "Sexuality in the Consciousness Raising Novel of the Seventies." *Journal of the History of Sexuality* 5 (4): 601–632.

Iacobbo, Karen, and Michael Iacobbo. 2004. *Vegetarian America, a History*. Westport, CT: Praeger.

Jones, Jill. 1996. *Hep-Cats, Narcs, and Pipe Dreams: A History of America's Romance with Illegal Drugs*. New York: Scribner.

Kanter, Rosabeth Moss. 1979. "Communes in Cities." In *Co-ops, Communes and Collectives: Experiments in Social Change in the 1960s and 1970s,* edited by John Case and Rosemary C. R. Taylor, 112–135. New York: Pantheon Books.

Kirk, Andrew. 2001. "Appropriating Technology: The Whole Earth Catalog and Counterculture Environmental Politics." *Environmental History* 6 (3): 374–394.

Kyle, Richard. 1995. *The New Age Movement in American Culture*. Lanham, New York: University Press of America, Inc.

Larsen, Ernest. 2005. "Junky and Important: The Collective Model in the Rearview Mirror." *American Quarterly* 57 (1): 223–236.

Levine, Larry. 1983. "New River Trading Co-op: A Venture into Good Food." *Southern Exposure* 11 (6): 44–47.

Lotchin, Roger W. 1990. "The Origins of the Sunbelt-Frostbelt Struggle: Defense Spending and City Building." In *Searching for the Sunbelt: Historical Perspectives on a Region,* edited by Raymond A. Mohl, 47–68. Knoxville: University of Tennessee Press.

Massing, Michael. 1998. *The Fix*. New York: Simon & Schuster.

Melton, J. Gordon. 1993. "Another look at New Religions" In *Annals of the American Academy of Political and Social Sciences.* Vol. 527, No. 1, 97–112.

Melton, J. Gordon. 1992. *Encyclopedic Handbook of Cults in America*. New York: Garland Publishing.

Meunier, Rachel. "The Farm. Communal Living in the Late 60s and Early 70s." December 17, 1994. http://www.thefarm.org/lifestyle/cmnl.html. Accessed July 18, 2006.

Miller, Randall M., and George E. Pozzetta, eds. 1988. *Shades of the Sunbelt: Essays on Ethnicity, Race, and the Urban South*. Westport, CT: Greenwood Press.

Miller, Timothy. 1999. *The 60s Communes: Hippies and Beyond*. Syracuse, NY: Syracuse University Press.

Mohl, Raymond A. 1990. "The Transformation of Urban America since the Second World War." In *Essays on Sunbelt Cities and Recent Urban America,* edited by Robert B. Fairbanks and Kathleen Underwood, 8–32. College Station: Texas A&M University Press.

Mungo, Raymond. 1980. *Cosmic Profit: How to Make Money Without Doing Time*. Boston: Little, Brown.

Patrick, Ted. 1976. *Let Our Children Go*. New York: Dutton.

Patterson, Alexander. 2000. "Terrasquirma and the Engineers of Social Change in 1970s Portland." *Oregon Historical Quarterly* 101 (2): 162–191.

Pike, Sarah M. 2004. *New Age and Neopagan Religions in America*. New York: Columbia University.

Plaskin, Glenn. 1984. "Calvin Klein; Playboy Interview." *Playboy* (May), http://store.soliscompany.com/caklplin.html. Accessed August 1, 2006.

The Religious Movements Homepage Project. http://religiousmovements.lib
.virginia.edu/. Accessed July 20, 2007.

Robinson, Ira E., and Davor Jedlicka. 1982. "Change in Sexual Attitudes and Behavior of College Students from 1965 to 1980: A Research Note." *Journal of Marriage and the Family* 44 (1): 237–240.

Ronco, William. 1974. *Food Co-ops: An Alternative to Shopping in Supermarkets*. Boston: Beacon Press.

Sager, Anthony P. 1979. "Radical Law: Three Collectives in Cambridge." In *Co-ops, Communes and Collectives: Experiments in Social Change in the 1960s and 1970s,* edited by John Case and Rosemary C. R. Taylor, 136–150. New York: Pantheon Books.

Schomburg Center for Research in Black Culture: Haitian Immigration 20th Century http://www.inmotionaame.org/migrations/. Accessed Aug 26, 2006.

Schulman, Bruce J. 2001. *The Seventies: The Great Shift in American Culture, Society, and Politics*. New York: Free Press.

Self, Robert O. 2003. *Race and the Struggle for Postwar Oakland*. Princeton: Princeton University Press.

Slocum-Schaffer, Stephanie. 2003. *America in the Seventies*. Syracuse, N.Y.: Syracuse University Press.

Spangler, David. 1976. *Revelation, the Birth of a New Age*. San Francisco: Rainbow Bridge.

Teaford, Jon C. 2006. *The Metropolitan Revolution: The Rise of Post-Urban America*. New York: Columbia University Press.

Thomas, Pauline Weston. "The 70s Disco Fashion: 1970s Costume History," and "1970s Punk Fashion History Development." Fashion-era.com, n.d. http://www.fashion-era.com/1970s.htm. Accessed July 25, 2006.

Torgoff, Martin. 2004. *Can't Find My Way Home: America in the Great Stoned Age, 1945–2000*. New York: Simon & Schuster.

Turner, Fred. 2005. "Where the Counterculture Met the New Economy." *Technology and Culture* 46 (3): 485–512.

Ueda, Reed. 1994. *Postwar Immigrant America: A Social History*. Boston: Bedford Books of St. Martin's Press.

Waterfield, Robin. 2003. *Hidden Depths: The Story of Hypnosis*. New York: Brunner-Routledge.

Whitsel, Bradley C. 2003. *The Church Universal and Triumphant: Elizabeth Clare Prophet's Apocalyptic Movement*. Syracuse, NY: Syracuse University.

Leisure and Popular Culture

OVERVIEW

Although often portrayed retrospectively as a decade of silly fads, the 1970s actually produced a rich and complex popular culture. Signature fashions that were later ridiculed, like platform shoes and brightly colored leisure suits, revealed the boldness and experimentation that marked the decade. Popular culture—the collective behavior and expressions of people, or the choices people make in consuming commercially produced cultural products—tells us much about the era. Political and social movements of the 1970s infiltrated popular culture to give it a more critical edge. The decade saw some of the most intelligently political music, film, and television ever created. The lifting of censorship restrictions allowed explorations of formerly taboo subjects, and the general air of openness infused American culture with new creativity. New forms of popular expression and consumption of the arts appeared that embraced this liberating atmosphere. For example, although much 1970s music, such as disco, punk, and glam rock, is often dismissed, critics failed to recognize the boundary-stretching efforts of the musicians and audiences.

Television viewing remained a primary pastime of Americans, and the 1970s represented a "golden age" of witty writing and acting. Concentrated in the three big commercial networks and national public television, much new programming explored social themes and problems and a broader diversity of characters, including single women and African Americans.

Television helped encourage the mass consumption of sporting events and made more evident the personalities of star athletes, including many African Americans. Social movements and countercultural trends of the 1970s influenced athletes to assert their autonomy, grow long hair, join together to strike and negotiate a bigger slice of game profits, and demand sexual and racial equality.

For African Americans, the decade presented the first opportunity since the civil rights revolution had ended legally sanctioned segregation to create popular culture for community and national audiences. Some have referred to the 1970s as the "Black Decade" for the outpouring of socially and culturally significant African American arts, film, journalism, literature, music, sports, festivals, and television. As critic Gene Seymour notes, the end of Jim Crow, although it failed to "purge racism from the country's psyche," did generate a "wave of pride" in African American culture and an unprecedented African American creative explosion (Seymour 2004, 28).

More cultural and leisure options were available to more Americans. Gays, lesbians, single women, young people, and others could openly mingle in integrated clubs and listen to or dance to a variety of music. Girls, women, and people of color could compete in school and professional athletics. Americans created ethnic associations, music festivals, and patriotic celebrations in their communities. They could purchase inexpensive paperback books exploring a range of topics, from science fiction to self-help programs. In the home, television offered more variety, including socially relevant comedy and sports programming.

Although often called the "Me" decade, as millions of Americans sought self-awareness and personal growth through various self-help groups, publications, and television shows like *Donohue,* the culture also critiqued this self-absorption, humorously, through Woody Allen's films and, seriously, through a variety of popular commentators. Although critics like Christopher Lasch argued that the decade's self-indulgence was damaging American social institutions, others found efforts to seek personal transformation and new forms of community critical for affecting social change.

As much as they reflected different tastes, these debates over the merits of various cultural trends often revealed the divisions in American society, which seemed to sharpen in the 1970s. The white male rock fan backlash against disco and African American farmers' protests of the nation's bicentennial celebration are two examples of how segments of the population contested what appeared to be broadly accepted cultural trends or events. Hollywood's pursuit of sex and violence on the screen, the gay and women's liberation movements and cultural challenges they presented, and what many saw as the drugs and decadence promoted by rock and roll all generated concerns among a growing number of Americans. The growing conservative movement often attacked these cultural developments as a sign of the failures of liberalism.

What many Americans saw as overwhelming dominance of certain discomforting values also reflected a growing commercialization of popular culture. As cultural expressions moved in many different and experimental directions, corporate consolidation and control simultaneously limited popular culture. The era of the blockbuster—in movies, books, and best-selling albums—stimulated similar sequels and stars in subsequent productions. Deals, profits, and audience potential, rather than artistic integrity or popular desires, often determined what was produced for mass consumption.

Notwithstanding these contradictions, the decade produced an impressive burst of creative activity. New artists exploring fresh themes, technologies, and genres struggled alongside the constraints of the powerful commercial side of cultural production. The editors of *Crawdaddy,* the quintessential cultural magazine of the 1970s, disagreed strongly with those who dismissed the decade as the "worst of times." The artists interviewed in the publication's pages, including Jack Nicholson, Mel Brooks, Patti Smith, Sly Stone, and many others reveal the cultural creativity of this important period and Americans' support of diverse forms of leisure.

TIMELINE

1970   The antiwar songs "Ball of Confusion" by the Temptations, and Edwin Starr's "War" top pop and African American music charts.

Jesus Christ Superstar opens on Broadway.

Big Bird of *Sesame Street* appears on a *Time* cover.

Janis Joplin and Jimi Hendrix die of drug overdoses.

George C. Scott refuses an Oscar for his starring role in *Patton.*

U.S. movie tickets drop from over 3 billion in 1950 to under 1 billion.

The Federal Communications Commission loosens network control of television production.

The Mary Tyler Moore Show about a single career woman begins popular seven-year run.

Phil Donahue launches his first talk show.

1971   *The French Connection,* Gene Hackman, and Jane Fonda win Oscars.

The New York Times publishes the "Pentagon Papers."

All in the Family begins its long-running television career.

In Washington, D.C., the Kennedy Center for the Performing Arts opens.

1972   *Ms.* magazine begins publication.

The movie *Deep Throat* starts the porn industry explosion.

The Washington Post begins Watergate reporting that will bring down President Nixon.

The Godfather sets a box office record of $1 million a day for the first month.

Major League Ball Players Association (MLBPA) calls a strike.

1973   *Burr,* by Gore Vidal, is a best-selling historical novel.

George Carlin's "Seven Dirty Words" results in court slap for Pacifica Radio.

Erica Jong shocks readers with her language and sexually liberated heroine in the best-selling *Fear of Flying.*

People magazine begins publication.

AP and UPI install computer terminals in all U.S. bureaus.

1974   *Carrie* is the first of Stephen King's blockbuster gothic novels.

The World's Fair is held in Spokane, Washington.

1975   Steven Spielberg's *Jaws* is the first film to earn more than $100 million.

Saul Bellow's comic novel *Humboldt's Gift* wins the Pulitzer Prize.

On television, *Saturday Night Live* begins its showcase of irreverent comedians.

1976   Alex Haley publishes the best-seller *Roots,* about his search for his ancestors.

American novelist Saul Bellow wins the Nobel Prize in Literature.

Barbara Walters is the first woman to anchor a U.S. network newscast.

The nation celebrates the bicentennial.

1977   As a TV miniseries, *Roots* draws 130 million viewers over eight nights.

Leslie Marmon Silko publishes *Ceremony*.

Elvis Presley dies in Memphis, Tennessee.

1978   Erma Bombeck publishes the best-seller *If Life Is a Bowl of Cherries, What Am I Doing in the Pits?*

Toni Morrison publishes the novel *Song of Solomon*.

Vietnam-themed films sweep the Oscars, with top awards going to *The Deer Hunter* and to Jon Voight and Jane Fonda for acting in *Coming Home*.

Games like Space Invaders draw teenagers to arcades.

1979   Eleven fans of the Who die in an oversold Cincinnati stadium.

Apocalypse Now presents a surreal portrait of Vietnam War.

SOUNDS OF THE 1970s: POPULAR MUSIC

Rock Searches for New Expression

By 1970, rock and roll, America's most popular music, sounded much different than it had in the 1960s. Musicians utilized new technology to produce better recordings, and they offered a broader variety of sounds, if usually divorced from live performance. Concepts, theatrics, new fusions of classical/jazz/rock styles, and politics became central to what Frank Moriarty referred to as the "decade of creative chaos."

Rock music expanded technological and creative boundaries, but it also lost some of its great 1960s icons. Janis Joplin and Jimi Hendrix died of drug overdoses in 1970, Jim Morrison of the Doors died in Paris, probably of an overdose, and Duane Allman, in a motorcycle crash in 1971. Although many of the bands of the 1960s had dissolved or lost key members to tragedy, many reconstituted themselves or, as solo artists, went on to have great influence on the development of rock in the 1970s.

Americans primarily heard their pop songs on AM radio, but in the late 1960s and early 1970s, the creation of new FM stations expanded listening choices. Hit rock songs often lasted 8–12 minutes, long past what had been acceptable by commercial AM radio stations, which were also more sensitive to potentially controversial lyrics. Cities often had multiple "underground" FM rock stations, which featured greater sound fidelity, uncut versions of songs, and fewer commercials.

Rock musicians of the 1970s not only sought new forms of production but also became bolder in their political expression. Crosby, Stills, Nash, and Young became one of the first bands to respond to the killings at Kent State with Neil

Members of Crosby, Stills, Nash & Young (left to right: Stephen Stills, Graham Nash, David Crosby, and Neil Young). Like other bands in the 1970s, the group used its popularity to raise awareness about political and social issues. (Henry Diltz/Corbis)

Young's song "Ohio" on the best-selling album of 1970, *Déjà Vu*. That same year, Steppenwolf released their politically charged album *Monster* about the moral decline of the United States. Bob Dylan protested the racially motivated conviction for murder of former middleweight contender Rubin "Hurricane" Carter with his 1975 hit song "Hurricane" and with concert fund-raising tours to assist his release. But as the war in Vietnam ended, music generally became less politically charged and more introspective than in the early 1970s. Despite many musicians' efforts to encourage young people to vote and elect George McGovern in 1972, President Nixon easily defeated the youth-oriented, antiwar candidate.

The "British invasion" of the 1960s, led by The Rolling Stones and The Beatles, continued in the 1970s with British "supergroups" like The Who, Blind Faith, Led Zeppelin, and others who had huge followings in the United States and played in large concert halls. The British influence of classical-infused and conceptual music, such as The Who's rock operas *Tommy* and *Quadrophenia* and Procol Harum's "A Whiter Shade of Pale," helped spur the popularity of "art" or "progressive" rock in the 1970s. Pink Floyd's 1973 album *Dark Side of the Moon* remained on the U.S. Top 200 charts for more than 14 years.

American and British musicians worked together in many rock bands and lived, toured, and sold records on both sides of the Atlantic. The blues-influenced British bands Deep Purple, Black Sabbath, and Led Zepplin and the Australian

Women and Rock

Despite women's political and social gains during the decade, rock and roll bands for the most part remained male. Fleetwood Mac was an exception. Lead singers Christine McVie and Stevie Nicks led the band to superstardom in the 1970s with their distinctive voices. The band's album *Rumours* (1977), which featured songs about the respective breakups between Nicks and McVie, and their band-member husbands, Lindsey Buckingham and John McVie, became one of the best-selling albums of all time.

Aside from a few rock sensations, women musicians found greater success on their own as solo artists and songwriters. Canadian Joni Mitchell, whose concerts and albums of the 1970s reached a large U.S. audience, sang introspectively of the highs and lows of relationships. While shunning the label "feminist," she represented for many women the efforts to reconcile independence and connectedness, and as singer-songwriter and guitarist, someone who broke into the 1970s male world of rock. Long-time songwriter Carole King, heavily influenced by 1960s African American pop and soul, also broke through the popular music scene in 1971 with her album *Tapestry,* which became the biggest-selling album of the year. Unlike Mitchell, her songs were less personal and more universal about women's experience, and she, too, gained a popular following among women. Carly Simon, with her marriage to singer-songwriter James Taylor in the spotlight in the 1970s, recorded numerous albums about love and family.

band AC/DC all found appreciative concert audiences, especially among young American white males. Often accompanied by boisterous stage antics and back-stage celebrations of drugs, alcohol, and sex, "heavy metal" became a term widely used by the early 1970s to describe the amplified rock and roll that emphasized technical guitar virtuosity and distortion. Aerosmith, a hard-working tour band from Boston, slowly built a devoted audience in the 1970s. The release of their fourth album, *Rocks,* in 1976 had many calling them "America's Rolling Stones." In addition to their Stones-level popularity, lead singer Steven Tyler pranced on stage to mimic Mick Jagger's singing style.

The British were not the only ones to infuse American rock with new sounds and ideas. Latino and Caribbean musicians also introduced rock to Afro-Caribbean rhythms. New York's Puerto Rican and Cuban musicians had long influenced jazz. Californian Carlos Santana introduced many rock fans to this music when he released his hit cover of New Yorker Tito Puente's "Oye Como Va" in 1970, mixing his distinctive psychedelic blues guitar with Latin grooves and instruments.

Another fusion music, reggae, brought a new sound and politics to rock from the Caribbean. Influenced by the rhythm and blues music heard from New

Theatrical and Glam Rock

Stage theatrics grew in importance in the 1970s as live concerts became ways for bands to promote their records, build and sustain fans, and experiment with new music. Frank Zappa and the Mothers of Invention pushed the limits of outrageousness and constantly created new sounds through the decade, including big band fusion, electric jazz rock, and bebop tango, all the while parodying American commercial culture, the bicentennial, politicians, and other rock groups. Alice Cooper, with heavy makeup and wild androgynous costumes, caught the attention of Zappa who signed him to his label, Straight Records. Cooper caught the rough rock scene of his Detroit home and became the master of "shock rock" in the 1970s, with a string of number one hits. Cooper reenacted scenes from his songs on stage, incorporating straitjackets and electric chairs, seeking to shock as well as entertain audiences.

British folksinger-turned-gender-bending rocker David Bowie became the most famous pop performer in the United States from 1975 to 1976, developing an androgynous look as well as music, and spearheading "glitter" or "glam" rock for his outrageous costumes, orange hair, makeup, elaborate sets, and special effects. Bowie was strongly influenced by American Lou Reed, from the legendary band Velvet Underground, who influenced both glam and punk rock in the 1970s. Bowie assembled an album and stage show, *The Rise and Fall of Ziggy Stardust and the Spiders from Mars* (1972), about a rock star trying to save the world, which met huge success. He continued to reinvent himself through the decade, tackling Philadelphia soul in *Young Americans* (1975), starring in the film *The Man Who Fell to Earth,* and collaborating with Brian Eno and his minimalist electronics in *Heroes* (1977).

British songwriter and pianist Elton John was one of America's leading performers of the 1970s, with his garish costumes, elaborately staged shows, and accomplished acting and singing. He had seven number one albums between 1972 and 1975, and was the focus of the tabloids and music magazines, which showcased his luxury home, outrageous outfits, friendship with John and Yoko, and bisexuality.

Orleans and Southern U.S. radio stations, Jamaicans produced their own local music that infused Afro-Caribbean rhythms with social messages. Especially through the wildly popular Bob Marley, reggae became a public symbol of Rastafarianism, a religious cult that personified Ethiopian emperor Haile Selassie as a god. Marley and Jimmy Cliff introduced reggae to many Americans through the film *The Harder They Come* (1972). Marley's radical "Get Up, Stand Up," recorded in 1973, became a clarion call for activists worldwide. Reggae's popularity declined after Marley's death in 1981, but it continued to influence rock and rap music.

Reggae reminded pop culture fans that rock music was international. Many of America's favorite pop stars of the 1970s, such as Rod Stewart and Elton John, were, after all, British. American rock, too, was heard around the world. The Swedish group ABBA was the most commercially successful group worldwide in the 1970s.

Jazz reasserted itself and influenced rock in the 1970s. Keyboardists Herbie Hancock and Keith Jarrett explored jazz/rock fusions, and jazz great Miles Davis assembled a legendary ensemble for his groundbreaking album *Bitches Brew,* which, when released in 1970, stymied many critics but mapped out future possibilities for jazz-rock fusion. The album earned a Grammy, made the *Billboard* pop Top 40, and became Davis's first gold record, signifying the reinstitution of jazz's connection to rock. British jazz guitarist John McLaughlin assembled some of the best American and international jazz and rock musicians into the experimental Mahavishnu Orchestra, which thrilled New York clubgoers and a larger audience when the album *The Inner Mounting Flame* was released in 1971. It hit rock music "like a tidal wave, altering [it] forever" (Moriarty 2003, 75). Other popular rock bands of the decade, including Chicago, Steely Dan, and Blood, Sweat & Tears, incorporated jazz instruments and styling in their music.

Many American bands deliberately distinguished themselves from their British counterparts by incorporating the distinctive American influences of country and soul in what was called "roots" music. John Fogerty's San Francisco band, Creedence Clearwater Revival, created a mythical Louisiana swamp sound. The last of the large Woodstock-style rock concerts took place in the summer of 1973 at Watkins Glen in upstate New York and featured the "all-American" bands the Grateful Dead, the Band, and the Allman Brothers.

Smaller rock music festivals attracted crowds in cities and towns throughout the United States during the decade, and other venues, such as clubs and halls, showcased local and international talent. One of the final episodes marking rock music in the decade occurred on December 3, 1979, when 11 fans were crushed to death in a stampede to enter Cincinnati's Riverfront Coliseum for a Who concert. The event haunted the band and the live music scene that was so critical to the creativity of the decade.

As much as rock dominated youth culture, other musical forms actually captured more Americans' attention and cash. Barbra Streisand, the Carpenters, and Neil Diamond had top-selling albums in the 1970s, although their songs were infused by rock rhythms. Cabarets, inspired by the 1972 hit musical film *Cabaret,* became popular clubs in cities, where people could listen to singers such as Rosemary Clooney or Tony Bennett. And early rock icon, Elvis Presley continued to be a huge star with an older crowd in places such as Las Vegas until his death in 1977.

Rock was experimental at the same time it became big business. By the mid-1970s, just six companies produced 80 percent of the best-selling records. Record production and promotion became more elaborate and expensive. Record sales boomed, and more groups sold in the millions. Fleetwood Mac's *Rumours* (1977), for example, became the best-selling album of the decade, selling 13 million. By 1980, the experimentation and the solo power of great drummers and guitarists represented by vinyl records in the 1970s made way for slicker production and new technology, including the first digital compact discs. The experimental underground radio stations also began disappearing by the end of the decade, making way for more commercial fare.

R&B and Cultural Fusion

The 1960s Motown sound gave way to multiple African American "sounds" in the 1970s. The last big act of Berry Gordy's Motown operation, the Jackson 5, featured the five oldest boys of the musically talented family of Joseph and Katherine Jackson. Lead by prepubescent singer Michael, the group reached a new and younger audience with a string of number one hits beginning in 1970. Motown's Marvin Gaye gained artistic control over his recordings, telling Gordy that he had to protest American government misdeeds. In 1971, Gaye released his jazz-inspired *What's Going On,* which became an artistic and commercial success, ruminating on social and environmental decay, the Vietnam War, and race relations. Gaye's break from Motown and the popularity of his more sophisticated lyrics and music marked a turning point for rhythm and blues in the 1970s. Along with Gaye, Stevie Wonder became a phenomenon in the decade, when he too gained creative control of his recordings from Motown. Wonder embraced the militancy of the era, reflected in his braided and beaded hair, dashikis, and social issues in his lyrics. He wrote, sang, played instruments for, recorded, and mixed his own songs. His popular LPs *Music of My Mind* (1972), *Talking Book* (1972), and *Songs in the Key of Life* (1976) were played all over the airwaves.

Wonder and Gaye were part of a movement of African American pop artists to engage with social issues during the decade, reflecting the influence of the black power and civil rights movements. The music was also commercially viable, and never before or since have so many African American voices dominated radio. War, the Temptations, the Staple Singers, and Earth, Wind & Fire commented on urban poverty, white flight, and war. The racially and gender-integrated Sly and the Family Stone released their 1971 album, *There's a Riot Goin' On,* which was more pessimistic than their late 1960s good-time music. Novelist and spoken-word performer Gil Scott-Heron released several politically pointed albums, including the famous *The Revolution Will Not Be Televised* (1974) and the hit song "Johannesburg" (1975). Scott-Heron's songs assessed white-owned corporate media, the superficiality of television and consumerism, and America's ignorance of the problems of inner cities.

The funky grooves of soul legend James Brown and the hip Sly and the Family Stone influenced new rhythms of the late 1970s, including funk, fusion, and rap. Long-time musician George Clinton expanded on Stone and Brown's funk, added a 40-member band, and staged spectacles with elaborate lighting and special effects. Stepping onto a stage from the smoking "Mothership" wearing white robes, the funk visionary Clinton celebrated the new black political order, the "Chocolate Cities" where African Americans now dominated, even as those cities were increasingly impoverished. But Clinton was more than a commentator; he creatively fused rock, jazz, and funk, and his two bands, Parliament and Funkadelic, performed marathon live concerts that outdid the extravaganzas staged by Kiss or David Bowie.

In addition to addressing new political themes, R&B sought new centers of production. Kenny Gamble, Leon Huff, and Thom Bell formed Philadelphia International Records in 1971 and helped form a new "Philadelphia sound" that included Teddy Pendergrass and other artists and a richer instrumental and rhythmic sound than Detroit's Motown. The O'Jays' hit "Back Stabbers" (1972) and the Spinners' "Could It Be I'm Falling in Love" (1973) made Philadelphia a music center. The August 1972 Watts Summer Festival, soul music's successful Woodstock, featured Memphis Stax Records stars the Soul Children, Isaac Hayes, the Staple Singers, and Johnnie Taylor, along with civil rights leaders like Jesse Jackson, but it also marked a shift in soul's power. Both Stax and Motown had moved to Los Angeles, rejecting their music's roots and attempting to become more like mainstream companies that could profit from larger commercial audiences.

The arrival of rock and roll in the 1950s and 1960s symbolized a growing generational divide among Americans, but it appeared to help erase the racial divide as young whites were attracted to black rhythm and blues. White musicians borrowed from African American R&B, and artists such as Jimi Hendrix, Janis Joplin, and Sly and the Family Stone defied categorization and appealed to both white and black audiences. But by the late 1970s music became more racially defined. In the early 1970s, rock and R&B audiences began to diverge, as FM "classic rock" stations played the longer songs of white rockers and disdained popular African American music. Soul music hit hard times. Isaac Hayes and Curtis Mayfield found greater success with film scores. Al Green emerged as one of the few successful soul/pop voices of the 1970s. Many R&B musicians, seeking to retain their popularity, created new niches. Aretha Franklin, Roberta Flack, and Barry White developed pop-oriented, jazzy, "soft soul" material for mainstream acceptance.

When rap music emerged in 1979, it rejected mainstream African American pop, the multiple identities and escape offered by disco, and the rhythm and blues ideals of integration and cultural pride to embrace black masculinity and emphasize the hard realities of urban life. For years, it remained high on the R&B

charts without gaining significant white audiences until the mid-1980s, reflecting the segregated music market of the late 1970s.

Disco

Disco grew out of late-1960s African American dance music and funk and the gay rights movement. Racially mixed gay discos popped up throughout New York and other large cities after the Stonewall rebellion, which fostered community and spaces for gay liberation, and African American and Latino pride. The scene rejected white macho rock and held out the lure of integration, crossing racial, gender, and cultural lines. With its uninterrupted, energetic music, same-sex dancers could meet, mingle, and dance freely. By 1973, *Rolling Stone* estimated there were about 2,000 disco clubs in the United States, a number that grew to over 15,000 by the end of the decade.

Unlike rock where the performers were central stage, disco relied more on dancers and DJs than musicians, turning the dance floor into the stage. DJs manipulated records to accentuate the bass and quickly transition between songs. The hustle, the main circular dance step of disco, emerged in New York around 1970 and was used in a group line dance, by couples, or as solo activity.

The disco craze naturally influenced musicians who wanted to appeal to the millions of Americans embracing the music. In 1974, the Jackson 5 recorded "Dancing Machine" at Motown, which sold 2 million copies. The integrated KC and the Sunshine Band had a string of disco hits in 1975, and Diana Ross, Barbara Streisand, ABBA, the Bee Gees, and many others recorded the sound that was sweeping America. Producer Jacques Morali created the Village People to appeal to gay disco audiences. Made up of three whites, two African Americans, and a Latino, the group parodied macho male stereotypes and sang songs replete with gay in-jokes, such as the hit "YMCA."

The music of Donna Summer, the "Queen of Disco," became ubiquitous in dance clubs. Born LaDonna Adrian Gaines, Summer had grown up singing in church; after high school, she joined the cast of *Hair* and toured and settled in Germany, where she became a pop singer. In 1975, Summer recorded "Love to Love You Baby," which became a huge radio and disco hit, mixing sounds of sexual pleasure with music in a long 17 minutes, perfect for the extended music desired by club dancers. She released several albums and a string of hits in the next few years, and her hard-edged and powerful voice made her one of the few recognized stars of disco music. Her 1979 album, *Bad Girls,* sold millions worldwide and won her a Grammy for the single "Hot Stuff." Twice Summer became the only woman ever to have two songs on Billboard's top three of the Hot 100 during the same week. She also symbolized liberated womanhood with her hits "Bad Girls" and "She Works Hard for the Money," energizing and inspiring women in particular on the dance floor.

The Village People (left to right: Victor Willis, Randy Jones, David Hodo, Felipe Rose and Glenn Hughes) in New York, 1979. The interracial band appealed to gay disco audiences. (Jean Louis Atlan/Sygma/Corbis)

The success of the 1977 film *Saturday Night Fever,* about Brooklyn working-class youths who lived for Saturday night dancing, triggered a disco craze. The music's characteristic pulsating beat and accompanying mirror balls above dance floors seemed to be everywhere. John Travolta emulators sported flashy dress, jewelry, and bravado.

New York's Studio 54 became a celebrity magnet, and clubs sprang up across the country. But the snob appeal of Studio 54, and numerous copycats, undermined disco's original inclusive ethos. When Nile Rodgers and Bernard Edwards, the creative forces behind the disco hit "Everybody's Dancing," were denied entrance to Studio 54 because of their towering Afros and platform shoes, they retreated to Rodgers's apartment in frustration and pounded out what became another disco hit of the era, "Le Freak."

Several scholars have attributed the increasing musical racial divide of the 1970s to the backlash by white male rockers to the disco phenomenon. On July 12, 1979, at Chicago's Comisky Park, young white baseball and rock fans notoriously burned 10,000 disco records and chanted "disco sucks!" Disco's popularity stimulated a backlash that often targeted its gay, working-class, Latino, and African American originators, and the music's increasing commercialization helped burn it out by 1980. Nonetheless, disco influenced techno, punk, and hip-hop music of the late 1970s and 1980s.

Punk and the Rejection of Hippie Rock

The word punk began appearing in popular music magazines like *Cream* in the early 1970s to describe the raw, distorted music of garage bands. But it quickly became a critical term used to characterize the outrageous behavior of youth who frequented New York nightclubs and hangouts that featured unsigned and noncommercial rock bands. As an artistic expression of a largely white and working-class culture, punk rockers—both performers and their fans—were staunchly realistic, antiauthoritarian, and nihilistic. Their attitudes stemmed from mounting frustration with the optimism of the 1960s counterculture and the growing cynicism toward the mass consumer culture of the 1970s, including the music establishment. They focused on illuminating the dysfunctions of modern capitalist life and rejecting the oppressive and conformist tendencies that perpetuated the circumstances.

By the mid-1970s, punk rock began to generate notoriety in both Britain and the United States. Understood as a reaction to the closed mindedness of the mainstream rock and roll establishment, punk rockers attempted to recapture the unrefined sound of bands like MC-5, the Velvet Underground, and Iggy Pop. Unlike Led Zeppelin, Pink Floyd, and the Grateful Dead, which rose to international fame through corporate sponsorship and commercial radio, punk rock developed its success through the intimacy of small venues and independent record labels. Punk relied on a devoted fan base to create self-sustained music scenes, smaller concerts, and an intimacy with audiences who often became as much a part of a show as the performers. Punk fans wore leather clothing, chains, and spiked hair and stage dived and slam danced at punk concerts.

Punk developed around the fringes of the abandoned and neglected areas of industrial society on the East and West Coasts. Cheap rents in the Bowery in New York City lured small-time club owners and rock promoters like CBGB. After an unsuccessful attempt to feature country, blue grass, and blues (hence the name CBGB), the club allowed unsigned bands that only played the music they wrote to perform, making CBGB a hot spot for fresh, original talent like the New York Dolls, Patti Smith, and the Ramones.

British bands propelled punk rock onto the international stage as a spectacle and fad. Influenced by the Ramones and other American punk artists, the Clash, the Stranglers, and the Sex Pistols enlivened the London Punk scene. Although hard to find in the United States, the Clash's first album, *The Clash,* became the biggest-selling import album in history. In 1977, the Sex Pistols toured America in support of their record *Never Mind the Bollocks, Here are the Sex Pistols.* The tour generated a great amount of media attention, which often sensationalized reports of violence and exposed many American youth to punk rock for the first time.

West Coast bands Black Flag, the Germs, the Circle Jerks and the Dead Kennedys helped spread punk at The Masque in Hollywood and the Mabuhay Gardens and On Broadway in San Francisco. The Dead Kennedys in particular made an impact on San Francisco, injecting wild left-wing sarcasm that attacked all sides of the political spectrum. Lead vocalist Eric Boucher (aka Jello Biafra) gained notoriety in 1979 when he ran for mayor of San Francisco against Diane Feinstein and Quentin Kopp. Biafra exposed the political process as a fiasco and took advantage of the media attention to mock politicians. On one occasion after Feinstein was seen sweeping the streets of San Francisco in front of a media crew, Biafra later showed up at her home with the press and vacuumed the leaves from her lawn. Biafra came in fourth place in the election with more than 6,500 votes.

Unlike the Sex Pistols, who signed with a major record label, many punk bands signed with small independent labels. Jello Biafra and the Dead Kennedys started their own label called Alternative Tentacles and eventually signed a number of punk and experimental bands in the 1980s. Greg Ghin, guitarist for Black Flagg, created the label SST.

The novelty of punk rock receded as the decade ended. The music establishment gradually incorporated bands into mainstream rock and offered an alternative to punk music that was seen as more commercially viable. The music known as New Wave, featuring acts like the B-52s, Talking Heads, and Devo, eventually drew attention away from the crude and informal origins of punk. Nevertheless, punk bands continued playing small venues and sustained a punk culture that was content without the media hype that presented the music as mere spectacle.

Country Western, Southern Rock, and the Symbolic South

Since the 1940s and the mass migration of whites and African Americans out of the South and to the North and West, country-western music had spread through the country via honky tonks and radio. In the 1970s, the counterculture and rock and roll infiltrated the genre. Inspired by the 1960s cultural rebellion, and resisting Nashville's control of the production of country western, the "Outlaws," including musicians Waylon Jennings and Willie Nelson, began creating music on their own terms, which included sporting long hair and recording in their home state of Texas. In the 1960s, singer-songwriter Nelson had defied the racism of the South by featuring Charley Pride in his tours, already establishing an "outlaw" reputation. Although he had many recordings, his *Red Headed Stranger* (1975) album combined country and gospel to explore themes of infidelity, vengeance, and redemption in a coherent narrative that became a commercial and artistic success. With songs that moved out of the country into the city and with their hit album *Wanted! The Outlaws* (1976), Jennings and Nelson produced a new crossover sound.

The Nashville rebels triggered a burst of creative country music centered in Austin, Texas, in the 1970s. Here country-rock and neowestern swing bands such as Asleep at the Wheel, and singer-songwriters such as Jerry Jeff Walker, Kris Kristofferson, and Michael Murphey recorded and achieved commercial success. Alternately called "hipbilly," "underground country," "redneck rock," or "progressive country," the new music spawned alternative country radio stations and concert venues throughout the nation as well as in southern cities. Austin shifted country power away from Nashville and became home to many performers and to a lively music scene at numerous clubs such as the Armadillo World Headquarters and Soap Creek Saloon, and at Austin's many outdoor festivals. The 1974 premiere of the PBS television series *Austin City Limits* extended the progressive country sound into millions of Americans' living rooms.

Other popular musicians, like Bob Dylan, had incorporated country sounds in their late 1960s and early 1970s recordings. Gram Parsons and Chris Hillman of the Byrds and later the Flying Burrito Brothers had successfully wedded traditional country music with hard rock. But it was the Allman Brothers and Lynyrd Skynyrd bands that made Southern rock popular in the early 1970s, reviving the African American blues and white country–infused influences of early rock and roll. Although embracing the long hair and rebelliousness of the counterculture, some bands also embraced white Southern conservatism. Lynyrd Skynyrd's signature "Sweet Home Alabama," written by lead singer Ronnie Van Zant, scolded Neil Young for criticizing white Southern men and represented a defiant defense of place and tradition. The band also defended white Southern conservatism, praising the likes of George Wallace and Richard Nixon.

Other Southern musicians created white blues bands, often evolving into hard rock blues bands. Edgar and Johnny Winter of Beaumont, Texas, each had several blues bands, including White Trash, which played at Harlem's Apollo Theater, before launching solo careers. ZZ Top of Houston, which incorporated Tex-Mex as well as hard-driving blues, became nationally known with the release of their third album *Tres Hombres* in 1972.

But more popular than the Southerners was a California group, the Eagles. Formed in 1971, their 1972 hit "Take It Easy" popularized country rock, a fusion of rock, blues, folk, and country western. San Francisco and Los Angeles spawned a host of musicians heard on alternative country radio stations in the early 1970s, including New Riders of the Purple Sage, Poco, Little Feat, and Jackson Browne.

Female singers, such as Linda Ronstadt, Bonnie Raitt, and Emmy Lou Harris, found success in country-blues rock and were very prolific with songwriting and successful albums during the decade. Even country singer Dolly Parton incorporated a rock beat in her 1970s songs.

ON VIEW: TELEVISION, FILM, AND FESTIVALS

The Golden Age of TV and New Images of American Society

In 1970, the Federal Communications Commission (FCC) enacted regulations to loosen network control of TV production and programming, which allowed a creative spurt by independent producers who directed their talents toward a more youthful audience, more cutting-edge content, and possibilities for syndication. During the decade, television reached its "golden age," with fine writing, acting, humor, and analysis of American social problems.

Humorists have often been more successful in subverting censorship to analyze society, but television remained cautiously trapped by McCarthyism through the rebellious 1960s. This was despite the fact that beginning in 1957, the U.S. Supreme Court had been upholding obscenity cases as protected by the First Amendment. The Smothers Brothers had provided topical political content in their variety hour program in the late 1960s, but a nervous CBS cancelled the show in 1969. Rowan and Martin's hip *Laugh-In* (1968–1973), with its fast-paced one-liners and stable of stars, was the only prime-time program at the turn of the decade with pointed social content; it remained on the air because of its dependable popularity.

In the 1970s, television ended its avoidance of realistic subjects to launch multiple successful, smart, urban comedies, especially on CBS. *The Mary Tyler Moore Show* (CBS 1970–1977) made a single career woman the most popular woman in America. Just as Mary Tyler Moore's career seemed on the skids after her successful debut on the 1960s *Dick Van Dyke Show,* her new show became a huge hit. Set in Minneapolis, Moore played Mary Richards, a producer of a local news show, with veteran newshound boss Lou Grant (Ed Asner). The series focused on comedic encounters in the workplace and in Moore's apartment, which her assertive and flamboyant Jewish neighbor Rhoda Morgenstern (Valerie Harper) frequently visited. Both Mary and Rhoda represented strong women characters surviving in the city without men. *Rhoda,* a spin-off, became the first major show in years to feature a Jewish character. Moore and her husband, Grant Tinker, founded MTM Enterprises and launched a string of successful, literate sitcoms that appealed to the educated American who had long disdained TV fare. In addition to *Rhoda,* the company produced *The Bob Newhart Show* and *Lou Grant.*

Another comedy series introduced in 1972, *M*A*S*H,* set the tone for the irreverent television culture of the decade. Co-creators/writers/directors Larry Gelbart and Gene Reynolds sought to capitalize on the popularity of the 1970 film of the same title, named for Mobile Army Surgical Hospital, about the dramatic-comedic misadventures of a team of American doctors in war-torn 1950s Korea.

All in the Family (1971–1979)

The quintessential 1970s television program that was hugely successful with both critics and viewers, *All in the Family,* was launched by producer Norman Lear as a pilot in 1968, modeled after a popular British sitcom that featured a working-class bigot. Fearing controversy, ABC turned down the pilot. CBS picked up a new pilot and the series in early 1971. Carroll O'Connor played the intolerant Archie Bunker; Jean Stapleton, his seemingly simple-minded but insightful wife Edith; Rob Reiner, his liberal student son-in-law, Mike Stivic; and Sally Struthers, his loving and hip daughter Gloria. Each week the family debated important issues of the day, including sex, race relations, religion, campus protests, the Vietnam War, economic exploitation, the presidency, fashion, and liberal politics. For example, when the African American family the Jeffersons moved into the neighborhood, Archie exploded, and numerous episodes dealt with Bunker's explicit racism and how the neighbors cunningly dealt with his ignorance. Bunker's convoluted logic in defense of his reactionary positions only highlighted and ridiculed those stances.

Rather than preaching to the audience, the show was well acted and snappy, with thoughtful and smart humor concerning timely critical issues. The program developed a devoted and large audience and became the number one series for five seasons, from 1971 through 1976, captivating 50 million viewers each week.

The show lost its controversial edge by the late 1970s, and in 1978, Rob Reiner and Sally Struthers left the cast. O'Connor kept his role going as he ran the neighborhood bar in a new series, *Archie Bunker's Place* (1979–1983).

There were several spin-offs from *All in the Family,* including *The Jeffersons,* where the African American family meets success and moves to a more upscale high-rise, and *Maude* (1972–1978). Beatrice Arthur played Maude, cousin of Archie Bunker, and a liberal feminist who kept her family together. The show addressed themes ranging from abortion to menopause to bankruptcy.

Despite its setting, its compelling antiwar humor captured large audiences as the unpopular war in Vietnam dragged on. Alan Alda, cast as the star character Hawkeye, helped shape the role to underscore the brutality and futility of battle. Even Lt. Col. Henry Blake, played by McLean Stevenson, ran a loose operation and tolerated the antics of Hawkeye and his fellow surgeon Trapper John (played by Mike Farrell after 1975), which included womanizing, drinking, and pranks on the rest of the unit, as well as humanistic encounters with Koreans. The character Klinger, played by Jamie Farr, wore women's clothing in a vain attempt to be sent home from the battlefield. *M*A*S*H* continued through 1983, lasting much longer than the actual war it covered, and continued through the decades to reach new generations in countless reruns.

The Mary Tyler Moore Show and *M*A*S*H* proved that social commentary could be not only broadcast but also popularly received by television audiences.

Saturday Night Live (1975–)

Saturday Night Live (SNL), introduced in 1975, followed two 1960s comedies with political stances, *Rowan and Martin's Laugh-In* and *The Smothers' Brothers Comedy Hour.* SNL attracted a youthful, cynical audience, and it targeted politicians and the drudgery of middle-class, suburban culture. When, in 1975, Johnny Carson announced that he no longer wanted reruns of his weeknight show played on the weekends, NBC entertained a pitch by writer Lorne Michaels for a Saturday night comedy modeled after *Laugh-In,* which would be live in front of a New York audience. The irreverent show became a hit, with parodies of newscasts, presidents, and pop stars. It influenced the development of comedy in subsequent decades, appealing to more youthful audiences with sexual and political innuendos.

Comedians Chevy Chase, Laraine Newman, Garrett Morris, Jane Curtin, Gilda Radner, Dan Aykroyd, John Belushi, and Bill Murray were among the original comedians of the Not Ready for Prime Time Players who made the 1970s show lively, edgy, funny, and smart. Each week a different celebrity guest-hosted, and, in addition to comedy sketches, the show featured a different musical group. The writers and cast combined the satirical with the silly, much like the British Monty Python's Flying Circus.

Lorne Michael's departure and a new cast in 1980 diminished SNL's political edge, despite the election of Ronald Reagan and what might appear to offer plenty of new material to mock. The show sustained and launched many comedians before they found success in film, other television, and radio, but it never had the universal youthful following or recognition as it did in its initial years in the mid to late 1970s.

Norman Lear created and produced in the early 1970s a number of successful comedies, including *All in the Family, The Jeffersons, Sanford and Son,* and *Maude,* which all had long lives and featured significant political content about race, class, the war, family relationships, and feminism.

Even the popular police show *Kojak* (1973–1978), starring Telly Savalas, explored the social conditions behind urban crime and racism in the criminal justice system. That police shows became the new "westerns" in the 1970s in providing a more complex understanding of violence and the "good" and "bad" guys reveals how Americans had come to understand life in their country in more nuanced ways.

In the new feminist age, the police genre provided women an opportunity to be as tough as men. Angie Dickinson played Sgt. "Pepper" Anderson in *Police Woman* (1974–1978), an edgy and liberated crime fighter. Although short-lived, *The Bionic Woman,* starring Lindsay Wagner, provided a model in the mid-1970s for the future glamorous action figure.

National Federation of Community Broadcasters (NFCB)

As television choices expanded in the 1970s, so did community radio stations that were volunteer powered and that offered noncommercial music, programming, and commentary. The NFCB formed in 1975 to serve and represent a growing number of community stations and grassroots efforts all across the country to begin new radio stations.

In 1973, a small number of community broadcasters then operating met in Seattle to develop a network to assist one another and to encourage others interested in building stations. Two years later, the National Alternative Radio Konvention (NARK) met in Madison, Wisconsin, to discuss the future of community radio. Representatives of some 40 community broadcast organizations agreed to form a national organization to represent community broadcasters and to influence national policy concerning noncommercial broadcasting. Several months later, the National Federation of Community Broadcasters was founded and established headquarters in Washington, D.C.

NFCB's initial mission was to help local stations with training manuals, obtaining FCC licenses, promoting the participation of minorities and women at all levels of broadcasting, and sharing programming tapes among member stations. The organization grew to advocate for the ideals and role of community radio and funding of local stations and projects. By the late 1970s and early 1980s, community radio had expanded dramatically, and the NFCB reached a membership of 75 stations and broadcasting groups.

Although many believed that *Charlie's Angels* (1976–1981) represented a step backward in its portrayal of women as sex objects, the stars, Kate Jackson, Farrah Fawcett-Majors, and Jaclyn Smith, were athletic and had adventures apprehending criminals, free from males bossing them around (their boss is never seen on screen). Tired of sexism in the Los Angeles Police Department, the women jump at the chance to work as private investigators. In its first season, almost 60 percent of American TV sets were tuned in to the show. As Anna Gough-Yates argues, although many feminist scholars saw the show as representative of a backlash against the feminist movement, the *Charlie's Angels* women embodied the sexual liberation of the single girl of *Cosmopolitan* rather than the more political *Ms.* The Angels pursued their careers rather than romance, lived alone, and depended on one another for companionship and solidarity. Yet they often used their sexuality, always in provocative or scantily clad costumes, as undercover fashion models, showgirls, or masseuses, to dupe criminals and bring to justice pimps and serial killers. It was the "commodity feminism" of the show, however—its emphasis on glamour, makeup, hairstyles, and clothes—that most disappointed feminists, even as female audiences found meaning in the Angels' version of liberation (Gough-Yates 2001, 97).

Television also launched new formats that reflected the introspective and self-help trends of the decade. In 1970, *The Phil Donahue Show* entered nationwide syndication as the first TV talk show. Donahue relocated the show's home base to Chicago in 1974. The program soon became a national phenomenon and demonstrated that popular television could emanate from the Midwest and involve ordinary Americans as both discussants and audience. Within a few years, the show was known simply as *Donahue,* and the host was one of the best-known Americans, spawning multiple talk-show imitations in subsequent decades.

The 1970s was also the golden age of public access television. In 1970, FCC Commissioner Nicholas Johnson published *How to Talk Back to Your Television Set,* which advocated the right of community groups to influence television programming and obtain limited public service airtime. This prompted a wave of local citizen groups to assert citizen interests in the airwaves, which were licensed to private businesses and provided monopoly regulation. Moreover, the Fairness Doctrine of the FCC required stations to provide programming that addressed issues of public importance and to ensure multiple perspectives aired on those issues. Public television ran strong in the 1970s, with hits such as the British dramatic series *Upstairs, Downstairs* and, for the younger set, *Sesame Street,* which combined the talents of Jim Henson's muppet-creating Creature Shop and the Children's Television Workshop. The integrated and multigenerational cast of *Sesame Street* helped children deal with serious themes as well as entertain with light-hearted humor in a fictional New York City neighborhood.

Prime-Time Ethnicity

In the late 1960s, television experimented with incorporating African Americans in a few key roles in *I Spy, Mission Impossible, Star Trek, The Bill Cosby Show,* and *Julia.* But these programs generally avoided civil rights themes and presented African American actors as universally upstanding, responsible, and middle class. In light of growing black militancy and frustration across the United States, late-1960s television promoted an integrationist model of "blacks just like whites." *The Mod Squad,* which ran from 1968 to 1973, was like other 1960s action shows that featured an African American character. But the character Linc Hayes, played by Clarence Williams III, presented a new street-smart and decidedly "black" figure, as part of a trio of former arrestees now working as hip undercover agents for the LA police.

Room 222, which premiered on ABC in 1969, featured as its star an African American professional, a history teacher, but it broached social themes. Each week the main character, played by Lloyd Haynes, wrestled with the trials of teaching urban youth at Walt Whitman High. The comedy/drama series with integrated cast met critical acclaim and won several Emmys in 1970 for broaching new subjects for television: sexism, racism, homophobia, and a teachers' strike. But audience interest declined after 1971, partly because of CBS movies shown at the same hour, and the series ended in 1974.

The success of these earlier programs, and the rising militancy of the black power and black pride movements, ushered in a "golden age" of African American programming, with an unrivaled number of African American cast and produced shows on television in the 1970s. In opening up new and diverse roles for African Americans, and in pursuing social content, television reached a new height of creativity and inclusion that attracted both white and black audiences.

Norman Lear and Bud Yorkin, recognizing the opportunity to reach mixed audiences, created a number of successful 1970s television shows that featured African American characters, including *Sanford and Son, Good Times, The Jeffersons, What's Happening!!, Carter Country,* and *Diff'rent Strokes. Sanford and Son,* with comedian Redd Foxx cast as the elderly junk dealer and a mostly black cast, became one of the most successful sitcoms of the decade. Foxx had worked the black "Chitlin' Circuit" for years and was well known in comedic circles for his raunchy humor that bragged of the black man's prowess over the white man. But he never broke into mainstream white audiences because he refused to moderate his language, so most came to know him through his television series. On *Sanford and Son,* which became NBC's most popular show from 1972–1976, Foxx incorporated African American oral traditions and folklore as well as his biting humor, minus his signature foul language. He brought black writers, performers, and comedians to a mainstream audience and addressed social issues relevant to African Americans at the time. It was one of the first shows to consider the urban African American underclass and problems with poverty, the police, and racism.

The greatest surprise success of the decade was the 12-hour miniseries *Roots,* based on the best-selling book by journalist Alex Haley, which aired on ABC in 1977. The multigenerational story about slavery told through the experiences of one family became the most watched program in television history, capturing 130 million viewers, most of whom were white.

Other nonfiction programming, including the PBS series *Black Journal* (1968–1977) and the music show *Soul Train,* which began broadcasting in 1970, appealed to African American audiences and reflected the networks' recognition of this important demographic for public service or advertising possibilities.

Asian Americans, Native Americans, and Latino Americans had less representation on 1970s television. *Chico and the Man,* broadcast on NBC from 1974 to 1978, was the first program to focus on a Mexican American community, an East Los Angeles barrio. But its Puerto Rican star Freddie Prinze, who played Chico Rodriguez, was controversial among Chicanos, and the lack of other Latino pro-

Scene still from the iconic 1970s television series Sanford and Son, *starring Red Foxx (left) and Demond Wilson. (Hulton Archive/Getty Images)*

gramming made Chicano groups suspicious and critical of what were perceived to be stereotypes presented by the show. After Prinze's suicide in 1977, the show never sustained its initial popularity. A non-Asian American, David Carradine, starred in the "Eastern Western" *Kung Fu,* from 1972 to 1975. Producers considered Bruce Lee for the part but saw him as too muscular—an intentional effort by Lee to counter the popular feminized view of Asians.

Television shows featuring people of color took place in the urban North and West, and representations of the mythic rural South, which featured whites only, declined in the 1970s. The rural themes and celebration of small-town life in the 1960s hit shows *The Beverly Hillbillies, The Andy Griffith Show, Petticoat Junction,* and *Green Acres* did not interest 1970s audiences, who looked for more socially relevant themes. The western, too, with its simplistic view of the world and celebration of the rural frontier, was absent from primetime by the mid-1970s, even though it had once dominated American TV.

There were some exceptions to the decline of rural, Southern content on television. *Hee Haw,* which premiered in 1969 and, in syndication, ran through

Did African American Comedy Television of the 1970s Stereotype?

Although the 1970s witnessed dramatic growth in the numbers of African American characters and programs, African American critics debated the value of what appeared on Americans' television screens. Many believed that some of the characters portrayed in some programs, especially the unemployed J. J., played by comic Jimmy Walker, on *Good Times,* perpetuated stereotypes of African Americans, something unacceptable in the Bill Cosby shows in the 1960s and 1980s. Some called the decade "the new age of minstrelsy" that reinscribed old stereotypes. Yet others criticized Cosby and the middle-class gloss of programs that denied the reality of life for most African Americans. They argued that much 1970s black TV presented a more complicated view of African Americans, with flaws, low-brow humor, and antics that many African Americans appreciated, regardless of white impressions. *Good Times,* for example, sought to present a sense of social consciousness that was missing from other programming. In fact, a survey in 1976 found that the three series with African American casts—*Sanford and Son, Good Times,* and *The Jeffersons*—were the top three favorite shows among African American audiences.

Scholars have recently revised the initial critical interpretations of African American sitcoms. Despite some stereotypical images, Christine Acham argues that African Americans used commercial television during the 1970s to articulate opposition to racism, control images about them, and present models of resistance. She notes that protests often revealed the "ideology of uplift" concerned about conveying positive African American images to white audiences (Acham 2004,5). Moreover, actors challenged the development of their characters and lines and disrupted traditional narratives about African American life. Many African American stars, including Esther Rolle and John Amos on *Good Times,* publicly criticized stereotypical elements of their show. Redd Foxx was one of the African American stars whom many criticized for perpetuating stereotypes, but he actually refused to accommodate white expectations for his character. Foxx famously walked off the set in 1974 because too few scripts were written by African Americans. His protest revealed that despite the plethora of shows appearing in the 1970s featuring African American actors, for the most part producers, writers, and directors were more often white.

the 1970s, plugged country content into the *Laugh-In* format. *The Waltons* became one of the most popular dramatic series of the 1970s. Set during the Great Depression of the 1930s, its rural farm family offered warm-hearted stories and homespun wisdom in the era of Watergate.

The New Hollywood

At the beginning of the decade, filmmakers and critics were optimistic about a "New Hollywood" that would usher in new aesthetics, technology, independence, democracy, and audiences. No longer did a few centralized studios control moviemaking, McCarthy-era censorship had been lifted, and television was no longer a foe but a partner. The 1970s witnessed what critic Pauline Kael called film's only "golden age" with a host of committed and idealistic artists and actors dealing with multiple serious social themes. Although film audiences were smaller than in the 1960s, 75 percent of moviegoers were under the age of 30, and those who were older were college educated, which pushed Hollywood to produce films and elevate stars that would appeal to these audiences. Actors like Jack Nicholson, for example, portrayed the generation's anarchistic values in *Five Easy Pieces* (1970) and *One Flew Over the Cuckoo's Nest* (1975). But if the success of Nicholson's earlier *Easy Rider* (1969) worried some that Hollywood would be overtaken by hippies, by the end of the decade, movies had become big business, with conglomerates purchasing studios for their "hit-making" potential.

Directorial rather than studio authority and the social movements that had pushed Americans to consider critical subjects opened filmmaking to new examinations of American society and mores in the 1970s. Films more often criticized the powerful, whether governments or corporations. Francis Coppola's *The Conversation* (1974) featured Gene Hackman as a surveillance man, who, like Richard Nixon, becomes obsessed with the practice that ultimately destroys him. Robert Redford's *All the President's Men* (1976) more explicitly explored the Watergate cover-up, based on the *Washington Post* reporters' account. Roman Polanski's 1974 film *Chinatown* also probed political corruption, a Water Department scandal in 1930s Los Angeles, and the depravity of capitalist greed. Comedians Woody Allen and Richard Pryor created and starred in films in the 1970s that analyzed American foreign policies, sexual mores, and racism. *The Big Fix* (1978) explored Moses Wine's (played by Richard Dreyfuss) role as an activist reliving the revolutionary 1960s. Paul Schrader's debut film *Blue Collar* (1978) portrayed class antagonisms in an auto plant, and his other film that year, *Hardcore,* featured George C. Scott as a father who was trying to save his daughter from destruction in a "snuff" film. *The China Syndrome* (1979), starring Jack Lemmon, Michael Douglas, and Jane Fonda, underscored how reliance on nuclear power threatened Americans' lives and environment.

The 1976 film *Network,* which swept the Academy Awards, even satirized the media and the celebrity culture that continued to sustain Hollywood. When long-time network news anchor Howard Beale (played by Peter Finch) is fired due to low ratings, he announces on the air that he will "blow his brains out" during an upcoming live broadcast and rants about media conglomeration. Ratings shoot up, reflecting the desperation of a viewing public for more populist arguments and sensational action, and Beale is granted his own show. He galvanizes the nation with his rant, "I'm as mad as hell, and I'm not going to take this anymore!" But if the film examines corporate ownership of the media and laments the passing of humanistic values, it, like many films of the 1970s, offers few solutions.

By the end of the decade, American filmmakers were openly confronting the Vietnam War that had ended in 1975. In 1970, the brazenly antiwar *M*A*S*H* and *Little Big Man* had used the themes of the 1950s Korean War and the 19th-century conquest of Native Americans to link current foibles in southeast Asia to previous U.S. imperial aggression. *Coming Home* (1978), Hal Ashby's film about returning Vietnam veterans who question both fidelity and patriotism, represented a string of late-1970s efforts to comment on the war that marked a generation. These films focused on the U.S. soldiers' and veterans' experiences and rarely contextualized the war or humanized the Vietnamese, whether friend or foe. In 1979, *Apocalypse Now* ended the decade with more ambivalence than the more explicit antiwar critiques that had opened the decade. Francis Ford Coppola described *Apocalypse Now* as more "operatic" and an "experience" than a movie. Its surreal portrait of war reflected a different kind of filmmaking and commentary.

Apocolpse Now represented a new kind of western, that former staple of Hollywood. The 1970s experimentation with this formerly dominant genre punctured old myths about the region and, more obliquely, the American imperial project. *Soldier Blue* (1970) examined cavalry atrocities. *Comes a Horseman* (1978), with Jane Fonda and James Caan, is set in the more modern West of the 1940s, and tells the story of two ranchers whose small operation is threatened both by economic hardship and the expansionist plans of a local land baron. Sam Peckinpah's bloody films, beginning with *The Wild Bunch* in 1969, ruptured the past innocent and clear good guy–bad guy delineations of the western myth. Mel Brooks' farcical *Blazing Saddles* (1974) parodied white corruption and bigotry in western settlement. Just as the African American character in *Blazing Saddles* challenged the notion of a "white" West and its racism, Sidney Poitier created the African American western, *Buck and the Preacher* (1972), to suggest the common interests of emancipated slaves fleeing the South and Plains Indians under attack by encroaching whites.

At the same time that Hollywood tackled serious themes, it also competed for declining audiences by producing tried-and-true genres to buttress profits. Sports and music appealed to the young. Sylvester Stallone's *Rocky* (1976) stimulated a series of sports films, and the successful 1970 concert film *Woodstock* was followed by the Mayles' Brothers film on Altamont. *Grease* (1978) and its celebration of the 1950s appealed to both older and younger audiences longing for more innocent times. *American Graffiti* (1972) and *Animal House* (1978), both set in 1962, bridged the nostalgic 1950s and 1960s with memorable soundtracks.

In 1977, *Saturday Night Fever* forever fixed disco as the sound of the decade in many Americans' memories.

Sequels and escapist horror films became other dependable Hollywood fare. *The Exorcist* (1973) and *Jaws* (1975) appealed to young audiences and distracted them from concerns of the times. *The Exorcist,* which fought and defeated imagined uncontrollable forces, proved that a box-office hit could be followed by a successful sequel. The great popularity of the British *Rocky Horror Picture Show* attracted young filmgoers to multiple midnight screenings, which became "events" where crowds dressed in character and shouted out lyrics and lines. The fiercely independent George Romero turned out a number of bloody films, including the popular *Dawn of the Dead* (1978), which had zombies frightening Americans in their favorite haunt, the shopping mall. *Invasion of the Body Snatchers* (1978) and *Alien* (1979) similarly frightened viewers even as they pulled them into theaters.

By the late 1970s, the new corporate film order asserted itself with predictable blockbusters rather than distinctiveness. The 1977 high-tech fantasies of *Star Wars* and *Close Encounters of the Third Kind* overcame earlier visions of the future that were more dystopian, as in *Soylent Green* (1973) and *Rollerball* (1975). And just as America's hegemony seemed to wane in the world, its denizens were subject to catastrophe on the screen, including tidal waves (*Poseidon Adventure,* 1972), urban skyscrapers on fire (*Towering Inferno,* 1974), and earthquakes (*Earthquake,* 1974). William Graebner argues that these films represented Americans' need to "hunker down" to survive economic decline, rising rates of divorce, and high energy prices.

New technologies made visual effects exciting to audiences, and screenings became happenings, which required Americans to see such blockbusters to join in ordinary conversations. Film studios engaged in super marketing so, regardless of film quality, new releases quickly earned big profits on the screen and in secondary commercial markets in everything from dolls to videocassette versions. By the end of the decade, the film, television, and music industries collaborated to win over consumers. They created spin-offs, associated one media form with another, and weakened the promise of independent statements of conscience that appeared at the opening of the decade. In 1979, most Americans rented escapist films, fleeing the realities of Watergate, Vietnam, and the energy crisis. Some attributed this trend to the growing conservatism of American audiences, others the profit motive and marketing of the industry, and some the new technological competition of cable and video.

The new Hollywood studios constructed "deals" that featured changing directors, actors, writers, and crews. Marlon Brando, who made millions for his small role in *Superman* (1978) reported that "there are no artists. We are businessmen" (quoted in Keyser 1981, 6). The major studios enhanced their profits through international distribution and growing worldwide demand. They also put the squeeze on local exhibitors by demanding 90 percent of the theater profits, which forced many local movie houses to close. The drive for profits, in fact, and the push toward more thrills, remakes, and sequels signaled the end of the "golden age."

Sex and Violence in Film

If Hollywood was less cautious about controversial political content, it wholeheartedly pushed sex and violence in bolder directions on the big screen. The film industry's Production Code, which had restricted the level of profanity, sex, and violence, changed to a new Classification and Rating System after 1968. The designations G, PG, R, and X separated adult from general audiences and expanded freedom of expression. By the 1970s, the bulk of Hollywood productions demanded parental discretion or an adult accompanying anyone under age 17. Francis Ford Coppola's 1972 film *The Godfather,* based on Mario Puzo's novel about postwar gangsters, represented this new direction of filmmaking. The big-budget, bloody tale of crime and capitalism swept the Academy awards that year.

Despite the liberal tilt of many 1970s films dealing with social themes, there also emerged films that portrayed American cities as crumbling into lawlessness and requiring repression and vigilante justice. Clint Eastwood's *Dirty Harry* films celebrated vigilantism, as the protagonist pursues child molesters and terrorists, despite being hampered by female partners and liberal mayors. Charles Bronson also embraced macho roles in films that called for retaliation, first in *Death Wish* in 1974.

A booming porn industry featured explicit sexuality, but more mainstream films also explored sexual infidelity and experimentation. *Shampoo* (1975), starring Warren Beatty and Julie Christie, represented the ambivalence of a generation about sexual mores including monogamy. In Paul Mazursky's *An Unmarried Woman* (1978), Jill Clayburgh stars as the jilted wife who must navigate the Manhattan singles world and reject the advances of men and remarriage to pursue her own dreams. The cult film *Harold and Maude* (1971) examined the meaninglessness of the rich, the Vietnam War, and social mores about gender, age, death, and relationships. Turning upside-down the standard older male–younger woman relationship model, the senior Maude, played by Ruth Gordon, shows a much younger Harold how to live life to its fullest outside customary social expectations.

Despite the era's focus on sex and sexuality, some films expressed discomfort with or struggled to accept homosexuality. One of *M*A*S*H*'s characters believes he is gay when he can't achieve an erection and plans on suicide, until the unit tricks him and places him in bed with a seductive nurse, restoring his manhood. The Shirley MacLaine character in *The Turning Point* admits that as a younger ballerina she had married her dancer husband to prove he was not gay.

Women and Film

Women regained some prominence on the screen during the 1970s, and a number of films reflected feminist themes. Jane Fonda's career in the 1970s reflected

Scene still from the 1971 comedy Harold and Maude, *starring Bud Cort and Ruth Gordon. Like other films of the decade, it explored social issues such as gender and age stereotypes, death, and the Vietnam War. (John Springer Collection/Corbis)*

changing roles for women as well as artists' connections to political events of the decade. First appearing as sexual fantasy in her 1960s films *Barbarella* and *Barefoot in the Park,* Fonda's growing feminist consciousness was apparent in 1971 in *Klute,* for which she won an Oscar for her role as an exploited call girl. Politically active Fonda and Vanessa Redgrave co-starred in *Julia* (1977), about the leftist writer Lillian Hellman and her political evolution during the 1940s struggle against fascism. *Julia* was one of the few films to focus on a serious relationship between two strong women. Anne Bancroft and Shirley MacLaine also starred as two friends in *The Turning Point* (1978), which explored the nature of relationships, loneliness, and the dilemma of the era for many women: the choice between career versus marriage. Bancroft also starred in *Lipstick* (1976) as a feminist lawyer prosecutor who had to defend the fashion-model rape victim from charges of provocative sexuality, reflecting the real-world attacks on rape victims' sexual history.

Although films of the 1970s featured more women stars than previous decades, sometimes their characters affirmed gender stereotypes. Some of the decade's most popular box-office female stars, such as Barbara Streisand, Goldie Hawn, and Raquel Welch often portrayed entertainers and sex goddesses rather than feminist figures. Diane Keaton, acclaimed for her acting in Woody Allen films of the decade, including *Annie Hall* (1977) and *Manhattan* (1979), oscillated between independence and vulnerability. In the 1977 film *Looking for Mr. Goodbar,* she plays a young woman, Theresa, who leaves her conservative Catholic family to live on her own in the city. Teacher by day, swinging single by night, she asserts her sexual freedom by picking up men. Just as she resolves to stop this reckless behavior, she is murdered by a man she picks up at a bar, who kills her for laughing at his inability to achieve an erection. Director Richard Brooks, like many commentators at the time, conflated women's liberation with sexual liberation, juxtaposing images of demonstrating feminists with Theresa's promiscuity. Anxieties over changing gender roles led many to believe that liberation may have freed women for more opportunities, but it also upset the "proper relationship between the sexes." The *Stepford Wives* (1975) similarly meet a pessimistic end. When Katharine Ross notices that her neighbors in her Connecticut suburb are eerily subservient to their engineer husbands, she discovers that the men have killed their wives and created in their place gynoids who happily cook, clean, and serve them. But she discovers the plot too late and loses this feminist battle; she is soon pictured mindlessly wandering grocery store aisles, another robotic Stepford victim.

Black Action Films

In 1971, Melvin Van Peebles released his low-budget, independent *Sweet Sweetback's BaadAsssss Song,* which marked the introduction of a new black film genre that subverted mainstream film narratives. In an era when African Americans were increasingly discouraged over the promise of nonviolent civil disobedience, the film's street-hustling hero, suddenly radicalized by aiding a young African American revolutionary who is beaten by white cops, meets violence with violence to defeat white corruption. Peebles wrote his own score and enlisted the new band Earth, Wind, and Fire to play it, and he found a few theaters in Detroit, New York, and San Francisco to show the film. *Sweetback* was hugely successful with African American audiences, who appreciated the male character's strength, authority, fashion taste, sexual prowess, and victory over "the Man." The film's commercial success demonstrated that an African American man could beat the white establishment rather than play traditional subservient or secondary roles on the screen. Nonetheless, Van Peebles charged that the X rating the film received reflected the racism of the system the film attacked. A year later, Gordon Parks Jr. directed *Super Fly,* which featured an African American gangster as a hero, outwitting both cops and drug lords, and again revealing the popularity of the new black action genre.

The *Shaft* series of the early 1970s emphasized physical daring along with traditional gangster themes. Shaft, played by Richard Roundtree, is a private investigator, neither cop nor criminal, who lives in the world of crime and is intimately familiar with his environment of New York City. The camera's focus on details of the city creates a sense of realism, even as cash and violence are the dominant themes. Shaft spends much of the film walking city streets, engaged in ordinary activities. The backdrop of institutional racism is apparent in ways that would not appear in a James Bond film. Despite his professionalism, for example, Shaft has difficulty hailing a cab. *Shaft* received an Oscar for Isaac Hayes' memorable score, and the film's success rescued MGM from a slump.

The number of and popularity of these films marked the 1970s as a black film decade, genre-twisting the white action films of the 1960s. Between 1970 and 1980, more than 200 films were released by major and independent studios that touted major African American characters and themes challenging "The Man." As Charles Kronengold notes, the films follow the gangster tradition in featuring characters who are articulate, elegantly dressed, and complex, despite their frequent turn to violence.

Although black and white audiences embraced these films, the NAACP and some other critics decried the violence and degrading images they believed perpetuated stereotypes, earning the genre the nickname "blaxploitation." But other African American artists defended the films. Fred Williamson, a former pro-football player and the star of many black action films, questioned the term "blaxploitation," asking who exactly was exploited.

Because of the predictability of action film plots, the African American films introduced other elements that attracted audiences, particularly fashion, urban life, and appealing soundtracks. In the Cleopatra Jones movies, the camera frequently pauses on star fashion model Tamara Dobson and her new outfits. Isaac Hayes, *Shaft*'s composer, was able to experiment with new production techniques, arrangements, and melodies, reflecting the early 1970s creative period in soul and funk. In a decade when R&B was losing its mass appeal, African American musicians sought musical parts in the films.

Unlike white action films, many black action films featured women as main characters. Actress Pam Grier appeared often as the African American heroine, most known for her roles in *Coffy* and

Soul singer and composer Isaac Hayes performs in Chicago, 1973. Like other African American artists, Hayes found new audiences by composing scores for the black action films of the 1970s. (John H. White/National Archives)

Foxy Brown (1974). Foxy "had attitude" and was popular with African American women for her courage, independence, self-confidence, and sexuality. In interviews, Grier noted that the films "redefined sexuality for America." Yet as Stephanie Dunn argues, Grier's characters often affirmed sexist and racist notions of the African American female as dangerously erotic, and the sexual violence in the films is only directed at women (Dunn 2003).

The popular representations of African American women and men reflected the shifting racial and gender politics of the 1970s. By the mid-1970s, the black action films had become formulaic and lost audiences. "White exploitation" film directors like Martin Scorcese, Brian DePalma, Francis Ford Coppola, and others found other genre opportunities, but the blaxploitation films became the fixed form that African American cinema of the 1970s was forced to follow, its directors having few choices for other work.

The Public Square: Fairs, Music Festivals, and the Bicentennial

Images of early 1970s rock festivals and the bicentennial celebrations of 1976 underscored the contrasting ways in which Americans came together in, and sometimes contested, public spaces. The diversity of leisure-time activities revealed the divisions and preferences among Americans by generation, race, and region.

Demographic and cultural changes, too, shaped the ways in which Americans gathered, paraded, and celebrated. The shrinking rural small town and growing suburbs meant that fewer people attended county fairs and more spent time in shopping malls. Gentrification and urban renewal also moved people out of some city neighborhoods, threatened community traditions, and fashioned new annual celebrations. For example, the popularity of rock festivals in the early 1970s, urban unrest, and efforts to revitalize the central city ushered in annual blues and music festivals in cities across the country in the 1970s. New traditions emerged as rural and urban places changed, ethnic groups asserted their identities, and new immigrants coalesced in efforts to perpetuate treasured practices and celebrations. Two of the decade's most well-known public events, the World's Fair and the nation's bicentennial, reflected the divisions and new concerns facing American society in the 1970s.

The 1974 Spokane World's Fair incorporated concerns from the decade in its theme: "Celebrating Tomorrow's Fresh New Environment." World's fairs in earlier decades had showcased emerging technology and hopes for the consumerist future, but the 1974 fair recognized a more sober reality. Technological change no longer surprised, and the limits of productivity, expressed by the oil and environmental crises, demanded new themes to attract visitors. Spokane,

Odunde Street Festival in Philadephia

The Odunde Street Festival in Philadephia was one of the new cultural festivals that emerged in the 1970s. Influenced by the black pride movement, a group of sisters and friends opened the Uhuru Hut, a boutique selling African clothes, jewelry, and arts, on South 23rd Street. Like many new African American–owned businesses, the shop sought to provide a gathering spot as well as to sell wares. One of the owners, Lori Hernandez, made a trip to Nigeria in 1972 and learned of the Oshun festival, held annually in honor of the river. She returned to Philadelphia determined to organize an African American festival by the city's river.

In 1975, the first Odunde (a Yoruba greeting for "Happy New Year") festival was held with the Hut as one of the sponsors. Women from the Southwest Center City Citizen's Council involved young people in marching, singing, dancing, and creating folk arts. The festival in the primarily working-class African American neighborhood grew rapidly each year, but by the late 1970s, the neighborhood faced a number of challenges. A citizens' coalition successfully fought off a planned expressway route that would cut through the area but could not halt small business owners on South Street from selling out to speculators, who used urban renewal (called "black removal" by locals) money to develop properties. An increasingly gentrified central city threatened to remove the festival, but organizers insisted on keeping Odunde rooted in its neighborhood.

Washington, represented the smallest city ever to host a world's fair. City businessmen had advanced the idea to accomplish two goals: to bring urban renewal to the dying downtown, and to clean up the Spokane River, which cut through the city and had become cluttered and polluted after a century of industrial development.

Expo '74 may have delivered a cleaned-up, 100-acre park to Spokane, but it was less successful in educating its 5.6 million visitors about environmental concerns. Critic Calvin Trillin noted that the American Petroleum Institute and National Coal Institute had prominent exhibits, but environmental groups had none. The American Pavilion included a display warning about auto fuel consumption, but the General Motors Pavilion featured a low-mileage camper van (Rettmann 1994, 13).

The 1974 Spokane World's Fair symbolized both the decade's contradictions and the end of 20th century American efforts to demonstrate uncritical faith in technology and the future. Where in earlier decades cities had vied for the privilege of hosting a world's fair, only Vancouver, British Columbia, and New Orleans attempted to host international expositions after 1974. Extensive commercial theme parks, such as Disney's Epcot, replaced the fantasy world of world's fairs.

On July 4, 1976, two years after President Nixon's resignation and a year after the fall of Saigon, the nation held a giant birthday party extolling the country's 200 years as a noble experiment in democracy. More than 60,000 public festivities celebrated the nation's past and future, with small towns especially staging elaborate old-fashioned pie-eating contests, parades, and town beautification campaigns. Red, white, and blue colors appeared everywhere—on community trashcans and fire hydrants and just about everything businesses sold. New York City, just recently bailed out from bankruptcy by the federal government, staged the most elaborate bicentennial celebration, filling its harbor with an armada of historic ships from 32 nations. The evening's massive fireworks show over the Statue of Liberty was viewed by millions who tuned in to one of the three national television networks that covered the display. In Washington, D.C., visitors celebrated a National Pageant of Freedom, and only small groups of demonstrators protested the affair. However, Philadelphia's law-and-order mayor, Frank Rizzo, scared away thousands of protestors as well as bicentennial parade participants when he claimed that his city would use force to stop any leftist violence.

Although for the most part festive and patriotic, bicentennial celebrations often had a somewhat ambivalent tone. Coming on the heels of the Vietnam War and Watergate, many Americans felt somewhat uneasy about unconditional

Tall ships anchored in New York Harbor in July 1976, part of the nation's 200th anniversary celebration. Millions of Americans celebrated the Bicentennial in over 60,000 public festivities. (National Oceanic and Atmospheric Administration)

Vortex Festival, Portland, Oregon, August 1970

In the summer of 1970, fearing that 50,000 protestors calling themselves the People's Army Jamboree would disrupt the American Legion national convention scheduled for Portland, Oregon, Gov. Tom McCall agreed to sponsor a week-long rock festival at a nearby state park. Approached by a small group of hippies who convinced him the festival would draw protestors away from the city, McCall agreed to devote state resources and encourage businesses to support the event. McCall set aside McIver State Park for the festival and ordered the police and Army National Guard to keep their distance as they maintained peace.

More than 100,000 young people attended the Vortex Festival, which was reported by the media to feature sex, nudity, drugs, and rock and roll. Dr. Cameron Bangs of Oregon City volunteered to oversee health care and kept a diary of his week, reporting that the biggest problem was LSD that caused panic among many concertgoers who were hallucinating for the first time.

Despite following on the heels of the underprepared Woodstock and violent Altamont festivals, Vortex illustrated how public officials could embrace the rock festival as a means of taming youthful energy. Organizers for the anti-Legionnaire protest were frustrated by the festival's ability to siphon away potential protestors. This revealed the tensions between the counterculture and radicals and signaled how the 1970s era of drugs and sexual liberation might distract young people from the pressing issues of the day, including the Vietnam War.

celebration of the nation's history. The bicentennial marked the competing notions of American political culture. In 1974, facing widespread criticism for partisanship, President Nixon disbanded the American Revolution Bicentennial Commission and turned over planning and payment responsibility to local and voluntary groups. State commissions raised funds from corporations and some tax revenues, and businesses used the celebration to market new products. Many observed these developments with some cynicism as communities scrambled to raise funds to support local activities.

Not everyone celebrated the nation's checkered past and present. Many African Americans, including some farmers in the South who protested continuing racial and economic injustices, refused to participate in the festivities. Others created alternative commemorations: 100,000 in San Francisco joined in a Gay Freedom Day parade, and Native American movement activists acknowledged an alternative holiday, the Battle of the Little Bighorn and the defeat of Gen. George Custer. Some used the opportunity to push for greater inclusion in understanding the past. The Afro-American Bicentennial Corporation formed in 1970 to lobby the government to include African American history sites on the National Register of Historic Places. Economist and activist Jeremy Rifkin, founded the

People's Bicentennial Commission in 1971 to reclaim the revolutionary character of the celebration. A growing conservative movement also used the bicentennial to criticize what they viewed as rising government power, likening everything from busing to taxes as oppressive.

If the bicentennial revealed divisions among Americans, it also stimulated an appreciation for family and local history and increased the number of museums and genealogical societies. The revival of traditional crafts such as quilting, the popularity of heritage tourism, and Alex Haley's best-selling novel *Roots* (1976) revealed an intense interest in the familiar and local, even if Americans were ambivalent about the national story. Christopher Capozzola finds "equal parts quest and escape" in how Americans observed the bicentennial, on the one hand searching for an imagined peaceful past while on the other hand avoiding bigger national questions (Capozzola 2004, 39).

In Print

Fact, Fiction, Fantasy, and Bookselling

In the same way that filmmaking expanded genres and took risks in the 1970s, even as it increasingly supported blockbuster hits, so too did book publishing experience a renaissance, expanding the range of literature produced as well as dramatically increasing volume of sales. The expansion of the U.S. population, its increased educational levels, and more leisure time all made book reading and new titles more popular. The expansion of book marketing and paperback sales made bookselling a profitable industry, and corporations actively sought to acquire publishing companies, initiating the pattern of corporate mergers and takeovers that accelerated through subsequent decades.

Best sellers, as John Sutherland reminds us, tell us much about a particular society at a particular point in time in revealing tastes of readers and marketing emphases of booksellers. The commercial machinery and consuming public, which was now international with ready translations, converged in the 1970s to sell millions of copies of Richard Balch's *Jonathan Livingston Seagull* (1970), James Michener's *Centennial* (1974), and Erica Jong's *Fear of Flying* (1973). The interests of the decade, including personal growth, history, and women's liberation, were reflected in the stories people wanted to read. The production of paperback best sellers and the growth of new genre lines, such as soft-porn historical romance for women readers, marked the decade.

Despite the protests by the Authors' Guild and other writers' groups over the increasing commercial ruthlessness of the industry, many writers accommodated the new trends. Mario Puzo, for example, wrote two well-received novels that netted few monetary returns until he decided to pitch a full-blown gangster saga to Putnam. *The Godfather* became one of the top paperback best sellers of all

Regional Writers: The Montana Gang

In 1974, Native American writer James Welch published *Winter in the Blood,* about the grim realities of reservation life and the possibilities of Native American community in northern Montana. Welch had studied writing with poet Richard Hugo at the University of Montana. The critical acclaim and popular success of Welch's first novel encouraged many other Montana authors that they could write about the place in which they lived. Norman Maclean, retired from the University of Chicago, published the successful novel *A River Runs Through It* (1976), about flyfishing and growing up the son of a minister in western Montana, which was nominated for a Pulitzer Prize. Ivan Doig's autobiographical *This House of* Sky (1978) about growing up on a sheep ranch in the state was nominated for the National Book Award. Through the 1970s, more attention came to Montana writers, who reached a public fascinated with exotic stories of the Mountain West and critics who recognized the power of literature about struggling people rooted in a real place.

Tom McGuane became known as the leader of the "Montana gang"—a group of writers, Hollywood celebrities, and artists—who settled in the 1970s in a valley north of Yellowstone National Park and had a significant impact on American cultural life. McGuane reached critical acclaim with *The Bushwacked Piano* in 1971, and his *Ninety-two in the Shade* was nominated for a National Book Award. He also nurtured and inspired visiting writers. Jim Harrison visited McGuane and wrote *Legends of the Fall* (1979), a compelling novella about Montana. In 1973, Richard Brautigan wrote the novel *The Hawkline Monster: A Gothic Western* in a rented tourist cabin at the Pine Creek Lodge and Store near McGuane's ranch. Brautigan was impressed with the machismo and success "Montana Gang" writers attained by turning their novels into movies. He sold the screenplay rights of *Hawkline* to Hal Ashby, director of the movie *Being There.* A year later Brautigan bought a 42-acre ranch near the Pine Creek Lodge and Store overlooking the Absaroka Mountains, near actors Peter Fonda, Jeff Bridges, and Warren Oates, film director Sam Peckinpah, and painter Russell Chatham.

Women writers found it difficult to break the Montana machismo mystique. Mary Clearman Blew became a noted short-story writer with her collection *Lambing Out* (1977), which countered the romance of Western life with struggling women in the ranchlands of central Montana.

time, and Puzo, and later Francis Coppola who made a film from the novel, admitted that they produced the popular book and movie to bankroll "better" projects. Also new were the sellers—in addition to purchasing from traditional bookstores, Americans picked up popular paperbacks such as *The Godfather, The Exorcist,* and *Love Story* from supermarkets and newsstands.

Fewer of these works were praised by literary critics, and fewer still gained the kind of long-standing attention that integrated their reading and discussion in colleges, universities, and journals. Literature experimented with new forms, challenging modernist concepts of boundaries and genres to embrace "postmodernism," which subverted and analyzed assumptions about universal truths. "Deconstruction," which had its first American boom in literary criticism in the mid-1970s, questioned the reliability of all kinds of assumptions, texts, and narrators. Writers like Joyce Carol Oates, Thomas Pynchon, and Kurt Vonnegut invoked the unconscious, social critique, skepticism, and dark humor. Yet other writers such as John Updike and Saul Bellow continued in the realistic tradition in the 1970s.

Literature also reflected the social and political interests of the era. Works examined technology, nuclear weaponry, and corporate or government dominance. Minority, gay/lesbian, and women writers wrote of poverty, discrimination, and oppression. Writers of color pushed a more militant analysis of race and culture in the United States, as represented by African Americans LeRoi Jones (Amiri Baraka) and Ishmael Reed, with *Mumbo Jumbo* (1972); Chicano novelist Rudoflo Anaya, with *Bless Me, Ultima* (1972); and Chinese American Frank Chin, with *Aiiieeeee! An Anthology of Asian-American Writers* (1974). Native American Leslie Marmon Silko's acclaimed *Ceremony* (1977) blended myth and the horrors

Artist Ron Blackburn paints an outdoor wall mural in downtown Chicago, 1973. The inclusive nature of public art made it integral to the Black Arts Movement, which sought to develop a national black culture and flourished in American cities in the 1970s. (John H. White/National Archives)

The Black Arts Movement

The Black Arts Movement was a loose network of African American artists and intellectuals who from the mid-1960s to the mid-1970s attempted in a variety of ways to develop or recover an authentic national black culture linked to African American popular culture. Many have described the Movement as "the cultural wing" of the Black Power Movement. Although often sharply divided over politics and aesthetics, Black Arts participants found enough common ground to produce national conferences, journals, cultural organizations, and widely read anthologies.

Some key anthologies that provided the intellectual framework for the movement in the 1970s included *The Black Woman* (1970), edited by Toni Cade Bambara, the first major African American feminist anthology; *The Black Aesthetic* (1971), edited by Addison Gayle Jr., which articulated a Black Arts theory and showcased the earlier influences of writers such as W. E. B. Du Bois and Langston Hughes; Stephen Henderson's *Understanding the New Black Poetry* (1972); *New Black Voices* (1972), edited by Abraham Chapman; and Eugene Redmond's *Drumvoices, The Mission of Afro-American Poetry: A Critical History* (1976).

The widespread rejection of the term "Negro" and the adoption of "black" as the designation of choice for people of African descent to indicate identification with both the diaspora and Africa is another enduring legacy of the Black Arts movement. *Negro Digest* changed its name to *Black World* in 1970, reflecting editor Hoyt Fuller's view that the magazine ought to be a voice for black people everywhere. The journal published an impressive range of quality poetry, fiction, criticism, drama, reviews, reportage, and theoretical articles, and gave out literary awards.

By 1970, Black Arts theaters, cultural centers, and organizations of nationalist-minded visual artists, writers, dancers, and musicians flourished in cities and college campuses throughout the country, including Barbara Ann Teer's National Black Theatre in New York, Baraka's Spirit House Movers in Newark, Val Grey Ward's Kuumba Theatre Company in Chicago, and Ron Milner and Woodie King's Black Arts Midwest of Detroit. In Los Angeles, the Ebony Showcase, Inner City Repertory Company, and the Performing Arts Society of Los Angeles (PALSA) thrived. BLKARTSOUTH, led by Tom Dent and Kalamu ya Salaam, grew out of the Free Southern Theatre in New Orleans and was instrumental in encouraging African American theater development across the South from the Theatre of Afro Arts in Miami, Florida, to Sudan Arts Southwest in Houston, and the formation of the Southern Black Cultural Alliance.

Poetry, drama, music (particularly avant-garde jazz), and public murals were the artistic genres that dominated the Black Arts Movement. This was due to the movement's close connection to Black Power politics and the fact that these forms were more accessible and easily performed at rallies, demonstrations, and other communal events.

Continued on next page

The Black Arts Movement, Continued

Influential Black Arts activists included writers Amiri Baraka, Ishmael Reed, and Askia Muhammad Touré; poets Sonia Sanchez and Nikki Giovanni; playwright Ed Bullins; critic Harold Cruse; and musicians Archie Shepp and Sun Ra. Many African American popular musicians were heavily influenced by Black Power and Black Arts. James Brown's hit "Say It Loud (I'm Black and I'm Proud)" became an anthem of the period. Many feminists criticized the movement for its hyper-masculinism and homophobia, but as James Edward Smethurst notes in his exhaustive study, the Black Arts Movement promoted women's work, women were often at the forefront of developing Black Arts projects, and women leaders openly challenged paternalistic views and actions, forcing many men to revise their ideological stances and even apologize for past sexist language.

The Black Arts Movement declined by the mid-1970s, along with the Black Power Movement and the Black Panther Party. Government repression of black militants, internal divisions, the economic recession that hit financially strapped African Americans communities particularly hard, and growing mainstream and commercial acceptance and demand for African American arts sapped the Black Arts Movement's fragile economic position. Larger success often weakened possibilities for the smaller, independent African American enterprises. For example, Ntozake Shange's *For Colored Girls Who Have Considered Suicide When the Rainbow Is Enuf,* opened on Broadway in 1976 even though it had been developed at Woodie King's New Federal Theatre of the Henry Street Settlement on the Lower East Side.

Nonetheless, the movement continued to influence artistic production over the next decades. It helped spawn the field of African American Studies as well as African American–oriented art galleries, theaters, book imprints, and academic book series. Many artists, such as Toni Morrison and various rappers, continued to embrace what was essentially a Black Arts stance in their work after the 1970s.

of war, and poet Joy Harjo, in *The Last Song* (1975), helped bring Native American poetry to a larger critical audience. Lesbian poet Adrienne Rich received the National Book Award in 1973 for *Diving into the Wreck* and shared her acceptance of the award with fellow nominees and African American writers Audre Lorde and Alice Walker, who also dealt with lesbianism, racism, patriarchy, and sexuality. Feminist criticism developed along with feminist literature. Elaine Showalter's *A Literature of Their Own* (1977) and Sandra Gilbert and Susan Gubar's *The Madwoman in the Attic* (1979) pioneered the study of women writers, even if focused on middle-class white women.

On the lighter side, Erma Bombeck, who wrote a syndicated humor column for many newspapers, became enormously popular in the 1970s. Her best-selling books, including *The Grass Is Always Greener over the Septic Tank* (1976)

Comic Books

Comic books, seeking to appeal to youthful readers influenced by social movements and the counterculture, revised the 1950s-era Comic Magazine Association of America code that prohibited subject matter that questioned police and government institutions or hinted at sex or drugs. By the early 1970s, comics incorporated socially relevant themes related to black power, the Vietnam War, women's rights, and critiques of authority figures. Former cold war figures such as Iron Man and Captain America underwent political conversions and focused on social problems rather than communists, and even questioned why the United States was fighting a war in Vietnam.

By the mid-1970s, comic book creators were casting about for new ideas as readership steadily declined. Inspired by the success of blaxploitation films, in 1972 Marvel introduced African American superhero *Luke Cage, Hero for Hire* who struggled against racism, pimps, drug dealers, and poverty in the inner city. Other efforts to introduce minority superheroes met less commercial success. Marvel's White Tiger, the first Latino superhero, remained a shadowy support figure to Spider-Man, and Marvel's first Native American superhero, Red Wolf, was discontinued after nine issues. Marvel met more success with its Chinese hero Shang-chi in *Master of Kung Fu,* which ran from 1974 to 1983.

With the influence of feminism in the 1970s, the comic book business naturally sought to introduce female characters and attract female readers. But much as white writers did not overcome stereotypes in their depiction of minority figures, so too were female superheroes often caricatured for their "women's lib" outlooks. Even Wonder Woman, praised by Gloria Steinem and turned into a popular prime-time television show in the mid-1970s, appeared to lose some of her power in the decade, represented by her concern with fashion. Other characters, such as the Cat and Night Nurse, offered more promising feminist roles, but the comic books did not sell well and were dropped after a handful of issues. White boys continued to be the main purchasers of comic books and determined the subject matter.

and *If Life Is a Bowl of Cherries, What Am I Doing in the Pits?* (1978), appealed especially to millions of women who struggled with childrearing and family life and who appreciated Bombeck's bittersweet humor and advice. Although Bombeck wrote about suburban family life and what seemed to be traditional gender roles, she was a strong supporter of the Equal Rights Amendment and campaigned for its passage.

The Age of Narcissism and the Search for Meaning

In the 1970s, the search for enlightenment, recovery, and self-improvement—represented by the hundreds of thousands of groups for women, gays, drug abusers, domestic violence victims, new parents, and the overweight, among others that sprang up during the decade—inspired the publication of self-help books. Inexpensive paperbacks readily available in bookstores and supermarkets offered to help readers obtain financial success, spiritual growth, healthier and thinner bodies, more satisfying sex, and more effective parenting. A 1978 article in the *American Psychologist* counted about 200 popular books on child care alone.

The burst of alternative religions and psychotherapies revealed an accelerated effort to find individual meaning and stability in life, which appeared in contrast to the collective sense of 1960s social change. But the 1960s and 1970s counterculture promoted personal liberation, and it was not surprising that efforts to achieve greater spiritual awareness and physical, mental, and emotional well-being would grow in the 1970s. The goal of the self-help movement was personal transformation as a way to affect social change, and publications outlined the humanizing revolution of the individual.

Many conflated the self-help trend with the New Age movement, but the latter focused on spirituality and redirecting religion largely from more patriarchal traditions to those that were feminist and egalitarian. Self-help, largely based on psychology, seeks to direct readers toward some knowledge about the self that will assist in helping them function more profitably within modern society.

Werner Erhard's "est" (Erhard Seminar Training) was an example of the self-improvement courses that operated through the 1970s. Erhard's training borrowed practices and principles from the numerous Eastern philosophies that had been introduced; est based its teachings on Zen training, Scientology, and the writings of Alan Watts. Erhard, formerly Jack Rosenberg, experimented with human potential movements in California in the 1960s and created his own approach in 1971, which involved intense est weekend training sessions that shouted insults at participants to help them "take responsibility" and acknowledge their self-transformation. The San Francisco est seminars graduated as many as 100,000 people by the late 1970s.

New voices in the field of psychology that focused on self-actualization and individual human potential became prominent and raised questions about psychoanalytic and behavioral theories and practices. In the 1960s, Abraham Maslow and other clinical psychologists reacted against the emphasis on behavioral and experimental psychology and created the Association for Humanistic Psychology. Rollo May's book *Love and Will* became a best seller in 1970 and one of the central psychological texts that reached a wide audience in the decade. An existentialist, May argued that modern society had distorted love and will and had created a more alienated, powerless society, where sex had replaced love. May recognized the value of the sexual revolution but proposed ways of reasserting a fuller expression of love.

Psychiatrist Eric Berne developed Transactional Analysis (TA) as a new method of conducting group therapy that provides group members concepts by which to analyze their interactions with one another. TA became a cultural phenomenon in the 1970s and appealed to many because of its populist character. One of Berne's students, Thomas A. Harris, wrote one of the books that defined the decade, *I'm OK, You're OK,* which was actually written in 1967 but made the best-seller lists from 1971 through 1973.

Another best-selling pop psychology book of the 1970s, *How to Be Your Own Best Friend,* by Mildred Newman and Bernard Berkowitz, revealed the attraction of self-attention in its title. Other best sellers of the decade—Jerry Greenwald's *Be the Person You Were Meant to Be* (1973), Wayne Dyer's *Your Erroneous Zones* (1976), Dr. Joyce Brothers' *How to Get Whatever You Want in Life* (1978), and Robert Ringer's *Looking Out for #1* (1977)—clearly emphasized the needs of the individual and countered the broader collective political spirit of the era.

Conservative and radical critics alike fired their disgust at America's obsession with self-help and, in their view, abandonment of traditional forms of community. Peter Marin described "The New Narcissism" in the October 1975 edition of *Harper's Magazine* as a retreat from morality, history, and community. Tom Wolfe, in his acerbic essay "The Me Decade and the Third Great Awakening" compared what he viewed as trivial and meaningless self-reflection to the mid-18th century enthusiastic religious revival: "Through group therapy, marriage counseling, and other forms of 'psychological consultation' they can enjoy the same Me euphoria that the very rich have enjoyed for years in psychoanalysis." The New Man, according to Wolfe, had created the "greatest age of individualism in American history!" (Wolfe 1976, 40). In his book *Psychobabble: Fast Talk and Quick Cure in the Era of Feeling* (1977), Richard Rosen criticized the self-help industry for applying psychological principles in a superficial way. Christopher Lasch found this turn to self as emblematic of the deep emptiness of American culture. In his book *The Culture of Narcissism* (1979), Lasch argued that the search for meaning had constituted an "antireligion" in elevating self above all others, weakening social ties, and incorporating a "narcissistic inability . . . to feel oneself part of a historical stream."

But critics tended to inflate the movement's silliest excesses rather than appreciate a genuine quest for meaningful community and self-fulfillment. For example, *Ms.* magazine began featuring self-help columns beginning in 1972, but these shifted the traditional focus of women's magazines from home and beauty concerns to personal transformation and liberation. So self-help often blended individualism with larger collective interests in sisterhood. The feminist movement's decentralized consciousness-raising activities reflected this larger trend in society and saw personal growth as liberating rather than viewing it as reactionary.

Whether the 1970s represented more self-indulgence than previous or subsequent decades is debated, but certainly, the oracles of wisdom seemed more prominent, due to the more aggressive mass marketing, chain bookstores, and consolidation of the publishing industry. As part of the expansive and exploratory mood of the decade, Americans turned to self-education and cooperative forms of self-help to improve society in ways that the political system had failed.

The Press

The 1970s is often remembered as the heyday of the American press, due in large part to Carl Bernstein and Bob Woodward's expose of the Watergate scandal in *The Washington Post,* later released as a book, *All the President's Men.* Bernstein and Woodward relied heavily on information from an anonymous source, "Deep Throat," identified as former FBI agent Mark Felt in 2006. The film *All the President's Men* (1976), starring Robert Redford and Dustin Hoffman, provided millions of Americans their impressions of newspaper work as serious and critical to a democracy. The popular and award-winning TV series *Lou Grant* (CBS 1977–1982), starring Ed Asner, reinforced the notion that serious ethical and social concerns preoccupied journalists.

The social ferment of the times, and some Supreme Court decisions, pushed the press to pursue more aggressively wrongs in American society. The 1971 Pentagon Papers decision ensured that newspapers could publish without gov-

Bob Woodward (left) and Carl Bernstein were the Washington Post *staff writers who investigated the Watergate case, April 29, 1973. Their work convinced many Americans that journalists should pursue serious social concerns. (Bettmann/Corbis)*

The "Underground" or Alternative Press

During the 1960s, an "underground" press emerged on college campuses and in cities to counter the prevailing news stories that relied on government officials' versions of events, especially regarding the Vietnam War. Borrowing the "underground" label used by antifascist presses during the Nazi occupations of the 1940s, the countercultural papers frequently battled with governmental authorities but were for the most part distributed openly and widely through a network of street vendors, newsstands, and alternative businesses. Usually associated with left-wing politics, the papers supported major movements for social, cultural, and political change and used their own published works to announce upcoming activities, critique government policies and the corporate economy, and suggest how to reshape society. By the 1970s, the "alternative" press included thousands of titles by antiwar GIs, Clergy and Laity Concerned, Students for Peace, women's liberation groups, Chicanas and Chicanos, the elderly, environmentalists, the Black Panthers, and many others.

Despite media consolidation, the alternative press thrived in the 1970s, although it lost strength by the end of the decade. The Vietnam War was a unifying theme of alternative tabloids, and the end of the war, along with counterintelligence government repression of groups like the Black Panthers, diminished the fervor of earlier publications. Nonetheless, student and community groups continued to produce local publications that addressed local concerns and issues ignored by the mainstream media.

ernmental interference. For years, journalists had pressed for First Amendment protection of their sources. In a trio of cases under *Branzburg v. Hayes* (1972), the U.S. Supreme Court ruled that news gathering deserved some First Amendment protection but that the press was required to help enforce laws and could not protect sources where criminal conduct was involved.

Despite the fleeting popularity of newspaper work, actual readership continued to decline in the 1970s as it had in the 1960s. Media consolidation also increased, which decreased competition and the kinds of investigative reporting that had made Bernstein and Woodward virtual celebrities. In response to this corporate consolidation, in 1976 the communications studies department at Sonoma State University began its Project Censored, where it awarded "alternative Pulitzer Prizes" for investigative reporting overlooked by the major news networks that feared offending owners and advertisers.

Although the public was unaware, during the 1960s and 1970s it was widely known among the press corps that the CIA had a close relationship with journalists. Increasing protests against the war and scrutiny of the intelligence agency led CIA director William Colby to limit these interactions by the mid-1970s. In

Crawdaddy (1971–1979)

The span of *Crawdaddy* in many ways reflected the cultural evolution of the decade as well as the possibilities for an alternative press created by young people on a shoestring budget to reach a national audience. Begun by Paul Williams at Swarthmore College in 1966 as a collection of record reviews, *Crawdaddy!* became the premier rock and roll magazine. But by 1969, the magazine faced financial troubles as increasing competition from *Rolling Stone* and other countercultural publications siphoned away readers and writers.

Then in 1971, rock and roll critics Peter Knobler and Greg Mitchell transformed *Crawdaddy* (without the exclamation point) from a "hippie-style, ineptly distributed, biweekly tabloid" to a national monthly magazine (Knobler and Mitchell 1995, 16). Knobler and Mitchell kept music at the center of the publication but also provided in-depth coverage of critical events of the day, whether investigating the Miss USA pageant or the Ford pardon of Nixon. *Crawdaddy* emphasized the art rather than commerce of music and devoted lengthy interviews to unknown but promising artists like Bruce Springsteen, Bonnie Raitt, and Patti Smith. Politically radical and skeptical of those in positions of power, the magazine also embraced offbeat humor, employing Abbie Hoffman as travel editor and including columns by William Burroughs and the Firesign Theater.

By the end of the 1970s, audiences became less appreciative of the magazine's efforts to mix progressive politics with cutting-edge cultural reporting. According to editors Knobler and Mitchell, younger people were embracing music by Black Sabbath and other groups that they could not appreciate. Financial difficulties, competition from the slicker *People* and *Rolling Stone* magazines, and the general conservative tide ended the magazine in 1979.

1975, Sen. Frank Church's (D-Idaho) Committee on Intelligence Activities revealed that agents had worked as editors, publishers, and reporters; the CIA had funded domestic and international news organizations and publishing houses; and it recruited or traded information with journalists. The journalists helped plant misinformation, recruit agents, and provide intelligence. For example, the CIA and its media sources worked furiously to prevent the election of Marxist Salvador Allende in Chile and then applied intensive propaganda to overthrow him in 1973 and install the dictator Gen. Augusto Pinochet.

Because of the Church committee disclosures, the agency enacted new guidelines to prohibit manipulation of the American media to influence public opinion. Colby's successor, George H. W. Bush, continued the policy but welcomed voluntary information from journalists. When Stansfield Turner became head of the CIA in 1977, under increasing congressional pressure, he issued stricter guidelines that were to prohibit U.S. media organizations from providing cover for or

Investigative Reporters and Editors (IRE)

Against the backdrop of Watergate and Seymour Hersh's 1970 Pulitzer Prize–winning examination of U.S. Army atrocities at My Lai in Vietnam, a group of journalists created the group Investigative Reporters and Editors (IRE). Formed in 1975 to promote the sharing of resources for this labor-intensive work, teams of reporters and editors offered each other clues, contacts, records, and patterns to uncover hidden or difficult stories. IRE was inspired by Bob Greene, a *Newsday* editor who had directed investigations of corrupt road-construction projects and the heroin trade, and the young investigative team of Harley Bierce and Myrta Pulliam at the *Indianapolis Star.*

In June 1976, the murder of IRE founding member Don Bolles of the *Arizona Republic* galvanized the group to pursue his killers and the story that he had been investigating. An anonymous caller had offered Bolles evidence of a major land fraud, but when no one showed up at the designated Phoenix meeting place, he returned to his car, which someone in the meantime had rigged with six sticks of dynamite. Bolles died 11 days after the explosion, and IRE sent a team of 50 reporters and volunteers to Phoenix. The group produced a 23-part series that exposed organized-crime influence and corruption in Arizona land projects, published in many newspapers across the country but, unfortunately, not in the *Arizona Republic.*

In addition to the Arizona Project, IRE organized conferences, seminars, and publications to stimulate the team style of investigative reporting. Based at the University of Missouri, the organization several decades later boasts more than 3,500 members.

conducting intelligence activities. There also emerged an air of suspicion among and about reporters and pressure to disavow any association with the CIA.

The strong relationship between public relations and the press, which became more prominent in the 1980s and 1990s, was exhibited famously in Anastasio Somoza Debayle, the Nicaraguan dictator supported by the U.S. government. During the 1970s, Somoza employed the New York PR firms Mackenzie and McCheyne and later Norman, Lawrence, Patterson, & Farrell to convince reporters that he was not such a bad guy. After the revolutionary Sandinistas came to power, President Reagan and the CIA created a "public diplomacy," or propaganda, machine to create sympathetic congressional and public support for the ex-*somocistas* organized into the Contras.

Rising postal rates in the 1970s also contributed to changing journalism and readership habits. The popularity of such long-standing mainstream magazines like *Life* diminished, but the in-store checkout-line *People* magazine became Time, Inc.'s biggest seller. Tabloids focusing on the sensational, especially the

Doonesbury

On October 26, 1970, Gary Trudeau launched the cartoon strip that would provide humorous and pointed social and political commentary about the decade and would reach readers of more than a thousand newspapers worldwide. The comic debuted in about two dozen newspapers. Begun earlier while a student at Yale, the strip's main character, Michael Doonesbury, was originally modeled after Trudeau. The cast of characters grew to include an assortment of earnest or disaffected young people who mostly inhabited Walden Commune but through the decades grew older and more far-flung.

Trudeau's characters sometimes operated in their own fictional world, at other times commented on current events or interacted with the leading political figures of the day. When in 1972 Mike and Mark set off on the road to discover America, they meet Ms. Joanie Caucus, on the run from husband and home. She accompanies them back to Walden Commune and moves in, working with children at a local day care center until she decides to study law. Joanie endures sexism in law school, manages an electoral campaign, and reveals the dilemmas facing women who combine career with motherhood.

Because of its strong political commentary, editors often shifted the strip to the editorial rather than comics page, or canceled the strip altogether. During the Watergate scandal, for example, one strip showed Mark on the radio with a "Watergate profile" of John Mitchell, declaring him "Guilty! Guilty, guilty, guilty!" A number of newspapers, including *The Washington Post,* removed the strip. In June 1973, the military newspaper *Stars and Stripes* dropped Doonesbury for being too political until hundreds of soldier-readers protested and the strip was reinstated. In February 1976, when character Andy Lippincott, a classmate of Joanie's, told her that he was gay, the *Miami Herald* suspended the comic strip. Despite frequent newspaper reluctance to run Doonesbury, in May 1975, the strip won Trudeau a Pulitzer Prize for Editorial Cartooning, the first strip cartoon to be so honored.

lives of celebrities, caught the attention of shoppers in ways that the older, more serious periodicals did not.

A more experimental form of journalism emerged in the 1970s, what Tom Wolfe called "New Journalism," in which some reporters and essayists experimented with a variety of literary techniques, mixing them with the traditional ideal of dispassionate, even-handed reporting. In addition to his own attempts to publish in this new style of journalism, Wolfe also edited with E. W. Johnson the collection *The New Journalism* (1973), which brought together pieces from Truman Capote, Hunter S. Thompson, Norman Mailer, and several other well-known writers, with the common theme of journalism that incorporated literary techniques and could be considered literature.

AMERICA'S FAVORITE PASTIME: THE SPECTACLE OF SPORTS

Commerce, Labor, and Politics in Sports

The success of professional sports in the 1960s initiated an era of expansion in the 1970s, with increased numbers of football and baseball teams, rival basketball and hockey leagues, and the embrace of the international sport new to the United States: soccer. Sports in general became more commercial, often with corporate rather than single owners. More Americans enjoyed sports from their living rooms on television rather than in bleachers and stadiums. As sports became more commodified, pressures grew in the 1970s to sustain winning teams. Even at the college level, coaches focused on winning to please alumni and college fundraisers at the expense of athletes, who often failed to graduate.

The AFL-NFL merged in 1970, which solidified football's growing dominance of sport and revealed television's importance to the game. Tickets for NFL games became big business; corporations bought up sections of season tickets, and sellout crowds became typical. Football's arrangements with TV networks also boosted its profits and fans. The merger brought restructuring of teams into the American Football Conference and the National Football Conference to achieve parity in television markets. CBS covered the NFC home games, NBC televised AFC home games, and ABC started "Monday Night Football." The largest audience ever—24 million Americans—watched Baltimore defeat Dallas in the January 1971 Super Bowl V. Television audiences grew larger through the decade, and in 1973 Congress even adopted legislation that required any NFL game that had been declared a sellout 72 hours prior to kickoff to be made available for local television. In 1978, the CBS telecast of Super Bowl XII made television history: 102 million people, the largest television audience ever for any show, watched Dallas defeat Denver at the Louisiana Superdome in New Orleans.

Even as corporate ownership, control, and marketing of sports events grew, athletes increasingly asserted political, economic, and cultural independence in the 1970s. Joe Namath, whose success with the New York Jets in the late 1960s increased the popularity of football, represented a new breed of athletes who challenged management, flamboyantly displayed their new wealth, and sported the long hair and political values of the counterculture. Soon, team owners capitulated to players' demands for autonomy over their own grooming, fashion, and behavior, and owners of the Oakland Athletics and the Oakland Raiders even encouraged the rebel image among players when they allowed mustaches and long hair.

In the 1970s, the NFL Players' Association sought a bigger piece of the new television wealth and more autonomy for players. In 1970 and 1974, the Association organized strikes and in 1975 won a court case that outlawed the draft. In

Dallas Cowboy cheerleaders rally the crowd as their team clinches a victory over the Denver Broncos in Super Bowl XII, January 15, 1978. The CBS broadcast generated the largest audience in television history. (Bettmann/Corbis)

1977, the Association and NFL Management Council ratified a collective bargaining agreement extending until 1982 that significantly raised salaries, improved benefits, and included a no-strike clause.

Baseball players also sought more control over their labor and an end to the hated reserve system. In 1970, Curt Flood, an African American who played for the St. Louis Cardinals, filed suit in U.S. District Court protesting his trade to Philadelphia and the reserve system that kept players bound to the team that originally signed them. He lost but appealed to the Supreme Court, the justices in 1972 ruled that baseball could retain its unique reserve system but encouraged Congress to resolve the issue.

In April 1972, the Major League Ball Players Association (MLBPA) voted overwhelmingly to stage on opening day baseball's first general strike. The issue was the pension plan and the owners' annual contributions, but the principle of the strike was power. MLBPA director Marvin Miller, a skilled labor attorney and negotiator, brought clarity to the players' argument and engendered resentment from the owners. Miller urged players to continue negotiating rather than going on strike because they had no strike fund and no public relations support, but the players' hatred of the owners' control was so visceral that they insisted on striking. Despite owners' intent to bust the union, they capitulated within two weeks because of disappearing revenues. The strike demonstrated to rank-and-file players that they held power, which set in motion the events that led to free agency. In late 1975, an arbitration panel ruled that pitchers Andy Messersmith of the Los Angeles Dodgers and Dave McNally of the Montreal Expos were free agents because they had played a full season without contracts. The historic decision ended the reserve system and allowed players to negotiate much higher salaries, which rose from 40 to 90 percent over the next decade.

Athletes also asserted their independence from management to speak out on important social and political issues of the day. NBA superstar Bill Walton used his celebrity status to address issues of social justice. As a player at UCLA, Walton had won the NCAA Player of the Year Award in 1972, 1973 and 1974. He

Soccer and the NASL

The 1970s became the decade for soccer as suburban and school youth leagues sprang up across the country and the nation's first professional league, the North American Soccer League, met temporary success. Soccer had long been the world's most popular sport, but it was only introduced professionally in the United States in the late 1960s. Because of so few skilled native players, close to 90 percent of NASL players and coaches came from Europe and South America. Yet American youth loved the sport, gaining confidence with kicking and dribbling on the field and clamoring to see pro players in action.

The sudden popularity of soccer led the NASL to expand from 9 teams in 1973 to 20 in 1975. Then, in the middle of the 1975 season, the New York Cosmos brought Pelé, the world's most popular player from Brazil, out of retirement to the Big Apple. Game attendance more than doubled. By the end of the decade, some of the world's best soccer players had signed with NASL teams. Despite soccer's growing popularity, by the 1980s the NASL was in trouble. Rapid expansion, the inability to acquire television contracts because of other sports' dominance, star player salaries, and the competition of the Major Indoor Soccer League that had since 1978 competed for players and fans, led to its dissolution in 1984.

then became the number one pick in the 1974 NBA draft by the Portland Trailblazers and led the team to a championship in 1977. He left the Trailblazers in 1979 for the San Diego Clippers and later the Boston Celtics.

Globalization affected sports like the rest of American life. The United States joined the rest of the world in embracing soccer by supporting youth leagues and the North American Soccer League (NASL), and it launched the World Football League (WFL) to introduce the world to America's favorite sport. The WFL formed in 1974, as labor troubles in the NFL delayed preseason games. It intended to include teams in Europe and Mexico but never expanded outside the United States. Its financial troubles lead the WFL to fold mid-season in 1975.

International relations changed through sports. In April 1971, the American Ping-pong team became the first Americans to visit China since the 1949 Communist revolution. They were invited to play exhibition matches. Through newspapers and television, their visit brought to Americans the sights of China and the team's impressions. Following their stay, Premier Chou En-lai invited more American journalists to visit, and the United States removed a 20-year trade embargo.

The Olympics had long represented a place of international political and athletic competition between the Soviet Union and the United States, albeit a less openly confrontational reflection of their Cold War rivalry. The 1972 political violence of the Munich Olympics revealed how small the world had become.

Monday Night Football

Television history was made in the fall of 1970 when football was first telecast on a weekday primetime slot. *Monday Night Football* on ABC transformed the habits of millions of Americans, especially men, as they switched from other television programs and quit bowling, eating out, or attending clubs or movies on Monday evenings to watch weekly games. The games became spectacles, with fans and host cities outdoing one another to greet the ABC commentators. Through the 1970s, sportscaster Howard Cosell and, to a lesser extent, fellow announcers Don Meredith and Keith Jackson attracted more acclaim than the football players.

Cosell brought his own brand of hyperbolic, literary commentary to the world of jock announcers. And he brought the "athletic revolution"—the more assertive efforts by African American athletes to end discrimination and the players' challenges to management—to a national audience. Cosell routinely criticized owners and the structure of organized sports and often identified with the counterculture. *Monday Night Football,* in fact, represented the decade's merging of countercultural and commercial values. The irreverence of Don Meredith, who openly stated he quit football because it was no longer fun and who alluded to his permissive values, including smoking pot, was another feature of the weekly broadcast. Yet the attraction of these rebels also meant high ratings and profits for ABC.

A group of terrorists broke into Olympic Village and held a group of Israeli wrestlers hostage. At the airport, German authorities engaged in a shoot-out with the terrorists and five were killed along with all the Israeli hostages. The 1972 Olympics seemed to represent the declining authority of the United States in the world. In addition to the tragedy of the killings and the direct assault on its Israeli ally, the U.S. basketball team lost to the Soviets, and many other American athletes lost their bid for gold medals. African American runners Vince Matthews and Wayne Collett protested the racism of the games and refused to stand at attention when they received gold and silver medals.

African American athletes, key to many U.S. competitions, saw the Olympics stage as an international platform from which to protest United States and Olympics committee policies, and other international athletes followed suit. Many Africans boycotted the Montreal Olympics in 1976, when the IOC refused to expel New Zealand for allowing its rugby team to play in apartheid South Africa. The boycott laid the groundwork for the subsequent U.S. boycott of the Moscow games in 1980 to protest the Soviet invasion of Afghanistan.

The international games also calculated growing television revenues into their plans and sought to exploit the American audience's desire for entertainment. Like the rest of sports, the Olympics faced controversy over athletes' drug use and product promotion, despite the amateur designation of the games.

The Dallas Cowboys Cheerleaders

The Dallas Cowboys, like other professional football teams in the 1960s, relied on cheerleaders to stimulate crowd enthusiasm for the game. The CowBelles and Beaux were high school students from Dallas/Ft. Worth who cheered the Cowboys to their 1971 Super Bowl Championship game. But president and general manager of the team Tex Schramm forever altered professional cheerleading in 1972 when he decided to change the image of his cheerleaders to boost attendance. Recognizing that television had made sports events into entertainment rather than solely an athletic competition, he recruited attractive female dancers and dressed them in provocative outfits to provide glitzy, choreographed half-time shows.

After the Dallas Cowboys introduced the cheerleaders during the 1972–1973 NFL season, other pro football teams duplicated the idea. When they weren't cheering at games, the Dallas Cowboy Cheerleaders were touring and performing, and they appeared on numerous television specials and movies. Partly because of the style and glamour of the professional cheerleaders, cheerleading at high schools and colleges became more sexualized in the 1970s and lost its former wholesome, athletic character.

Ethnicity and Race in Sports

The concentrated struggles of African American athletes from the 1940s through the 1960s to gain equal access to America's playing fields and courts began to pay off by the 1970s. More college and professional sports teams recognized the skills of talented players, regardless of race or ethnicity. As former tennis star Arthur Ashe notes in his history of African Americans in sport, by the mid-1970s most white schools had younger and more experienced coaches, who replaced older racist coaches and actively recruited talented African American players. As a result, in the 1970s over 60 percent of Heisman Trophy winners and 30 percent of NFL players were African American (Ashe 1988).

Still, despite the increase of African American and Latino players in professional sports, they were not represented in management and lagged behind in salaries. In the 1970s, social scientists began to research whether sports had provided an avenue of mobility as was often assumed. They concluded that athletes of color were generally in peripheral positions, such as wide receivers and defensive backs or positions in the outfield and were less likely to move on to managerial or coaching roles after retirement. In 1974, Frank Robinson became the first African American manager of a major league team, the Cleveland Indians. He joined the Cincinnati Reds in 1956 and was named MVP while with them and later with the Orioles. He left the Orioles in 1971 for the Los Angeles

Dodgers, then played for the California Angels in 1973 until he was named playing manager of the Cleveland Indians. He later managed the Giants and Orioles in the 1980s. It was not until 1981 that Dennis Green became the first African American football coach at a predominantly white college, Northwestern. And black quarterbacks were few, which led many NFL players to decry the discrimination and claim that prejudiced coaches still did not believe African Americans could play "thinking" positions.

Yet African American stars rose in all fields. Orenthal James "O. J." Simpson gained more yards as an offensive runner for the Buffalo Bills than any player in history, from 1972 to his retirement in 1977. He became a football icon, and his record helped to boost the NFL and its TV ratings. On April 8, 1974, Atlanta Braves player Hank Aaron made baseball history by hitting his 715th home run to break Babe Ruth's 39-year-old record. But fame came at a price for African American players, and Aaron began receiving hate mail as he neared breaking the white player's old record. He retired after the 1976 season; he held the all-time record in home runs, extra base hits, total bases, and runs batted in.

Athletes could also gain even greater attention and admiration for their outspokenness. When superstar baseball player Reggie Jackson joined the New York Yankees in 1977, he famously sparred with coach Billy Martin, who resented that an African American man had so much wealth and attention. Claimed Jackson, "I don't know how to be subservient" (Ashe 1988, 35). Yet Jackson helped the Yankees defeat the Dodgers in the 1977 World Series and in Game 6 hit three consecutive home runs.

Latino athletes also gained prominence in baseball. Puerto Rican Roberto Clemente helped solidify a bond among Latin American players, regardless of nationality. Clemente had joined the Pittsburgh Pirates in late 1957 and became a star in the 1960s. He batted .414 in 1971 as he helped the Pirates win the World Series against the Baltimore Orioles, and he was named MVP. He batted his last and 3,000th major league hit on September 30, 1972; on December 31, 1972, he died on a small plane that crashed as he was helping take supplies from Puerto Rico to Managua, Nicaragua, to earthquake survivors. Widely admired by Latino players, seven years after Clemente's death, Panamanian Manny Sanguillen noted his and others' devotion at the outset of the 1979 World Series: "Anything we do in this series, we are doing for Roberto" (Regalado 2002,19).

By the 1970s, African Americans had become the major stars of and dominated professional basketball. Americans welcomed professional sports as a diversion from Vietnam and other concerns of the decade, and recognizing the popularity of the sport, ABC television renewed its National Basketball Association (NBA) contract. As cities vied for more teams, the American Basketball Association (ABA) and NBA competed for players, and salaries rose. Yet some ABA teams resisted African American prominence in the sport. Dallas, for example,

Franco's Italian Army, Franco Harris, and the Pittsburgh Steelers, 1971–1979

The significance of ethnic identity and the fluidity of ethnic/racial categories were revealed in the popularity of Pittsburgh Steelers running back Franco Harris. Born to an African American serviceman and an Italian immigrant war bride, Harris identified as African American, growing up in a predominantly black neighborhood of New Jersey. He also embraced the Italian language, foods, and mores taught by his mother. After a successful college football career at Penn State, he was drafted by the Pittsburgh Steelers in 1972 and moved to a city with a large population of Italian Americans. By the 1970s, however, the Italian character of Pittsburgh had begun to fade as upward mobility and Italian–African American tensions over urban renewal had increased migration away from the "Little Italy" East Liberty neighborhood. Learning of Harris's Italian heritage, a group of Pittsburgh Italian Americans created a fan club they called "Franco's Italian Army" and created a visible cheering section in Three Rivers Stadium.

For the next five seasons, the large fan club/ethnic association reflected the rise of the "New Ethnicity," or the revival of ethnic pride among white European immigrant descendents. It also reflected the tensions among ethnic/racial groups over identity: Pittsburgh's African Americans resented the claiming of Harris as Italian and often confronted Franco's Army at games. Harris, whose stardom continued to rise as offensive rookie of the year in 1973 and most valuable player as he led the Steelers to their first Super Bowl victory in 1975, tried to negotiate between the two groups, but the conflicts remained until the army disbanded after his trade to the Seattle Seahawks in 1980.

removed four African Americans from its 11-man roster to appease white audiences, and leagues struggled with finding qualified white players. The ABA and NBA merged in 1975, the same year Moses Malone became the first high school player to skip college to go directly to the NBA. New basketball star Lew Alcindor, who had been named Rookie of the Year of the Milwaukee Bucks in 1970, shocked many fans when in 1975, after he was traded to the LA Lakers, he announced that he had become a Muslim and a had new name: Kareem Abdul-Jabbar. Aside from some fans' disapproval of African American players' defiance, stories abounded of players from humble beginnings becoming rich in basketball careers, and the media emphasized their free-spending habits and moralized about their irresponsibility and poor business acumen. Basketball hoops appeared in every neighborhood schoolyard, housing project, and urban park as many young African Americans aspired to attain professional status as a way to gain access to the American dream.

African American youths play basketball at Stateway Gardens high-rise housing project on Chicago's South Side, May 1973. Basketball became increasingly popular during the decade as it generated larger team and television fans. (John H. White/ National Archives)

Title IX and Gender Equity

Women's sports were transformed in the 1970s as Title IX of the Educational Amendments Act of 1972 prohibited sexual discrimination in schools and colleges receiving federal aid. The Association for Intercollegiate Athletics for Women (AIAW) formed in 1971 to govern women's athletics and, after Title IX was passed, encouraged funding for a comprehensive athletic program. In 1975, the Department of Health, Education, and Welfare adopted an implementation program that required institutions to expand women's sports programs. But the men's athletic establishment, especially the National Collegiate Athletic Association (NCAA) and its university allies with big intercollegiate sports programs, launched a well-financed opposition to the changes. This coalition argued that men's sports generated revenues for universities and that women students did not request more sports programs for themselves. In response, some 60 women's groups, ranging from NOW to the American Association of University Women to the Girl Scouts, formed the Education Task Force to lobby for Title IX implementation.

The NCAA ultimately determined it would be best to control rather than oppose women's athletics, and it soon blocked AIAW's access to the financial

Title IX of the Education Amendments of 1972, P.L. 92–318 (enacted June 23, 1972)

"No person in the United States shall, on the basis of sex, be excluded from participation in, be denied the benefits of, or be subjected to discrimination under any education program or activity receiving Federal financial assistance."

"The Battle of the Sexes": Billie Jean King Versus Bobby Riggs (1973)

Boasting that a middle-aged man could beat a woman in her prime, former tennis champ Bobby Riggs defeated Margaret Court in a match on Mother's Day 1973. Billie Jean King, who had broken the record for most Wimbledon championships and had been *Sports Illustrated*'s first Sportswoman of the Year, challenged Riggs to a match held at the Houston Astrodome on September 30. Riggs had claimed that women players were not as talented as men and therefore did not deserve equal billing or prize money. Billed as the "Battle of the Sexes," the match in which King trounced Riggs drew the largest crowd ever to watch tennis. It also demonstrated how the media drew attention to particular sporting events, as the match was broadcast on television to millions around the world. In addition to generating interest in the skills of a woman athlete and her ability to defeat a seasoned male player, the television coverage boosted the appeal of professional tennis.

In addition to being a champion tennis player, Billie Jean King was an articulate and outspoken advocate of equal rights and equal pay for women athletes. In 1970, she and other top women players threatened to boycott a West Coast tournament that offered 12 times the prize money for male winners. Gladys Heldman, publisher of *World Tennis* magazine, organized an alternative tournament in Houston and obtained Phillip Morris sponsorship to beef up the women's prize money. This became the Virginia Slims Circuit, which in 1971 had 24 tournaments. King and many feminists, however, felt uncomfortable with a cigarette company sponsoring women's athletics, and the slogan "You've Come a Long Way, Baby," trivialized women's liberation efforts. In 1973, King helped form the Women's Tennis Association, which soon came to agreement with the United States Lawn Tennis Association, that made women's prize money equal to men's at the U.S. Open.

Women and Boxing

As women asserted themselves in the worlds of professional, collegiate, and high school sports, many deliberately pursued training in still off-limits contact sports such as boxing. Although there were scattered exhibitions and bouts between women boxers before the 1970s, the decade experienced a burst of interest in and was highlighted by many women's boxing "firsts." Many states lifted bans on women's boxing, issued boxing licenses, and sanctioned matches.

The publicity surrounding these first-time licenses encouraged other women to join the sport. In 1975, Caroline Svendsen received the first documented boxing license in the United States in Nevada, followed in 1976 by boxer Pat Pineda, who became the first woman to be licensed in California. In 1978, after an ongoing lawsuit in the state of New York, three high-profile women boxers, Cathy "Cat" Davis, Jackie Tonawanda, and Marian "Lady Tyger" Trimiar received their boxing licenses. Davis became a popular, if controversial, subject for news stories in the late 1970s after her 1977 match with Margie Dunson in Fayetteville, North Carolina, right after a ban on the sport was lifted. The first woman boxer on the cover of *Ring* and *People* magazines, Davis was criticized for having greater promotional than athletic skills, especially when more talented female African American fighters did not receive the same hype and coverage.

Several determined male coaches and promoters helped boost girls' and women's boxing. Doyle Weaver, a boy's boxing team coach in Pleasant Grove, Texas, and a firm supporter of the women's rights movement sweeping the country decided that he was not going to coach at all unless girls were allowed to participate. In 1968, he started the Missy Junior Gloves Boxing Club, the first of five boxing clubs in Texas that allowed girls to box. When Weaver moved the Missy Junior Gloves to Duncanville in 1974, he had as many as 100 club participants. Yet despite his outspoken and eloquent defense of "Girls as Equals," Weaver was disappointed that the Missy Junior Gloves girls would spar with boys boxing in Amateur Athletic Union tournaments, but the actual AAU tournaments forced the girls to the sidelines. Weaver also tried to get the girls admitted to Golden Gloves without success.

Called the "Father of Women's Boxing in America" by *Boxing Illustrated,* Bill Dickson made the Hyatt Lake Tahoe a center for the women's sport in the late 1970s. He regularly brought to the hotel world-class boxers such as "Squeaky" Bayardo, Julie "Machine Gun" Mullen, LaVonne "Snow White" Ludian, and Toni Lear Rodriguez.

St. Paul, Minnesota, hosted the World's First Women's Amateur Boxing Championships on May 12, 1978. Claire Buckner, a St. Paul mother of three and theater arts major at the University of Minnesota, became Minnesota's first AAU woman champion in a four-bout card. But just a month earlier women fighters had to insist on their right to a state championship. The AAU tried to block the bout, and the University of Minnesota Women's boxing club and founder Bill Paul protested through the media. After negotiations, the AAU director sanctioned the event.

Women and Boxing, Continued

In 1975, Eva Shain became the first woman granted permission by the New York State Athletic Commission to judge pro fights. She judged her first professional fight on Thanksgiving Eve in 1975, and two years later became the first woman to judge a World championship bout (Muhammad Ali versus Earnie Shavers) and the first to appear in Madison Square Garden.

---

resources connected to national championships, thus marking the demise of the women's organization. Before its departure, the AIAW played an instrumental role in passing the Amateur Sports Act of 1978, which resulted in the U.S. Olympic Committee increasing opportunities for female athletes.

Title IX changed the face of school athletics. In 1970–1971 only 7.4 percent of students participating in high school interscholastic sports were girls; by the 1978–1979 school year, 31.9 percent of the athletes were girls. During the same period, intercollegiate sports offered to women doubled, and their portion of the athletics budget increased from 1 to 16.4 percent. By the end of the decade, the NCAA instituted national championships for women in cross-country track and volleyball, to be followed by other sports in the early 1980s. Title IX also opened the door for women in areas outside sports, where more attention was given to equal admissions, access to courses and degree programs, scholarships, and other opportunities available from universities.

BIOGRAPHIES

Muhammad Ali, 1942–

Champion Boxer

One of sport's most flamboyant, popular, and controversial figures of the decade, Muhammad Ali reclaimed his title as "greatest champion" after losing his eligibility to box in 1967 when he refused to be inducted into the U.S. Army to fight what he viewed, as an African American Muslim, an immoral war in Vietnam. The World Boxing Association revoked his title, and he was sentenced to five years in prison for draft evasion. He fought the sentence in court, and in 1970, the city of Atlanta granted him a license for a fight. He won handily, and in 1971, a Manhattan judge ordered the New York Athletic Commission to restore Ali's license to fight heavyweight champion Joe Frazier in Madison Square Garden. Frazier won, but later that year Ali's conviction was set aside by the U.S. Supreme Court.

Ali, who had earlier changed his name from Cassius Clay when he converted to Islam, had a special relationship with Howard Cosell, the noted 1970s ABC sports broadcaster. Cosell, who announced his matches in his own flamboyant way, defended the fighter for his stance against the draft. For his defense of Ali, Cosell received thousands of hate letters, often calling him "nigger-loving Jew bastard" (Hietala 1995, 141).

Ali struggled to regain his heavyweight title, knocking out Jimmy Ellis, Ken Norton, and Frazier in matches in the early 1970s. But his real comeuppance came in 1974 in the world championship match held in Kinshasa, Zaire, against George Foreman. The match reflected African American efforts to reconnect with Africa during the decade. It also became a symbol of Ali's popularity among African Americans, who admired his firm opposition to a white man's war with Vietnam, despite the cost to his own fame and fortunes. In typical witty fashion, Ali called his strategy "rope-a-dope," where he wore down Foreman by leaning against the ropes with gloves in front of his face before knocking him out. Ali was the "world's greatest" once again. His match with Joe Frazier in the Philippines in September 1975, dubbed "The Thrilla in Manila," ended in Ali's favor after 14 brutal rounds and was hailed by many sports aficionados as "the greatest" fight in history.

In addition to his principled stand against a war that had become overwhelmingly unpopular by the early 1970s, Ali was admired as a symbol of racial pride. African Americans often reveled in his arrogance, confidence, and defiance of the white power structure. Ali used his title and celebrity status to openly champion his blackness, civil rights, and African American cultural and athletic contributions to the United States.

Robert Altman, 1925–2006

Filmmaker

M*A*S*H (1970) was Altman's first big success after years of laboring in television and films. Although set in Korea, *M*A*S*H*'s thinly veiled attack on the U.S. war in Vietnam inspired a popular television series in the decade. Altman next deconstructed the great American western in *McCabe and Mrs. Miller* (1972), which took place in a cold, wet, and ramshackle Pacific Northwestern mining town where confinement and darkness contrasted to the genre's expansive vistas and sunshine of the Southwest. John McCabe (Warren Beatty), an entrepreneurial vagabond, moves to the depressing mining camp to establish a brothel. Together with the shrewd Mrs. Miller (Julie Christie), a professional madam with years of experience, they start a booming business and a blossoming relationship that soon is destroyed by rapacious capitalists seeking to control the mines and town.

Altman was a favorite among actors, who appreciated the freedom he allowed them to develop characters and scenes. His style was distinctive, often employing huge casts and encouraging improvisation and overlapping dialogue. This sometimes worked and sometimes did not, and his prodigious efforts resulted in years of obscure films before a hit would appear. Altman's popular film *Nashville* (1975) crammed a large cast who improvised in their dealing with adulteries, betrayals, disillusionments, and assassination during a political rally in the capital of country music. Altman directed a series of other 1970s films with less commercial success, if critically acclaimed, and left his mark on the decade through his Lion's Gate Films, encouraging other young filmmakers with bold projects that ran against the increasing corporatization of filmmaking in the 1970s.

Arthur Ashe, 1943–1993

Champion Tennis Player and Author

Born in Richmond, Virginia, Arthur Ashe received the support of Dr. R. Walter Johnson, who had begun a training program for young African American tennis players and had helped Althea Gibson break the color barrier to become the world's best player in the late 1950s. Awarded a tennis scholarship by UCLA, Ashe won a number of college titles in the 1960s. Fighting segregation in the United States and South Africa, Ashe was named to the U.S. Davis Cup Team and helped recapture the cup from Australia in 1968. That year he became the first African American male to win the U.S. Open Tennis Championship.

Ashe became a world-renowned figure in the 1970s, winning the Australian Open in 1970, the French Open in 1971, and Wimbledon in 1975. In 1979, he suffered a heart attack and retired from professional tennis. He continued to work for tennis instruction in public parks and to assist young minority athletes, and he researched and wrote a definitive history of African American athletes in America. He contracted the HIV virus, most likely from a blood transfusion in surgery, and died of AIDS in 1993.

Tony Brown, 1933–

Television Journalist

Brown was born in Charleston, West Virginia, and received B.A. and M.A. degrees from Wayne State University in Detroit. As president of the national Association of Black Media Producers, Brown had challenged the licenses of 36 radio and television stations in Detroit and other cities for neglecting the concerns of African Americans. He became the host of the long-running PBS series *Black Journal* in June 1970. Brown brought articulate and often controversial guests to the show, who defined for themselves the important political, cultural, and social issues to address, winning the respect and attention of a large African American fan base. When white station managers refused to air particular controversial segments, Brown encouraged letter-writing campaigns from his base to pressure the station to air the show. Because Brown often attacked the Nixon administration, in 1973 the Corporation for Public Broadcasting, now with a Republican majority on its board, refused to continue to fund the program. But the cancellation of one of the only black programs on public television engendered protests from African American communities across the country, and the corporation was forced to restore funding and address its own racial practices by instituting an affirmative action plan.

Despite his popularity among African American viewers, producer Brown struggled to retain funding, episodes, and station outlets for the next few years. In 1977, with the underwriting of the Pepsi Corporation, he decided to move *Black Journal* to commercial television. Brown returned the show to PBS in 1981.

Although primarily known for his journalism and called "Television's Civil Rights Crusader," Brown was the founding dean and professor of the School of Communications at Howard University. As the honorary chairperson of the National Organization of Black College Alumni, Inc., Brown spearheaded a movement to preserve black colleges. He initiated scholarship committees for African American students and participated in numerous civic and educational boards. He also initiated efforts to expand the numbers of qualified African Americans in the field of communications.

Al Green, 1946–

Pop Rhythm and Blues Artist

One of the last and the best of the great soul singers, Al Green's career took off in the 1970s after the 1960s heyday of soul. Born west of Memphis, Green performed with his brothers in a gospel quartet near his Arkansas hometown and in Michigan when his family moved there. Green connected with Willie Mitchell, who owned Hi Records in Memphis, and his 1970 song "Let's Stay Together" topped both R&B and pop charts.

Green continued to produce hits through the decade with his distinctive songwriting and singing. He combined soul, country-western, and Motown into his own polished sound. His romantic songs, including top 10 hits "Tired of Being Alone" and "Call Me," and his intimate and erotic stage manner attracted many women fans who threw gifts of underclothing onto the stage. When in 1974 one of his girlfriends burned him with hot grits and shot herself, Green turned back to religion, starting his own church in Memphis. He continued to tour, but when he escaped serious injury after falling off stage in 1979, he set aside the gold chains and flashy pop-star lifestyle and devoted himself mainly to gospel music. Gospel and contemporary Christian music were becoming popular in the late 1970s, and Green helped punch it with soul.

Toni Morrison, 1931–

Writer

One of the strongest literary voices to emerge from the decade was Toni Morrison, who examined the African American experience in new and compelling ways. Morrison was born Chloe Anthony Wofford and grew up in the Midwest, where her family helped her gain an appreciation for African American storytelling, songs, and folktales. She earned degrees at Howard University (B.A., 1953) and Cornell University (M.A., 1955) and, while teaching at the predominantly black Texas Southern University in Houston, learned that African American culture was a serious discipline rather than just family reminiscence. She returned to Howard to teach from 1957 to 1964, became influenced by the civil rights movement, married and had two children, and joined a writers' group. In 1965, Morrison divorced and left her teaching job to become an editor for Random House in New York. While her sons slept, she started writing and decided to turn a short story for her writers' group into a novel.

In 1967, Morrison became a senior editor at Random House, and while editing books by prominent African Americans like Muhammad Ali, Andrew Young, and Angela Davis, she submitted her own novel to various publishers. *The Bluest Eye* was finally published in 1970, and although it received much critical acclaim, it was not commercially successful. The novel concerns a victimized adolescent African American girl who is obsessed by white standards of beauty and longs to have blue eyes. From 1971 to 1972, Morrison taught English at the State University of New York at Purchase while she continued working at Random House. In 1973, she published her second novel, *Sula,* which focused on a friendship between two adult African American women. It achieved widespread success and was excerpted in *Redbook* women's magazine, and it became an alternate selection by the Book-of-the-Month Club and was nominated for the 1975 National Book Award in fiction.

Morrison's third novel focused on strong African American male characters based on her own sons. *Song of Solomon* (1977) won the National Book Critics Circle Award and the American Academy and Institute of Arts and Letters Award. Morrison was also appointed by President Jimmy Carter to the National Council on the Arts. In 1981, she published her fourth novel, *Tar Baby,* which features interaction between black and white characters. Noting her influence on literature through the 1970s, she appeared on the March 30, 1981, cover of *Newsweek* magazine.

Patti Smith, 1946–

Rock Singer and Songwriter

A rock critic turned poet/performer, Patti Smith emerged from the New York punk club subculture to find a larger audience. Originally from New Jersey, Smith had

Rock musician Patti Smith, performing in 2006. Smith's raw sound and social themes contributed to the growth of punk clubs and culture on east and west coasts in the 1970s. (Daigo Oliva)

written album covers, lyrics for Blue Oyster Cult, and articles for *Cream* magazine. She embraced New York's art scene with her roommate, photographer Robert Mapplethorpe.

Her debut album, *Horses,* recorded in Hendrix's Electric Lady Studios in 1975, boldly fused three-chord rock with her lyrical writing to break into punk rock. The next year, she recorded another successful album, *Radio Ethiopia.* Her raw sound and emotional delivery often reworked familiar lyrics such as Van Morrison's "Gloria" into hard rock. Her concerts were memorable for her band's experimentation that changed from night to night.

Smith recognized the role that she and the Ramones played as "pollinators" of the new punk culture and supported the American debut of British bands like the Clash. She intended to "stir up people" to change music culture and create more democratic spaces outside the commercial scene for artistic expression. Her popularity revealed that the punk genre had more room for strong women than conventional rock.

Bruce Springsteen, 1949–

Rock Musician

Son of a bus driver and secretary who struggled to make ends meet, Bruce Springsteen grew up in gritty New Jersey working-class communities in decline, and he sang about the lives of men and women he knew. In 1972, Springsteen first recorded with his band, the E. Street Band, and challenged the promise of America as he sang about those who suffered from the boredom of their jobs or deindustrialization and unemployment. With his album *Born to Run* rising to the top of Billboard charts in 1975, Springsteen became a major star, featured on the covers of both *Time* and *Newsweek* in October. His recording career was held up for three years in litigation over management rights, but numerous singers including Patti Smith and the Pointer Sisters recorded his songs in the 1970s.

Springsteen's folk-rock music followed in the tradition of Woody Guthrie and Pete Seeger, singing about ordinary people and their struggles. Like them, he too was politically active and supported environmental, antinuclear, and anti-apartheid causes, and he often laced his long concerts with punchy political commentaries. His legendary concerts with the E. Street Band won a fiercely loyal fan base. At the end of the decade Springsteen's double album, *The River,* featured many hit singles with his brooding and uplifting lyrics.

Flip Wilson, 1933–1998

Comedian

Although African American comedians had been playing black and white clubs in the 1960s, television provided the medium to cross over to a large mixed audience. Flip Wilson had the most successful comedy variety series in television history from 1970 to 1974. Born Clerow Wilson in New Jersey, he adopted the nickname "Flip" from his flippant style of joke telling while serving in the Air Force. After a decade of working clubs, Wilson broke through on television as a favorite and frequent guest of Johnny Carson in the late 1960s. NBC recognized Wilson's popularity and gave him a variety show, which featured a traditional range of comedy, dance, guest stars, and Wilson's unique characters, including Reverend LeRoy of the Church of What's Happening and the sharp Geraldine Jones, with her signature phrase, "What you see is what you get!"

After his successful burst onto the comedy scene, Wilson left the entertainment industry to raise his children and faded from the limelight, never reviving his early stardom. Wilson's humor was considered nonthreatening for white audiences, rarely pushing them to reconsider critical social and racial issues. Nonetheless, he represented a major African American star heading a popular comedy hour and regularly featured black artists as guests.

REFERENCES AND FURTHER READINGS

Abzug, Robert H. 1996. "Love and Will: Rollo May and the Seventies' Crisis of Intimacy." In *The Lost Decade: America in the Seventies,* edited by Elsebeth Hurup, 79–88. Aarhus, Denmark: Aarhus University Press.

Acham, Christine. 2004. *Revolution Televised: Prime Time and the Struggle for Black Power.* Minneapolis: University of Minnesota Press.

Armao, Rosemary. 2000. "The History of Investigative Reporting." In *The Big Chill: Investigative Reporting in the Current Media Environment,* edited by Marilyn Greenwald and Joseph Bernt, 35–50. Ames: Iowa State University Press.

Ashe, Arthur. 1988. *A Hard Road to Glory: A History of the African-American Athlete since 1946*. New York: Warner Books.

Bailey, Beth. 2004. "She 'Can Bring Home the Bacon': Negotiating Gender in Seventies America." In *America in the 70s*, edited by Beth Bailey and David Farber, 107–128. Lawrence: University Press of Kansas.

"Blaxploitation: A Soulful Tribute to the Genre." http://www.blaxploitation.com/. Accessed December 8, 2006.

Campbell, Michael, and James Brody. 1999. *Rock and Roll: An Introduction*. New York: Schirmer Books.

Capozzola, Christopher. 2004. "'It Makes You Want to Believe in the Country': Celebrating the Bicentennial in an Age of Limits." In *America in the 70s*, edited by Beth Bailey and David Farber, 29–49. Lawrence: University Press of Kansas.

Ciotola, Nicholas P. 2000. "Spignesi, Sinatra, and the Pittsburgh Steelers: Franco's Italian Army as an Expression of Ethnic Identity, 1972–77." *Journal of Sport History* 27 (2): 271–289.

Cobly, Paul. 2001. "'Who Loves Ya Baby?' *Kojak,* Action and the Great Society." In *Action TV: Tough-Guys, Smooth Operators and Foxy Chicks*, edited by Bill Osgerby and Anna Gough-Yates, 53–68. London: Routledge.

Dunn, Stephane. 2003. "Foxy Brown on My Mind: The Racialized Gendered Politics of Representation." In *Disco Divas: Women and Popular Culture in the 1970s*, edited by Sherrie A. Inness, 71–86. Philadelphia: University of Pennsylvania Press.

Echols, Alice. 2002. *Shaky Ground: The '60s and Its Aftershocks*. New York: Columbia University Press.

Epstein, Jason. 2001. *Book Business: Publishing Past, Present, and Future*. New York: W. W. Norton.

Friedman, Norman L. 1978. "Responses of Blacks and Other Minorities to Television Shows of the 1970s about Their Groups." *Journal of Popular Film and Television* 7 (1): 85–101.

Gelder, Lawrence Van. "Pauline Kael, Provocative and Widely Imitated New Yorker Film Critic, Dies at 82." *New York Times,* June 11, 2008. http://query.nytimes.com/gst/fullpage.html?res=9E04E2D61639F937A3575AC0A9679C8B6. Accessed June 10, 2008.

Gough-Yates, Anna. 2001. "Angels in Chains? Feminism, Feminity, and Consumer Culture in *Charlie's Angels*." In *Action TV: Tough-Guys, Smooth Operators and Foxy Chicks*, edited by Bill Osgerby and Anna Gough-Yates, 83–99. London: Routledge.

Graebner, William. 2004. "America's *Poseidon Adventure:* A Nation in Existential Despair." In *America in the 70s,* edited by Beth Bailey and David Farber, 157–180. Lawrence: University Press of Kansas.

Hietala, Thomas R. 1995. "Muhammad Ali and the Age of Bare-Knuckle Politics." In *Muhammad Ali: The People's Champ,* edited by Elliott J. Gorn, 117–153. Urbana: University of Illinois Press.

Hyatt, Wesley. 2006. *Emmy Award Winning Nighttime Television Shows, 1948–2004.* Jefferson, North Carolina: McFarland & Co.

Kaluma ya Salaam. "Historical Overview of the Black Arts Movement." *Modern American Poetry Online Journal.* http://www.english.uiuc.edu/maps/blackarts/historical.htm. Accessed December 27, 2006.

Keyser, Les. 1981. *Hollywood in the Seventies.* San Diego: A. S. Barnes & Co.

Knobler, Peter, and Greg Mitchell, eds. 1995. *Very Seventies: A Cultural History of the 1970s, from the Pages of Crawdaddy.* New York: Fireside.

Kodish, Deborah, Lois Fernandez, and Karen Buchholz. 1996. "The African American Festival of Odunde: Twenty Years on South Street." *Pennsylvania Folklife* 45 (3): 126–133.

Kronengold, Charles. 2000. "Identity, Value, and the Work of the Genre: Black Action Films." In *The Seventies: The Age of Glitter in Popular Culture,* edited by Shelton Waldrep, 80–123. New York: Routledge, 2000.

Lasch, Christopher. 1979. *The Culture of Narcissism: American Life in an Age of Diminishing Expectations.* New York: W.W. Norton.

Love, Matt. 2004. *The Far Out Story of Vortex I.* Pacific City, OR: Nestucca Spit Press.

Marc, David. 1989. *Comic Visions: Television Comedy & American Culture.* Malden, MA: Blackwell.

Masar, Brenden. 2006. *The History of Punk Rock.* Detroit: Lucent Books.

McCain, Gillian, and Legs McNeil. 1997. *Please Kill Me: The Uncensored Oral History of Punk.* New York: Penguin.

Miller, Douglas T. 1996. "Sixties Activism in the 'Me Decade'. In *The Lost Decade: America in the Seventies,* edited by Elsebeth Hurup, 133–143. Aarhus, Denmark: Aarhus University Press.

Moriarty, Frank. 2003. *Seventies Rock: The Decade of Creative Chaos.* Lanham, MD: Taylor Publishing.

"1970s Bestsellers." Cader Books. http://www.caderbooks.com/best70.html. Accessed December 22, 2006.

Regalado, Samuel O. 2002. "Hey Chico! The Latin Identity in Major League Baseball." *NINE: A Journal of Baseball History and Culture* 11 (1): 16–24.

Rettman, Jef. 1994. "Fairs and Celebrations in the Pacific Northwest." *Pacific Northwest Forum* 7 (1): 3–21.

Reynolds, Simon. 2006. *Rip It Up and Start Again: Postpunk 1978–1984.* New York: Penguin Books.

Roman, James. 2005. *From Daytime to Primetime: The History of American Television Programs.* Westport, Conn.: Greenwood Press.

Seymour, Gene. 2004. "The Black Decade: Why the 1970s Were a Turning Point in African-American—and all American—Culture." *American Legacy* 10 (3): 28–36.

Smethurst, James Edward. 2005. *The Black Arts Movement: Literary Nationalism in the 1960s and 1970s.* Chapel Hill: University of North Carolina Press.

Starker, Steven. 1989. *Oracle at the Supermarket: The American Preoccupation with Self-Help Books.* New Brunswick, NJ: Transaction Publishers.

Sutherland, John. 1981. *Bestsellers: Popular Fiction of the 1970s.* London: Routledge.

Tasker, Yvonne. 2001. "*Kung Fu:* Re-orienting the Television Western." In *Action TV: Tough-Guys, Smooth Operators and Foxy Chicks,* edited by Bill Osgerby and Anna Gough-Yates, 115–126. London: Routledge.

Tucker, Stephen R. 1984. "Progressive Country Music, 1972–76: Its Impact and Creative Highlights." *The Southern Quarterly* 22 (3): 93–110.

Wandersee, Winifred D. 1988. *On the Move: American Women in the 1970s.* Boston: Twayne.

Werner, Craig. 1998. *A Change Is Gonna Come: Music, Race & the Soul of America.* New York: Penguin.

Wiener, Jon. 1984. *Come Together: John Lennon and His Time.* Urbana: University of Illinois Press.

Wolfe, Tom. 1976. "The 'Me' Decade and the Third Great Awakening." *New York* (Aug 23): 26–40.

Women Boxing Archive Network. http://www.womenboxing.com/historic.htm. Accessed January 15, 2007.

The Economy, Work, and Society: Crises and New Directions

OVERVIEW

Economic uncertainties and concerns about the country's future and its role in the world arose alongside the pop culture image of the carefree and creative 1970s. In the post–World War II period Americans had enjoyed a booming economy that together with union strength boosted an unprecedented number of people into the middle class. But in the 1970s, American global hegemony weakened, and a series of economic shocks hit Americans. New global competition hurt U.S. manufacturing, unemployment increased, and interest rates and inflation rose. The GNP and real incomes fell. On the international stage, too, the end of the Vietnam War, the OPEC oil embargo, and the fall of the Shah of Iran indicated that the United States could no longer easily manipulate world affairs. These new developments not only affected the ways in which Americans earned their living and their level of prosperity but also how they organized to change society, lived in their homes and communities, and pursued leisure.

By 1973, real wages and incomes had stagnated and even declined given inflation, and inequalities in wealth became more pronounced. Family incomes grew only because Americans worked longer hours and women and teenagers joined the waged workforce in larger numbers. Although our assessments of the 1970s as the watershed for the decline of post–World War II prosperity are made in hindsight, Americans at the time felt uncertainty and fear that their and their children's lives would not improve. The American Dream, or hopes for an ever-improving standard of living, disintegrated in the decade. The unusual economic advantages that Americans had experienced for so long were now threatened by other forces, including Arab oil countries and multinational corporations. Even that icon of the American Dream—the single family home—moved beyond the grasp of many Americans. For the first time, the proportion of people under age 55 who owned a home dropped dramatically after 1973. Education had also long represented a route to improved economic status. But with the economy less able to absorb high school and college graduates, prospects and enrollments diminished. Investment in public education also began to decline.

The very nature of work changed as agricultural and unionized, blue-collar jobs declined and white-collar work expanded. During the 1970s, only one manufacturing job was created for every 7.5 service-related jobs. Americans increasingly worked in sales, government, finance, recreation, and food service instead of production. Clericals became the largest single occupational group. But the move away from manual labor did not mean that Americans' work lives improved. Unionized workers in the postwar period, which represented up to 35 percent of the workforce, enjoyed health and retirement benefits and job security. But these jobs typically excluded women and minorities, who faced lower wages and fewer benefits in the workforce and an inadequate social safety net.

By 1977, inflation and unemployment had weakened the labor movement and strengthened the political mobilization of American business. In 1972, chief executive officers of major corporations established the Business Roundtable for the purpose of formulating positions about the economy and business and effecting public policy. Roundtable members believed that the U.S. economy would be healthier if there was less unwarranted intrusion by government into business affairs and that could be achieved if CEOs were more directly involved in government policy making. Labor, on the other hand, became less politically influential. Congressional and campaign finance reforms weakened the Democratic Party and its union supporters. Republicans successfully appealed to the interests of working- and middle-class Americans by capitalizing on Democratic identification with programs to help minorities and the poor and then attacking government programs in general. The labor movement failed to pass effective full-employment legislation, and support for New Deal liberalism in general—the rights of labor unions, wage and hour laws, unemployment compensation, aid to the elderly and families with dependent children, and other aspects of the social welfare state—declined.

Many hoped that the technological advances that helped boost the economies of Western Europe and Japan would also reshape American industry and consumer society. Scientists and engineers made great leaps in understanding the structures of nature and in developing new technologies that could treat diseases or process information. Technology advocates who saw breakthroughs in alternative energy or space exploration believed it was possible to create new tools to solve dilemmas arising from modern life and to develop cutting-edge commercial enterprises.

Faith in technological progress, however, was also challenged by technological disasters during the decade. Nuclear power, once touted as a source of clean energy to substitute for scarcer oil, became disfavored as construction cost overruns, near meltdowns, and threats to groundwater stymied further plant development. Rising skepticism of policymakers and corporations that grew from witnessing Vietnam War, Watergate, and environmental debacles challenged the idea that technology could improve life.

The dramatic economic changes that characterize more recent times—corporate downsizing, deindustrialization, globalization, decline in unions, income gaps, job insecurity—have their roots in the 1970s. A main difference for people in the 1970s, however, was that they believed this economic insecurity was temporary. Americans lived through and remembered the postwar boom and expected that someone or something could return the country to the golden age of prosperity, whether it was technological innovation or a silver-tongued politician.

TIMELINE

1970	*Dandridge v. Williams* Supreme Court case upholds state-determined ceilings for welfare recipients.
	Arkansas Community Organizations for Reform Now (ACORN) is established.
	The United Construction Workers Association forms in Seattle to compel all-white unions to recruit minority workers.
	The Occupational Safety and Health Act (OSHA) is passed to improve workplace safety.
	The Agricultural Act offers subsidies to limit crop production and develop exports.
	U.S. postal workers go on strike, initiating public-service worker militancy in the decade.
1971	*Wyman v. James* Supreme Court decision rules that welfare recipients cannot refuse caseworker entry to homes without losing benefits.
	Amtrak is created.
	Griggs v. Duke Power decision by Supreme Court rules that employers must take affirmative steps to increase minority employment even if hiring practices were nondiscriminatory.

The Attica prison rebellion in New York results in 43 deaths.

1972   The Business Roundtable is created.

The AFL-CIO refuses to endorse Democratic presidential candidate George McGovern.

The Coalition of Black Trade Unionists forms.

Miners for Democracy defeat United Mine Workers (UMW) president Tony Boyle.

The Equal Employment Opportunity Act is passed to deter discrimination in employment.

President Nixon's Family Assistance Plan (FAP), which would guarantee a minimum income to all families with children, dies in the Senate.

Latina workers begin two-year strike at Farah Manufacturing Company in El Paso.

Young autoworkers at General Motor's Lordstown, Ohio, plant lead wildcat strike to protest accelerated assembly-line production.

1973   In response to U.S. support of Israel in Yom Kippur War, Arab states ban export of oil to the United States, which increases price of oil by 350 percent.

Senate passes National Energy Emergency Act authorizing President Nixon to require conservation measures.

NASA launches Skylab.

E. F. Schumacher publishes *Small Is Beautiful: A Study of Economics as if People Mattered*.

President Nixon ends the system of fixed currency exchange rates.

Independent truckers lead a nationwide wildcat strike.

1974   The worst recession since the 1930s begins.

The National Welfare Rights Organization folds.

The Employee Retirement Income Security Act is passed to protect pensions.

After 84 days in outer space, the crew of Skylab 4 returns to Earth on February 8.

The Consent Decree forces the United Steel Workers of America and the steel industry to promote African American workers.

The Energy Reorganization Act creates the Nuclear Regulatory Commission.

Most OPEC nations end a five-month oil embargo against the United States.

1975 The Apollo-Soyuz Test Project brings together American astronauts and Soviet cosmonauts.

The L-5 Society is founded to promote space colonization.

HBO establishes cable TV service.

1976 In *Gregg v. Georgia,* the Supreme Court allows states to reinstate the death penalty under strict guidelines.

Bill Gates and Paul Allen create the software corporation Microsoft.

The first biotech company, Genentech, is established.

1977 The first *Star Wars* film is released.

President Carter calls the energy crisis the "moral equivalent of war," calls on Americans to lower thermostats in winter to 65 degrees, and creates the Department of Energy.

The Coal Employment Project is created to advocate for women miners.

NASA abandons plans for *Enterprise* space shuttle.

Steve Jobs and Steve Wozniak introduce first commercially successful Apple computer.

1978 Republicans defeat in the Senate a bill to improve National Labor Relations Board (NLRB) elections for greater worker protection.

The Pregnancy Discrimination Act is passed.

Solar energy enthusiasts celebrate the first "Sun Day" on May 3.

1979 The nuclear reactor incident at Three Mile Island in Pennsylvania shakes the nation's support of atomic power.

OPEC raises oil prices and gas lines form again in the United States.

Independent truckers strike to protest rising fuel costs.

President Carter addresses the nation about the need to conserve, restrain affluence, and unite to solve the energy crisis.

Residents of the blue-collar suburb of Levittown, Pennsylvania, riot over high fuel prices.

GLOBAL AND DOMESTIC CHALLENGES

Global Economy, Global Competition

Since World War II, the United States had enjoyed economic dominance of the world, but beginning in the 1970s, it met global challengers for markets and resources. Recovered from the war's destruction, Japan and Europe had rebuilt industries with new technology and educated workers to achieve greater productivity than U.S. manufacturing. Unburdened by military spending, the countries devoted capital to building industry and human resources. The U.S. share of the world's manufacturing exports dropped from 32 percent in 1955 to 18 percent in 1971, and imports to the United States rose in these same years from 3.5 to 6 percent. Americans bought Japanese radios, televisions, steel, and, by the 1970s, automobiles. Imports of autos increased from 1.3 million in 1970 to 2.3 million in 1979 while domestic production rose less steeply. Increasing imports from developing nations like Korea, Mexico, and Brazil also competed in the U.S. market at a time when U.S. consumers already had plenty of refrigerators, radios, and toasters.

Corporations reacted to this increasing competition by attempting to streamline operations and hold down labor costs while improving productivity. This "lean and mean" strategy of reducing the workforce rebuilt profits at the expense of investing in labor and advanced technology to make the American economy more globally competitive. Newer production methods allowed Japanese car manufacturers, for example, to produce high-quality cars with new features in fewer labor hours than American manufacturers. Auto and steel, the bedrocks of the industrialized economy, began to decline and eliminated hundreds of thousands of jobs. Managers intensified production, which led to rising industrial accident rates, and increased the numbers of supervisors, which swelled corporate bureaucracies at three times the rate of Japan and Germany. U.S. corporations also cut labor costs by relocating to nonunionized states and developing countries. New plants, called maquiladoras, appeared in a new "free-trade" zone on the northern Mexico border to take advantage of cheaper labor; by the mid-1970s, more than 600 U.S. factories were in operation there. Nonetheless, despite these dramatic cost-cutting measures, the rate of business failures increased in the 1970s.

There were a number of factors that prevented the U.S. economy from bouncing back until well into the 1980s. President Nixon continued to expend enormous amounts for the war in Vietnam without raising tax revenue, which fueled inflation. A growing glut of American dollars on world money markets led the

United States to end its maintenance of the dollar at a fixed exchange rate. Increasing imports of oil, automobiles, and electronics led to a balance of payments problem, and the U.S. devalued the dollar in 1971. By 1973, President Nixon ended the system of fixed exchange rates, devised at Bretton Woods in 1944, to allow the exchange rates between the dollar and other currencies to fluctuate in response to markets. This resulted in high inflation and the steady decline of the dollar's value through the 1970s, revealing how artificially inflated its value had become when the United States dominated the world economy.

The oil crises of 1973 and 1979, and a mid-decade recession drove up costs of production, shrank profit margins, and made investors more hesitant. The first oil crisis, in fact, appears to mark a watershed in American economic history: after 1973, the U.S. economy grew by just 2 percent a year, down from the historic average of 3.4 percent a year following World War II. Average weekly earnings, adjusted for inflation, peaked in 1973, and productivity began to decline. Other nations, also experiencing higher energy prices, did not experience the same declines as the United States.

OPEC Oil Embargo and the Energy Crisis

In 1973, OPEC, in response to U.S. support of Israel in the Yom Kippur War, dramatically increased oil prices. Already faced with a faltering economy, the United States plunged further into a recession, and high energy costs fueled inflation and deficit spending. By late 1973, the phrase "energy crisis" had entered the lexicon, and it haunted the remainder of the decade, affecting society and politics as well as the economy. Americans worried about the nation's ability to control world events. The growing environmental movement warned about a culture of excess that had failed to recognize limits to the Earth's production of natural resources.

The Nixon administration had neglected to pay attention to rising American consumption of oil while domestic production had declined, which increased U.S. dependence on foreign sources of oil. By 1973, the country had doubled its importation of oil from the previous decade to 33 percent. Because of gasoline shortages, President Nixon introduced a system of rationing, where those with license plates ending with either an odd or even number could buy gas only on odd or even-numbered days. But the energy crisis failed to generate significant new domestic sources or conservation; by 1977, 50 percent of the nation's oil came from abroad. Nixon's price controls had kept domestic oil prices below the world average, and the lack of conservation measures increased domestic use of energy.

In 1975, President Ford announced measures that would stimulate domestic production of oil. He proposed that Congress decontrol domestic oil prices and raise tariffs on Middle Eastern oil. But Congress refused to allow the president

Gas stations abandoned during the fuel crisis in the winter of 1973–1974 were sometimes used for other purposes. This station at Potlatch, Washington, was turned into a religious meeting hall. Signs painted on the gas pumps proclaim "fill up with the Holy Ghost . . . and Salvation." (National Archives)

to raise prices immediately and in a compromise bill gave the president authority to decontrol prices over a longer, 40-month period.

OPEC's actions temporarily ended the country's love affair with the automobile. Higher gas prices and long lines of cars inching their way to gas pumps became the most visible signs of the crisis. In the prosperous postwar years, cheap petroleum had fueled the American economy, and the auto had symbolized the country's economic and social mobility. Although Americans were just 5 percent of the world's population, they drove 40 percent of the world's autos. Owning a car and a home served by multiple freeways and subdivision streets represented middle-class status. But with the energy crisis, the American car became a gas-gulping hazard to the economy, environment, and the nation's world stature. Teenagers halted honored past practices such as "cruising." Many young people adopted the moped, long used in Europe, to get around within cities. Many Americans considered alternatives to driving or began carpooling to work to save on costs and to adjust to rationing.

Other daily and business practices were altered. Fuel and advertising companies had to switch from messages of consumption to that of conservation. The crisis stimulated many communities to bolster mass transit. Government agencies and families lowered thermostat temperatures in the winter and raised them in the summer to cut down on energy costs. New businesses sprang up to exploit new energy sources such as wind and solar.

Threatened by foreign competitors, especially Volkswagen and Toyota, with their energy-efficient, small 4-cylinder cars, and congressional mandates to improve fuel efficiency, American car manufacturers began to redesign many cars. One of the most popular small cars, the Ford Pinto, was first introduced in 1971 and manufactured through 1980. However, the Pinto became associated with safety problems because the car's design allegedly allowed its fuel tank to be easily damaged in the event of a rear-end collision, which sometimes resulted in deadly fires and explosions. Because of accidents, Ford faced major lawsuits, criminal charges, and a costly recall of all affected Pintos. Ultimately, American interests in conservation and dramatically altering the car culture proved temporary. As gas prices leveled off at 60 cents a gallon in spring 1974, demand for small cars dropped.

Increasing oil prices affected different regions of the country in different ways. Oil-producing areas like Texas, already becoming influential because of political power shifting to the Sunbelt, became wealthier while the automobile-producing upper Midwest and oil-consuming Northeast were further hurt by the energy crisis. Coal-producing areas in the Mountain West and Appalachia experienced new growth, and miners won new concessions in their 1974 contracts. Because of new demand for coal, mine operators were forced to raise wages and streamline the grievance procedure.

Despite the increase in passenger air travel during the decade, airlines experienced difficulties due to rising fuel costs and deregulation. Railroads also suffered financial problems, including the bankruptcy of the major Penn Central Railroad in 1970. Because of the vital nature of rail transportation, the government created two corporations, Amtrak in 1971 to operate intercity passenger lines, and Conrail in 1976, which consolidated six major northeastern rail companies, including Penn Central, to manage freight transport.

President Carter had been preoccupied with the energy crisis since taking office in January 1977, but his efforts to enact long-term solutions met political trouble. His administration created a new Department of Energy in 1977, but the agency made few significant strides in developing alternative energy sources. The 1979 Islamic revolution in Iran that overthrew the U.S.-friendly shah, the failure of OPEC's efforts to regulate oil prices and production, and rising world consumption sent oil prices spiraling upward again. Once more, small Japanese cars sold like hotcakes, and the American auto industry struggled to meet new fuel and emissions standards.

The 1979 crisis once again created long gas lines, frustrated consumers, and angry truckers, whose livelihoods became threatened by escalating fuel costs. On June 23, residents of the model blue-collar suburb of Levittown, Pennsylvania,

Truckers' Strikes

The OPEC oil crisis, rationing, and the subsequent lowering of the speed limit to 55 miles per hour to enforce gas conservation pushed many independent truckers close to financial ruin. Most goods in the United States were transported by tractor-trailers, with less than 25 percent of commercial freight moved by water or rail. So in December 1973, truckers led a wildcat strike without the support of either the American Truckers Association or the Teamsters Union. Truckers used the citizens' band (CB) radio to spread the word about the protest and unite a far-flung group of otherwise independent operators to shut down major transportation arteries through massive traffic jams.

CB radios played an instrumental role in the truckers strike as well as in trucker culture in the 1970s. CBs became affordable, under $150, and convenient to install beneath a truck dashboard or in a glove box; by 1976, an estimated 16 million were in use. Truckers used the radios to communicate with each other and to listen to police radios to determine when they could safely exceed the speed limit without getting caught. Because police could also listen to radio chat, truckers developed a continually changing slang to dodge law enforcement. Sam Peckinpah's film *Convoy* (1978) featured a populist hero with the handle of Rubber Duck, played by Kris Kristofferson, who led a convey that broke the speed limit and out-witted federal officers' surveillance.

The strike elicited sympathy from many Americans, and popular culture made the independent trucker into a temporary American hero, celebrating his independence and resistance to bureaucrats and authority figures. C. W. McCall's song "Convoy," which celebrated CBs and life on the road, became a number one hit in 1976. A series of films about truckers, led by *Smokey and the Bandit I* (1977) and the popular TV show *Dukes of Hazard* (CBS 1979–1984), seemed to supply 1970s consumers with an updated version of the western, this time on the highway rather than the trail.

Again, in mid-1979 as gas prices rose dramatically, 100,000 independent, long-haul truckers pulled off the road. Some angry truckers pulled their rigs in front of distribution centers and refineries to block shipments, exacerbating the gasoline shortage. Violence broke out in 23 states when some truckers shot at nonstriking truckers, injuring several and killing one. Nonstriking truckers received death threats on their CB radios. Governors in at least nine states called out the National Guard, and Gov. Fob James of Alabama ordered armed escorts for truck convoys and urged truckers to arm themselves against violent strikers.

Federal officials condemned trucker violence and stepped up FBI investigations, but they also began addressing trucker concerns by urging states to increase both weight limits on trailer loads and the availability of diesel fuel. They also began deregulating the industry to allow independent truckers to haul freight carried only by licensed companies. This deregulation for the independents, however, paved the way for more intense competition in the trucking industry, leading to further deunionization, lower wages, and more stressful working conditions, which were ultimately more damaging to the trucker lifestyle than the 1970s energy crisis.

President Jimmy Carter's
"Crisis of Confidence" Speech (July 15, 1979)

Faced with national economic problems including a recession, inflation, and rising oil prices, on July 15, 1979, President Carter addressed the nation about its future and difficult choices. A devout Christian who was concerned about the role of morality in personal and public life, Carter suggested that the excesses of affluence had plunged the nation into crisis. He claimed that Americans had a "crisis of confidence," built on the growing pessimism around events of the previous two decades. Efforts to solve the energy crisis could revive national unity and provide a "new sense of purpose."

Carter and other Americans were influenced by the spate of books written in the 1970s that warned of the economic and environmental problems that excess abundance and consumption produced. Carter was especially persuaded by the writings of three popular intellectuals—Christopher Lasch, Daniel Bell, and Robert Bellah—who moralized about how mass consumption and self-indulgence threatened basic values in American society. In 1979, the president invited the three men to discuss their writings and incorporated their thoughts in the speech he was composing about the energy crisis.

Although intended to be reassuring, the address was one of the most debated presidential policy speeches of the decade. What was later called his "malaise" speech, Carter reached the largest audience while in office; more than 65 million Americans heard it. The speech represented competing visions of America's future and warned of the trade-offs between economic growth and environmental protection.

Although Carter's popularity rose immediately following the speech, his reorganization of his administration and attacks from left and right on the details of planned solutions to the energy crisis soon brought his approval ratings to new lows. In the months that followed, the Iranian hostage crisis remained unresolved, Sen. Ted Kennedy launched a challenge to Carter's Democratic Party renomination, and the Soviet Union invaded Afghanistan. Criticisms of the speech reflected the difficult and transitional time for Democratic political leaders. Carter inherited the legacy of Vietnam and Watergate, which made Americans suspicious of presidential power. Moreover, Republican challenger Ronald Reagan offered confidence and cheery optimism in contrast to Carter's sermonizing and realistic appraisal of tough choices facing the nation's future.

erupted in anger over higher prices, and the next day some young people torched several cars and destroyed a gas station. Police had to subdue the riot and impose a curfew, but the violence revealed that many white working-class Americans felt their relative affluence was under assault by foreign threats, big oil companies, and a changing economy.

An Economic Conundrum: Stagflation

The decade began ominously with a recession that raised unemployment to almost 6 percent in 1971 while President Nixon tried to control runaway inflation through wage and price controls. This combination of high unemployment and high inflation, which became known as "stagflation," remained a persistent problem through the 1970s. Stagflation perplexed economists, who expected low unemployment during periods of high consumer demand and inflation, and policymakers, who alternated rhetoric about which needed most attention depending on whether attempting to satisfy business or workers.

Presidential administrations of the decade wrestled with the conundrum. President Nixon's New Economic Policy of 1971, which sought to rein in inflation with wage and price controls and ended the exchange of dollars into gold to allow the dollar to float against other currencies, had limited success. The 1973 oil crisis ushered in the most serious recession since World War II. Abiding by conservative principles, President Ford focused on inflation rather than unemployment, calling for cuts in government spending, a tax increase, and volunteer efforts by Americans to save more and spend less. But the program, Whip Inflation Now (WIN), failed to win over most Americans, and Republicans lost badly in the midterm elections of 1974. In 1975, the president proposed a large tax cut and moratorium on any new federal spending. But Ford met resistance by Congress and could not implement major changes, and inflation and unemployment reached record postwar highs.

President Carter believed the country should tackle the unemployment problem and proposed to Congress an economic stimulus package that included public service employment, a small tax cut, and a $50 cash rebate to all Americans to stimulate consumer spending. While wrangling with Congress over terms of the measure, inflation crept upward. The president then reversed his strategy to focus on inflation, calling for tax cuts and spending limits. This alienated many fellow Democrats who supported spending on social programs, including jobs programs that would lower unemployment rates. By 1979, inflation reached 20 percent, the trade deficit increased, another recession pushed up unemployment, and federal revenues declined.

Stagflation and economic uncertainties required American families to adjust their habits. Workers' take-home pay fell, and more members of the average household entered the workforce. Unemployment hovered around 8 percent, but the rate of joblessness for African American and Latino workers was almost twice the national average. Nonetheless, worker productivity increased during the decade, and workers became more skilled. The demands of a nonindustrial economy required more years of education; college-educated workers increased from 21 percent in 1970 to 32 percent in 1980.

Concerns about jobs and the economy also made many Americans less willing to pay taxes, especially when they believed that those tax revenues did not serve their interests but only government bureaucrats and unproductive welfare recipients. Corporations also struck back, claiming that movements to hold business more accountable for pollution and worker safety drove up costs of production, and they called for rolling back regulations and reducing tax burdens. The tax revolt that began in California and a new conservative movement that advocated less government spending on nonmilitary programs changed American political culture by the late 1970s.

Deindustrialization and American Workers

Deindustrialization—the closure of manufacturing plants across the United States—devastated working-class communities and cities in the late 1970s. Large corporations often bought out older steel or mining firms and then used short-term profits to invest in more lucrative operations, such as chemicals, oil, and real estate and they then "divested" or shed the now unprofitable manufacturing operation. Attempting to remain competitive in the world, other manufacturers relocated plants in lower-wage and nonunion areas, often in the South or outside the United States. For the first time since the 1930s, downward mobility became a reality or possibility for many working families. The wage gap increased, too, with larger differences between high and low-income earners, a shrinking middle class, and after a decade of decline, growing numbers of poor. Job growth in the decade centered in the service and retail sector of the economy, which paid lower wages than traditional manufacturing and remained largely nonunionized.

Entire communities felt the impact of industrial shutdowns. For example, the steel mills along the Mahoning River west of Pennsylvania had for 100 years employed generations of workers, and families had deep roots in the communities that sprouted by the mills. Beginning in the late 1970s, mills began shutting down and laying off thousands of workers. The impact of deindustrialization was felt greatest in the "Rust Belt," or the industrial North, while textile towns in the South and logging and mining towns in the Pacific Northwest also reeled from the effects of automation, declining resources, global competition, and shutdowns.

Labor unions could no longer assume their continued recognition in the new economic climate. Citing intensified competition, corporations could insist on lowering wages, reducing benefits, and eliminating jobs. Desperate to hang onto jobs, workers and unions agreed to concessions and lost many hard-won gains, such as cost-of-living increases and job security. Vulnerable industrial communities offered tax incentives in the hope of keeping employers intact. As economists Charles Craypo and Bruce Nissen note, after 1975 employers took advantage of the changing economic and political environment to either relocate production operations elsewhere or develop new tactics to defeat unions at the bargaining table.

Housing adjacent to the U.S. Steel Plant in Birmingham, Alabama, 1972. Industry-based communities were hit particularly hard during the economic downturn of the early 1970s. (National Archives)

The loss of thousands of manufacturing jobs hit the working poor particularly hard. Minority and women workers, following union and company seniority clauses as the "last hired, first fired," suffered disproportionately because they had struggled for decades to gain access to industrial jobs only to see the opportunities disintegrate. The gap in pay between whites and African Americans had been narrowing in the early 1970s, but partly because of these declining opportunities, the gap widened again later in the decade.

As many sectors of the economy deindustrialized, agriculture became more industrialized and concentrated. Although in 1970 almost a third of American workers were employed in food-related jobs, a very small percentage were engaged in actual agricultural production; most worked in food processing and grocery. By 1980, the combined employment in agriculture, forestry, and fisheries declined to just 3.5 percent in the United States. New technology and more powerful farm implements reduced labor needs and led those farmers who had the capital to expand their operations and smaller farmers to sell out to them. Overproduction in the 1960s that threatened prices led Congress to pass the Agricultural Act of 1970, which offered subsidies to limit crop production and develop exports. Through the decade, small farmers, who represented most of the country's 2.5 million farms, faced increasing financial difficulties, including bankruptcies. Rising fuel costs and inflation that decreased the value of crops led many farmers to protest with their tractors in the nation's capital. Through the decade, about 50,000 farms per year went out of production, ending two centuries of the American family farm ideal and shifting to more industrialized production.

THE WORLD OF WORKERS IN THE FACE OF ECONOMIC DECLINE

Labor Union Victories and Defeats

The 1970s brought both victories and defeats for American workers. Women and minorities claimed rights to jobs that had formerly excluded them, and public sector workers organized in large numbers, expanding the potential ranks of unionized workers. Workers led union democratization movements and more aggressively pursued contract negotiations and work stoppages to improve wages and conditions. But shifts in the economy and the political weakening of labor unions also spelled the decline of labor's position and the percentage of American workers organized. Although union membership increased slightly during the decade, the overall share of organized workers declined from 31 to 25 percent of the workforce. Unions lost members in the 1970s as heavy industries downsized, and they failed to galvanize new workers and faced many new legal and political obstacles. The labor movement's decline that began in the 1970s would continue over the next three decades.

Total employment increased by nearly 15 percent from 1973 to 1979, mostly in service occupations, with clerical jobs, which employed primarily women, representing 25 percent of that increase. But even with job expansion, the unemployment rate steadily rose through the decade. African Americans had an unemployment rate twice as high as the rate for whites, and together with other minorities did not experience employment gains during the 1970s due to recession and deindustrializing urban economies. Although wages increased steadily through the 1970s, when adjusted for inflation, real income for working Americans fell.

Workers responded to declining job conditions and inflation by participating in major strikes, averaging about 285 a year during the decade. More than 2 million

Female picketer outside Mt. Sinai Hospital in New York is one of more than 30,000 technical, service, and maintenance workers who walked off the job at 48 of the city's hospitals, November 1973. (Bettmann/Corbis)

auto, airlines, communications, U.S. Postal Service, railroad, and longshore workers led major strikes in 1970–1971 alone. To counter the effects of inflation on their wages, workers made cost-of-living allowance (COLA) clauses one of their central demands for labor contracts in the decade.

Public employees made historic gains in the 1970s. Teachers, hospital workers, and local government employees, who had been largely unorganized in the postwar period, recognized that collective bargaining could serve them as it had blue-collar workers in the previous three decades. As the service sector of the economy increased, too, the numbers of public-service workers who wanted blue-collar union benefits grew. Ethnic public workers in New York City led the unionization drive in the 1950s and 1960s that stimulated efforts across the country in the 1970s to obtain union recognition. In 1970, when postal workers refused to work, President Nixon declared a national emergency in this first nationwide strike of government employees in U.S. history. By the early 1970s, unions like the American Federation of State, County, and Municipal Employees (AFSCME) and the American Federation of Teachers (AFT) had organized millions of public employees.

But even as public employees gained more power, the cities in which they worked increasingly faced fiscal crises, which increased residents' and officials' resentments of the unions that had helped win their pay increases. Democratic mayors, long supporters of labor unions, often clashed with public employees as they tried to balance budgets and keep their cities solvent while avoiding unpopular tax increases. When in 1975 President Ford refused to provide federal loan guarantees to New York City, which faced bankruptcy, the city forced a wage freeze on its municipal unions.

The strains between unions and cities revealed larger breaks in the old labor–liberal Democratic Party political coalition. Since the New Deal, Americans had generally recognized that as unions boosted wages for their members, they lobbied for minimum wage, health care, and the welfare state, which kept other families secure. As the old New Deal coalition fragmented, many younger workers and other Americans failed to recognize the value of unions to organized and unorganized workers alike. They no longer felt unity and allegiance to the Democratic Party, which they believed had abandoned them. The New York City construction workers who assaulted antiwar demonstrators in 1970 and the resistance of many unions to racial and gender diversity symbolized the social conservatism of many blue-collar workers. AFL-CIO president George Meany's refusal to endorse liberal Democratic presidential candidate George McGovern in 1972 revealed ideological as well as strategic divisions in the labor-liberal coalition. With 54 percent of the union vote going to Nixon, the 1972 election put in relief the ideological and cultural divisions among American workers.

As working-class solidarity declined, conservatives accelerated their assaults on unions and helped businesses gain greater political power in the 1970s. The construction industry helped form the Business Roundtable in 1972, which encouraged firms to set up subsidiaries that hired non-union labor, essentially deunionizing the building trades over the next few decades even though it faced no global competition. In addition to its financial clout, big business realized in the mid-1970s that there were no real penalties for antiunion actions, and there were rewards for violating labor laws. Although illegal, a company could fire an employee for organizing a union, knowing that the complaint process through the National Labor Relations Board (NLRB) moved slowly and allowed the company time to intimidate others from organizing. Manufacturing operations could more easily shut down and move, thus jeopardizing jobs and pressuring workers to accept lower wages. Even as some economists insisted that layoffs were more likely a result of mechanization than direct global competition, the threat of shutdowns created a new mindset among workers about whether they should directly challenge employers.

Despite the Democratic Party's control of Congress during the decade, labor made few legislative gains. In the mid-1970s, Labor Subcommittee chair Frank Thompson pushed for labor law reform that would put teeth in the laws governing collective bargaining. The bill sailed through the House but lost by one vote in the Senate, with Democrat Russell Long of Louisiana not supporting it. Congress never again came so close to supporting rights of workers. In 1978, the AFL-CIO also lost an effort to make a modest reform in NLRB union certification procedures. Government policies focused on job retraining rather than job creation, and policymakers failed to acknowledge structural changes in the economy that kept so many Americans below the poverty line. Deregulation of major industries such as trucking, airlines, and communications in the late 1970s further eroded labor's position. When giant automaker Chrysler faced bankruptcy, President Carter's Democratic administration and the UAW pushed union members to accept wage cuts, layoffs, and other concessions to keep the automaker afloat. Soon other companies exacted similar concessions.

Court decisions also weakened the state of labor during the decade. In 1970, the Supreme Court ruled that work stoppages during the life of a contract were

Union Militancy and New Left Organizing

As the Vietnam War wound down and the New Left movement fractured, many radicals gravitated to the labor movement to try to revive its militant potential. Antiwar and student movement radicals brought to the workplace their counter-cultural values and a critique of capitalism, union bureaucracy, racism, and sexism. They found support in a number of local unions, including New York's Hospital Workers Local 1199, and nationally in the United Electrical Workers, the United Farm Workers, and AFSCME. Other New Left intellectuals, who began to have influence in academic and activist circles, attacked modern American unionism as collaborating too closely with employers. Jeremy Brecher's 1972 book, *Strike!*, and Alice Lynd and Staughton Lynd's 1973 book, *Rank and File,* celebrated worker militancy while also criticizing institutional unionism.

Influenced by other democratic social movements sweeping the country, many union insurgents tried to dismantle authoritarian structures of their unions and revive rank-and-file control. Miners for Democracy toppled the corrupt United Mine Workers president Tony Boyle in 1972, and Teamsters for a Democratic Union emerged to try the same, although unsuccessfully, in their giant union. Different protest movements within the USWA began to join together to demand greater union democracy and militancy. Older CIO radicals teamed up with younger leftist activists who had been hired in the early 1970s to build a national alliance called Steelworker Fightback. The group reached out to minority and women workers, won elections to local offices, and by 1975 challenged the International by running its own slate of officers.

Other rank-and-file movements emerged to challenge workplace conditions where union leadership failed. In March 1972, autoworkers at General Motors' Lordstown, Ohio, plants walked off the job for three weeks to demand more humane production. The young workers sported long hair, smoked dope, and sought interracial solidarity, representing a generational challenge to traditional blue-collar culture. They also vigorously challenged GM's accelerated assembly line to produce the Vega to compete with foreign imports. The strike led the business press and Nixon administration to raise alarms about growing alienation and insurgency among American workers.

Women and workers of color sought to reshape the labor movement to consider their demands for equity. The Coalition of Black Trade Unionists formed in 1972 to struggle for civil and employment rights both within and outside the labor movement. The Coalition of Labor Union Women and groups like 9 to 5 and Stewardesses for Women's Rights organized for recognition and to address specific gender issues in the workplace.

But despite increasing labor militancy in the 1970s, employers still held the upper hand in a changing economic and political climate. In an impressive interracial organizing drive in North Carolina, textile unions targeted the large anti-union firm J. P. Stevens to open up the South to organized labor. Stevens vigorously resisted the organizing drive, repeatedly breaking labor laws and inspiring other

---

Union Militancy and New Left Organizing, Continued

firms to employ strong-arm tactics to defeat unions. In 1976, to gain media attention and public support, the Amalgamated Clothing and Textile Workers Union (ACTWU) initiated a boycott of the company's products. A corporate campaign staged shareholder protests and pressured financial backers to urge a settlement. The union struggle also inspired the Oscar-winning film *Norma Rae* (1979). Under pressure, in October 1980 Stevens managers finally settled, and the union eventually organized 3,500 Southern workers at 12 textile mills. But the gains were fleeting, since the South remained stubbornly antiunion and the rapid decline of clothing manufacturing and the loss of jobs after the 1970s deteriorated organizing possibilities. Many labor activists also sought to persuade their unions to oppose the Vietnam War, although the AFL-CIO and its president George Meany remained steadfastly supportive of Nixon's war policies until the war's end in 1975. Left-leaning unions such as the United Electrical, Radio and Machine Workers of America (UE) and the International Longshoremen's and Warehousemen's Union (ILWU) were already protesting the war as early as 1966. The United Auto Workers, under the leadership of Walter Reuther and then Leonard Woodcock, publicly opposed the war in the1970s.

---

illegal. By 1981, in *First National Maintenance Corporation v. NLRB,* the Court ruled that companies did not have to bargain over "entrepreneurial" decisions, such as closing plant production, and in *NLRB v. Yeshiva University* (1980) limited the kinds of workers, such as private college teachers, who could organize under the National Labor Relations Act.

Organizing against Racism

The civil rights movement continued to focus on institutional racism in the workplace and within unions in the 1970s. African Americans launched protests at many white work sites, whether urban construction sites where craft unions had failed to hire African Americans, or within large industrial workplaces where militant workers organized to attack both union and management for failing to promote them.

Many black workers formed caucuses to challenge discriminatory treatment within their unions. Detroit's African American autoworkers, who in the 1970s saw working conditions decline, staged a number of wildcat strikes to demand attention from their own union, the UAW. In 1973, the League of Revolutionary Black Workers organized a series of walkouts in Detroit Chrysler plants to criticize the union's complicity in perpetuating degrading conditions in the auto "plantation."

Right to Work

Reeling from its late 1960s failure to repeal section 14(b) of the Taft–Hartley Act—the legislative amendment allowing states to restrict the requirement that a worker must become a member of a union if his/her workplace is unionized—organized labor in the 1970s went on the offensive in several states to defeat the amendment and obtain greater union security.

Efforts to repeal right-to-work became central in Democratic Party struggles to curb both the defection of white unionists to George Wallace and liberals to the antiwar George McGovern. In 1972, McGovern's opponents, Edmund Muskie and Henry "Scoop" Jackson, criticized his 1966 vote against repeal of section 14(b). After McGovern's nomination for the presidency, the AFL-CIO largely distanced itself from his candidacy and devoted resources to maintaining a friendly Democratic Congress. A shrewd President Nixon convinced Republicans not to make opposition to 14(b) repeal a platform plank, diluting workers' opposition to his reelection.

With the issue removed from presidential politics, labor leaders took their fight to the states, even to those with small union populations. In the early 1970s labor pollsters in Arkansas, Kansas, and other states found that their populations were supportive of union security if the confusing language "right to work" could be clarified. Labor activists in Nebraska, Alabama, and Utah tried to obtain an agency shop amendment in the mid-1970s; Wyoming and South Dakota's labor movements tried to repeal state right-to-work laws; and Louisiana and Oklahoma defeated efforts to add such a law. The National Right to Work Committee, in fact, despite its victory in defeating 14(b) repeal, was on the defensive in the 1970s to fend off these state initiatives.

By 1976, with growing public dissatisfaction with Republican leadership, the struggle moved back to the national level. The labor wing of the Democratic Party criticized candidate Jimmy Carter's ambivalence about repeal of section 14(b). Carter was forced to change his position and chose respected labor supporter Sen. Walter Mondale of Minnesota as his vice presidential running mate. But Carter's small margin of victory, and his interest in maintaining southern state support, kept organized labor from launching a full-blown national campaign in an increasingly conservative climate. In 1977, labor leaders agreed to support the Carter administration's proposal to make labor law reforms without repealing 14(b). The House of Representatives passed a bill to increase NLRB and representation election efficiency and to provide protections to workers subject to employer antiunion discrimination. But in response to intense business lobbying, the Senate balked when the bill reached it in 1978, and the bill died because of Republican filibusters.

In 1979, Louisiana elected its first Republican governor since Reconstruction, David Treen. The new governor had made right-to-work part of his campaign and pushed through the measure. The end of the decade put organized labor on the defensive again, and a changing economy and political climate made improbable its efforts to achieve union security through repeal of Taft-Hartley.

Farah Strike, El Paso (1972–1974)

In March 1972, when workers at Farah Manufacturing Company's San Antonio plant were fired for joining a union-sponsored march in El Paso, Texas, more than 500 of them walked off their jobs; 5,000 El Paso workers followed on May 9. The mostly Latina workers at Farah protested their low wages, poor working conditions, and lack of job security. When the strike was declared illegal, the Amalgamated Clothing Workers of America (ACWA) led a national boycott of Farah products, supported by the AFL-CIO. The strikers enlisted the aid of women's groups and the Catholic Church, and much like the UFW boycott of grapes, won the support of celebrities and others who helped put the strike in the media limelight.

In addition to outside support, the strikers mobilized families and community to develop strike strategies, create pickets, and organize food and clothing donations for fellow strikers. They won support of many local residents by going door to door, and some collaborated with other striking workers in El Paso, such as those from the ASARCO mill, by walking picket lines.

Still, the two-year strike took its toll on residents and divided the city. Farah was El Paso's largest industry, employing 10,000 workers in five factories. In some cases, the political tension became personal, pitting members from the same household against one another. Other Latina workers from El Paso and Ciudad Juárez replaced striking workers.

In early 1974, the NLRB forced the company, weakened by the boycott, to allow union organizing and sign a union agreement with the women workers. Yet despite the workers' victory, the Farah plants were in decline along with other U.S. clothing manufacturers and most closed in the 1980s.

Following the victory of the Farah strike, some women continued to be activists in El Paso supporting efforts of workers' rights. Some women participated in Unidad Para Siempre and joined study groups focusing on Marxist literature and labor history. Others became shop stewards or helped workers with grievances on behalf of local unions.

In 1969, African American workers in Pittsburgh, Philadelphia, Chicago, and Seattle halted major federally funded construction projects by disabling equipment and blocking workers from their jobs, and they demanded that contractors hire African American workers and contractors. Their actions brought about the enforcement of affirmative action on local governments, industries, and unions.

In 1970, the United Construction Workers Association (UCWA) formed in Seattle to force historically all-white unions to recruit minority workers. Following their protests, the U.S. Justice Department filed suit against the unions, and in June 1970, federal district court judge William Lindberg ruled that Seattle's building trade unions were in violation of Title VII of the 1964 Civil Rights Act, and the construction industry would have to implement an affirmative action program. Lindberg created a board representing all parties, the Court Order Advisory Committee (COAC), to decide how to implement the order. But as Trevor Griffey writes, the COAC prevented the UCWA from participating. In response to its inaction to hire African American workers, in summer 1972, UCWA members led dramatic protests that closed down I-90 and area construction sites. Judge Lindberg then gave UCWA two seats on COAC and significant oversight over union apprenticeship programs.

Following its legal victories, the UCWA exported its organizing strategies to Denver, Oakland, Little Rock, Tulsa, and Austin to mobilize African American workers to combat discrimination in the building trades. UCWA also helped militant Filipino youth organize the Alaska Cannery Workers Association in 1973, and with the Northwest Chapter of UFW founded the Northwest Labor and Employment Law Office (LELO) to aid grassroots labor activists in pursuing Title VII lawsuits.

Court decisions in the 1970s supported affirmative action measures by employers to mitigate institutional racism and increase minority hiring even if they had not practiced discrimination. Unions generally supported these hiring practices unless they threatened the treasured seniority system, which the labor movement held as a central protection. The seniority systems that unions had struggled to protect often failed minority workers who were the last to be hired and first to be fired. Conservatives recognized how labor and civil rights activism could be at odds over this issue. President Nixon's Philadelphia Plan of 1969 and 1970 helped stiffen union resistance against affirmative action. In the face of rising unemployment and cuts in federal jobs programs, the Plan established job quotas for minority workers in federally supported construction projects. The plan generated few jobs for African Americans but created much hostility among white construction workers. As Nelson Lichtenstein points out, successful affirmative action suits were often won as industries mechanized and laid off workers. Even as the proportion of African Americans and Latinos increased in various industries, their real numbers shrank as the job prospects for all working Americans became more bleak.

The sanitation workers strike in Memphis in 1968 that had involved Martin Luther King Jr. in his last civil rights action before his assassination encouraged the growth of public employee unionism. AFSCME grew to more than half a million workers by 1973, linking its growth to increasing African American political power in the nation's cities. But as cities confronted increasing fiscal pressures, even African American mayors faced off against urban unions. In 1977, Mayor Maynard Jackson of Atlanta, whose roots with the civil rights movement ran deep, refused to raise AFSCME workers' wages, defeated a long strike, and fired hundreds of city workers.

The success of AFSCME, which doubled its membership in the 1970s as it organized health care, sanitation, and other public service workers, challenged the AFL-CIO leadership for its failure to organize these sectors of the economy. Dominated by women and minority members, AFSCME threatened to shift its clout outside the AFL to join with other large non-affiliated unions such as the UAW, Teamsters, or National Education Association, reflecting tensions that remained through the decade over the failure of organized labor to grant more power to underrepresented workers.

African American Steelworkers

In 1964, African American steelworkers formed an organization to protest discrimination within the United Steelworkers of America (USWA) called the National Ad Hoc Committee of Concerned Steelworkers. Although the USWA proclaimed racial equality, African American activists had not advanced above local union offices. Since its founding in the 1930s, Steelworker organizers and officers had reached out to black workers, but anticommunist fervor in the 1950s had pushed the union to the right and many activists who had fought for equality were expelled. After Ad Hoc's formation, it led pickets at international conventions to insist that the union fight discrimination and demanded African American representation on the Executive Board. Their pressures convinced USWA president I. B. Abel to recruit more blacks for staff positions, and in 1976, USWA appointed an African American to a policy-making position on the executive board.

In the early 1970s, Ad Hoc recruited more African American workers, including many women who had recently been hired as part of Title VII mandates. One of the female newcomers, Mississippi-born Ola Kennedy, became a leader of Ad Hoc. Kennedy believed that principles should override desires to be promoted and resisted efforts to include African American USWA staff in the organization, insisting that Ad Hoc retain its rank-and-file mission. She began calling for more women to be hired in the plants and cofounded the District 31 Women's Caucus, a group of militant women steelworkers who advocated for greater inclusion of women in union leadership positions.

Ad Hoc and African American workers sued both U.S. Steel and USWA for supporting a racist promotion system. The resulting Consent Decree of 1974, an agreement between the steel industry and union, allowed workers to transfer out of dead-end jobs with their seniority intact, which had the effect of reducing segregation in the mills. For example, many African Americans suffered health problems and high rates of cancer from the least desirable workplace where they were concentrated, the coke plant. The Consent Decree was the union's response for past discrimination and allowed African Americans to move out of departments that offered few promotional opportunities.

Yet many African American steelworkers decried the limited gains of the Decree. They protested the paltry reparations, about $300 per worker, for past wage discrimination, and the ability of lower-seniority white workers to hold their jobs. Many white workers, on the other hand, convinced that African American workers were gaining at their expense, claimed "reverse discrimination." Unwilling to recognize past injustices against their black co-workers, white workers became eager to blame "preferences" as the industry downsized.

Even as Ad Hoc dissolved as a national network, individual members and regional African American caucuses filed hundreds of lawsuits against companies and the union for discrimination. But African American steelworkers never regained the power they reached in the mid-1970s. Without pressure from below, USWA failed to continue to add African American staff, and the decline of the industry in the 1980s diminished the numbers of black workers and weakened their former militancy. The steel industry's dramatic decline ended job opportunities and limited the effectiveness of affirmative action measures. By the mid-1980s, employment dropped 50 percent. Despite seniority, many African Americans worked in sections of the plants that were first shuttered. The rapid fall of the steel industry also severely impacted African American and Latino communities in the industrial heartland.

Women Workers

The changing economy that made it difficult for families to survive on the incomes of one breadwinner pushed many more women into the paid workforce. The feminist and civil rights movements encouraged women to venture into formerly male-only occupations. Many efforts by African American workers to challenge discriminatory practices of business and unions led the way for women to demand employment rights. For example, the Consent Decree of 1974 won by African American steelworkers allowed women to be hired in the male-dominated steel industry.

Women became bus drivers, miners, and pipefitters, challenging old stereotypes about "women's work." Yet, as Karen Olson found in her interviews with women steelworkers in Pennsylvania, they endured much resistance from male co-workers who intended to keep their industries or occupations male preserves. But deindustrialization challenged the male breadwinner ideal and the mills' "cult of masculinity" more directly; as thousands of steelworkers were laid off, wives became chief breadwinners in the retail trade, financial services, and public sectors of the economy. Women dramatically increased their workforce participation in the 1970s, but by the end of the decade, they still clustered in sex-segregated jobs and still averaged just 59 percent of men's wages. Two-thirds of all workers earning minimum wage were women. And their numbers in the skilled trades such as carpentry and welding did not increase at all during the decade.

Women workers increasingly brought Title VII–based complaints and lawsuits against employers and unions in the early 1970s, compelling both to adopt compliance measures to eliminate discrimination. As Dennis Deslippe finds, unions responded to these charges in different ways. The United Packinghouse Workers of America (UPWA) resisted job reclassifications to remedy past discrimination partly because of declining employment and plant shutdowns in the 1970s. The International Union of Electrical Workers (IUE), conversely, actively pushed local unions to comply with Title VII and pursue antidiscrimination plans for its women members. IUE worked to close the wage gap between male and female employees, and when big employers like General Electric failed to make changes, pursued redress through EEOC and the courts. IUE members, in fact, led the comparable-worth pay movement that emerged in the 1970s.

Woman coal miner at the Bullitt Mine in Big Stone Gap, Virginia, 1979. The 1972 Equal Employment Opportunity Act opened the male-dominated occupation of mining to women. (National Archives)

Yet tensions persisted between the EEOC and unions until the late 1970s, especially over time-honored seniority clauses. Many union men and women saw liberal feminist goals to institute affirmative action as antithetical to efforts to treat all workers equally. Relations improved with the courts' upholding of seniority systems and the appointment of labor-sympathetic Eleanor Holmes Norton as EEOC chair in 1977. Holmes Norton quit naming unions along with employers in charges and lawsuits and worked with unions more closely to resolve discrimination issues.

In addition to breaking down barriers in male-dominated occupations, women organized in traditional female workplaces. In 1971, hundreds of mostly African American middle-aged workers attended the first National Committee for Household Employees conference. Through the decade, domestic workers in Atlanta and Detroit worked to raise wages, and nationally the Fair Labor Standards Act was amended to include household employees in minimum wage coverage. Female flight attendants formed independent unions and in 1972 organized Stewardesses for Women's Rights. In 1973, clerical workers organized 9 to 5 to draw attention to working conditions, including sexual harassment.

Title VII, Affirmative Action, and the Equal Employment Opportunity Act of 1972

Section VII of the Civil Rights Act of 1964 created the Equal Employment Opportunity Commission (EEOC) to end employment discrimination and promote programs to make equal employment opportunity a reality. Two executive orders from President Johnson required government contractors and educational institutions receiving federal funds to develop affirmative action programs to overcome the effects of past societal discrimination. But the Commission did not obtain litigation authority until 1972, which made it largely ineffective in its early years.

A mere handful of successes in forcing employers to comply with equal employment legislation prompted the federal government to intervene actively on behalf of those minorities protected under the law. In 1970 and 1971, federal courts upheld President Nixon's 1969 Philadelphia Plan. The plan responded to racial inequalities in the workforce by requiring contractors who worked on federally funded projects to set goals for hiring minorities. The plan had an impact, yet only those who worked on projects wholly or partially funded by the federal government enjoyed its benefits.

In 1971, Congress conducted public hearings on proposed amendments to Title VII and concluded that "employment discrimination is even more pervasive and tenacious than . . . Congress had assumed . . . [when] it passed the 1964 Act." Congress found widespread discrimination in both the private and public sectors, continued concentrations of women and minorities in the lowest paid positions and industries, and discrimination in pay and promotion. It became clear that the original EEOC act, relying on conciliation and voluntary compliance, was inadequate. Based on these findings, Congress passed the Equal Employment Opportunity Act of 1972 to provide the Commission with litigation authority and an expanded jurisdiction.

The decade of the 1970s as a whole saw significant progress in the development of and enforcement of employment discrimination law, legal protections extended to millions of persons, and the elimination of many discriminatory practices. For example, African American steelworkers used Title VII to file discrimination suits against the steel industry and USWA and won Consent Decrees in 1974 and 1975 to increase the number of women and minorities hired and promotions for long-time workers. However, the EEOC's expanded reach also created an overwhelming backlog of unresolved cases.

Affirmative action's relative effectiveness in creating more diverse workforces caught the attention of university students and faculty across the country, who pressured schools to recruit minority applicants. Success varied among recruitment programs; some remained effective until national enthusiasm waned in the late 1970s and turned into controversy. In 1978, the Supreme Court ruled on *Regents of the University of California v. Bakke* in which it held that the University of California, Davis medical school admissions program violated the equal protection clause in its use of quotas for minorities. However, affirmative action propo-

> ### Title VII, Affirmative Action, and the
> ### Equal Employment Opportunity Act of 1972, Continued
>
> nents applauded the Court's consent for universities to use race as a factor in admissions if they so chose.
>
> Affirmative action was envisioned as a temporary remedy that would end once there was a "level playing field" for all Americans. Yet despite the EEOC's judicial and legislative victories in the 1970s, entrenched racial discrimination remained, and many Americans after the *Bakke* case came to resent those efforts to level the playing field, regarding them as "reverse discrimination."

Women joined and became more prominent in labor unions in unprecedented numbers in the 1970s, just as their numbers increased in the paid work force. As Dorothy Sue Cobble notes, women workers had been at the forefront of the feminist movement beginning in the 1950s. The decline of male-dominated industrial jobs and the unionization of the service sector also dramatically increased the numbers of women in unions. In 1974, some of these female unionists formed the Coalition of Labor Union Women (CLUW) in Chicago and pledged to end sex discrimination in the workplace, organize more women workers, and encourage women's leadership. Olga Madar, who in 1966 became the first woman executive board member-at-large in the UAW, was elected as the first president of CLUW. Although the numbers of women in union leadership grew, they still did not represent the proportion of women union members as a whole. For example, although women made up 66 percent of the Amalgamated Clothing and Textile Workers, only 15 percent of officers and board members were women.

Women unionists were initially divided over the ERA, some workers fearing that hard-won protective laws would be dismantled. But women in the garment, restaurant, and other trades who benefited from protective legislation gradually came to see what women workers in automobile and other industries had recognized: that equality, or "rights, not roses," would best serve their economic interests. Because of members' pressures, the AFL-CIO endorsed the ERA in 1973; in 1977, the labor federation moved its convention site from Florida to Washington, D.C., because of CLUW complaints that the state had not yet endorsed the ERA.

Women Miners

In the 1970s, federal mandates opened coal and hard-rock mining jobs to women, and for the first time since World War II, women entered mines in Arizona,

Montana, and Appalachia. The 1972 Equal Employment Opportunity Act gave the EEOC the power to order appropriate affirmative action and to initiate court action against offending employers. Although hard rock mining reeled from global competition, declining ore sources and facilities, and scarce jobs, coal mining experienced a temporary boom because of the 1973 oil crisis. Nonetheless, through the mid-1970s, women were often hired by companies only because they filed complaints with state agencies that enforced equal employment statutes. They still represented less than 1 percent of coal miners. In 1977, women in the UMW created the Coal Employment Project (CEP) to combat discrimination, work on health and safety issues, and form an international network of coalfield women. The group initiated a class-action lawsuit through the Department of Labor's Office of Federal Contract Compliance Programs against 157 coal companies over discrimination in hiring. Settled in 1978 and 1979, the court action provided back pay to women denied jobs and opened up mining jobs for women throughout Appalachia. The CEP held its first national conference of women coal miners in 1979.

As Suzanne Tallichet found in her interviews with women miners in southern West Virginia, women suffered the dangers and harassment of work underground because of the superior wages. In mining communities, conflicts sometimes emerged between miners' wives and women miners, as in the case of Logan, West Virginia, when in 1974 wives protested the local mine's hiring of women as potential threats to their husbands' wages and security. Women miners had to prove daily to their male co-workers that they were capable workers, and they had to endure hazing, verbal and sexual harassment, and lack of access to better jobs. With the coal production slowdown and mechanization in the 1980s, many of these "pioneer" women lost their jobs or quit.

Workers and the Environment

During the 1970s, workers, unions, and their environmentalist allies brought attention to workplace hazards and industrial pollution and helped pass new environmental legislation. Rank-and-file concerns over working conditions in hazardous industries pressured union leaders to push for tougher environmental regulations and make health and safety concerns chief priorities in negotiations with employers. Many unions supported the UFW efforts to restrict highly toxic pesticides used in the fields through their boycott of California grapes. The UAW, the United Steel Workers of America (USWA), the UMW, and the Oil, Chemical, and Atomic Workers (OCAW) were instrumental in passing the Clean Air Act and OSHA in 1970, the Clean Water Act in 1972, the Safe Drinking Water Act of 1974, the Toxic Control Substances Act of 1976, and the Superfund Act in 1980.

OCAW's 1973 strike against Shell Oil represented a successful effort to gain environmentalist groups' support for worker issues. Unlike other industrial unions that were losing membership in the 1970s, OCAW's militant stance on workplace health and safety helped increase its members from 161,000 in 1965 to 175,000 in 1971. In January 1973, when Shell remained one of the last oil producers to settle a contract adding safety measures, 5,000 workers walked off the job. OCAW announced a national boycott of the oil giant and received endorsement from 11 of the nation's largest mainstream environmental organizations. The union realized a boycott was necessary to push Shell back to the bargaining table and hoped to mobilize consumers by emphasizing their concerns about chemicals in the workplace and the environment. By April, OCAW claimed that the boycott had worked to sharply decrease demand for Shell products. But with a weakened union treasury and some workers demanding an end to the walkout, Shell exacerbated internal divisions by negotiating with a Texas local that wanted to settle. Out of reserve funds, OCAW ended the strike on June 4.

The Shell strike represented a growing labor–environmental alliance in the mid-1970s, something forgotten by many who, at the end of the century, believed that the interests of the two groups were diametrically opposed between jobs and the environment. OCAW did not achieve all its goals, but it raised public awareness of hazards in the workplace, pressured OSHA to adopt stricter standards for exposure to various chemicals, and led the oil industry to accept union participation in critical health and safety matters. In 1975, environmentalists joined labor's effort to pass the Humphrey-Hawkins full employment bill.

But the turn in the economy after the mid-1970s and employers' claims that pollution control measures resulted in plant shutdowns and layoffs frightened many unionized workers. Job security became organized labor's primary concern, and environmental activists focused on defending environmental regulations from conservative attack. For example, steelworkers in Gary, Indiana, became more reluctant to push environmental reform as the steel industry became threatened by imports and USWA cooperated with management to preserve jobs. But as in other industries in the early 1970s, younger rank-and-filers pushed for reforms. When labor leaders neglected to welcome the volunteer services of area scientists to monitor pollution, rank-and-file workers joined with scientists to form the Calumet Environmental and Occupational Health Committee (CEOHC) in 1972. CEOHC leafleted steelworkers about the dangers of industrial fumes. By late 1972, Gary workers formed Workers for Democracy, modeled after Miners for Democracy, to pursue the improvement of factory conditions and demand more OSHA inspections. Ed Sadlowski's campaign for district director in 1973 sought to put pollution issues into the collective bargaining process.

Gary workers also helped form a multiracial and multiclass environmental coalition to curtail coke oven pollution, both inside and outside the steel plant. With citizen pressure in the early 1970s, the Gary Air Pollution Control Division used the threat of EPA litigation to motivate U.S. Steel to negotiate. By 1975, the company had reduced coke emissions by rebuilding oven doors and improving furnace maintenance. But it took advantage of the economic downturn to intimidate citizens and preserve its control over the local environment. By the late 1970s, Gary's unemployment rate had crept up to 14 percent, and the company threatened to shut down various operations if forced to comply with new pollution control measures.

Despite the passage of significant state and national legislation to protect workers and the environment during the 1970s, workers and states pulled back from enforcement when manufacturers threatened plant closures. In Anaconda, Montana, for example, the site of one of the world's largest smelters, officials backed off compliance when the Anaconda Copper Mining Company threatened to shut down operations. Safety conditions in smelters remained among the worst in U.S. industry through the 1970s, although companies invested millions of dollars in cleaning up operations. When the Chilean government expropriated the Anaconda Company's properties there in 1971, the company immediately requested revisions in air standards to sustain its Montana smelter. Montana's governor made allowances, but state environmental groups sued the EPA to enforce sulfur dioxide standards, and the company sued EPA for an in-

Smelter of the Anaconda Copper Mining Company in Anaconda, Montana. Industrial jobs and communities declined in the late 1970s with layoffs and shutdowns. (Library of Congress)

Occupational Safety and Health Administration (OSHA) 1971

The passage of the Occupational Safety and Health Act and in 1971 the creation of the agency, OSHA, within the Labor Department to administer its provisions, ushered in a new era in protecting workers from harm on the job. The act established for the first time a nationwide, federal program to protect almost the entire workforce from job-related death, injury, and illness. OSHA focused on developing standards for noise, toxic metals, carcinogenic chemicals, and other hazards. For example, it issued a standard for vinyl chloride in 1974 when a virtual epidemic of liver cancer suddenly became evident among exposed workers.

Through the 1970s, OSHA was criticized by labor leaders and workers for not adequately enforcing health and safety measures, and by businesses for demanding too many expensive reforms. Small businesses in particular complained about the onerous costs of compliance, and industry executives decried OSHA's interference in their day-to-day operations. With Republican and Democratic administrations, the agency's bureaucrats responded to political pressures to reduce red tape and costs while at the same time pursuing stricter enforcement of health and safety measures.

After his inauguration in January 1977, President Carter sought to streamline OSHA by reducing regulations and applying more "common sense." He appointed Eula Bingham, a scientist with extensive background in worker health issues, to head the agency. Although she indicated her support for a flexible process in evaluating economic impacts, Bingham held that economics should not be a paramount consideration in setting safety and health standards. Nonetheless, Carter's Council of Economic Advisers and anti-inflation campaign prevented Bingham from issuing many new occupational health regulations, and OSHA revised a number of safety regulations.

Despite organized labor's opposition, business successfully increased political pressures to limit OSHA's powers. In 1978, the Senate passed an amendment to an appropriations bill exempting workplaces with 10 or fewer employees from safety inspections, provided that they had good safety records. The House defeated the amendment, but it was revived in 1979 and passed.

junction so it could keep operating. Despite Montana's strict Clean Air Act, the state issued repeated variances to the smelter for emissions until its final shutdown in 1980. While it operated, the smelter achieved less than 30 percent control of its sulfur dioxide emissions, far below the federal Clean Air Act requirement. Despite alarming statistics about high lung cancer rates and arsenic levels in soil and hair, workers and unions reluctantly allowed infractions in order to preserve jobs. Natt Strizich, USWA Local 6002 president, noted that he

Historians' Debate: Why Did Workers Lose Power in the 1970s?

Many labor historians view the 1970s as a pivotal period in explaining the political realignments of the late 20th century and the declining position of American unions and workers. Many have claimed that President Reagan's firing of air traffic controllers in 1981 marked the end of postwar labor power, but other scholars, including Joseph McCartin, contend that antiunionism had been mounting in the 1970s along with a growing acceptance of using replacement workers during strikes. In 1970, President Nixon, recognizing a powerful labor movement, negotiated with and did not harshly penalize striking federal PATCO and postal workers. But by April 1977, Atlanta's mayor Maynard Jackson, long-time civil rights activist and former labor sympathizer, threatened to fire and replace striking sanitation workers. McCartin shows how by the mid-1970s mayors dealt with growing fiscal crises by uncompromising union negotiations. But inflation fueled worker militancy just as it fed an antitax movement keen on reducing government spending. Though many public sector workers were too necessary to fire outright, sanitation workers had become more vulnerable as technology reduced crew sizes and cities contracted with private companies to remove trash. Two years later, the city of San Antonio defeated a strike by its Latino sanitation workers. Many urban Democratic administrations threatened to replace or actually replaced striking public workers so that by the late 1970s workers more often hesitated to use strikes as a bargaining lever (McCartin 2005).

The Democratic Party's inconsistent support of labor's cause in the 1970s reflected the stresses felt by the old New Deal coalition. Nelson Lichtenstein notes that despite public sector union activism and liberal control of Congress, labor actually lost political influence and failed to achieve even modest labor-law reforms. Economic pressures and a rising conservative movement convinced many Democratic policymakers that they should reward businesses with tax cuts without granting labor more influence (Lichtenstein 2002).

The labor movement made many mistakes, too. The strategy of unions after World War II to rely on "pattern bargaining," or capital's willingness to accept increases in wages and benefits across industries as a cost of doing business, came to a screeching halt in the 1970s as the globalization of trade made labor costs more competitive. Because unions had focused on organizing blue-collar jobs that were more susceptible to international competition, the share of organized workers quickly shrank. As Lichtenstein notes, because postwar unions failed to organize "within a broader political arena" and pursued gains for members rather than wider social goals, they became more irrelevant to many Americans (Lichtenstein 2002, 130). Jefferson Cowie claims that the increase in unemployment and slip in real earnings marked the "beginning of a fundamental transition in the equity of the postwar political economy," where class lines became more pronounced, and "the interests of the organized and unorganized diverged more dramatically" than ever (Cowie 2004, 84). But, Cowie warns, we must not contrast

Historians' Debate: Why Did Workers Lose Power in the 1970s?, Continued

the seventies so neatly with previous decades when labor relations appeared to work better. The oil shock, inflation, and recession may have "stripped the nation of a relatively thin veneer of working-class identity," revealing a greater gap between organized workers and other Americans (Cowie 2005, 95, 100).

The U.S. labor movement's failure to embrace social change and collaborate with other social movements also weakened it. AFL-CIO support for the Cold War and the war in Vietnam alienated student and civil rights activists. Moreover, most labor leaders resisted opening union-protected jobs to women, African Americans, and Latinos. AFL-CIO president George Meany even withheld support for the 1972 Democratic candidate George McGovern because of his liberal, antiwar views. Nelson Lichtenstein argues that the "rights consciousness" of the 1960s that led individual workers to resolve disputes through experts and the courts weakened possibilities for participatory union democracy. Attention to affirmative action, for example, did little to mitigate discrimination and unemployment among minorities, as traditional labor liberal goals for full employment and union power might have. And this strategy failed to grapple with the structural crisis. Workers may have been able to enforce rules about gender and racial equity, but they lost job security as corporations downsized (Lichtenstein 2002).

But not all historians see workers losing ground during the decade. Dorothy Sue Cobble observes that the 1970s marked the decline of the "old" New Deal working class and the rise of the "new" working class involving pink-collar women, minorities, and public-sector workers. By the 1980s, she notes, women constituted close to a majority of the largest public employee unions, including AFSCME, SEIU, the NEA, and AFT. Women's entry into blue-collar jobs also increased their percentage of the unionized workforce, from 23 percent in 1970 to 33 percent in 1983. This new working-class had not yet fully developed its workplace strategies to contest growing power or exercise its new class politics in the electorate (Cobble 2005). Dennis Deslippe also contends that though their own unions declined in strength over the decade, women's status in the workplace and in unions improved in the 1970s. From 1970 to 1975, the number of collective bargaining agreements that included antidiscriminatory clauses grew from 46 to 74 percent (Deslippe 2000).

Jefferson Cowie argues that capital flight did not always satisfy corporate desires to control labor. He traces how RCA fled union militancy in New Jersey, then Indiana, then Memphis, before moving to Ciudad Juárez in 1970. Even with a repressive government, young women workers of Mexico also began mobilizing to improve their working conditions. (Cowie 1999). But not until the WTO protests of the late 20th century would U.S. labor recognize that cross-border organizing could strengthen its faltering position.

and others had to worry about feeding their kids "tomorrow" rather than what might happen to their health in 20 years (Mercier 2001, 197). By the 1980s, the decline of labor-environmental coalitions and industrial retrenchment from pollution control reflected the growing power of industry to exert control over workers and the political process by threatening to shut down plants.

PERSISTENCE OF POVERTY
AND UNEMPLOYMENT

Organizing against Poverty

Despite President Johnson's 1960s "War on Poverty," antipoverty agencies noted that less than half of the nation's low-income residents were receiving any kind of public assistance. Yet poverty rates were at an all-time low by the early 1970s, which suggested that such assistance helped. The impetus of the civil rights movement and the promise of new social programs to uplift many from desperate circumstances led many antipoverty activists to mobilize for rights to housing, health care, and welfare during the 1970s.

The strong postwar industrial economy that had pulled many white and black Southerners north and west began to falter in the 1970s, just as many African Americans and Latinos had gained access to industrial jobs. Deindustrialization and white flight to the suburbs had left many central cities with a diminished tax base, decaying infrastructure, and a growing population living in poverty. Almost one-third of African Americans, 25 percent of Latinos, and 49 percent of female-headed households with children under age 18 lived in poverty. Access to relief benefits relieved some of the hardship. In 1960, fewer than 800,000 families accessed less than $1 billion in Aid to Families with Dependent Children (AFDC); in 1972, 3 million families received $6 billion in aid.

Abandoned housing on Chicago's South Side, May 1973. With white flight to the suburbs and the decline of urban industrial jobs in the 1970s, the nation's older cities were increasingly inhabited by low-income African Americans and Latinos. (John H. White/National Archives)

National Welfare Rights Organization
(1967–1974)

In 1966, protestors marched in 25 cities demanding adequate welfare support, and a year later activists from a dozen states met in Chicago to launch the National Welfare Rights Organization (NWRO). George Wiley, a former Congress of Racial Equality (CORE) director, who had established the Poverty Rights Action Center in Washington, D.C., and had helped develop community welfare organizing efforts, became director of NWRO.

To make certain that the organization was not taken over by middle-class "do-gooders," NWRO restricted membership to people with incomes below the poverty line. By 1969, it had more than 30,000 members in 100 cities. In the early 1970s, NWRO expanded its influence, winning support and funding from churches, civil rights groups, foundations, and unions, and attracting media attention. But during this period, NWRO also lost some of its militancy, with some of its visible welfare-mother leaders going on speaking tours instead of organizing others to storm or picket welfare offices.

When President Nixon introduced the Family Assistance Plan (FAP) to replace welfare programs with a federally guaranteed annual income, NWRO initially supported the move. But when congressional conservatives began making the program more restrictive, NWRO activists, along with some liberal Democrats and conservative Republicans, worked to defeat the Nixon bill.

NWRO continued to work for an improved guaranteed income bill and presented a Poor People's Platform at the 1972 Democratic Party national convention. But President Nixon tapped into the conservative backlash and attacked "welfare cheaters," damaging Democratic candidate George McGovern's efforts to advocate a $4,000 guaranteed income.

By the mid-1970s, the welfare rights movement suffered many attacks and lost organizing strength, and it became less effective. Although it was a multiracial movement, frequent media images of militant African American women occupying welfare offices sharpened an emerging racist backlash against welfare costs and welfare activism. Moreover, despite the large numbers of Americans living below the poverty line, it was difficult for people without resources to sustain organizations and to influence politicians.

In many respects, NWRO suffered from too much organization and the desires of individual leaders in key states such as New York and Massachusetts to remain in power. NWRO neighborhood, city, and state affiliates each elected leaders, and sometimes they felt threatened by new members and had little incentive to organize mass numbers of people into their organization. AFDC mothers dominated the groups and seldom organized or included the working poor. Backing away from a factional struggle that would have diversified the membership but endangered the survival of NWRO, founder George Wiley resigned in December 1972 and formed a new multiconstituency group called the Movement for Economic Justice.

Continued on next page

National Welfare Rights Organization (1967–1974), Continued

In the 1970s, most of the funds raised for NWRO went to its national office and to expensive political lobbying, and little to local organizing efforts. In the fall of 1974, executive director Johnnie Tillmon announced a fundraising campaign that would raise $1 million a year, relying on small donations from the poor. But few responded to the call, and within a few months, NWRO was bankrupt and closed its national office.

Despite its decline, NWRO left an important legacy. It raised awareness about income distribution and the obligation of the state in providing minimum sustenance for the nation's citizens, empowered thousands of poor women, and helped train a generation of organizers who carried NWRO's militant and democratic techniques into other community movements. But it failed to mobilize the millions of poor Americans to halt the growing attack on welfare or the upward distribution of wealth.

Labor unions, poor people, and their middle-class advocates launched the Citizens' Crusade Against Poverty (CCAP) in the late 1960s that brought together more than 100 organizations to demand an expanded War on Poverty. Welfare Rights Organizations (WROs) also grew to about 500 in 1970, but they tended to pursue grievances of individual members rather than to create mass organizations. By the early 1970s, groups including the Campaign for Adequate Welfare Reform Now expanded this vision to demand a guaranteed income.

Frustrated by their lack of access to jobs and income, poor people in northern cities organized "for the sheer right of survival" (Piven and Cloward 1979, 265). Cloward and Piven argued that if more eligible poor people would demand their rights to public assistance, the crisis situation would force the federal government to enact a comprehensive income program. Large concentrations of urban poor in the northern states and the Democratic Party's dependence on these states for political power indicated that disturbances could lead to wholesale change in the system to more effectively address the needs of the poor.

But President Nixon's 1972 reelection campaign marked a turning point in curbing sympathy for the poor. He and other conservatives tapped into a white backlash against African American gains and rising welfare rolls. In television ads, he warned that if McGovern were elected, the Democrats would put half the country on welfare. Politicians in many states and the Department of Health, Education and Welfare began calling for audits of recipients to curtail abuse and to implement eligibility restrictions.

The Arkansas Community Organizations for Reform Now (ACORN)

ACORN represented the most successful and visible effort of the decade to create a broad-based, multiracial, locally based organization to advocate low-income
concerns. In June 1970, NWRO organizer Wade Rathke went to Little Rock to try
to organize such a group as a test case for a broader national effort. Poor people
in Little Rock organized to successfully demand that Governor Winthrop Rockefeller set up a program to distribute used furniture and clothing. ACORN brought
together the working poor and welfare recipients to campaign for free school
lunches, public housing, and emergency hospital care.

ACORN broadened its work to appeal to moderate-income homeowners to
improve declining neighborhoods in Little Rock. The energy crisis and subsequent
efforts by utility companies to raise rates generated many protest activities.
ACORN's utility rate campaigns were popular with a larger public and convinced
many politicians to support rate reforms. But ACORN's rapid growth inevitably
led to tensions within the organization, especially on whether to focus on local or
national issues. The broadening of issues to appeal to a broader coalition created
splits in the movement, with some prominent welfare rights leaders severing ties
with ACORN. By 1977, the association's board concluded that ACORN's mission
went beyond specific neighborhoods to the needs of its low- and moderate-income
constituencies.

ACORN's model of organizing, with its intensive door-to-door recruitment and
fundraising, spawned similar groups in more than 40 communities across the
country between 1975 and 1980. For example, the Citizens Action Program in
Chicago halted an inner-city freeway and pressured banks to offer more mortgage
loans to low-income residents. Massachusetts Fair Share organized homeowners to
protest insurance and property tax inequities.

Changing Views of Poverty

The sympathy that Michael Harrington and Lyndon Johnson elicited for America's poor in the mid-1960s began to change dramatically in the early 1970s.
Policy experts, pundits, and politicians began to portray those in poverty as per-
sonally responsible for their plight and characterized the programs that mar-
ginally assisted them as unfairly burdening the middle class. Courts in the 1970s
also moved away from viewing welfare benefits as inherent rights to ruling that
they were set by legislation. The weakened economy of the early 1970s and
declining average family income contributed to the abrupt turn in Americans'
attitudes towards helping the poor. Analysts and policymakers also focused
on reforming the welfare system rather than creating more equitable economic

Mississippi Freedom Farm Corporation
(1969–1974)

Civil rights activist Fannie Lou Hamer, known for her work with the Student Non-violent Coordinating Committee (SNCC) and for representing the Mississippi Freedom Democratic Party, turned her attention to a project that would make poor people economically self-sufficient. In her native Sunflower County of the rural Delta, 70 percent of the mostly African American population lived on $1,000 or less a year, far below the poverty line of $2,000. Hamer began the Freedom Farm by convincing the Sunflower County chapter of the National Council of Negro Women to donate 50 pigs. Families could then receive a pregnant female pig from the farm's "bank," and return the pig once it had delivered offspring for the family to raise and later slaughter.

The Freedom Farm expanded in the early 1970s to develop a number of projects to benefit poor people in the area. The farm purchased about 700 acres of land that was used to raise vegetables for needy families and cash crops, cotton or soybeans, to make land payments. In 1971, the Farm provided food, shelter, transportation, and medical aid to some 300 families who were made homeless by tornadoes that ripped through Sunflower County. Taking advantage of low-cost FHA and farm mortgages, and with the assistance of local African American and white contractors, the Farm also started a housing cooperative that provided 70 affordable homes by 1972. The Freedom Farm also developed a high school scholarship program and a business development loan program.

During the five years it operated, the Freedom Farm served more than a thousand families a year. Tens of thousands of Mississippi residents had lost their farm jobs to mechanization in the late 1960s, and these were the primary constituents of the project. Although the Freedom Farm's goal was to help poor people become self-sufficient, it also helped them access the new food stamp program instituted in the county in 1970, what activists viewed as an entitlement to survival.

Despite its successes, the Freedom Farm began experiencing serious financial difficulties in 1973, and the experiment ultimately ended in 1974. Hamer had been an indefatigable organizer and fundraiser for the project, but the work took its toll on her health. Celebrities such as Harry Belafonte and college groups, labor unions, classrooms, and audiences who heard Hamer on programs such as the *Donahue* show, contributed tens of thousands of dollars to the Freedom Farm. Large and consistent donors, such as Wisconsin's Measure for Measure and the American Freedom from Hunger Foundation, also supported the project. Poor crop yields due to bad weather, pressures of back taxes and delinquent land payments, and poor management all contributed to the farm's decline. The Freedom Farm represented one of many cooperative visions that failed in the 1970s, but it also underscored the desperate plight of many poor Americans and their desires for economic self-sufficiency and the creation of alternatives to the welfare system.

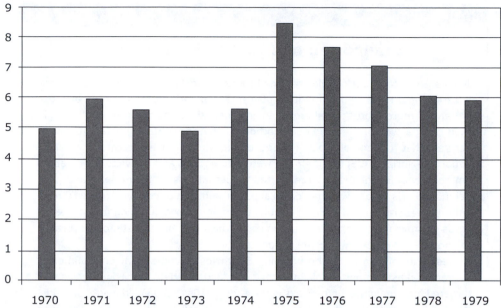

Figure 5.1 *The U.S. Unemployment Rate (percent), 1970–1979.* Source: *U.S. Department of Labor.*

policies as the American economy offered fewer opportunities to the working poor and working-class Americans.

The federal War on Poverty and the welfare rights movement through the 1960s had more than doubled the percentage of poor people receiving benefits, from 20 percent in 1959 to 50 percent in 1970. Many pointed to the fact that poverty still persisted despite federal programs, which proved that the War on Poverty "didn't work." Yet the antipoverty programs that began in the mid-1960s did reduce poverty levels in the United States, despite funding competition brought by escalating costs of the Vietnam War. By the mid-1970s, even in a declining economy, the poverty rate dropped to an all-time low of 11 percent, from 20 percent just a decade earlier in the prosperous 1960s.

Through the 1970s, presidential administrations struggled with ways to overhaul, streamline, and create more effective welfare programs; critics focused on the system's waste and abuses. President Nixon promised to dismantle the War on Poverty, but economic stagnation, inflation, and rising unemployment put more demand on programs such as Food Stamps, and social spending steadily increased. Nixon, who routinely spoke against federal solutions to the intractable problem of poverty, proposed the Family Assistance Program (FAP), which promised to radically alter the welfare system by providing a guaranteed minimum income floor to families. The legislation's defeat by an odd coalition of conservative southerners and welfare rights activists led many to give up on the idea of eliminating poverty.

Environmental Justice Movement

Just as America's poor people bore the brunt of a declining economy, deindustrialization, and harsher treatment by policymakers and the media, they also experienced more than their share of environmental degradation and pollution in their homes, workplaces, and neighborhoods. As Andrew Hurley notes, it was no accident that "the age of ecology corresponded with the rise of environmental inequality" (Hurley 1995, 172). Air and water regulations and the victories of labor-environmentalist coalitions often shifted industrial wastes to the land and poor neighborhoods. Those who had political power and wealth could more easily navigate bureaucracies and political entities to prevent toxic dumping in their backyards or move from the polluted urban core, which left more waste to affect racial minorities and other low-income residents.

Residents of barrios in the booming Southwest faced similar environmental degradation as did poor people in decaying industrial cities. East Los Angeles was targeted for a major set of freeways in the early 1970s that divided neighborhoods, erected barriers that destroyed local commerce, eliminated housing, and spewed millions of tons of particulates from slow-moving autos. David Diaz notes that Latino and Latina residents of other expanding Sunbelt cities, including Phoenix, San Antonio, San Diego, El Paso, and San Jose, also saw their barrios targeted for freeway construction. Despite their public protests, residents lacked the political power to halt city and state transportation agency plans, and through their displacement lost cultural connections as well as affordable housing.

Other coalitions of workers, low-income residents, and urban environmentalists joined during the decade to address the problems of industrial pollution that affected all residents. In 1970, Richard Hatcher, the first African American mayor of Gary, Indiana, told a group of white environmentalists trying to preserve a lakeshore that for African Americans the chief ecological issues were overcrowded housing and poor sanitation. Though this comment put in relief the lack of race and class-consciousness of the mainstream environmental movement, Hatcher stressed that the nation had the resources to defeat both poverty and pollution. Numerous grassroots groups echoed this claim as they launched the environmental justice movement.

Nixon's second administration implemented stricter eligibility, work requirements, and cost reductions for federal assistance. Policymakers dismantled programs that advocated for the poor and working poor, such as Community Action and the Office of Economic Opportunity, and absorbed less controversial programs within the federal bureaucracy. After the defeat of Nixon's FAP proposal, analysts began to push another Income Supplement Program to replace welfare with work incentives and to devolve social services to the states. After presidents Nixon and Ford emphasized the need to decentralize poverty programs, in

August 1977, President Carter proposed a more expensive welfare program that would encourage work by creating publicly funded jobs. But anti-inflation efforts soon overcame efforts to provide employment.

Although social spending for, and the needs of the poor, grew in the 1970s, as Alice O'Connor finds, much of the spending was directed to "poverty research." Federal funding for the social sciences and policy analysts to evaluate programs and create more efficient bureaucracies grew from $3 million in 1965 to nearly $200 million in 1980. Yet, as O'Connor concludes, poverty analysts retreated from the goal of ending poverty to absorb the political imperatives of welfare reform. Entrenched in government programs or dependent on federal grants, they followed the lead of policymakers. They found it more efficient and politically expedient to advocate income maintenance rather than plan more equitable economic policies, even as the 1970s economy increasingly failed working-class and middle-income Americans as well as the poor.

One of the results of this crackdown on costs was revealed in 1974 when a judge found that more than 100,000 poor, mostly minority, women were sterilized each year under the threat of removal of welfare benefits. Women's rights advocates stressed the hypocrisy of federal efforts to pay for sterilization but not provide a range of contraceptive options, including abortion, for the poor. In the early 1970s, many policymakers supported legalized abortions—not in support of women's rights but to reduce welfare expenditures.

In the 1970s, many Americans turned away from both the ideals of social justice and the facts about welfare assistance. Instead of acknowledging that benefits for the poor were actually falling rather than rising, many chose to believe what pundits and others claimed were abuses and bad choices by the poor. Resentments grew over perceived privileges that welfare mothers received over their working-women counterparts. Politicians routinely slandered welfare recipients. For example, Gov. Ronald Reagan called them "lazy parasites." The media helped foster an image of disproportionality in the public's mind and linked poverty with race. As the percentage of minorities living in urban areas increased from 36 percent to 48 percent in the 1970s, white Americans increasingly began to associate poverty with people of color. As Gwendolyn Mink and Rickie Solinger point out in their book about the history of welfare policy, 75 percent of media images presented about welfare profiled African Americans, creating the distinct impression that they benefited to a much greater extent than their white counterparts when in reality the majority of welfare recipients were white.

Welfare or Work? Debates over Income Guarantee and Full Employment Legislation

In 1969, Republican president Richard Nixon proposed as his solution to runaway welfare costs an omnibus Family Assistance Plan (FAP) that would guarantee a minimum income to all families with children. Many liberals and welfare-rights advocates supported the precedent of a guaranteed income and federal aid to the working poor, something that other western industrialized nations already supplied. But other progressives and feminists divided over how to improve poor women's lives, and their debates about appropriate family roles in the 1970s reflected the tensions between those who wanted to abolish gender differences in federal solutions and those who emphasized the realities of women's roles as mothers. Many commentators, politicians, and activists clung to the male breadwinner ideal and emphasized the need for jobs programs for men so that wives would not have to go on welfare. They claimed that by providing families with working fathers a minimum income, FAP would promote family stability. Even the NWRO supported the creation of 3 million jobs for male heads of families.

But soon welfare supporters criticized the low minimum income, which would lower benefit levels for many AFDC recipients, and the work requirements that made few provisions for child care, and they fought for the defeat of FAP. NOW followed NWRO's lead and opposed FAP because of its emphasis on family patriarchy while other women's groups and advocates for the poor supported the idea.

Beginning in 1971, the primarily white and middle-class League of Women Voters made support for the poor its primary legislative goal, and it formed coalitions, educated citizens, lobbied for higher benefits, and developed a volunteer corps to help welfare applicants. While opposing the "workfare" and other drawbacks of FAP, the League worked to secure compromise legislation enshrining the major principles of a federal guaranteed income. League officers accused the NWRO of ignoring the needs of the millions of working poor who would see their incomes increased under FAP, and the possibilities of a federal minimum income erasing the racial income stratification in the South. The NWRO represented AFDC recipients largely from high-benefit states, the League pointed out, and it claimed that FAP legislation would help a much larger segment of the poor.

The concept of a guaranteed family annual income died in the U.S. Senate in October 1972. Conservatives opposed FAP because they claimed it cost too much; welfare rights and many liberal groups rejected it because it would offer too little. Conservative Southern representatives used their power in the congressional committee structure to defeat the plan because even an income as low as $1,600 for a family of four would have damaged the low-wage structure of the South. And the president himself lost interest in supporting the bill, even as compromises were proposed.

Feminists remained conflicted at the International Women's Year Conference in 1977 and had difficulty agreeing on a welfare resolution. Many believed that insisting on welfare mothers' right to full-time motherhood would close off jobs programs and opportunities for other women to become self-sufficient.

In 1977, Democratic president Jimmy Carter proposed the Program for Better Jobs and Income (PBJI), claiming the employment program would not add any costs to the welfare budget. PBJI was similar to FAP in that it guaranteed a job to each family's "primary wage earner," reinforcing the traditional family model that kept women at home. But this time, women's groups were more unified in their recognition of welfare as a feminist issue. Organizations such as NOW, League of Women Voters, Women's Lobby, and the National Women's Political Caucus testified before Congress and met with administration officials to protest sex discrimination in benefit levels. The economic downturn, "feminization of poverty," and increasing reality of two-income family wage earners motivated these organizations to advocate full employment as an alternative to welfare. This emphasis on work also grew from the inability to implement policies compensating household labor and childrearing. As NOW lobbyist Pat Leeper noted in 1977, the Carter Administration's "wishful thinking" about the male family breadwinner kept women "dependent and underskilled" (Chappell 2002, 169). Yet this position still did not address the reality that most women in poverty had family responsibilities.

Through the 1970s, more pundits and politicians came to argue that welfare fostered a "culture" of dependency and that work and family stability could

Rev. Jesse Jackson, founder of Operation PUSH (People United to Save Humanity), addresses supporters of the Humphrey-Hawkins Bill for full employment, January 1975. (Library of Congress)

rehabilitate the poor. But little funding followed for jobs programs. Sen. Hubert Humphrey of Minnesota and Rep. Augustus Hawkins, who represented the high-unemployment district of Watts in Los Angeles, recognized that focusing on full employment could mend the frayed New Deal coalition by linking civil and economic rights. The mid-1970s recession, the worst since the Great Depression of the 1930s, had pushed unemployment rates close to 10 percent. Hawkins recognized that job security was beyond an individual's control, and society, through the federal government, could temporarily lessen suffering through jobs programs. He and Humphrey introduced the Humphrey-Hawkins Bill in 1974, which required the president to submit each year a plan for full employment, including federal jobs programs in the public and private sectors. Civil rights groups and the AFL-CIO made it their legislative priority, and after four years of struggle, the bill became law. But the Carter administration and conservatives drained it of its substance, requiring business incentives and commitments to balanced budgets. Full employment lost support as the administration, Congress, and the Federal Reserve focused on reducing inflation. Efforts to make the federal government the employer of last resort were defeated much like a similar effort in 1946. The tolerance of high unemployment and layoffs grew during the 1970s, marking an end to the collective ethos that had for 30 years marked an effort to "lift everyone's lot" (Uchitelle 2006, 128).

Managing the Poor: The New Prison-Industrial Complex

The protests, uprisings, and changing cultural mores of the late 1960s and early 1970s had led many Americans to want to restrain what they viewed as threats to the social order. In response to this sentiment, Congress passed a massive federal crime bill in 1968 that created the Law Enforcement Assistance Administration, which began channeling matching grants to states, thus fueling accelerated efforts to arrest and incarcerate. Appealing to the "silent majority," Richard Nixon had warned against rising crime rates and a society run amok by the demands of workers, minorities, and the poor. Nixon and other politicians promised to "get tough" on crime, reinforcing the belief that increased imprisonment would effectively control crime. Because of this changing attitude and the decline in faith in rehabilitation, state and federal prison populations doubled during the 1970s. Even greater increases would follow in the 1980s with additional crime bills and President Reagan's tough stance on drugs, marking a new era in the history of American incarceration.

At the same time that the criminal justice system expanded jail and prison populations in the 1970s, concerns for civil rights and liberties led many of those who were incarcerated to use the courts to challenge prison officials in their treatment. The courts provided new definitions regarding the rights of due process, including inmates' rights to communicate with an attorney and to practice

Attica Prison Rebellion (1971)

On September 9, 1971, a fight at Attica Correctional Facility in New York sparked an uprising in which 1,200 inmates took over the prison. Holding 38 guards as hostages, the African American, Latino, and white prisoners demanded 30 reforms, including improved conditions, healthier food, the hiring of more minority guards, and a promise of amnesty to all involved in the rebellion.

For four days, the inmates ran the prison, conducted negotiations with numerous officials, and repeated their demands to reporters. The inmates allowed a Citizens Observers Committee to join the negotiations and to observe treatment of hostages and reach a peaceful conclusion. Civil rights lawyer William Kunstler pleaded with Gov. Nelson Rockefeller to come to Attica, negotiate with them, and grant more time because prisoners would not harm any hostages as long as negotiations continued.

Despite Kunstler's and others warning that the state's effort to forcibly suppress the rebellion would result in a massacre, Governor Rockefeller refused to consider amnesty and after five days sent state troopers to retake the prison. State Corrections Commissioner Russell Oswald claimed he had pledged to meet 28 of 30 of the prisoner demands but felt that the situation was deteriorating, with prisoners making weapons and accelerating the possibility of violence. On September 13, 1,700 U.S. Army, state, and National Guard troopers stormed the prison from the air and ground. Officers stationed on the prison's roofs fired more than 2,000 rounds of ammunition in six minutes, killing 29 inmates and 10 hostages. A commission that investigated the incident later called this the "bloodiest encounter between Americans since the Civil War" (Gonnerman, 2001).

After the New York State Correction Department recaptured Attica State Prison, it took weeks for reporters, lawyers, clergymen, and medical teams to enter the prison and piece together fragmentary reports about what happened. Meanwhile, because state officials claimed that inmates had cold-bloodedly slit the throats of eight hostages, many Americans came to see the Attica prisoners as "animals" and "outlaws" who left the prison authorities little choice but to use force. One letter to the editor of *The New York Times* on September 19 summed up the feelings of many Americans who saw the prisoner rebellion as reflective of a deteriorating society and called for a crackdown on crime and dissent: "Rampant permissiveness, long afflicting our society, easily penetrates penitentiary walls" (Yamin 1971).

Eventually, a local coroner, reporters, and lawyers who interviewed eyewitnesses refuted officials' claims. After the Attica invasion, prison guards sought revenge, beating and torturing the inmates and executing one. Frank "Big Black" Smith recounted in an oral history interview that he and his fellow prisoners were forced to run through a gauntlet over broken glass, then "five officers beat me and broke my wrist and opened my head up and knocked me just about out, played shotgun roulette with me, and dumped me on the floor in the [prison] hospital" ("Attica Revisited").

Continued on next page

Attica Prison Rebellion (1971), Continued

The final death toll for the uprising was 43, including three prisoners killed by their fellow inmates. Over the next three years, many more chapters were added to the story of Attica, as the state indicted more than 60 prisoners for crimes ranging from sodomy to murder. Despite the National Lawyers Guild and other groups pressing charges against state police officers and prison guards, the state refused to prosecute them. After a 27-year legal battle, New York State finally compensated the 502 former prisoners who were injured, who shared an $8 million settlement. In the wake of this settlement, the families of the hostages formed their own organization, the Forgotten Victims of Attica.

one's religious faith. The courts forced many state prisons to comply with federal oversight during the decade until improvements in inmate treatment were made.

The numbers of opponents to the death penalty grew in the early 1970s along with concerns over racial disparities in the sentencing of individuals. A series of court challenges found that people of color and the poor received a disproportionate share of death sentences, which led the Supreme Court in 1972 (*Furman v. Georgia*) to essentially ban the death penalty. The Court determined that application of the death penalty, especially in the South, amounted to arbitrary sentencing and was was "cruel and unusual" in its discriminatory patterns. For the next four years, there was effectively a moratorium on the death penalty, but because the Court did not outright declare it unconstitutional, states rewrote their capital punishment laws to meet the Court requirements. In *Gregg v. Georgia* (1976), the Court allowed the death penalty if states guided jurors to distinguish between crimes and held two different hearings, one to determine guilt or innocence and the other to decide the sentence.

Still, a disproportionate number of African Americans and Latinos from poor, urban neighborhoods and the rural South were in prison. Although African Americans represented just 11 percent of the total U.S. population, they represented over half of prison inmates. Activists like Amiri Baraka and Angela Davis articulated the racial and class dimensions of incarceration.

On January 16, 1970, prisoner George Jackson and two others were charged with murdering a guard in retaliation for the killing of three African American activists by another guard at California's Soledad prison. Isolated in solitary confinement for 23 hours a day, Jackson studied political economy and radical theory and wrote two books, *Blood in My Eye* and *Soledad Brother,* which became best sellers and brought him worldwide attention. On August 7, Jackson's 17-year-old brother, Jonathan, burst into a Marin County courtroom with an automatic weapon and took Judge Harold Haley as a hostage to demand freedom for the three "Soledad Brothers." However, Haley, two other prisoners, and Jonathan Jackson were killed as they attempted to drive away from the courthouse. Activist Angela Davis was charged with providing a shotgun for the crime. Two weeks later, three days before he was to go on trial, George Jackson was gunned down in the prison yard at San Quentin during an escape attempt. The fate of the Soledad brothers and the Attica prison rebellion a year later drew attention to conditions of the nation's prisons, especially overcrowding, and the grievances of African American militants.

TECHNOLOGICAL DREAMS

Reaching New Galaxies

If the country's economic situation appeared dire and protests more desperate, technological developments in the 1970s offered improvement in how Americans lived, worked, and played. Even knowledge of and travel in space became

Design for a space colony known as "Stanford Torus," developed by NASA Ames Research Center and Stanford University, 1975. Americans retained their fascination with space travel even as their support for NASA declined. (Don Davis)

Brig. Gen. Thomas P. Stafford (left), and Soviet Maj. Gen. Andriyan G. Nikolayev in the Soviet Soyuz spacecraft simulator during the Apollo-Soyuz Test Project, 1975. (NASA)

a realistic goal rather than science-fiction fantasy. Knowledge of the solar system grew rapidly in the 1970s even as the federal government trimmed its space explorations. The ill-fated Apollo 13, which safely returned to Earth after equipment failure in April 1970 prevented a landing on the moon, did not end crewed explorations of space. Apollo 14 and 15 in 1971, then Apollo 16 and 17 in 1972, took scientists to the Moon where they successfully explored lunar valleys and mountains and returned with rock and soil samples. But because of the expense of crewed missions, the Vietnam War that siphoned funds away from NASA, and the geopolitical achievement of U.S. technological superiority over the Soviets, subsequent Apollo missions were cancelled.

Although astronaut space flights were more glamorous, NASA's robotic explorers, including Mariner 9 that circled Mars in 1971, Pioneer 10 that neared Jupiter in 1973, and Mariner 10 that flew by Venus and Mercury, became the most efficient way to explore space and determine planetary composition. Each sent back to Earth thousands of remarkable images of the planets. Probes launched in the decade took photos of the Sun and Venus, landed on Mars and Mercury, observed Jupiter, and flew close to the rings of Saturn. Some scientists claimed that the Voyager missions to Jupiter, Saturn, Uranus, and Neptune were the most

Skylab

NASA envisioned future space flights using Earth-orbiting space stations and a shuttle system and in May 1973 launched its giant laboratory, Skylab. Teams of astronauts made three visits to Skylab, first for 28, then 59, and finally 84 days, until February 1974. They carried out more than 100 scientific experiments. NASA was especially interested in the effects of extended periods of weightlessness on humans, and the lab demonstrated that humans could live and operate effectively in space for long periods of time. Shortly after the May 14 launch, the station's thin meteorite shield and two solar panels were torn loose. The Skylab 2 mission was launched on May 25 with a crew that erected a parasol-like structure to shade the station and allow the crew to tolerate the inside temperature.

Scientists expected the space station to remain in orbit at least until 1981, but because of increased solar activity that created a drag, it reentered the Earth's atmosphere in July 1979. Fortunately, Skylab broke up as it fell over the Indian Ocean and Western Australia, avoiding inhabited areas. Critics inside and outside NASA accused the agency of failing to launch a shuttle mission to boost it into a higher, more stable orbit, allowing astronauts to continue to study the effects of space on the station. Astronauts who worked on the station believed that each mission improved the station's operations and, at the end of the third and final mission, on the remote chance that someone else would enter, they left food and film at the front of the hatch. Others in NASA welcomed the end of Skylab, fearing that continued efforts and costs to continue it would have diverted the agency from other projects, including more advanced stations. But funding decreases and a focus on short-term shuttle flights ended American efforts to establish permanent stations. The Soviet Union, the first to establish a space station in 1970, continued to focus on long-duration missions and launched a series of subsequent Salyut stations in the 1970s and early 1980s. In 1986, the Soviets launched the first module of the Mir space station.

significant feats in space exploration history. Their surprising discoveries of phenomena such as the 300-year-old storm, the Great Red Spot, and Jupiter's four large moons captured scientists' imaginations. From Earth, new telescopes spotted new moons, and astronomers discovered a black hole, stars that emit X-rays, and the speed of the Milky Way.

Yet these discoveries did not capture the public imagination as much as did the first Apollo moonwalk in 1969, and the decade lacked the optimism that accompanied 1960s space travel. By the mid-1970s, waning public interest and a declining economy led President Nixon to direct NASA to focus on a reusable orbital vehicle, or space shuttle, instead of crewed planetary exploration. Funding for NASA declined during the 1970s, and its focus became more commercially practical rather than "reaching for the stars." For example, the 1970s NASA

Space Travel and Popular Culture

If popular and congressional support for NASA declined in the 1970s, fantasies about space travel, life, and battles continued to capture the popular imagination as they had for generations. Americans could figuratively enter new galaxies through a spate of new science-fiction literature and films.

Although the popular television series *Star Trek* ended in 1969, its popularity continued in the 1970s through countless reruns, fan groups called "Trekkies," and among the counterculture who valued the show's currency, multiethnic cast, and antiwar critiques. In 1976, following a letter-writing campaign by fans, President Ford and NASA named the prototype space shuttle *Enterprise* after the fictional starship.

In 1975, filmmaker George Lucas conceived of two trilogies about power, politics, sin, and redemption in a high-action adventure in another galaxy in the 21st century. Although several movie studios turned down the idea of the films, 20th Century Fox backed Lucas, and when it was released in May 1977, the first *Star Wars* film (later renamed *Star Wars Episode 4: A New Hope*) was enormously popular and became the most successful film in North American history. Fans eagerly awaited the release of subsequent films in the series over the next several decades.

Other popular movies about space travel revealed encounters with planets and creatures that portrayed a nightmarish vision of voyaging into the unknown. *Beneath the Planet of the Apes,* the sequel to the popular film *Planet of the Apes,* was released in 1970 and was followed by three more sequels over the next three years as well as a short-lived television series in 1974. The movies were based on the premise of astronauts lost in space and crashing onto the surface of an unknown planet where "lower" primates have surpassed the intelligence of humankind, creating a civilization that cages and enslaves human beings like animals. The popularity of the series was followed by merchandise, including action figures, board games, and comic books.

Alien (1979) explored similar dystopic themes with strange space creatures as murdering stowaways. The movie was phenomenally successful and popularized the space-horror genre that sparked the generation of similar films through the next decades. *Alien* also introduced perhaps the first space-age female heroine, Ripley, played by Sigourney Weaver.

missions benefited the aerospace industry, and improved satellite technology helped advance weather forecasting and telecommunications.

The value of space orbits also became more contested in the 1970s. In a decade of a declining economy and rising unemployment, many Americans wondered why the United States should be devoting scarce resources on space science rather than domestic needs. The whole notion of "progress," which had once convinced Americans that they could accomplish anything and their lives

Space Enthusiasts and the L5 Society

Along with the profusion of science fiction in print, television, and film were groups organized to support space travel and living, partly organized to defend public expenditures for NASA in light of growing criticism. In 1975, Carolyn and Keith Henson of Tucson, Arizona, founded the L5 Society to promote the space colony ideas of Dr. Gerard K. O'Neill. O'Neill envisioned huge rotating space habitats that would be located on the L4 and L5 Lagrangian points of stable gravitational equilibrium located just outside the Moon's orbit. In 1974, he published a paper on the subject, "The Colonization of Space," which appeared in the journal *Physics Today,* and he organized a Conference on Space Manufacturing Facilities held at Princeton. With O'Neill's blessing, the Hensons corresponded with attendees, organized the L5 Society, and published their first newsletter. In it, they stated "The L-5 Society is being formed to educate the public about the benefits of space communities and manufacturing facilities, to serve as a clearinghouse for information and news in this fast developing area and to raise funds to support work on these concepts where public money is not available" (Brandt-Erichsen).

Local chapters formed immediately in response to the Hensons' appeal. After receiving a copy of the newsletter in the summer of 1976, Gregory R. Bennett of Seattle formed the Northwest L5 Society because he and Carolyn Henson decided there were not enough members in any one state to form a stable organization. Local chapters were autonomous and defined chapter activities and became the major recruiting force for the L5 Society. Bennett gave public lectures on space industrialization and the L5 Society's vision at venues like the SeaCon '76 science fiction convention held in Seattle in September 1976.

Local chapters and the national L5 Society often split on priorities, with locals wanting to focus on private development and L5 emphasizing political lobbying to prevent any form of sovereignty, private property, or environmental degradation in outer space that would make space colonization impossible. In 1986 the Society, which had grown to about 10,000 members, merged with the 25,000 member National Space Institute.

During the 1970s space proponents did not represent ideological convergence but rather a range of enthusiasts from left to right. For example, NASA received relatively bipartisan support over the decades, and the publisher of the *Whole Earth Catalog* was inspired to publish Gerard K. O'Neill's book *Space Colonies.* Later, the pro-space activist community became characterized as stridently libertarian and antigovernment.

would continue to improve, underwent greater scrutiny beginning in the 1970s. Writers and philosophers who had warned of the limits of growth gained traction during the 1973 oil and environmental crises. For the first time, many wondered whether American society might deteriorate rather than necessarily move toward a better future.

Space activist movements grew in this context to revive the idea of progress and place humanity's future hopes in space development. Groups such as the L-5 Society viewed space as a provider of infinite resources and an endless source of innovation and new knowledge.

Begun as a weapon in the Cold War, by the 1970s, the space exploration program became a symbol of international cooperation. In July 1975, the much publicized Apollo-Soyuz Test Project brought together three American astronauts and two Soviet cosmonauts. But if the project was symbolic, it was expensive and had little scientific value, negating NASA goals of holding down costs through cooperative ventures.

Dreams of future space ventures were dashed by the failure of NASA to launch the heralded space shuttle *Enterprise*. Named for the famous space vehicle in *Star Trek,* the shuttle became the victim of contractor cost-overruns and an increasingly stingy Congress and President Carter. NASA awarded the orbiter contract to Rockwell International in 1972, and *Enterprise* tested successfully in 1976 and demonstrated that a shuttle spacecraft could fly and land like aircraft. NASA planned five orbiters in the shuttle fleet but in late 1977 abandoned plans to upgrade the *Enterprise* for space flight. Through the 1970s, the Office of Management and Budget pressured federal agencies to reduce spending, and NASA faced particular scrutiny for repeated funding appeals for the shuttle program. In 1985, the *Enterprise* was shipped to the Smithsonian for preservation and display.

In addition to challenges to meet costs of its space programs, NASA was slow to recognize the currency of 1970s social movements. It did not admit women and African Americans to its astronaut corps until the late 1970s, and it did not tap into the momentum of the environmental movement to focus more on Earth's environment, although much of the Skylab program was devoted to Earth observation.

Other New Worlds: The Personal Computer

Stewart Brand, creator of the *Whole Earth Catalog* and inspiration to thousands who sought to live more simply and self-sufficiently, was one of the first observers to claim that "computers are coming to the people" (Ceruzzi 1998, 207). In 1972, Brand witnessed people at the Stanford Artificial Intelligence Laboratory playing a computer game, Spacewar, on the large PDP-10. As computer historian Paul Ceruzzi notes, Brand recognized the allure of the PDP-10 and the sensation that users had an individual relationship with the computer because it allowed saving information to and from personal files or tapes. The evolution of the personal computer in the 1970s grew from the convergence of technological advances in semiconductors with the intellectual desire to bring computing to individuals.

In 1970, Xerox Corporation established the Palo Alto Research Center to investigate applications of the new information technology, and Robert Noyce opened Intel nearby, forming the nexus of what became known as the country's center of technology, "Silicon Valley." Through the work of Dr. Ted Hoff Jr., Intel advertised the first microprocessor, or computer chip, in *Electronic News Magazine* in 1971, launching what many called the computer revolution.

It was the proprietor of a small model-rocket hobby shop in Albuquerque, New Mexico, H. Edward Roberts, who launched the first accessible personal computer. Roberts advertised his $400 MITS Altair 8800 minicomputer in the January 1975 issue of *Popular Electronics* as the "world's first minicomputer kit." Only serious hobbyists could assemble and use the Altair. Although Roberts tried to sell it for serious applications, users created an extensive social network to expand its possibilities and play games.

Paul Allen showed his friend Bill Gates the *Popular Electronics* issue and the two decided to write a Beginner's All-purpose Symbolic Instruction Code (BASIC) software that would make the Altair more interactive and accessible for the novice computer user. The pair had attended private high school together in Seattle and had learned programming before heading to Harvard. In the late 1960s, capital-intensive new computer companies found it difficult to remain solvent through renting expensive computer time to engineering companies and others. Before it folded in 1970, one of these companies, Computer Center Corporation, or C-Cubed of Seattle, gave teenager Bill Gates ample time on its computer in exchange for eliminating system bugs.

Gates and Allen abandoned college to develop software for MITS, then in late 1976 created their company, Microsoft, to sell an improved version of the Altair BASIC. In a 1976 "open letter," Gates complained to hobbyists about their making copies of his BASIC without compensation. In 1978, Microsoft moved from Albuquerque to Bellevue, Washington, a Seattle suburb, and established "the ethic of charging money for software" as it established its early dominance of the new industry (Ceruzzi 1998, 240).

In 1977, Radio Shack introduced the inexpensive TRS-80 in its stores and brought personal computers to a mass audience. That same year, Steve Jobs and Steve Wozniak introduced the Apple II,

Apple Computers cofounder Steve Jobs poses with the Apple II computer, 1979. Jobs and associate Steve Wozniak helped launch the computer revolution. (Ralph Morse/Time Life Pictures/ Getty Images)

which exceeded its predecessors in performance, graphics, and ability to house interactive games, and soon provided floppy disk use. IBM had first developed the floppy disk to store and transfer data in 1971 and, once reduced in size to 5.25 inches in 1976, it became widely used.

By 1978, Intel and Motorola had made strides in creating faster and more efficient microprocessors. Their chips, which could process data in 32-bit words, were chosen by Apple and IBM for their personal computers. By the end of the 1970s, computers had become accessible to large numbers of Americans.

The Internet also had its roots in the 1970s. Set up as a cross-country link for the U.S. Department of Defense's Advanced Research Projects Agency Network (ARPANET), the project's first international connection, with Norway, occurred in 1973. The first email program was invented in 1971, and in 1975, Telnet became the first commercial equivalent of ARPANET.

Alternative Technology

Although many Americans placed great faith in the promises of technology, a growing environmental movement made clear that technological and industrial innovations had also caused environmental problems. Chemical wastes and industrial and auto emissions had damaged air, land, and water, but companies claimed cleanup would damage the economy.

Nuclear power had once promised clean and efficient energy as a solution to limited fossil fuels. But in the 1970s, public opposition grew over cost and safety issues, and by the time of the Three Mile Island accident in 1979, nuclear power plant construction had ended and some existing reactors were mothballed. Especially in Pacific Coast states, demands for citizen involvement and oversight of nuclear plans led to commissions, hearings, and initiatives. In one of the first of these efforts, in 1970, voters in Eugene, Oregon, defeated a proposal by the city's public utility to construct a nuclear plant. Aware of earthquake dangers, Californians refused to approve a half-dozen nuclear sites sought by utilities. When electric companies moved eastward to the region's less-inhabited and arid interior to find sites, they met opposition from unlikely coalitions of agribusiness owners concerned about depletion of water sources and environmentalists. By the late 1970s, antinuclear activists in Bakersfield, California, and Skagit County, Washington, organized citizens to reject plant proposals. Yet these activists had to narrow their ambitions. The Western Bloc, a coalition of antinuclear activists, was unable to pass initiatives that shut down existing nuclear plants. They were more successful with initiatives that banned waste transportation or storage or defeated new plant proposals. For example, in response to voter-supported Proposition 15, the California legislature in 1976 passed a bill that halted new plant construction unless the U.S. Department of Energy found appropriate solutions to the problem of radioactive waste disposal.

Activists pressed for limits and regulations as one strategy for curbing technological damage to the environment. Concerns about the safety of nuclear power led Congress to pass the Energy Reorganization Act in 1974, which created the Nuclear Regulatory Commission. Earlier, in 1970, Congress passed the Clean Air Act, which required the automobile industry to reduce hydrocarbon and carbon monoxide emissions by 90 percent or risk federal fines. The Act also provided tax incentives to companies to switch to clean fuels.

The expense, safety, and pollution concerns associated with nuclear and petroleum technologies led many Americans influenced by the environmental movement to search for renewable alternatives. The "appropriate" or alternative technology (AT) movement was an intellectual as well as social movement. In the mid-1960s, British economist E. F. Schumacher and several others called for new development strategies that would consider the needs of poorer countries without damaging the environment and wasting resources as had western industrial countries. Schumacher created the Intermediate Technology Development Group to put into practice in both First and Third Worlds, and his 1973 book *Small Is Beautiful: A Study of Economics as if People Mattered* was immensely popular with American youth.

The communal or "back to the land" movement of the 1970s also influenced a growing AT movement, best characterized by the popularity of Stewart Brand's *Whole Earth Catalog,* which provided ideas and tools for alternative technology. Hundreds—or by some estimates, thousands—of AT groups formed in the United States in the 1970s. Rather than creating technological "fixes" to solve environmental problems, these groups advocated nonpolluting technology that used renewable resources. Intellectuals Murray Bookchin, Herbert Marcuse, and young environmentalists influenced by AT broke with those in the counterculture and environmental movements who equated technology with planetary destruction. They advocated small-scale and accessible *appropriate* technologies that, instead of harming the environment, could counter the dangerous military-industrial technocracy.

Other divisions emerged between ecological proponents of alternative energy who critiqued industrial society and advocated dramatic societal shifts to reduce consumption, and policymakers who believed new forms of energy could support continued growth. Solar advocacy groups, which proliferated in the 1970s, ranged from groups like the Bio-Energy Council, which included corporate vice presidents among board members, to the Domestic Technology Institute in Evergreen, Colorado, which advocated more decentralized solutions. A range of environmental groups, including the Audubon Society, Friends of the Earth, and the Sierra Club added to the chorus of groups promoting greater government support for solar and wind energy.

On May 3, 1978, solar energy enthusiasts around the world celebrated the first "Sun Day," to usher in what they hoped would be a new energy era powered by the sun. Denis Hayes, the organizer of the nation's first Earth Day, organized

Modular solar-heated home near Corrales, New Mexico, 1974. During the 1970s, the alternative energy movement blossomed in tandem with concern about limited resources and unsustainable growth. (National Archives)

Sun Day in the United States. Hundreds of events around the country demonstrated the sun's efficiency including the five-mile-long "solar clothes dryer" strung between Miami and Key Biscayne.

President Carter embraced the solar craze, boosting America's solar budget by $100 million, installing a solar hot water system on the White House, and declaring that the United States could obtain 25 percent of its energy from solar, wind, and other renewable energy resources by the year 2000.

Advocates of AT linked the need for changes in social arrangements to the adoption of "soft energy," or energy efficiency and renewable energy technologies. They warned that corporations could sell solar heaters while still resisting activists' efforts to create an alternative society of greater equality and participation. Many believed that solar energy was becoming a "false panacea" for long-term energy problems. Ecological solar advocates distrusted both big corporations and big government, seeing solutions for the environmental crises in smaller, environmentally sustainable communities. But most policymakers rejected this more radical philosophy and saw solar as one tool to help meet growing energy needs. In 1973, John Love, President Nixon's chief energy official, linked energy consumption to prosperity: "Americans are the greatest energy users in the history of the world. . . .What a tribute that is to our intelligence and innovativeness" (quoted in Laird 2003, 49).

Washington Public Power Supply System Scandal

Washington Public Power Supply System (WPPSS), or what would later become known as "Whoops," was a municipal corporation that allowed publicly owned utilities to pool resources to build power generation facilities. As energy demands increased in the early 1970s in the growing Pacific Northwest, the Bonneville Power Administration, which provided cheap hydropower from Columbia River dams to public utilities, told the utilities that costs would increase. WPPSS made plans to build a series of nuclear plants, most on the federally operated Hanford Nuclear Reservation in arid central Washington, and signed up utilities to share costs. Construction began on the first plant in 1971, and by 1974, WPPSS had committed to five reactors. By the end of the decade, huge cost overruns and delays, and increasing concerns over nuclear plant safety, led to public demands to halt further construction. In January 1982, anticipating costs of $23.8 billion to complete the five plants, the WPPSS board stopped construction on four of the plants and defaulted on $2.25 billion in bonds. The largest municipal bond default in U.S. history left Northwest utility-rate payers the burden to repay and no new power generation.

WPPSS managers pointed to rising inflation, Nuclear Regulatory Commission safety changes that increased costs, heavy rains that washed away much of the excavation work for two projects, and lack of coordination between designers and various building contractors as the main culprits for the plants' problems. But historian Daniel Pope finds that the WPPSS debacle reflected weaknesses in other large-scale, high-technology projects. WPPSS managers had little nuclear plant expertise and inefficient methods of enforcing contractual agreements. The "interactive complexity" of multiple contractors and monitors, combined with pressures for fast-track construction on a complicated venture and bond financing that generated inaccurate information about power needs, helped doom the project.

The WPPSS disaster revealed how faith in technological solutions to the energy crisis crumbled under increasing skepticism in the 1970s. The environmental movement had initiated questions about nuclear plant safety, and public concern grew through the decade. The Washington Environmental Council, which threatened to sue Seattle City Light to require an environmental impact statement on the nuclear plants, agreed instead to the utility's proposal to establish a Citizens' Overview Committee that included leading environmentalists to examine the needs for power and the best ways to provide it. In 1975, the citizens' committee concluded that investment in nuclear power was unnecessary, and conservation measures could meet new energy needs. The Seattle City Council then voted not to participate in WPPSS 4 and 5.

New Technologies and Daily Life

The 1970s not only fostered the information age through computer production and space exploration but also altered commercial and social interactions as new technology entered daily life. Americans embraced ways of dealing with daily needs more quickly. The pocket calculator by the mid-1970s had become a small, inexpensive tool for consumers to calculate large volumes of information. Families bought disposable diapers at supermarkets, shopped at malls that housed multiple stores, and dined more frequently at fast-food restaurants. In 1972, Wendy's, which Dave Thomas opened in Columbus, Ohio, in 1969, pioneered the use of the "drive-thru" window to allow customers to purchase and pick up their food without having to leave their cars. McDonald's and other fast-food chains soon adopted the window service. Americans sought food convenience at home, too. By 1975, sales of microwave ovens exceeded sales of gas ranges.

If the 1970s was a decade of narcissism, as many critics claimed, new products catered to consumers' desires. Whether installing waterbeds at home, or tuning in portable Walkmans when commuting or exercising, Americans sought comfort and pleasure. New technologies allowed people to create their own private entertainment spaces, whether enjoying a Walkman outdoors, 8-track tapes in the car, or an array of new audiovisual choices through cable television and videocassette recorders (VCRs) at home.

New technology clearly benefited commercial enterprises in improved efficiency and in catering to Americans' accelerated desires to acquire an array of new consumer products. The microprocessor used in computers controlled programmable elements of automobiles, washing machines, cash registers, gas pumps, and other equipment used in daily life. Lasers became a part of daily commerce, as more products used bar codes for store accounting. The National Association of Food Chains pushed for a common standard code that could be read by computers in the market's checkouts to increase productivity, given the small profit margin in the food industry and inflation pressures of the decade.

New consumer electronics also demonstrated Japanese firms' rising dominance of the U.S. market in the 1970s. In 1971, Sony began selling its first VCRs, which quickly became the most popular consumer electronics product of the decade. The VCR allowed Americans to watch videotapes on their television sets and to record television programs for later viewing. The machines presented new choices to viewers who could watch movies at home or fast-forward through commercials in their recorded favorite shows. Until the mid-1970s, rival companies marketed differently designed VCRs with incompatible formats. By the end of the decade, Sony's Betamax VCR declined as JVC's VHS system became the dominant VCR. JVC, a Matsushita subsidiary, had aggressively moved to increase production capacity over other firms and dominated the European electronics market; the dominance of VHS in tape rentals ensured its success in the United States.

Cable Television

By the early 1970s, a coalition of community groups, educators, Nixon adminis-tration officials, and cable industry representatives, believing in the technologi-cal, educational, and commercial potential of cable television, lobbied the FCC to loosen its regulations on cable's expansion to new markets. After the FCC issued its plan for cable development in 1972, cable companies could import programs via microwave and expand service, even though the extent of programming re-mained restricted. Companies began testing pay-per-view systems in New York and Redondo Beach, California, but these quickly went out of business. In 1972, Home Box Office (HBO) offered to Wilkes-Barre, Pennsylvania, customers sports-casts on a "pay cable" basis using microwave relays. In 1975, HBO, now a sub-sidiary of the large Time, Inc. media empire, became the first national service by using a communications satellite to distribute its signal and a flat-rate billing method. Its first satellite telecast was the Muhammad Ali versus Joe Frazier fight from Manila in September 1975.

Although the major broadcasters feared cable competition, a series of First Amendment court cases by the cable industry to eliminate FCC restrictions re-sulted in a U.S. Court of Appeals decision in 1977 that ruled that the FCC had ex-ceeded its authority. By the late 1970s, Showtime and The Movie Channel began competing with HBO for cable viewers, and the three big networks saw an end to their dominance of television programming.

An interest in gaming had propelled early interest in computers in the 1970s, and video games appeared in arcades, bars, and shopping malls to entertain boys and young men in particular. The first home video game system, Odyssey, was introduced by Magnavox in 1972; it allowed a variety of hockeylike and maze games. Game-maker Nolan Bushnell created Atari in his home, and Sears began to market it in 1975; a year later, he sold his company to Warner Com-munications for $28 million, revealing the rapidly growing popularity of video games.

In the field of medicine, new technologies allowed physicians to find and diagnose human diseases with more precision. The computed axial tomography (CAT) scanner, invented in 1972 by Godfrey N. Hounsfield, combined multiple X-rays to record data and create a three-dimensional image of the body. At the same time, magnetic resonance imaging (MRI) was introduced to use radio waves, rather than radiation, to examine soft tissue areas to determine the lo-cation of unhealthy cells. Like CAT and MRI scans, ultrasonography, or the use of high-frequency sound waves, became another noninvasive way to evaluate body textures and fluids. Expectant mothers began to rely on ultrasound tests as a matter of course to monitor the health of the fetus.

Boeing 747

Commercial air travel, which had grown in the 1960s, became transformed with the introduction of the Boeing 747, called the "Jumbo Jet" for its massive size and wide body, in 1970. After Pan Am's inaugural flight between New York's John F. Kennedy International Airport and London Heathrow Airport, other airlines, including Trans World Airlines, Japan Airlines, Lufthansa, United, TWA, and American, rushed to bring their own 747s into service to better compete in transatlantic and domestic long-haul passenger travel. Once reserved for the privileged, the lower-cost and speedy form of travel was affordable to more Americans in these planes that could seat more than 400 passengers.

The 50,000 Boeing production workers, mechanics, engineers, and administrative staff who built the 747 were called "The Incredibles" for completing it to meet purchaser deadlines in less than two years. Boeing had to borrow heavily to fund the project and build a special larger factory north of Seattle in Everett. Its Everett employees increased from 190 workers in early 1967 to 14,950 at the time of the airplane's launch.

But despite the technological feat and initial excitement over producing the largest passenger jet of its time, employees soon faced the trauma of massive layoffs. Boeing had trouble getting orders when the country fell into economic recession in the early 1970s and laid off 63,000 workers in the Puget Sound region over a three-year period. So distressed was the local economy that residents recall during the early 1970s a billboard near Sea-Tac Airport stating, "Will the last person leaving Seattle—turn out the lights." The Boeing layoffs signaled a changing economy where workers could no longer expect job security and where technological advances did not ensure profitability.

At the time, aerospace engineers and others thought that the 747 would eventually be replaced by supersonic transport (SST) aircraft, including the European-made Concorde. The oil crisis and rising fuel costs dampened enthusiasm for the noisy and inefficient SSTs. Fuel efficiency became more critical after the mid-1970s, as passenger numbers declined with the stagnating economy, and many airlines dropped their 747s for smaller, more efficient wide bodies. Nonetheless, Boeing enjoyed a monopoly in producing the large passenger aircraft for the next three decades until the European Airbus was introduced.

Advances in enzymology, which allowed scientists to manipulate DNA molecules with more precision, led to the transformation of genetics research and microbiology in the 1970s, creating the field of biotechnology. The blending of empirical and applied science led to commercial applications, especially regarding health, food production, and industrial materials. Scientist Herbert W. Boyer and entrepreneur Robert A. Swanson established the first biotechnology company, Genentech, in 1976.

The Neutron Bomb

The neutron bomb reflected both the ambivalence about and the persistence of faith in technology. The idea for an enhanced radiation warhead as a weapon in the Cold War had been discussed since the 1950s, but President Carter announced support for the weapon's development in 1977. By the late 1970s, however, increased criticism of nuclear power and weapons heightened moral outrage over the bomb's purpose to kill people and leave property undamaged. Antinuclear advocates seized on this imagery to protest the insanity of nuclear weapons, and critiques of the neutron bomb appeared in popular fiction and music. ABC's science fiction television show *Battlestar Galactica* incorporated the bomb in an episode where humans discover that the Eastern Alliance destroyed the inhabitants of a planet with a neutron bomb but all the buildings were left intact. Punk bands like the Weirdos and the Dead Kennedys leveled pointed attacks of the bomb in some of their songs. Critics abroad claimed the bomb symbolized the U.S. obsession with property and callousness toward human lives. In the face of vigorous opposition from Americans, NATO, and the Soviets, Carter dropped plans to develop the N-bomb, only to be reversed by Ronald Reagan when he became president in 1981.

As some technologies and industries, such as nuclear power plants, were becoming more regulated, deregulation of other industries aided technological developments and consumers. Senators Howard Cannon and Ted Kennedy helped pass in Congress the Airline Deregulation Act of 1978, which intended to create better prices for consumers through greater competition. However, instead of increasing the number of airlines, the competition may have reduced airlines in the market and did not always lower prices, especially as fuel prices increased dramatically. Still, more Americans in the 1970s relied on air travel to get to destinations more quickly.

BIOGRAPHIES

Eula Bingham, 1929–

Assistant Secretary of Labor, OSHA, 1977–1980

An occupational health scientist at the University of Cincinnati with a doctorate in zoology, Eula Bingham brought stability to OSHA, serving a full four-year term during Jimmy Carter's presidency, after six assistant secretaries had headed the agency since its establishment in 1970. Bingham was an authority on occupational disease and on cancer-causing substances, so even though she had never worked directly for organized labor, unions admired her vigorous efforts to protect workers' health. Women's groups also applauded Carter's appointment of Bingham.

Bingham was sensitive to the charges that OSHA was preoccupied with "frivolous, irrelevant rules and regulations" and staged new publicity about OSHA's programs and policies that would follow new "Common Sense Priorities" and focus on the most serious problems of the workplace (U.S. Dept. of Labor). Bingham also sought to simplify safety rules and help small businesses comply with them. In 1977, the agency redirected its resources to inspect the industry groups with the most serious health and safety problems, not the smaller and less risky businesses, and increased the number and quality of its health inspections and voluntary employer/worker education programs.

Bingham managed to patch together better relations with both business and labor, and her supporters prevented Congress from cutting OSHA's budget. Labor unions especially appreciated her serious approach to major workplace hazards, increasing inspections and levying much stiffer fines for violations.

Yet repeatedly during Bingham's tenure, OSHA came into conflict with the Carter Administration and Congress over regulations. Business pressures to reduce the costs of compliance steadily increased, and Bingham found it difficult to implement her goals of cleaning up carcinogens and improving worker health. Philosophical about the roadblocks she faced, especially after 1977, Bingham expressed hope in grassroots pressure to improve occupational safety and health in the next decade. But the election of Ronald Reagan in 1980 signaled that worker safety would not be a priority in national politics. Bingham returned to her research at the University of Cincinnati, published widely on the effects of carcinogens in the workplace, and continued to serve on multiple national public health panels.

César Chávez, 1927–1993

United Farm Workers of America Leader

The 1960s struggles of low-wage farm workers in California, under the leadership of César Chávez, by 1970 won contracts with table grape growers and raised wages by 10 percent. Yet the vast majority of farm workers remained unorganized. In the 1970s, the United Farm Workers (UFW) faced tremendous struggles and organized hostility, but under Chávez's leadership, it emerged stronger and moved into the mainstream of the labor movement.

An immediate challenge came within the labor movement itself. Growers in the Salinas Valley responded to United Farm Workers of California (UFWOC) successes in organizing lettuce workers by signing contracts with the International Brotherhood of Teamsters. Chávez appealed to the AFL-CIO to stop the Teamsters because an earlier accord between the two unions had granted juris-

United Farm Workers union leader César Chávez delivers a speech, 1972. (National Archives)

diction of the fields to the UFWOC, but president George Meany refused to act. Chávez asked California governor Ronald Reagan to order fair elections among farm workers, but Reagan refused. UFWOC cofounder Dolores Huerta led successful negotiations with some growers, including winning a contractual prohibition of DDT and other harmful pesticides, but most growers refused to negate contracts with the Teamsters. Chávez then called for a general strike and national boycott of the lettuce industry, but the union faced legal injunctions, violence, and the imprisonment of Chávez. In April 1971, the state supreme court ordered Chávez released from prison and declared the boycott legal. In 1972, the union became fully recognized within the AFL-CIO and changed its name to the United Farm Workers.

The union movement in California frightened growers elsewhere, and in May 1971, the Arizona legislature and Gov. Jack Williams passed a bill that would impede farm worker organizing. The UFW launched a recall campaign and voter registration drive, and Chávez began a 24-day fast. His fast attracted celebrity and media attention. While the recall effort failed, the political mobilizing within a few years elected Mexican American state legislators and the state's first Mexican American governor, Raúl Castro.

President Nixon, a former California congressman, tried to hamper the UFW's new political and organizing clout by assisting the Teamsters. In April 1973, Teamsters negotiated new contracts with growers at 10 cents an hour less than the

UFW rate of $2.50. UFW called a strike, and opponents terrorized UFW pickets. By the fall of 1973, the violence and loss of contracts forced UFW to call another boycott. Chávez targeted Gallo for the boycott because it had signed a contract with the Teamsters, and in February 1975, led supporters on a 110-mile march from San Francisco to Gallo headquarters in Modesto.

Chávez also achieved a major legislative victory for farm workers in California. After gaining support from the state AFL-CIO, the Democratic Party, and Gov. Jerry Brown, in May 1975 the UFW saw the state adopt the Agricultural Labor Relations Act, which gave farm workers the right to strike, boycott, and vote for the union of their choice. In 1975, UFW won 55 percent of elections, the Teamsters another 33 percent, both significantly raising wages for farm workers.

After 1975 new economic and social pressures hurt the UFW and led Chávez to tighten his control of the union. The end of the antiwar movement, the decline of the civil rights movement, economic recessions, rising unemployment, and deindustrialization hurt the union movement as a whole. Chávez met these challenges by quashing dissent within the union and crushing independent farm worker unions such as the Texas Farm Worker Union. In 1977, he expelled many organizers and volunteers who had worked for years on various UFW campaigns and boycotts; in 1978, most of the legal staff resigned. Despite criticisms of Chávez of nepotism, inability to tolerate dissent, embrace of New Age therapies that many felt did not belong in the labor movement, and failures in organizing, he continued to envision bold campaigns to organize and expand the rights of farm workers. The lettuce strike of 1979, which won wage increases for lettuce workers to $5 an hour, became the most successful effort in UFW history. Yet the new economic pressures and rising conservatism in American society, and Chávez's autocratic style, contributed to the union's decline in the 1980s.

Steve Jobs, 1955– , and Steve Wozniak, 1950–

Apple Computer Founders

In 1975, Steve Wozniak reconnected with friend Steve Jobs at a meeting of the Homebrew Computer Club in Palo Alto, California. They decided to build and sell a small computer that could be used by people not familiar with electronics. A year later, they introduced the Apple I to the Club, and over the next year sold over 500 of the machines. Over the next decades, Apple computers would engender fierce loyalty by computer enthusiasts and make the iconoclast founders two of the richest businessmen in the United States.

Wozniak and Jobs early shared a passion for electronics, and Wozniak designed his first computer in 1963. The two met in 1971 and worked together on programming, phone, and game projects before building their first computer.

After Apple I, Wozniak and Jobs steadily improved the design, graphics, and functions so that by 1980, the Apple II had many of the features of contemporary computers and was the leading personal computer until IBM introduced its PC in 1981. The first Apple II, introduced in 1977, made it possible for the non-technically inclined to bring a computer into their home and easily use it.

Amory B. Lovins, 1947–

Alternative Energy Guru

An experimental physicist educated at Harvard and Oxford, Amory B. Lovins rose to prominence during the energy crisis of the 1970s. While in Britain, Lovins became fascinated by Snowdonia National Park in North Wales, and in 1971 wrote a book about these endangered wildlands for Friends of the Earth. He became increasingly interested in energy strategy, initially through his research on climate, and published *World Energy Strategies* in 1974. Lovins's ground-breaking essay, "Energy Strategy: The Road Not Taken?" published in a 1976 issue of *Foreign Affairs,* called for lifting the barriers to energy efficiency and solar technologies and ending subsidies of the huge and centralized nuclear and coal industries. He urged that the United States follow a "soft energy path," shifting the focus from how to obtain and supply more energy to methods of adapting the appropriate scale of energy at the cheapest cost.

Lovins further outlined these controversial ideas in his 1977 book *Soft Energy Paths: Toward a Durable Peace.* Traditional energy suppliers initially attacked the economic and technical feasibility of the soft-path concept, and critics dismissed him as an anti-industrial, social idealist. But the energy industry eventually adopted his philosophy that renewable energy could be profitable, without the hard path's prohibitive costs and risks. In 1982, Lovins co-founded with his first wife, L. Hunter Sheldon, the Rocky Mountain Institute to foster the efficient and restorative use of resources.

Tyree Scott, 1940–2003

Seattle Union and Civil Rights Activist

In 1969, Tyree Scott joined Seattle's Central Contractors Association (CCA) in an effort to lobby for federal construction contracts that had been controlled by white unions and contractors. Recognizing Scott's leadership abilities, the Seattle Branch of the American Friends Service Committee (AFSC) asked him to organize the United Construction Workers Association (UCWA) in early 1970, which would focus on combating union racism. Scott and the UCWA successfully won the right to help enforce an affirmative action ruling to desegregate Seattle's building trades unions. He recognized the need to collaborate with government agencies and groups such as the Seattle Urban League to advance worker and civil rights issues.

Scott emblemized the activist mantra, "think globally, act locally." In addition to his commitment to fellow African American construction workers, in 1972 Scott helped found the Northwest Labor and Employment Law Office (LELO), which pursued civil rights and workplace justice. He also became committed to the idea of unifying diverse oppressed people of the world into a global movement for racial and economic justice. He was active in Seattle's Third World Marxism community, and from 1973 to 1980, together with other UCWA leaders, he helped coordinate the Seattle Workers Group. From 1977–1979, Scott served as the co-chair of the AFSC Third World Coalition, a national racial justice organization.

Johnnie Tillmon, 1927–1995

Welfare Rights Activist

Born into a sharecropping family in Scott, Arkansas, Johnnie Tillmon knew hard work and poverty from an early age. During World War II, she moved to Little Rock to attend high school and work in a local munitions factory. She then worked in a laundry for 15 years before moving to California as a single parent of six children. In 1963, after applying for public assistance to enable her to care for her children, she organized other women in the Nickerson Gardens Housing Project, who then formed the Aid to Needy Children (ANC) Mothers Anonymous of Watts. Several years later, she was elected to the newly formed Los Angeles County Welfare Rights Organization and then to the presidency of the California Welfare Rights Organization (CRWO). In 1971, Tillmon moved to Washington, D.C., to become associate director of NWRO and Executive Director after George Wiley's resignation in 1972.

In spring 1972, Tillmon published an article in *Ms.* that became a famous articulation of "why welfare is a women's issue." Tillmon explained that women's liberation may be important to middle-class women, but to poor women, it meant "survival." Women were "the worst educated, the least-skilled, and the lowest-paid people there are." Because they were responsible for children, they had to be dependent on welfare. Tillmon compared welfare to "a super-sexist marriage." The "man," or the state, could "cut you off anytime he wants," but one had to give up everything, including control of one's own body, to receive public assistance. She noted that "poor welfare women will really liberate women in this country" through their advocacy of a Guaranteed Adequate Income, which would eliminate gender and age from welfare categories to grant aid to any poor people who needed it (Tillmon 1972).

Many in the welfare rights movement, however, criticized Tillmon and claimed her charisma and fame overshadowed local organizers' efforts to expand the membership and militancy of NWRO. They believed that Tillmon and other leaders focused on legislative objectives and press conferences at the expense of the membership base.

Tillmon struggled to locate funds to keep NWRO afloat. When NWRO folded in 1974, Tillmon returned to Los Angeles, were she resumed her community organizing in Watts and continued to help welfare recipients until 1991, when diabetes caused her health to fail.

Kenneth White, 1926–

Navajo Labor Activist

A carpenter who was employed at the Navajo Power Plant near Page, Arizona, Kenneth White became a leading labor activist and advocate for Navajo workers. White was born on the Navajo reservation in a traditional family that raised sheep, but World War II drew him into the wage economy. Like many Native American workers, he traveled to other states and held a variety of jobs in a munitions depot, an ice plant, and for the railroad. After he returned to the reservation and married, he accepted the Bureau of Indian Affair's (BIA) relocation program, moved his family to Los Angeles, and started a job at the Chrysler plant. There he became active in the United Auto Workers, but during a long strike, he was drawn back to the reservation, where he wanted to raise his children, rather than in urban California.

On the Navajo Indian Reservation, many Navajos and the Tribal Council had discouraged union organizing because they believed unions had upheld racial job segmentation and would hire white union members instead of Navajos. By the 1970s, however, BIA and Navajo tribal officials began to see that unions might help Navajo workers find skilled jobs, such as with the Four Corners coal gasification plants near Shiprock, New Mexico. Colleen O'Neill notes that by encouraging unions to adopt preference clauses and giving Navajos priority in jobs on the reservation, the tribe could expand the Indian workforce, turning to unions to implement what companies had failed to do in their leasing agreements (O'Neill 2005). Although Arizona was a "right-to-work" state, Indian reservation projects adhered to national labor agreements that required contractors to hire union laborers. With several large construction projects on the reservation in the 1970s, the number of Navajo union members increased from about 50 in 1950 to 6,000 in 1977.

When Kenneth White returned to the reservation, he found many construction jobs, joined the Carpenters Union, and became the shop steward at the power plant, operated by Arizona Public Service and California Edison and subcontracted by Bechtel Corporation. White soon noticed that some Navajos were losing their jobs to non-Indian union workers. In 1973, he testified before the U.S. Civil Rights Commission about how Navajos faced job discrimination. White criticized employers' attitudes toward Navajo cultural practices and worked to create greater understanding of those practices and more flexibility in the workplace. Especially in winter, when children were in school, men were needed at home to help care for sheep and cattle. At other times, Navajo men needed to return home to attend to ceremonial functions. White urged employers to understand when workers had to take time off and should not fire them for absenteeism.

White also criticized the racism of trade unions and charged that they made it difficult for Navajos to join by requiring long trips to Flagstaff to sign up at the union hall, or respond to referrals because many Navajos lacked telephones. In response to these struggles with both management and unions, White and other Navajo workers formed the Navajo Construction Workers Association (NCWA) to advocate for them. The NCWA was designed not to compete with national unions but to address specific concerns of Navajo workers. White's complaints led the tribal council to create the Office of Navajo Labor Relations, with White as the first appointed compliance officer. He played a central role in expanding skilled labor opportunities for Navajos beginning in the 1970s. In fact, since the mid-1970s, Navajos have served as presidents of the United Mine Workers Local in Window Rock.

REFERENCES AND FURTHER READINGS

Adamson, Madeleine, and Seth Borgos. 1984. *This Mighty Dream: Social Protest Movements in the United States*. Boston: Routledge.

Anderson, David M. 2005. "Levittown is Burning! The 1979 Levittown, Pennsylvania, Gas Line Riot and the Decline of the Blue-Collar American Dream." *Labor: Studies in Working-Class History of the Americas* 2 (Fall): 47–65.

"Attica Revisited: A Talking History Project." http://www.talkinghistory.org/attica/index.html. Accessed July 24, 2007.

Boeing History. http://www.boeing.com/history/. Accessed July 18, 2007.

Brandt-Erichsen, David. "The L-5 Society." http://www.nss.org/settlement/L5news/L5history.htm. Accessed July 17, 2007.

Ceruzzi, Paul E. 1998. *A History of Modern Computing*. Cambridge, MA: MIT Press.

Chappell, Marisa. 2002. "Rethinking Women's Politics in the 1970s: The League of Women Voters and the National Organization for Women Confront Poverty." *Journal of Women's History* 13 (4): 155–181.

Cobble, Dorothy Sue. 2005. "A 'Tiger By the Toenail': The 1970s Origins of the New Working-Class Majority." *Labor: Studies in Working-Class History of the Americas* 2 (Fall): 103–114.

Cowie, Jefferson. 1999. *Capital Moves: RCA's Seventy-Year Quest for Cheap Labor*. Ithaca, NY: Cornell University Press.

Cowie, Jefferson. 2005. "Portrait of the Working Class in a Convex Mirror: Toward a History of the Seventies." *Labor: Studies in Working-Class History of the Americas* 2 (Fall): 93–102.

Cowie, Jefferson. 2004. "'Vigorously Left, Right, and Center': The Crosscurrents of Working-Class America in the 1970s." In *America in the Seventies,* edited by Beth Bailey and David Farber, 75–106. Lawrence: University Press of Kansas.

Craypo, Charles, and Bruce Nissen, eds. 1993. *Grand Designs: The Impact of Corporate Strategies on Workers, Unions, and Communities.* Ithaca, NY: ILR Press.

Day, Dwayne A. 2006. "Exploring the Social Frontiers of Spaceflight." *The Space Review: Essays and Commentary about the Final Frontier,* September 25. http://www.thespacereview.com/article/713/1. Accessed July 17, 2007.

Deslippe, Dennis A. 2000. *"Rights, Not Roses": Unions and the Rise of Working-Class Feminism, 1945–80.* Urbana: University of Illinois Press.

Diaz, David R. 2005. *Barrio Urbanism: Chicanos, Planning, and American Cities.* New York: Routledge.

Gall, Gilbert J. 1988. *The Politics of Right to Work: The Labor Federations as Special Interests, 1943–1979.* New York: Greenwood Press.

Garvey, Ed. 2005. "Corrupt Political Process, Not Labor, Is to Blame." *Capital Times* (Madison, Wisc.) August 2.

Gonnerman, Jennifer. 2001. "Remembering Attica: Thirty Years Later, the Story of America's Worst Prison Riot Continues." *Village Voice,* September 5–11. http://www.villagevoice.com/news/0136,gonnerman,27855,1.html. Accessed July 23, 2007.

Gordon, David M. 1994. "Chickens Home to Roost: From Prosperity to Stagnation in the Postwar U.S. economy." In *Understanding American Economic Decline,* edited by Michael A. Bernstein and David E. Adler, 34–76. New York: Cambridge University Press.

Gordon, Robert. 1988. "Shell No! OCWA and the Labor-environment Alliance." *Environmental History* 3/4 (October): 460–484.

Griffey, Trevor. "United Construction Workers Association." Seattle Civil Rights and Labor History Project. http://depts.washington.edu/civilr/ucwa.htm. Accessed August 20, 2007.

Harrison, Bennett, and Barry Bluestone. 1988. *The Great U-Turn: Corporate Restructuring and the Polarizing of America.* New York: Basic Books.

Hoing, Emily. 1997. "Striking lives." *Journal of Women's History* 9 (1): 139–157.

Hoing, Emily. 1996. "Women at Farah Revisited: Political Mobilization and Its Aftermath." *Feminist Studies* 22 (2): 425–452.

Horowitz, Daniel. 2005. *Jimmy Carter and the Energy Crisis of the 1970s: The 'Crisis of Confidence' Speech of July 15, 1970*. Boston: Bedford/St. Martin's.

Hurley, Andrew. 1995. *Environmental Inequalities: Class, Race, and Industrial Pollution in Gary, Indiana, 1945–1980*. Chapel Hill: University of North Carolina Press.

La Botz, Dan. 2006. *César Chávez and la Causa*. New York: Pearson Longman.

Laird, Frank N. 2003. "Constructing the Future: Advocating Energy Technologies in the Cold War." *Technology and Culture* 44 (1): 27–49.

Lee, Chana Kai. 2000. *For Freedom's Sake: The Life of Fannie Lou Hamer*. Urbana: University of Illinois Press.

Lichtenstein, Nelson. 2002. *State of the Union: A Century of American Labor*. Princeton, NJ: Princeton University Press.

Lipsitz, George. 1988. *A Life in the Struggle: Ivory Perry and the Culture of Opposition*. Philadelphia: Temple University Press.

Lovins, Amory B. 1977. *Soft Energy Paths: Toward a Durable Peace*. New York: Penguin.

Madrick, Jeffrey. 1995. *The End of Affluence: The Causes and Consequences of America's Economic Dilemma*. New York: Random House.

Magdoff, Harry, and Paul M. Sweezy. 1977. *The End of Prosperity: The American Economy in the 1970s*. New York: Monthly Review Press.

McCartin, Joseph A. 2005. "'Fire the Hell Out of Them': Sanitation Workers' Struggles and the Normalization of the Striker Replacement Strategy in the 1970s." *Labor: Studies in Working-Class History of the Americas* 2 (Fall): 67–92.

Mercier, Laurie. 2001. *Anaconda: Labor, Community, and Culture in Montana's Smelter City*. Urbana: University of Illinois Press.

Minchin, Timothy J. 2005. *"Don't Sleep with Stevens!" The J. P. Stevens Campaign and the Struggle to Organize the South, 1963–80*. Gainesville: University Press of Florida.

Mink, Gwendolyn, and Rickie Solinger, eds. 2003. *Welfare: A Documentary History of U.S. Policy and Politics*. New York: New York University Press.

Moore, Marat. 1996. *Women in the Mines: Stories of Life and Work*. New York: Twayne.

Mullen, Megan. 1999. "The Pre-history of Pay Cable Television: An Overview and Analysis." *Historical Journal of Film, Radio and Television* 19 (1): 39–56.

National Aeronautics and Space Administration. http://history.nasa.gov/. Accessed May 24, 2007.

Neal, Valerie. 2002. "Bumped from the Shuttle Fleet: Why Didn't *Enterprise* Fly in Space?" *History and Technology* 18 (3): 181–202.

Needleman, Ruth. 2003. *Black Freedom Fighters in Steel: The Struggle for Democratic Unionism*. Ithaca, NY: ILR Press.

Oberg, James. "Skylab's Untimely Fate." *Encylopedia Astronautica*. http://www
.astronautix.com/articles/skyyfate.htm. Accessed May 24, 2007.

O'Connor, Alice. 2001. *Poverty Knowledge: Social Science, Social Policy, and the Poor in Twentieth-Century U.S. History*. Princeton, NJ: Princeton University Press.

Ogunseitan, Oladele A. 2006a. "Genetics Research." In *The Seventies in America,* edited by John C. Super, 406–407. Pasadena, CA: Salem Press.

Ogunseitan, Oladele A. 2006b. "Inventions." In *The Seventies in America,* edited by John C. Super, 484–488. Pasadena, CA: Salem Press.

Ogunseitan, Oladele A. 2006c. "Space Exploration." In *The Seventies in America,* edited by John C. Super, 843–846. Pasadena, CA: Salem Press.

Olson, Karen. 2005. *Wives of Steel: Voices of Women from the Sparrows Point Steelmaking Communities*. University Park, PA: Penn State University Press.

O'Neill, Colleen. 2005. *Working the Navajo Way: Labor and Culture in the Twentieth Century*. Lawrence: University Press of Kansas.

Orsini-Meinhard, Kirsten. 2007. "And the Planes Just Keep Rolling . . ." *Seattle Times,* July 6. http://seattletimes.nwsource.com/html/snohomishcountynews/
2003773059_boeing04n1.html. Accessed July 23, 2007.

Packer, Jeremy. 2002. "Mobile communications and Governing the Mobile: CBs and Truckers." *The Communication Review* 5:39–57.

Patterson, James T. 1994. *America's Struggle Against Poverty, 1900–1994*. Cambridge, Mass: Harvard University Press.

Piven, Frances Fox, and Richard A. Cloward. 1979. *Poor People's Movements: Why They Succeed, How They Fail*. New York: Vintage Books.

Pope, Daniel. 1990. "Environmental Constraints and Organizational Failures: The Washington Public Power Supply System." *Business and Economic History* 19:74–82.

Schumacher, E. F. 1973. *Small Is Beautiful: A Study of Economics as if People Mattered*. New York: Harper & Row.

Slocum-Schaffer, Stephanie A. 2003. *America in the Seventies*. Syracuse, NY: Syracuse University Press.

Tallichet, Suzanne E. 2006. *Daughters of the Mountain: Women Coal Miners in Central Appalachia*. University Park, PA: Penn State University Press.

Tillmon, Johnnie. 1972. "Welfare Is a Women's Issue." *Ms.* (Spring). http://www
.msmagazine.com/spring2002/tillmon.asp. Accessed July 27, 2007.

Uchitelle, Louis. 2006. *The Disposable American: Layoffs and Their Consequences.* New York: Knopf.

U.S. Department of Labor. "Eula Bingham Administration, 1977–1981: Of Minnows, Whales and 'Common sense'." http://www.dol.gov/oasam/programs/history/osha13bingham.htm. Accessed August 22, 2007.

"Washington Public Power Supply System." *HistoryLink.org: the Online Encyclopedia of Washington State History.* http://www.historylink.org/essays/output.cfm?file_id=5482. Accessed July 16, 2007.

Wellock, Thomas. 2005. "Atomic Power in the West." *Journal of the West* 44 (1): 45–54.

White, Myles. 1996. "25th Anniversary for Microprocessor." *Toronto Star,* November 17. http://www.computerwriter.com/archives/1996/sf171196.htm Accessed November 25, 2006.

Yamin, Robert J. 1971. Letter to the editor, *The New York Times,* September 19.

Zeman, Scott C. 2004. "Confronting the 'Capitalist Bomb': The Neutron Bomb and American Culture." In *Atomic Culture: How We Learned to Stop Worrying and Love the Bomb,* edited by Zeman and Michael A. Amundson, 65–80. Boulder: University Press of Colorado.

Political Culture and American Society

By Josh Ashenmiller

OVERVIEW

The biggest change in American politics during the 1970s occurred in the area of ideology. Before 1970, liberalism reigned supreme. By 1980, conservative Ronald Reagan won the presidential election and the Republican Party won a majority of seats in the Senate. From 1980 through the early 21st century, Bill Clinton was the only Democrat who occupied the Oval Office, and he conspicuously avoided describing himself as a liberal. In popular parlance, terms such as "liberal," "feminist," and "environmentalist" acquired connotations of extremism.

In 1970, liberalism was the philosophy that the U.S. Government bore ultimate responsibility for the nation's economic performance, for the protection of elected governments around the world, and for the promotion of equal rights among all citizens. The conservatism that unseated liberalism did not oppose these endeavors. In fact, many conservatives' stated goals were exactly the same. But conservatives fiercely criticized the way liberals tried to reach those goals. What liberals presented as enlightened regulation, conservatives deemed authoritarian control. In liberals' preference for peaceful negotiations, conservatives perceived weakness and betrayal. And where liberals attempted to rectify discrimination, conservatives decried policies of "reverse discrimination" and "enforced morality." Throughout the 1970s the conservative critique mounted, and eventually replaced liberalism as the norm.

Not all Americans abandoned liberalism and embraced conservatism. Nor did the change happen all at once. Millions of voters chose Democratic legislators and Republican presidents on the very same ballot. Politicians such as Sen. Henry Jackson (D-Wash.) managed to stay in office by arguing for increased militarism *and* increased efforts to end discrimination and protect the environment. In the overall narrative of politics in the 1970s, however, the rise of the conservatives was the most salient development.

Behind the ideological changes of the 1970s were changes in who had access to political power. The right to vote, for example, spread further and deeper than it ever had before—into the South, across the color line, and down the age scale. Energetic social movements increased the political power of women, African Americans, homosexuals, and Latinos. Even so, voter turnout and party allegiance continued to decline. Voters organized themselves into effective lobbying groups around vital issues. At the same time, public opinion polls showed that many Americans felt that government had been taken over by "special interest groups" who subverted the democratic process. The 1970s were a decade when the politics of inspiration and the politics of cynicism were remarkably intertwined.

In foreign policy, the United States began the decade bogged down in an unwinnable war in Southeast Asia and ended the decade stuck in a seemingly endless hostage crisis in the Middle East. Both events were body blows to Americans' self-confidence, which had been nurtured by victory in World War II and by the self-righteous rhetoric of the Cold War. By the end of the 1970s, foreign policy makers and average citizens seriously doubted whether U.S. foreign policies should follow lofty ideals or focus narrowly on economic and security interests.

After decades of speculation as to when the South would catch up with the rest of the country, by the end of the 1970s, the rest of the country had begun to resemble the South. Legalized segregation was a thing of the past, but policy debates took on a Southern accent. Voters elected more and more politicians who championed the long-held Southern ideals of limited federal government and rugged individualism. Observers who had grown used to liberals in national office were stunned by the election of Ronald Reagan and wondered if it might be a fluke. It was no fluke, but rather the result of a concerted, nationwide effort to make conservative values appealing to the average voter.

From the White House to the streets of Boston, the various groups that made up the conservative movement did not agree on how to retake government from the liberals. Nor did they agree on how to run it once they had it. But their disparate messages added up to a simple message to the public: liberalism is dead. By liberalism they meant the belief that the federal government bore the fundamental responsibility for the security of its citizens. Conservatives countered that citizens were better off providing for their own security, individually and in groups. In the conservative vision, the role of government should be as small as possible—just enough to defend the country and allow the free market to operate. Whatever their differences, all conservatives rallied around Ronald Reagan's main campaign theme. "Government is not the solution to our problems," he said. "Government is the problem."

TIMELINE

1970
President Richard Nixon signs the National Environmental Policy Act.

Supreme Court clears "Chicago Seven" of rioting charges.

The first Earth Day celebration takes place on April 22.

Nixon announces that U.S. forces have invaded Cambodia.

In May, four antiwar protestors are killed by the National Guard at Kent State; two are killed by police at Jackson State.

Democrats lose two seats in the Senate but pick up nine House seats and keep the majority in both chambers.

The Environmental Protection Agency begins operating.

1971
Joint U.S.–South Vietnamese forces invade Laos.

In *Swann v. Charlotte-Mecklenburg,* the Supreme Court okays busing between cities and suburbs as a means of school desegregation.

Nixon advisers form "the Plumbers."

The Supreme Court decides *Lemon v. Kurtzman,* which cuts off government funding to Catholic schools.

The Supreme Court rules against the Nixon Administration in *Pentagon Papers* case.

States ratify the 26th Amendment, which lowers the voting age to 18.

To control inflation, Nixon announces 90-day wage and price controls.

The week-long Attica Prison uprising ends when guards storm the yard, killing 43.

1972
Nixon visits China.

Nixon tries to declare moratorium on school busing.

Congress passes the Equal Rights Amendment (ERA).

FBI Director J. Edgar Hoover dies, ending 48-year term in office.

Third-party candidate George Wallace is shot by Arthur H. Bremer and is paralyzed.

Nixon and Brezhnev sign the ABM Treaty, a result of the SALT I negotiations.

The Watergate burglary takes place on June 17.

Nixon signs Title IX of the Education Amendments.

Congress passes the Water Pollution Control Act.

Phyllis Schlafly organizes the STOP-ERA movement.

President Nixon is reelected by a landslide. Republicans gain 12 House seats and Democrats gain two Senate seats. Democrats still have majority in both houses.

Nixon orders the bombing of North Vietnam to resume.

1973   Nixon announces voluntary wage and price controls.

The Supreme Court's *Roe v. Wade* decision partially legalizes abortion.

The United States and North Vietnam sign the Paris Peace Accords. Congress ends the draft.

The Senate forms a committee to investigate the Watergate crimes.

The American Indian Movement occupies Wounded Knee, South Dakota, by force.

Nixon announces a "price freeze" on retail goods.

Chilean president Salvador Allende is assassinated in a CIA-backed coup.

Egypt and Syria invade Israel on the Jewish holy day of *Yom Kippur.*

Henry Kissinger and Le Duc Tho receive the Nobel Peace Prize.

Nixon fires his advisers in the "Saturday Night Massacre."

The OPEC Oil Embargo begins.

Watergate burglars are sentenced to prison. G. Gordon Liddy gets 20 years.

Congress authorizes the construction of the Alaska Oil Pipeline.

Gerald Ford sworn in as vice president, replacing Spiro T. Agnew.

1974   Patty Hearst is kidnapped by the Symbionese Liberation Army.

Judge Arthur Garrity orders busing to desegregate Boston public schools.

President Nixon resigns on August 9.

President Gerald Ford choses Nelson Rockefeller to be vice president.

Ford pardons Nixon on September 8.

Democrats gain 49 House seats, 3 Senate seats, and maintain majority.

A Senate committee investigates the CIA role in 1973 Chilean coup.

1975   H. R. Haldeman, John Ehrlichman, and John Mitchell are indicted for the Watergate cover-up.

Ford signs the Jackson-Vanik Amendment, which links foreign aid to human rights.

The Khmer Rouge takes power in Cambodia, initiating a four-year genocide.

South Vietnam surrenders to North Vietnam.

Fifteen U.S. Marines die in the *Mayaguez* incident.

Patty Hearst is captured by police on September 18.

In September, President Ford survives two assassination attempts in same month.

After previously denying aid, Ford agrees to help New York City's finances.

The Senate committee finds the CIA had a role in 1973 Chilean coup.

With the blessing of the United States, the Indonesian Army invades East Timor.

1976   The Supreme Courts strikes down portions of 1974 Federal Campaigns Act.

The United States celebrates its bicentennial, July 4.

Orlando Letelier, former Chilean ambassador to the United States, is killed by a car bomb in Washington, D.C.

In a pre-election debate, Ford mistakenly says that Poland is free of Soviet influence.

Gov. Jimmy Carter (D-Ga.) wins the presidential election. Democrats gain one seat in House and maintain majority in both houses.

Milton Friedman wins the Nobel Prize for Economics.

1977   Utah firing squad executes a prisoner, the first execution in United States since 1972.

President Carter pardons those who evaded the draft during the Vietnam War.

Carter cuts U.S. foreign aid to countries that violate human rights.

Mass arrests of protestors are made outside a Seabrook nuclear plant in New Hampshire.

New York City suffers a blackout, July 13–14.

Congress creates the Department of Energy.

Carter signs Panama Canal Treaties on September 7.

The International Women's Year Conference convenes in Houston.

1978   California voters soundly reject Proposition 6, a plan to ban gay schoolteachers.

The Supreme Court hands down *University of California Regents v. Bakke,* which limits affirmative action.

Native Americans stage the "Long March" from San Francisco to Washington, D.C.

Israel and Egypt sign the Camp David Peace Accord on September 17.

Democrats lose 15 House seats and 3 Senate seats but retain majority in both houses.

Almost 1,000 Americans die in Jonestown, Guyana, mass suicide.

San Francisco mayor George Moscone and supervisor Harvey Milk are assassinated.

Cleveland, Ohio, defaults on its municipal bonds.

1979   The United States officially recognizes China.

An accident occurs at Three Mile Island nuclear power plant, near Harrisburg, Pennsylvania on March 28.

Carter and Brezhnev sign SALT II on June 18.

OPEC raises oil prices.

Carter delivers the televised "Crisis of Confidence" speech on July 15.

Iranian Hostage Crisis begins on November 4.

Arthur McDuffie is killed by Miami police officers, whose acquittal later sparks three days of riots in May 1980.

Congress authorizes a $1.5 billion loan to Chrysler Corporation.

Soviet troops invade Afghanistan on December 24.

NIXON, THE SILENT MAJORITY, AND THE CULTURE OF SURVEILLANCE

Cultivating the Silent Majority

When the 1970s began, Richard Nixon was beginning his second year as president. He won the 1968 election by a slim majority that many observers took to be a repudiation of the New Left social movements of the 1960s. In contrast to the loud protests against racial and sexual discrimination, and against the Vietnam War, a "silent majority" of American voters showed their strength in numbers by voting for Nixon, or so he claimed. Nixon's main goal in office was to cultivate this silent majority in order to achieve a more lopsided victory in 1972.

President Richard Nixon, the 1968 victor, did not begin using the phrase "silent majority" until a few months after his inauguration. But the idea guided his campaign and his five and a half years in office. His most memorable 1968 campaign slogan was a pledge to restore "law and order" to the nation, which had been rocked by protest movements and urban violence. With the assassination of Dr. Martin Luther King Jr. in 1968, riots erupted in 100 cities, claimed 39 lives, and required 79,000 National Guard troops. Nixon's "law and order" pledge was more than a traditional campaign promise to punish criminals. It also implied that the incoming administration would take steps to neutralize the New Left and the Democrats who supposedly encouraged it.

Southerners, solidly Democratic since the Civil War, were the largest silent majority bloc Nixon sought to seduce. The 1964 Republican candidate for the White House, Sen. Barry Goldwater (R-Az.), won five traditionally Democratic Southern states, pioneering a strategy that later Republicans found to be successful. Instead of attacking federal civil rights reforms directly and defending segregation, Republicans argued that federal regulation of public schools, city transit lines, and even public swimming pools was unconstitutional. It violated every state's right of self-determination and granted excessive powers to Congress and federal agencies. In 1968, campaign adviser Kevin Phillips told Nixon that the time was ripe to hammer home the states' rights message in order to win. For many Americans, voting for Nixon was a way to put a brake on the expansion of federal authority over everyday life. Except for Texas, the Democrats lost the South in 1968 and 1972.

President Richard Nixon campaigns for reelection in Ohio on October 28, 1972.
Nixon called the voters who swept him to victory the "Silent Majority." (National
Archives)

Once in office, Nixon clothed the old states' rights warhorse with a new garb,
which he called "new federalism." It was a nebulous concept, but it implied
slowing down civil rights oversight and offering state governments more latitude
in spending federal funds. New federalism continued once Nixon was in office.
The Nixon administration used the budget process to erode civil rights regulations. At the same time, Nixon proclaimed a results-oriented approach to ending racial discrimination. One pro-Nixon editorial summed up the administration's
civil rights policy in one word, "Jobs" (Kotlowski 2001, 98). Nixon also thanked
his Southern constituents by nominating to the Supreme Court Judge Clement
Haynsworth of South Carolina and G. Harrold Carswell of Georgia. Even the
fact that the Senate rejected both nominees aided Nixon's strategy. It placed Nixon
in the role of the champion of many white voters who felt that the Democratic
Party had become an auxiliary of the NAACP.

Nixon cultivated his image as a political outsider fighting for the rights of
working Americans, but he was hardly a true outsider. He had spent his career
in Washington politics and as a lawyer at a New York City firm. But his proximity to those nodes of power only deepened his resentment of the class of
people who seemed most comfortable in it—the wealthy, northeastern, prep-

schooled, Ivy League aristocrats personified by the Kennedy family. Nixon never forgot that his first electoral defeat came at the hands of a Kennedy in 1960. To settle accounts, it was not enough for Nixon just to come back from obscurity to win the presidential election in 1968. He wanted to exact revenge on the Kennedys and their ilk by turning their voters against them and bleeding the Democratic Party dry.

Dismantling New Deal/Great Society Liberalism

Nixon was not driven by an ideological mania for rolling back liberalism. Instead, he was mostly concerned with securing a lasting voting majority for the Republican Party. He repealed Great Society and New Deal programs only to the extent that such repeals earned votes for Republicans.

Nixon slowed the desegregation of public school districts, a process initiated by the Supreme Court in 1954. Nixon was not bold enough to defy desegregation per se, but he courted the votes of white voters who lived in districts slated for busing. Nixon instructed his cabinet members to end a policy whereby local school districts that desegregated too slowly saw their federal funding disappear. Nixon restored this funding, provoking an immediate outcry from civil rights leaders. Nixon portrayed himself as the reasonable compromiser between two extremes—the school districts and the civil rights leaders. He ignored the fact that recalcitrant school districts were breaking the law. Although his funding strategy was only temporary—any future president could cut off funds just as easily as he had restored them—it suited Nixon's purposes because, in the eyes of voters, he was standing up for the silent majority against the liberals. The ploy lasted long enough to win votes.

After 1970 school desegregation became a national issue, no longer just a Southern issue. In the 1971 *Charlotte v. Mecklenberg* decision, the Supreme Court allowed busing students to end "de facto" segregation, that is, schools that were mostly of one race because of their surrounding neighborhoods. Violent anti-busing protests soon followed. Irish American parents in Boston picketed in front of local high schools and threw rocks at the school buses bringing in African American students. They blamed liberals for "playing God" with their personal lives. Nixon won points for largely staying out of the melee and reassuring voters that he stood for "no forced integration" (Kotlowski 2001, 3).

In busing, and in almost every other case where a liberal reform created a heated conflict, Nixon starved a liberal program of funding, then let public opinion batter it as another example of liberal "social engineering." For example, the Fair Housing Act of 1968 directed the Department of Housing and Urban Development (HUD) to make sure that low-income housing was part of any residential construction projects receiving federal funding. Fearing that such housing would attract the very low-income minority residents that their customers were fleeing, homebuilders balked at the requirements. Nixon's HUD reinterpreted the Act's rules to say that the federal government could not use funding as a lever, so the requirement went unenforced. Policies such as these appealed to middle-class and working-class citizens who sought low-crime, low-diversity schools and neighborhoods. Nixon became the hero in the virtual South, the rapidly growing rings of suburbs around every U.S. city.

Rhetorically, Nixon took care not to attack liberal desegregation policies directly. He then hired brilliant young speechwriters to write memorable invective for his vice president, Spiro Agnew. Agnew memorably savaged liberal Democrats as "an effete corps of impudent snobs" who felt they could rearrange society to suit their theories. Agnew stayed in the headlines with his alliterative jabs, going after the "pusillanimous pussyfooters" and "nattering nabobs of negativism" who criticized Nixon for abandoning the civil rights movement (Chafe 2007, 375). With Agnew, the assault on liberalism hit its rhetorical stride. Instead of defending segregation, he attacked desegregation. And it seemed to work. As one White House aide remarked, "The President really believes in the southern strategy—more than he believes in anything else" (Blum 1991, 337).

He had reason to believe. In 1968, Nixon won 31.7 million votes for president. In 1972, he won 46 million and carried every state except Massachusetts and the District of Columbia. The silent majority seemed to be growing.

Reducing Poverty, Protecting the Environment, and Cultivating the Arts

President Nixon succeeded in turning the tables on the liberal Democrats, but he did not succeed in dismantling all their policies. In part, these policies survived because Nixon did not oppose them. He saw them primarily as factors that determined elections rather than as visions of how society and government should interact. The result of Nixon's peculiar vision was that some liberal goals, especially ending poverty, protecting the environment, and subsidizing the arts, survived Nixon's term.

Of all the liberal reforms, the "War on Poverty" was singled out by doctrinaire conservatives in the Republican Party as an egregious federal intrusion into the labor market and as a program that distorted poor people's incentive to find work. Conservatives attacked the Office of Economic Opportunity (OEO), Volunteers in Service to America, the Community Action Program, Upward Bound, the Jobs Corps, the Neighborhood Youth Corps, and the Model Cities plan for their underlying theory. Instead of creating more jobs, conservatives asserted, the programs would block the efficient workings of the labor market and leave low-wage workers dependent on government welfare programs.

Elected officials in big cities came to despise the War on Poverty, whose funds went right past them and into the coffers of community action committees and jobs programs. Mayors wanted to get credit from their voters for jobs programs, so they resented the federal government's high-handedness. Even Democratic mayors broke from liberals in Washington over this challenge to their ability to distribute patronage.

Urban voters were also embittered by the War on Poverty. Low-wage workers living just above the poverty line resented the liberal effort to help people just below the poverty line, often nonwhites. Racial animosity and class antagonism combined into a rage against liberals for appearing to give handouts to people who did not deserve them. The Northern working-class found common cause with Southerners who voted against liberal reforms. Both groups opposed giving away tax-supported benefits to the nonwhite and the poor.

Eventually, Nixon and his budget planners starved the War on Poverty to death, zeroing-out the OEO's budget in 1974. Controversially, Nixon's budget office impounded over $8 billion in congressional appropriations for poverty programs. Nixon instructed his staff to support antipoverty reforms in public, but only up until the point where they might actually get enough votes to pass Congress. At that point, the White House backed off and let the plan die in committee.

Despite Nixon's decommissioning of the OEO, other battalions in the War on Poverty helped many poor people survive the ailing economy of the 1970s. Food stamps, subsidized housing, education, and subsidized medical care helped millions of Americans move out of poverty, even as inflation and unemployment rose to record levels. At the beginning of the 1960s, more than 22 percent of the U.S. population lived below the poverty line. After a decade of robust economic growth, this number was down to 12 percent. The poverty rate then fluctuated between 11 percent and 12 percent in the 1970s, a time when poverty rates should have shot up. At a time when families below the poverty line needed a safety net the most, the War on Poverty's remaining troops fought on despite their commander's attrition tactics.

When it came to environmental protection, Nixon tried to claim the issue as his own. Never much of an outdoorsman, Nixon still recognized the grassroots energy behind the environmental movement. He also recognized that both of his likely challengers in the 1972 election, Sen. Henry Jackson (D-Wash.) and Sen. Edmund Muskie (D-Maine), were years ahead of him on the environment issue. Nixon attempted to upstage Jackson by signing the senator's National Environmental Policy Act (NEPA) on national television on New Year's Day 1970. He told reporters that the 1970s would be the decade in which the United States repaid its debt to nature. Recent oil spills in California and burning rivers in Cleveland contributed to the national drive to protect nature, climaxing with the April 1970 Earth Day. "It is literally now or never," Nixon said (*The New York Times,* January 2, 1970).

With his signature on NEPA still fresh, Nixon took a number of positions in line with the growing environmental movement. Privately, Nixon's advisers hoped that this might be the one issue that could make Nixon appeal to young voters.

Student activists mostly despised him for continuing the war in Vietnam. The 27th Amendment, ratified in 1971, expanded the youth vote by lowering the voting age to 18. In part to grab the attention of the young, Nixon helped create the Environmental Protection Agency, helped stop the Cross-Florida Barge Canal and the supersonic transport (SST) jet, and signed the Clean Air and Endangered Species Acts. After his 1972 reelection, Nixon backed off protecting nature. He vetoed Senator Muskie's Water Pollution Control Act, a veto that Congress overrode. Nixon and Congress reacted to the 1973 OPEC oil embargo by quickly authorizing the Alaska Oil Pipeline, described as the largest construction project in the world and the future source of the 1989 *Exxon Valdez* tanker disaster.

Behind the scenes, Nixon decided to use environmental protection to drive a wedge between liberal groups. Adviser H. R. Haldeman wrote that Nixon increasingly felt that his environmental crusader image was dangerous. He got criticism from environmentalists for being too timid, and criticism from business leaders for being too radical. Unsure, he fell back on his political instincts. He would depict environmental protection as too costly for average Americans. "It has to be put in terms of environment versus jobs," he told Haldeman, repeating a refrain that foreshadowed countless future efforts to repeal or weaken environmental protection (Haldeman 1995, July 5, 1971)

For Nixon, bread-and-butter economic issues were the path to the voters' hearts. Thus, he did not pay much attention to the quietly growing network of federal programs to sponsor communication and the arts. The Corporation for Public Broadcasting, with its radio network NPR and television network PBS, expanded throughout the 1970s, adding local affiliates and producing highly rated educational programs such as "The Electric Company," "Sesame Street," "Nova," and "Cosmos."

Nixon also did nothing to stop the growing budget of the National Endowment for the Arts (NEA), a Great Society reform from 1965. The NEA made thousands of grants to ballet companies, playwrights, folklorists, painters, photographers, and museums. Early NEA grants often went to works that celebrated the civil rights movement, such as the play about boxer Jack Johnson, "The Great White Hope." Criticism of this type of grant did not go very far. But by the 1980s, once the conservative movement was a national force, critics of the NEA nearly killed off the agency entirely after it funded art exhibits with strong homosexual themes. Nixon's presidency was not a dress rehearsal for every act of the revolt against liberal reform.

More than a Bungled Burglary: The Watergate Scandal

The Watergate Scandal began before dawn June 17, 1972, when Washington, D.C. police arrested five men for burglary. They were apprehended in the Watergate offices of the Democratic Party. The burglars were rifling through files, taking microfilm photos of documents, and planting listening devices. It was not immediately obvious that the five men worked for President Nixon, but investigative work by reporters revealed this fact over the next several months. In the middle of Nixon's reelection campaign, the burglars' White House link would have been a bombshell, but the press needed time to prove the allegation, and the public needed time to absorb it. Thus, the full weight of the scandal did not come crashing down around the president until 1974.

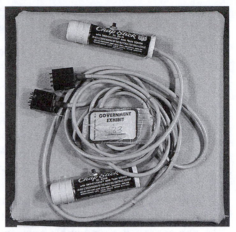

Government Exhibit 133 from the Watergate hearings: Chapstick tubes with hidden microphones used by G. Gordon Liddy and E. Howard Hunt at the time of the Watergate burglary. During 1973–1974 many Americans watched the televised Watergate hearings that revealed malfeasance in the Nixon White House. (National Archives)

The Watergate scandal shocked Americans, but not because it revealed Nixon to be a devious politician. They already knew that. He had red-baited his way into the Senate, rescued his vice presidential job by threatening—on national television—to orphan his family's dog, and attacked the loyalty of every Democrat who criticized the Eisenhower administration. The Watergate revelations were new because they revealed Nixon to be in control of a criminal network. Nixon's operatives used extortion to raise campaign funds from wealthy individuals and large corporations, laundered money, intimidated and spied on so-called enemies of the White House, and sabotaged the campaigns of Democratic challengers. The shock of Watergate was that the Nixon administration so cavalierly broke laws and abused power. A memo from one Nixon aide put it bluntly, "we can use the available federal machinery to screw our political enemies" (Schlesinger 1989, 258).

Millions of dollars moved through a secret slush fund operated by the Committee to Re-Elect the President (CREEP). The Watergate burglars came out of a sort of commando unit called "the Plumbers," so named because their job was originally to stop leaks, that is, government employees who gave classified information to the press. By the time of the Watergate burglary, Nixon's men had committed numerous felonies, such as breaking into the office of the psychiatrist of Daniel Ellsberg, the man who had leaked the *Pentagon Papers.*

For all the crimes committed by members of CREEP and the Plumbers, very few of them ever faced indictment or conviction. In fact, the articles of impeachment drawn up in Congress focused mostly on the "obstruction of justice" charge. In other words, Nixon and his men were in trouble for trying to cover up the crimes

The Pentagon Papers

Daniel Ellsberg was a Defense Department analyst who supported the war in Vietnam as a necessary battle in the war against communism. But by 1970, he had changed his mind. An analyst for the RAND Corporation, he participated in authoring a 7,000-page secret history of U.S. involvement in Vietnam. Among other conclusions, the report noted that every president, from Eisenhower through Nixon, had consistently misled the American public about how deeply the United States was involved in the fighting between North and South Vietnam. The report was never meant for public consumption, only for internal Defense Department use. Ellsberg smuggled out the entire report through RAND security checkpoints, one section at a time in his briefcase. He photocopied the sections late into the night, and then returned the sections to work the next morning. When he began leaking the photocopies to the press in early 1971, the report acquired the nickname, "The Pentagon Papers."

On June 13, 1971, several newspapers, led by *The New York Times,* began publishing the Pentagon Papers. At the behest of the Nixon administration a federal court enjoined the newspapers from further publication, and the Justice Department prosecuted Ellsberg for espionage. Nixon also harassed Ellsberg secretly by hiring a group of burglars to break into Ellsberg's psychiatrist's office to look for materials that would ruin Ellsberg's reputation. Nixon miscalculated. Instead of discrediting Ellsberg and taking the Pentagon Papers story off the front page, it became the biggest news story of the summer of 1971. Newspapers covered it extensively as an attack on freedom of the press. Ironically, the Nixon's administration's mania to plug Ellsberg's leak ignored the fact that the Pentagon Papers themselves were somewhat exculpatory. As Nixon had argued in the past, he was not responsible for getting the United States into the Vietnam War and he was hardly the first president to lie about it.

The Supreme Court settled the Pentagon Papers case quickly, handing down *New York Times v. U.S.* on June 30, 1971. In a 6–3 decision, the Court ruled that the White House effort to block publication of the Pentagon Papers was "prior restraint" of the press, and therefore a violation of the First Amendment. Ellsberg was vindicated, and the antiwar movement and the newspapers celebrated a triumph. Nixon was convinced that the press was out to get him. He decided to make the burglary of Ellsberg's psychiatrist's office a model for a new group of secret White House operatives, the Plumbers. The Pentagon Papers thus began the chain of events that led to the Watergate scandal.

more than they were for the crimes themselves. Nixon was slow to realize this because he spent most of 1973 trying to keep special prosecutors, congressional Democrats, and reporters away from witnesses who could testify about the crimes committed by CREEP and the Plumbers. This effort became more difficult as witnesses demanded higher and higher payments to keep their mouths shut.

All the President's Men: Cover-up and the Press

During the nearly 26 months between the botched burglary and President Nixon's resignation, the Watergate scandal received an enormous amount of attention in the press and on the major television networks. Without a doubt, the story merited the coverage, but part of the reason for the spotlight was the role journalists themselves played in the dramatic story.

Washington Post reporters Bob Woodward and Carl Bernstein put themselves at the center of the story. Indeed, Woodward's account of the duo's investigation, *All the President's Men,* appeared in bookstores just a few months after Nixon waved farewell from the helicopter on the White House south lawn. Two years later, a Hollywood film version of the book starred Dustin Hoffman and Robert Redford and won four Academy Awards. The film's enduring utility as a Watergate scandal primer combined with periodic coverage of the anniversaries of Nixon's resignation to refresh the public's memory of Watergate.

In addition, the story remained a fresh news story because for three decades, Woodward and Bernstein refused to name their main government source, a man who fed them tips in exchange for anonymity. The reporters referred to him only as "Deep Throat." A cottage industry developed over the next three decades, dedicated to guessing Deep Throat's identity. In 2005, at the age of 92, Deep Throat allowed Woodward and Bernstein to reveal his name. At the time of Watergate, Mark Felt had been associate director of the FBI.

Deep Throat meeting the reporters in a shadowy underground parking garage was just one of many Watergate images that became iconic. President Nixon was surrounded by shadowy advisers and soldiers of fortune who formed "the Plumbers" and "CREEP." Nixon ordered the "Saturday Night Massacre," during which he fired both his attorney general and the independent investigator probing the scandal. The famous White House tapes contained the unexplained "18-1/2-minute gap," and the tape transcripts contained numerous "expletive deleted"-s. "I am not a crook," declared Nixon during a press conference in 1973, nine months before resigning. The televised Watergate hearings recalled the long-remembered McCarthy hearings, with dogged congressmen such as Sen. Sam Irvin (D-N.C.) determined to find the truth behind the White House smokescreens.

Watergate thus left the news media with a ready-made script for how to cover presidential cover-ups. Secret sources, denied allegations, congressional investigations, and the refrain, "How much did the president know, and when did he know it?" became familiar mileposts during the Iran-Contragate, Nannygate, Whitewatergate, and Monicagate scandals that plagued the Reagan and Clinton administrations. The second Bush administration had all of these examples in mind when it adopted a strategy of restricting reporters' access to the White House. But even it could not avoid the scandal surrounding the exposure of a covert CIA agent, Valerie Plame, in what became reflexively known as "Plamegate." The news media's coverage of the presidency is still greatly influenced by the Watergate scandal.

Any remnants of Nixon's credibility went up in smoke in the White House tapes controversy. Sen. Sam Ervin's (D-N.C.) investigative committee discovered that Nixon had installed a voice-activated tape-recording system in the Oval Office. Thus, there existed an audio record of Nixon discussing the Watergate cover-up. Nixon refused to make the tapes public until forced by a court injunction. His initial refusal had two fatal flaws: first, it seemed like there was something on those tapes he wanted to hide, and, second, it seemed as though he was doing everything he could to obstruct the Watergate investigation. When transcripts appeared in newspapers in the summer of 1974, readers were amazed at the high number of "expletive deleted"-s and gaps in the record—especially a famous 18-1/2-minute gap that Nixon blamed on his secretary.

By the end of July 1974, the House of Representatives had passed three articles of impeachment. They were not for burglary, money laundering, or extortion but rather for obstruction of justice, abuse of power, and contempt of Congress. Aides warned Nixon that the Senate would likely vote to convict Nixon on all three charges, which would force him from office. To avoid that spectacle, Nixon chose to resign on August 9, 1974. Voters expressed their displeasure with Nixon's party when they elected 54 new Democratic members of Congress in the 1974 midterm elections. Even Gerald Ford—whom most people agreed was an honest, decent person—could not escape the wrath of the Watergate-scorned public, especially after he pardoned Nixon. Voters turned Ford out of office in 1976 in favor of the hitherto-unknown governor of Georgia, Jimmy Carter.

The Watergate affair came at a critical juncture in the 1970s. It coincided with the final U.S. military withdrawal from Vietnam, impeded the resurgence of the Republican Party, and heightened the suspicion of elected officials that more and more Americans adopted as a default mode. In the second half of the 1970s, distrust of government found ample reasons to spread and magnify. Factories closed throughout the Midwest, the price of food and gasoline skyrocketed, and American leaders seemed to capitulate to the rulers of so-called Third World countries. When Ronald Reagan won the election of 1980 by identifying the federal government as the source—not the solution—to the country's problems, he reaped a bountiful harvest of public support from soil well sown by the Watergate affair.

Culture of Surveillance

The sensational story of the White House tapes reflected a growing trend, a growing "culture of surveillance." All of Nixon's advisers and visitors to the White House were taped, whether they knew it or not, by an automatic, voice-activated system. With a conservative administration in power at the start of the 1970s, most of the groups of citizens under surveillance were activists on the political left.

Historians' Debate: Where Does Nixon Fit In?

After Watergate, journalists and scholars weighed in on the meaning of what they had just witnessed. Many, such as historian Arthur Schlesinger Jr., declared Nixon's resignation to be the end of "the imperial presidency." Post-Watergate Congresses bristled with investigative committees and bills limiting executive power.

More recently, the debate among historians shifted. For one thing, the Reagan administration showed that presidents still managed to evade congressional oversight; for another, the rise of conservatism has stood out in bold relief. Historians began to debate the question: was Nixon the first of the conservatives or the last of the liberals?

For Allen Matusow, John Morton Blum, William Chafe, and Bruce Schulman, Nixon was clearly a conservative, counterrevolutionary force against the revolutionary, left-wing impulses unleashed during the 1960s. These scholars focus on Nixon's active courting of the "silent majority." Every policy he adopted, from affirmative action to environmental protection, seemed calculated to stoke debate among factions of the Democratic Party, and to discredit liberals in the eyes of the average voter. By trying to accommodate black nationalists, women's liberationists, and a host of other extreme groups, the Democrats seemed to be turning into a radical, left-wing fringe. Centrist voters turned to Nixon as a moderate alternative.

Other historians have taken issue with this account. As Joan Hoff, Dean Kotlowski, Donald Crichtlow, and Matthew Lassiter have argued, historians should reconsider their depiction of Nixon as a conservative who fooled voters into thinking he was a moderate. According to them, many of Nixon's policies appealed to voters on their merits alone, not just because they stood out against a liberal foil. These historians object to labeling Nixon as a conservative because doing so gives the impression that Nixon was part of the Barry Goldwater–Ronald Reagan wing of the Republican Party, which triumphed in 1980. In reality, these scholars point out, right-wing Republican activists despised Nixon as a "me-too" politician who tried to follow public opinion. Nixon was not a member of the grassroots right because he did not share its arch antistatist ideology. Nixon was not part of "America's right turn," these scholars argue. Rather, he was "a detour."

It is also possible that Nixon was an accessory to the conservatives' rise, regardless of whether he was a true believer. Because of the Watergate fiasco, the American public lost faith in the federal government, a trust already eroded by the Vietnam War. That lack of trust was deadly for liberalism, which relied on government action. Although it was difficult to perceive at the time, Watergate functioned as a huge victory for political conservatives who learned how to capitalize on voters' spent faith in the federal government. Nixon's resignation was not so much a cleansing of the system as it was an indictment of all politicians. As cultural historian Stephen Paul Miller put it, Watergate made Nixon "a kind of human sacrifice" to voters' distrust of their leaders (Miller 1999, 38).

By coercing indicted members to spy for the government, the FBI devastated some of the most militant protest groups, including the Black Panther Party, the America Indian Movement, and the Weather Underground. Several Native American leaders and black nationalists perished in gun battles with police. Several more activists served long prison terms even though the FBI and police had broken laws to gain evidence against them. Increased surveillance, and even persecution, was the fulfillment of Nixon's "law and order" campaign promise. The liberal Democrats had not endorsed radical militants of the New Left. In fact, New Left activists frequently identified liberals as their foe for continuing the Vietnam War and for compromising in pursuit of reform. But the surveillance crackdown made the activists of the 1960s seem like criminals on the run in the 1970s.

Expansion of the Political Franchise

Working from within the System

Throughout the country, sweeping changes were transforming the ways politics affected the lives of everyday Americans and how leaders at the very top operated. Some called it the "new politics" of the 1970s. It was new because it brought previously disfranchised groups into the process of elections, policy making, and governance. City councils and congressional committees in the 1970s simply had more women, more people of color, and more homosexuals than had previously been the case. In San Antonio, for example, a large Mexican American community had been shut out of politics for years by citywide elections. Switching to a district election system put several Mexican Americans on the city council.

For decades, most Americans had contact with politics through their local party precinct captain. The two major parties had elaborate hierarchies connecting the top national leaders with neighborhood captains in cities, towns, and counties. In presidential election years, the hierarchy sprang into action. Local party officials competed to be selected as delegates to their parties' national conventions, the scene of intense, lengthy debates over the platform and the nominees for president and vice president. In "smoke-filled rooms," the most powerful members of state and local governments traded favors. The delegates were primarily white and male.

Because this arrangement had been in place since the 19th century, it did not seem ripe for change until the 1970s. Beginning in 1964, grassroots activists challenged the traditional leaders of both major parties and accused them of putting compromise and bargaining ahead of the principles that motivated voters. The Goldwater Republicans took over the San Francisco convention. The Mississippi Freedom Democrats challenged party rules that maintained white supremacy.

By 1970, leaders in each party faced a dilemma. On the one hand, they felt that grassroots activists would pull their parties toward an ideological extreme and alienate moderate voters. They also recoiled from the press coverage of the elections in the 1960s. Television captured dramatic footage of activists being shoved to the side by their own party. On the other hand, grassroots activists brought a tremendous amount of energy to the national parties that could translate into new voters. They often angrily identified party leaders as their main adversaries, igniting what they called a "life-or-death war" within the Democratic and Republican parties (Reichley 1992, 344). The parties sought to harness that energy before it destroyed them.

The Democrats were the first to change their nominating process. In 1971, the party adopted the reforms recommended by a commission chaired by Sen. George McGovern (D-S.D.) and Rep. Donald Fraser (D-Minn.). The McGovern-Fraser reforms changed the way the Democrats chose delegates for the national convention. Instead of the smoke-filled rooms and members-only caucuses, the states now held primary elections. Primary voters chose which candidate they wanted the national convention to nominate. The new rules required each state's delegates to represent the primary results at the conventions. Delegates could no longer arrive at the convention "uncommitted," ready to wheel and deal for personal gain in exchange for their vote.

Young woman casts her ballot during the 1972 Illinois presidential primary. The 27th Amendment, ratified in 1971, expanded the youth vote by lowering the voting age to 18. (Bettmann/Corbis)

More often than not, the choice of the nominee was a fait accompli based on the outcome of the primary elections. Party officials strove to make the convention a well-managed event that minimized conflicts. From smoke-filled rooms, the emphasis shifted to balloon-and-confetti-filled convention halls, where party members wildly applauded their candidate in front of television cameras. No longer making the final decision, conventioneers merely ratified the primary election winners. In 1972, there were 23 states that held Democratic primaries, which accounted for 49 percent of the convention delegates. By 1980, the number of primary states had increased to 35, tying 81 percent of the delegates to a specific candidate.

The switch to primary elections was not the only reform the Democratic Party enacted during the 1970s. Each state delegation also had to take "affirmative steps" to ensure that its pool of delegates mirrored the ethnic make-up of the state's population (Reichley 1992, 345). Thus, the Mississippi delegation had to be 50 percent African American, and all state delegations had to be 50 percent female. The effect of these changes on the convention was rapid. The 1976 and 1980 conventions were noticeably more diverse than the 1968 convention. The Democrats still nominated white men to run for president, but the presence of nonwhite delegates in 1976 helped give the nomination to Jimmy Carter, a Southern governor with a record of civil rights reform. And not long after the 1970s ended, the presence of female delegates helped Geraldine Ferraro become the first major-party nominee for vice president in 1984.

Even the Republican Party reformed itself during the 1970s, a testament to the power of social movements to change the two major parties. Its Delegates and Organization Committee enacted a series of similar reforms: 50–50 male-female delegations and diversity targets for the party's various councils and committees. By 1980, the Republicans held one more primary than did the Democrats, with 36 primaries determining 78 percent of the convention delegates. The major parties were beginning to keep pace with changes occurring in society as a whole.

Both parties' embrace of primary elections had diffuse effects. Because state party leaders no longer had as much control over delegate selection, the national party leaders assumed greater power. No longer could one faction or one person—such as the Southern Dixiecrats or Chicago mayor Richard J. Daley— exercise effective veto power at the national convention. Paradoxically, as national party leaders increased their power and influence, the power and influence of the parties themselves declined. Primary voters mattered more, and local party organizations mattered less, which had the effect of weakening the bonds that many voters had with their neighborhood party organization. Public opinion polls tracked a gradual but steady decline in the number of voters who identified themselves strongly as Republicans or as Democrats, from 75 percent in the 1950s to 60 percent by 1980.

African American Victories

In 1970, Congress took up the question of whether to reauthorize the Voting Rights Act of 1965. The data showed just how much the Act had changed America. Across the South, millions of African Americans were registering to vote and turning out in large numbers on Election Day. For the first time since the Reconstruction Era, large numbers of African American congressmen, state legislators, mayors, governors, city council members, and sheriffs were winning elections. Congress voted easily to reauthorize the Act that seemed to be working.

The 1970s saw a continuation of the steady improvement in the economic lives of African Americans. On the whole, they were still worse off than the rest of the population, but their wealth and status were growing. White family incomes increased 69 percent during the 1960s. African American families, whose incomes still lagged behind, saw a 109 percent increase over the same years. In 1970, this still left African American families earning, on average, only 61 percent of the average white family. But there was no doubt that African Americans were becoming upwardly mobile. While only 20 percent of African American families earned middle-class incomes in 1940, by 1980 a majority (55 percent)

Bus provided by the Sixth Avenue Baptist Church in Birmingham, Alabama, takes African American voters to the polls on primary election day, May 1972. (National Archives)

of African American families resided in the middle or middle-upper class. These economic gains combined with the ongoing enforcement of the Voting Rights Act to make African Americans a powerful voting constituency.

If the 1970s were the moment in which African Americans "arrived" politically, then it was a cruel hoax. The recession undermined their newfound power in many ways. Because of the great migrations of the early 1900s, African Americans were a mostly urbanized group. Unfortunately for them, the 1970s were a time of acute financial crisis for most large U.S. cities. This was especially true of cities in the Midwestern "rust belt," so-called because so many factories were closing and deteriorating behind chain-link fences. Not only were steel and auto companies abandoning cities but also middle-class residents fled to the suburbs. High urban unemployment and its offshoots—crime, decaying neighborhoods, poor schools—drove to the suburbs millions of citizens who could afford to move. What they left behind were cities with an even lower per capita income and a shrinking tax base.

The signs of the urban crisis were literally on the front page throughout the 1970s. During one four-year period, 40,000 acts of arson were recorded in the South Bronx, a neighborhood that epitomized the hollowed-out urban core. Even viewers of *Monday Night Baseball* saw footage of the Bronx burning. The rest of New York City was not faring much better. The city teetered on the edge of bankruptcy in 1975, which forced the mayor to ask President Gerald Ford for federal assistance, who denied the request. The *Daily News* famous headline ran the next day: "Ford to City: Drop Dead!" (Barlett 1998, 177). The headline seemed prophetic in the summer of 1977, when an electric blackout caused two nights of looting and rioting. And New York was lucky. New York came close to bankruptcy but never fell into it. Cleveland, Ohio, was not so lucky. Once an industrial powerhouse, Cleveland was devastated by closing factories and middle-class flight to the suburbs. The city defaulted on its municipal bonds in December 1978.

The 1970s were an inauspicious time, then, for African American leaders to emerge as a major force in urban politics. Being elected mayor of a major American city in the 1970s was something like being made captain of a sinking ship. Nevertheless, many of the mayors elected then were the first African American mayors in their cities' histories, and many of them served several consecutive terms, which demonstrated their popularity with voters even in the worst of economic times.

While African American mayors battled urban decline during the 1970s, other black leaders were building permanent institutions at the national level. In 1969, three members of the House of Representatives—Shirley Chisholm (D-N.Y.), William Clay (D-Mo.), and Louis Stokes (D-Ohio)—founded the Congressional Black Caucus. Although the Caucus only began with 9 members, it doubled to 18 by 1980. Like a majority of African Americans, black members of Congress were almost all Democrats, so the Caucus quickly became a powerful force in

African American Mayors

In 1967, Richard Hatcher and Carl Stokes became the first African American mayors of Gary, Indiana, and Cleveland, Ohio, respectively. In 1973, Tom Bradley, Maynard Jackson, and Coleman Young became the first African American mayors of Los Angeles, Atlanta, and Detroit, respectively. Lionel Wilson did the same in Oakland, California, in 1977. And Birmingham, Alabama—where police dogs had attacked marching African American schoolchildren in 1963—elected its first African American mayor, Richard Arrington, in 1979.

The personal histories of these mayors resembled the history of millions of African Americans. Tom Bradley was born in Texas to a family of sharecroppers, and his grandparents had been born slaves. His family found steady work and an escape from Jim Crow—if not from racism—in southern California. Bradley became the longest-serving mayor in Los Angeles history, winning election five times. Richard Arrington's parents were Alabama tenant farmers who were determined to escape the sharecropper's crushing debt. They moved to Birmingham to work in the steel mills. Mayor Arrington also served 20 years. Some African American mayors were elected in cities such as Atlanta that had black majorities. But some, such as Bradley in Los Angeles, won in cities with a large white majority.

Handling racial politics was always a delicate issue for African American mayors in the 1970s. Their constituents in the black community were often deeply suspicious of local government. Oakland's working-class African American neighborhoods, for example, were the scene of several incidents of police brutality in the 1960s. The Black Panther Party for Self-Defense responded by patrolling the police officers. In Detroit, the home of the Nation of Islam, African American militancy was an established force, which put Mayor Young under the close scrutiny of non–African American citizens who criticized the way he spent redevelopment funds.

The first generation of African American mayors had some success in lessening the rage that ghetto residents expressed during the urban uprisings of the 1960s. Riots were fewer during the 1970s, even though unemployment, inflation, and crime rates generally rose throughout the decade. African American mayors had remarkable success at getting their police departments to hire more black officers, which no doubt healed some of the wounds between the police force and the neighborhoods. But in the end, budgetary necessities hamstrung even the most talented leaders. Detroit's Mayor Young was in a typical situation in 1978, trying to negotiate a fair contract with the city's unions while the city's tax base continued to dwindle. He made the hard choice to give the union members a raise, but cut the size of the city's police force. The result was an uptick in violent crime in 1979 and 1980, grimly symbolized by hoodlums' transformation of Halloween into "Devil's Night," a spasm of burglary, vandalism, and arson that became a dreaded Detroit tradition well into the 1980s.

the Democratic Party, helping to keep civil rights reform a major part of the party platform even as the civil rights movement declined in influence.

African American representation on Capitol Hill also received a boost from the judiciary. A series of court rulings ensured that dozens of congressional districts contained black majorities. These districts often elected African American congresspersons, but not without controversy. Republicans claimed that Democrat-controlled state legislatures had gerrymandered the districts in order to ensure an African American election victory. Criticism came also from the left. Some civil rights activists saw majority–African American districts as a way of segregating the African American vote and containing it, resulting in only token representation. Conservative activists termed the whole exercise pernicious "social engineering" that treated voters as pawns and violated the value of color-blindness by paying too much attention to voters' color. The conservative critique bore fruit after the 1970s, as conservative federal judges slowly chipped away at the majority–African American districts. The Congressional Black Caucus was forced to spend much time literally defending its home turf rather than pushing for further civil rights reform.

By the end of the 1970s, black leaders had made their mark in politics, but their prominence did not necessarily mean that all African Americans had escaped poverty and institutional racism. Indeed, behind the success stories was a story of increasing despair and alienation for a large percentage of African Americans. In the 1970s, scholars and journalists began using the term "underclass" to describe the urban, poor, nonwhite population that seemed to have slim prospects for social mobility and political power. Sociologists estimated that at least 30 percent of the African American population spent the 1970s sinking deeper into poverty, a sad counterweight to the 55 percent of blacks who had achieved middle-class status. Moving out of the underclass was almost impossible during the prolonged recession. Despite government-sponsored hiring programs, African Americans were largely stuck in their historic position as the "last hired" when the economy was booming, and "first fired" when the economy was slumping. The 1970s slump hit African American workers harder than it hit other groups, and showed the limits of political success in an adverse economic climate.

Women in Politics

Textbooks, popular films and televisions shows frequently depict the 1970s as a high water mark for the women's rights movement, and in politics women increased their numbers and influence. The signs of women's growing political clout were everywhere, from the Astrodome-filling conferences, to the growing number of females giving stump speeches, to the decade-long fight for the Equal Rights Amendment (ERA). But not all female political leaders were feminists. By

1980, ratification of the ERA had stalled, a symbol of the cultural shift away from feminism and women's liberation. In fact, female 1970s conservatives helped translate the growing popular discontent with liberal reform politics into votes for conservative Republican candidates.

As with the story of African American political gains, a stark economic reality underlay the political gains made by women during the 1970s. As well-paying jobs became scarce for unionized men, the competition for entry-level work increased, which left many women at a disadvantage. Even though some women of the 1970s appeared in new places—on previously all-male Ivy League campuses, on trading floors in New York and Chicago, and on election ballots—the vast majority of women were funneled into professions and occupations that society as a whole had deemed "women's work." "Pink collar" jobs such as nursing, teaching, typing, and waiting tables paid less than comparable "men's jobs." The 1980 Census found that 80 percent of women working full-time jobs clustered in just 20 of the 420 listed occupations. The problem was much broader than the existence of "glass ceilings" in a few professions. There were cultural and social barriers to women's economic progress.

The economic situation was even worse for women who could not hold down a full-time job, especially single mothers with young children. From 1970 to 1980, there was a 39 percent increase in the number of female-headed families living below the federal poverty line. As divorce and out-of-wedlock birth rates increased throughout the 1970s, millions of women found themselves applying for federal relief. The rolls of Aid to Families with Dependent Children swelled from 3 million in 1960 to 11 million in 1980. The public and academic perception of poverty changed along with this trend. Whereas Kennedy-era social scientists focused on the geographic pockets of poverty, scholars in the 1970s began seeing a correlation between sex and socioeconomic status. Many called it the "feminization of poverty." Because political power and economic power often reinforced each other, the 1970s were a contradictory period for women in American politics.

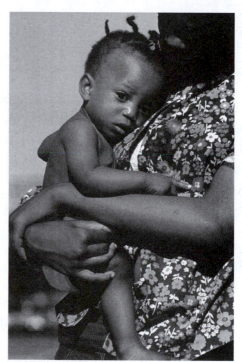

South Side Chicago mother and child living in low-income housing, 1973. Poverty affected women in disproportionate numbers during the 1970s, giving rise to the term "feminization of poverty." (John H. White/National Archives)

A time of increasing influence for some women was also a time of increasing political marginalization for others.

Nevertheless, for women who aspired to political office or who just wanted to be active in elections and in policymaking, the 1970s seemed full of possibilities and role models. The National Organization for Women (NOW), headed by Eileen Hernandez, Wilma Scott Heide, Karen DeCrow, and Eleanor Smeal, increased its membership and launched ambitious initiatives. NOW helped sponsor the ERA campaign, which required exhaustive lobbying in every state capital. NOW also carried out an aggressive legal strategy to force government agencies and private employers to adhere to the equal opportunity provisions of Title VII in the 1964 Civil Rights Act. The legal strategy yielded mixed results in high profile cases—better working conditions for female flight attendants but no improvement for retail saleswomen who wanted to sell on commission. But without a doubt, feminists put the question of fairness squarely on the political agenda in the 1970s. This was a huge political advance from the 1960s, when activists faced ridicule for protesting the Miss America Pageant.

Youth in Politics

In May 1970, students protesting Nixon's invasion of Cambodia went into a fury after National Guard troops shot and killed four young protestors at Kent State University in Ohio, and state troopers killed two protestors at Jackson State University in Mississippi. In response, over 4 million students went on strike, shutting down over 900 campuses nationwide. The spring 1970 semester never ended, and many schools remained closed until the fall. The decade thus began with an extraordinary degree of political passion and mobilization among the nation's young people. By the end of the decade, however, youth participation rates in politics had plunged precipitously. There were several reasons for this, including the end of the Vietnam War, the Watergate scandal, and the stagnant economy.

The social movements of the 1960s had kindled in many young people a desire to be active in politics, but even more immediately, the Vietnam War draft heightened the political consciousness of the youth. By 1970, the military was calling up 30,000 draftees every month in order to continue the fighting in Southeast Asia. College students campaigned heavily for antiwar candidates, such as Sen. Eugene McCarthy (D-Minn.) in 1968 and Sen. George McGovern (D-S.D.) in 1972. Neither senator won, but young voters won a victory in 1971 when Congress passed the 26th Amendment, which lowered the voting age from 21 to 18, the same age that males became draft-eligible. Newly enfranchised, 50 percent of voters aged 18 to 24 cast ballots in the 1972 presidential election, compared with 57 percent for the overall eligible voter population. Both of these percentages declined over the course of the 1970s. In 1976, 54 percent of eligible voters turned out, but only 44 percent of the 18-to-24 segment. By 1980, the percentages were down to 53 percent and 42 percent, respectively.

If the 1970s had begun with such a high level of political activism among young people, why did their voting rates decline? First, voting rates declined among all age groups, so it is not surprising that young voters were part of the trend. Second, young voters who supported antiwar candidates were profoundly disappointed when their favorites lost over and over to candidates such as Richard Nixon, who intensified the Vietnam War. For some, disappointment led to disengagement from politics. Third, New Left activists were some of the first to perceive that American political culture as a whole was shifting to the right. The chances for bringing about New Left reforms through national elections grew slimmer by the year. Fourth, with the end of the Vietnam War, the main source of leftist youth political activism disappeared.

The antiwar movement was difficult to sustain after 1973, when the Nixon administration signed a peace treaty with North Vietnam and ended the draft. The coalition of left-wing activists was splintering into several factions, some of them violent, radical, and anarchist. The Black Panther Party was a symbol of young defiance, but by the mid-1970s, many of its leaders were serving prison sentences or had been killed by law enforcement officers. Chicago Black Panther chairman Fred Hampton was 21 when police officers shot him in an early morning raid on his home. Even the venerable Students for a Democratic Society (SDS) fell apart at its 1969 convention. Anarchists calling themselves "The Weathermen" launched a campaign of violent revolution not only to end the war but also to bring down the capitalist order. The Weathermen carried out several terror attacks during the 1970s, including bombs that destroyed the U.S. Congress mailroom and part of the New York City Police headquarters. Several Weathermen leaders went to prison after robbing and killing the driver of an armored car in 1982.

By the end of the 1970s, in the eyes of many Americans, the radical youth of the New Left were discredited. Journalists noted that American campuses had quieted down considerably. Students recognized the poor state of the economy and devoted themselves to their studies, a sharp contrast to the students of the 1960s who often skipped classes and stayed up all night organizing rallies and protests. Some of the most politically active young people during the 1970s were, in fact, conservatives. William F. Buckley's Young Americans for Freedom, founded in 1960, grew in numbers throughout the 1970s and fought to drive liberals from the Republican Party. In the 1970s, many of the most successful— and most conservative—future leaders of the Republican Party, including Lee Atwater, Karl Rove, Grover Norquist, Rick Santorum, and Jack Abramoff, cut their teeth in the political battles of the College Republicans. At the beginning of the 1970s, most people assumed that young, politically active citizens were most likely liberals or leftists. But by the end of the decade, they were more likely to be conservatives.

FOREIGN POLICY FAILURES AND DILEMMAS

Defeat in Vietnam

After 1954, the United States was heavily involved in the defense of South Vietnam from the communist and nationalist government of North Vietnam. President Nixon took office in 1969 pledging to bring "peace with honor," meaning that the United States would eventually get out of Vietnam but would not simply abandon South Vietnam to the communist forces. More than 30,000 U.S. soldiers had died in the fighting, and another 20,000 more would die before the final pullout in 1975. The war's prolonged denouement drove the final nails into the coffin of liberal foreign policy, giving rise to a more hard-headed philosophy of neoconservatism.

Nixon called his withdrawal strategy "Vietnamization," meaning that the United States would train and equip the South Vietnamese military to fight on its own. Vietnamization implied a gradual, but not hasty, reduction in U.S. involvement. At the same time, though, Nixon was openly stepping up the aerial bombing of North Vietnam and secretly invading Cambodia and Laos. The bombings and invasions cost Nixon a great deal of public support. The largest mass demonstrations against the Vietnam War occurred during Nixon's presidency, including the nationwide student strike that followed the Kent State and Jackson State shootings.

Nixon defended the invasions and bombings as part of the Vietnamization strategy. Bombings would force North Vietnam to negotiate. Invading Cambodia and Laos would deprive communist troops of a haven and a supply center. But to many Americans, both actions looked like escalations of the war, not steps toward peace.

Nixon's war policies earned criticism from the left and right. New Left protestors saw Nixon as a conservative militarist. They held countless rallies and marches, and committed acts of civil disobedience, such as shutting down recruiting stations and burning draft cards. Conservative critics saw Nixon as a liberal—and worse, amateur—militarist. Nixon's first move was to use more firepower. Conservative critics such as Sen. Henry M. Jackson (D-Wash.) and Phyllis Schlafly objected to the escalation because they saw Vietnam as a distraction from the real enemies, Russia and China. Communist countries, critics argued, supported North Vietnam to make the U.S. military bleed itself to death in an inconsequential war.

The conservative understanding of the Vietnam War as a needless sideshow to the main event far outlasted the temporary critics on Nixon's right, the so-called war hawks. During the war, the hawks called for more troops. But in the years after 1975, many of them came to a new understanding—a neoconservative stance. To the neoconservatives, the Vietnam War was a mistake not because it was immoral but because it weakened the United States in the global

Vietnam War protester holds a sign reading "Air murder is still murder!" outside Moffett Field Naval Air Station in California, February 1971. (National Archives)

struggle against communism. Neoconservatives sought to modify the liberalism of John F. Kennedy, whose inaugural address promised to "meet any challenge." The neoconservatives contended that the United States should only meet direct challenges, not indirect threats such as North Vietnam. By the late 1970s, the neoconservatives gained increasing influence among policymakers and members of Congress.

Liberal critics pounced on Nixon for taking an interest in the court martial of Lt. William Calley, who ordered his troops to massacre several hundred civilians in the village of My Lai in 1968. After Lieutenant Calley received a life sentence in April 1971, Nixon ordered him released from prison, which began an appeals process that eventually reduced his sentence to three-and-a-half years' house arrest. Editorials, street protestors, and members of Congress lambasted Nixon for the cover-ups and the leniency, and as a result, he was politically unable to intensify U.S. fighting after the 1971 Laos invasion.

Even without Lieutenant Calley, the *Pentagon Papers,* or Watergate, Nixon probably would have had no choice but to withdraw U.S. troops. By 1971, opinion polls showed that 71 percent of Americans felt that the war was a mistake, and 58 percent considered it immoral to continue fighting. Nixon adviser Henry Kissinger and North Vietnam's Le Duc Tho signed the Paris Accords in January 1973. Tho and Kissinger shared the Nobel Peace Prize, but Kissinger did not win any prizes with the American public. The final U.S. troops left South Vietnam in April 1975.

Invasion of Cambodia

When Nixon decided to invade Cambodia in 1970, he could hardly have imagined the chain of events that would follow. More than just a haven for Vietnamese communists, Cambodia was complicated society that was emerging from the colonial era full of internal conflicts and tensions. Cambodia's hereditary monarch, Prince Norodum Sihanouk, tried to remain neutral in the Vietnam War. But North Vietnam built bases and supply lines in Cambodian territory. Sihanouk also tried to repress an internal communist revolt led by Pol Pot, leader of the Khmer Rouge, a group inspired by Marx, Lenin, and Mao. Impatient with Sihanouk, the United States supported Lon Nol, who took power in a coup in 1970 and used American supplies to bomb Khmer Rouge–held parts of the country.

For years, U.S. military leaders had wanted to invade Cambodia in order to destroy the "Asian Pentagon," a rumored communist command post located somewhere in the Cambodian jungle. The 1970 invasion uncovered no such post, only a few scattered weapons caches and bunkers. The invasion cost Nixon dearly at home, because it unleashed a new wave of antiwar protests. More importantly for Cambodia, the American invasion intensified its own civil war. North Vietnam supplied and funded the Khmer Rouge while the United States did the same for Lon Nol and the Cambodian military. The continued American bombing of rural areas caused many Cambodian citizens to align with the Khmer Rouge against the military government. The United States gradually pulled out of both South Vietnam and Cambodia at the same time. Saigon and Phnom Penh fell within days of each other in the spring of 1975.

Once in power, Pol Pot's Khmer Rouge closed off Cambodia from the outside world and began genocide. Believing that only the rural peasantry could form the revolutionary vanguard of a new society, the Khmer Rouge executed or imprisoned anyone who seemed to be urban, middle class, or well educated. Cambodians who wore eyeglasses quickly learned to dispose of them. In an attempt to erase all vestiges of colonialism, the Khmer Rouge outlawed private property, private enterprise, currency, banking, religion, and western medicine. They declared 1975 to be the "year zero," and they mercilessly slaughtered or starved to death anyone who impeded their goal of an agrarian, classless, communist utopia. Ironically, the genocide stopped when the communist government of Vietnam invaded in 1979 and sent Pol Pot into hiding. At the time of the Khmer Rouge's rise to power in 1975, there were just over 7 million Cambo-

Protests: Hardhats, Soldiers, and Students

By 1970, the anti–Vietnam War movement was at least three years old. In the early 1970s it got even bigger. New outrages, such as the invasions of Cambodia and Laos, energized the protestors. Before the 1970s, most protests were carried out by college students or college-aged individuals, many of whom were eligible for conscription and thus highly motivated to protest the war. On several college campuses, prowar youth also staged demonstrations to counter the antiwar protests and voice their support of the U.S. fight against communism. After 1970, two new groups joined the protests: war veterans and construction workers.

The prowar demonstration that became known as the "hard-hat riot" began in New York City in May 1970, just a few days after the Kent State shootings. In response to the shootings, antiwar activists marched down Wall Street and festooned a statue of George Washington with flags of the Viet Cong, the communist rebels in South Vietnam. About 200 construction workers—many from the World Trade Center construction site, wearing hard hats and waving American flags—drove the protestors way from the statue by force. President Nixon was quick to exploit the situation, recognizing the hard-hat workers as members of the "silent majority." After the melee, he rushed to New York City to pose for photos wearing a hard hat and laughing with construction workers. Quietly, to improve their image, New York's construction unions organized a peaceful march of 100,000 members a few weeks later.

One year after Kent State and the hard-hat riot, Vietnam Veterans Against the War staged a massive protest in Washington, D.C. Hundreds of them tossed their military medals onto the steps of the Capitol. Dozens more, including future senator John Kerry, told the Senate Foreign Relations Committee about the atrocities they had witnessed or committed. Active-duty military personnel made indirect protests. Officers in Vietnam reported increased levels of insubordination and drug use. In 1970, the Army suspected that 65,000 U.S. soldiers were using illegal drugs. Also in that year, 200 officers were attacked or killed by their own soldiers. The practice became so common that soldiers created a name for it, "fragging," because the preferred mutiny method was to roll a fragmentation grenade into the officer's tent.

dian residents. Between 1.2 to 3.3 million perished in the genocide, which made it proportionately the worst of the 20th century.

Cold War "Thaws"

Many people hoped that the 1970s would begin a new, less-dangerous phase in the Cold War. A new word circulated to refer to America's relations with communist countries—"détente," a French term meaning "loosening." The United

The Paris Peace Agreement (1973)
and the Fall of Saigon (1975)

The official end of the Vietnam War defied President Nixon's campaign slogan, "peace with honor." It was neither peaceful nor honorable. North Vietnam and the United States started peace negotiations in Paris in 1969 but did not sign a final agreement until January 1973. Nixon had hoped to conclude the talks in time to help his reelection in November 1972. Even so, he won by a landslide without a treaty. Nixon and Kissinger knew they had little chance of actually saving South Vietnam. Their main hope was to secure a "decent interval" between the peace treaty and the takeover of the South by the North (Herring 1996, 277).

One last bombing campaign did not budge the North, so Kissinger and his counterpart, Le Duc Tho, signed a treaty. But Nixon did not gain much approval in U.S. opinion polls, which showed widespread dissatisfaction with his policies. South Vietnam president Nguyen Van Thieu was also disappointed in Nixon, feeling that he and Kissinger had ignored his needs during the treaty negotiation. He did not sign or even endorse the treaty but only said he would not actively oppose it.

In retrospect, the four years of talks between the United States and North Vietnam seem like a cruel hoax. During that period, the fighting and bombing raged unabated. More than 500,000 North Vietnamese and pro-North rebels in the South died in battle, along with more than 100,000 South Vietnamese deaths. More than 20,000 American troops died between 1969 and 1973. The treaty ended America's direct role in the fighting, but Nixon supplied President Thieu with one billion dollars in military equipment with which to hold off the North. In 1975, Thieu possessed the fourth largest air force in the world, even though this was a war in which air superiority did not lead to victory. The flow of American money and arms soon ran dry. The post-Watergate Congress defied President Ford's request for an additional $300 million in aid for 1974.

The end came quickly for South Vietnam. In the spring of 1975, it took North Vietnam only 55 days to capture the whole country and fulfill its decades-long ambition to make Vietnam unified, independent, and completely decolonized. Still over-confident, U.S. officials in the South delayed evacuation planning until the last minute. The United States got its people out of Saigon before the city fell and evacuated 150,000 South Vietnamese citizens who had collaborated with the Americans and thus feared for their lives. Even so, thousands of South Vietnamese searched frantically for a way out of the country. Corrupt officials auctioned off exit visas to the highest bidder. Taking off from embassy rooftops, American helicopter crews had to remove desperate civilians who were clinging to the skids, a striking image broadcast to American television viewers. South Vietnamese helicopter pilots tried to land on U.S. carriers floating offshore. Finding no room to land, they jumped out and ditched their helicopters in the South China Sea, risking their lives for the chance to swim to a U.S. vessel.

Images such as these haunted the American public for the rest of the 1970s and for some time after. By May 1975, North Vietnam controlled the whole country and renamed Saigon as Ho Chi Minh City after its revered former leader. There was no way for Americans to take pride in the endgame of the Vietnam War.

States signed several important treaties with the Soviets during the détente era. But by the end of the decade, tensions between the United States and the Soviet Union had tightened once again.

In 1970, U.S.-Soviet relations were hardly amicable. Hard-line militarists in the Soviet leadership had forced out Premier Khruschev and installed a leader much less willing to compromise with the West, Leonid Brezhnev. The "Brezhnev Doctrine" was a policy of openly supporting communist rebels fighting against Western regimes in foreign countries. This brought the United States and the USSR into direct conflict in North Vietnam, where U.S. pilots dodged anti-aircraft fire from Soviet "advisers."

Nixon's 1972 visit to the People's Republic of China (PRC) brought the Soviets back to the negotiating table. Although ideological allies, the USSR and the PRC had grown distrustful. Chairman Mao always chafed at the marching orders sent to him from Moscow, and the two Red Armies clashed several times

President Richard Nixon meets with Chinese Communist Party Chairman Mao Zedong during his historic visit to China in 1972. The visit provided a memorable symbol of the "thawing" of the Cold War and initiated some cultural exchanges between the two powerful nations. (National Archives)

Human Rights and Foreign Policy

The notion that the Helsinki accords led directly to the rise of overt challenges to Soviet authoritarianism is overstated. Eastern Europeans had resisted Soviet rule for decades. But with the Helsinki Accords, dissidents behind the Iron Curtain had a new weapon in their struggle. Soviet rulers had committed themselves on paper to uphold human rights. By the late 1970s, the Soviet-controlled government of Poland was having a difficult time keeping a lid on Lech Walesa's Solidarity labor movement. Even dissidents inside the Soviet Union, most notably Andrei Sakharov, became international figures for challenging the Soviets' heavy-handed imprisonment and persecution.

In the United States, the new focus on human rights marked a definitive breaking point between the early 1970s and the late 1970s. At the beginning of the decade, Henry Kissinger adhered to a policy of realpolitik, a German term meaning that the United States should be concerned with only its direct military or economic interests. Furthering idealistic goals, such as spreading democracy and opening markets across the globe, should be a secondary consideration. As far as Kissinger was concerned, it was irresponsible for American policy makers to link another nation's human rights record to its relations with the United States.

Presidents Ford and Carter departed from realpolitik, as the Helsinki Accords indicated. Carter's national security adviser, Zbigniew Brzezinski described himself as a "realist" in foreign policy, but secretly he encouraged Carter to make human rights a hallmark of his administration. Carter and Brzezinski openly urged dissidents in Eastern Europe to speak out against their governments, increased the range of Radio Free Europe propaganda, and supported Pope John Paul II, a native of Poland who was an implacable foe of communism.

To say that the Cold War entered a thawing period during the 1970s is not really accurate. The United States and the Soviet Union made some progress in arms control and human rights. But these treaties had drawbacks, such as the multiple-warhead exception to the SALT agreement. Taking into account the rest of the world outside the United States and the USSR makes it difficult to accept the word détente at face value. The United States treated China with careful, polite diplomacy but subjected less-powerful countries to aerial bombardments or repressive puppet regimes. Hundreds of thousands died fighting U.S. troops in Southeast Asia, and tens of thousands more died in other proxy wars between the United States and the Soviet Union. Thinking that superpower relations were "thawing" may have comforted Americans who were uncomfortable with the disastrous pullout from Vietnam. But to soldiers and civilians caught in crossfires, fleeing civil wars, or suffering under the heel of repressive regimes in Africa, the subcontinent, East Asia, and Latin America, the era of détente did not provide much comfort.

Realpolitik

In reality, détente was only a public display of friendliness between the super-powers. Behind the façade, each side bankrolled murderous proxy wars in the name of reducing the influence of the other side. Most directly, the United States and the USSR clashed in Southeast Asia, where Soviet aid helped Marxist revolu-tionaries in Vietnam, Laos, and Cambodia. Nearby Maoist rebels in Indonesia and the Philippines also received Soviet and Chinese support. The wrenching conflict between India and Pakistan over Bangladesh in 1971, although primarily a Hindu-Muslim conflict, also acquired a Cold War cast when each superpower supported a separate side. India's reliance on Soviet funds for hydropower development made India a suspect state in the eyes of American policymakers. The Soviets also inserted themselves in the Arab-Israeli conflict by arming Syria, Jordan, and Egypt in their fighting against American-backed Israel. The USSR moved into Africa under the aegis of helping native peoples fight imperialism. Soviets helped communist insurgents in Ethiopia and Angola, and had a hand in wars in Zambia, Mozambique, and Rhodesia. And of course, the USSR maintained its support of Cuba, just 90 miles from the United States. The Soviets also assisted other Latin American communist movements, in Brazil, Uruguay, Argentina, Chile, Peru, El Salvador, and Nicaragua.

Wherever it could, the United States rushed to prop up governments battling Soviet-aided insurgencies. Under Kissinger's realpolitik, the United States did not flinch when this meant arming and funding repressive and violent governments. Over the objections of his own ambassador, Nixon backed the Pakistani military regime's brutal crackdown on its eastern province, which eventually became in-dependent Bangladesh. Most famously, Nixon and Kissinger continued the policy of assassinations and coups to oust governments that seemed left leaning. So when Salvador Allende won election as president of Chile in 1970 and began a series of socialist reforms, the United States helped organize the officers' coup that assassinated Allende and installed the Gen. Augusto Pinochet dictatorship that lasted until 1998. The United States also attempted to assassinate Cuban leader Fidel Castro on several occasions.

President Ford was appalled to learn of the assassination policy, and he gave orders to bring the practice to a halt. But Ford continued the policy of supplying money and military hardware for despotic rulers who allied with the United States and fought against communist rebel groups. The United States officially supported General Suharto of Indonesia, a military strongman who had seized power in a 1965 coup. To crush a bothersome ethnic minority, in 1975 Suharto's forces in-vaded the province of East Timor under the pretense of stamping out a Marxist insurrection. Throughout the 1970s, the United States similarly supported the dic-tator of the Philippines, Ferdinand Marcos.

Nixon and China

In the 1991 installment of the *Star Trek* film series, Mr. Spock convinces Captain Kirk to make a peace agreement with his long-time evil foe, the Klingons. At first Kirk rejects the suggestion, noting that he has spent his whole career fighting the Klingons. "There is an old Vulcan proverb," Mr. Spock counters. "Only Nixon could go to China."

President Richard Nixon's ballyhooed visit to the People's Republic of China in February 1972 proved the wisdom of Mr. Spock's proverb. It seemed improbable that Nixon, who had built his career as a staunch anticommunist, would ever do a favor for a communist nation. But then, how could anyone else be the first to go to China? If President Kennedy or Johnson had made the first diplomatic overture to Chairman Mao, Republican critics—certainly Nixon himself—would have pounced on the Democrat for coddling the enemy. With his credentials, Nixon's China visit made him appear "statesmanlike" and earned him praise in history books. It also exploited the growing distrust between China and the Soviet Union. The visit left the Soviets wondering about China's commitment to communism.

There were other reasons for Nixon's visit. The trip served to distract public attention from the Vietnam War and put at least one feather in the president's foreign policy cap before the 1972 election. Nixon's handlers timed the trip so that Air Force One touched down in Beijing during prime-time television hours in the United States. American newspapers carried front-page photos of Nixon shaking hands with Mao and touring the Great Wall with the first lady. The United States was now a tentative ally with the largest nation on earth.

The visit provided memorable images but very little substance. The two countries agreed to establish a cultural exchange program, to provide American manufacturers limited access to the Chinese market, to allow China and Taiwan to settle their differences without U.S. interference, and to pave the way for full-scale diplomatic relations by the end of the 1970s. There was no mention, however, of the reasons why the United States had denied recognition to the People's Republic for so many years. There was no mention of the millions killed during the Cultural Revolution and invasion of Tibet, or of the proxy wars fought in North Korea and North Vietnam. Both sides benefited from the visit. China's government received an important boost to its legitimacy, and Nixon gained praise at home and improved leverage with the Soviet Union.

over central Asian and Siberian borders. Fearing that the United States and the PRC were making a separate peace, the Soviets agreed to begin negotiating with the United States to reduce the size of each country's nuclear arsenal. The Strategic Arms Limitation Talks (SALT) began in 1972 and continued throughout the 1970s. They produced some real results. In 1972, both sides agreed to outlaw biological weapons and antiballistic missiles, which meant that neither side would

Panama Canal Treaty and Backlash

Dozens of major historical figures were responsible for the 1978 treaty in which the United States agreed to turn over control of the Panama Canal to the government of Panama in 1999. But President Jimmy Carter got most of the blame. Aside from the Iranian hostage crisis, no other foreign policy event provided Carter's conservative opponents with more ammunition to attack him.

President Theodore Roosevelt considered the Panama Canal to be his prized diplomatic trophy. He boasted of wresting the isthmus from Colombia in 1903 in order to expedite canal construction, completed in 1914. For the next 50 years, the Canal Zone was governed by a police force of American troops. In 1964, several Panamanians died in clashes with Canal Police, which set off days of rioting that left 20 dead. Many Panamanians resented the fact that Canal Zone profits went overseas to foreign governments. President Johnson sent a negotiator to Panama to restart talks toward a new agreement for the Canal Zone.

The talks concluded with the Torrijos-Carter Treaties of 1977, which Carter considered consistent with his overall defense of human rights and opposition to colonialism. The treaties did not completely deny the United States a role in managing the Canal. In fact, they explicitly allowed the United States to use military force if any nation, including Panama, threatened the canal's neutrality and open access. Carter spent a great deal of his political capital getting the U.S. Senate to ratify the treaties. His public relations push worked, as 68 senators voted for them in March 1978. Even conservative commentator William F. Buckley supported Carter's treaties.

But the canal turnover was red meat for Carter's foes. They derided it as a giveaway that weakened U.S. influence over Latin America, where left-wing social movements were brewing. The treaties were a bludgeon for conservative Republicans to use in the 1978 and 1980 elections. Senators Strom Thurmond (R-S.C.) and Jesse Helms (R-N.C.) denounced the treaties as near-treason before applauding crowds, as did presidential candidate Ronald Regan. Public opinion polls showed 77 percent of respondents objected to giving the Canal Zone to Panama. Reagan's objection was a blunt appeal to those voters: "We built it, we paid for it. And we intend to keep it" (Schulman 2002, 200).

develop weapons that could destroy the other side's incoming missiles. In that way, deterrence was ensured.

But in another sense, the SALT treaties produced meaningless results. Both sides claimed a historic victory when they reached an agreement to stop adding more long-range missiles to their arsenals. It was presented as an end to the arms race. But the treaty did not put a cap on the number of atomic weapons in the world. Each side mastered the technology of MIRVs, or Multiple Independently Targeted Reentry Vehicles. A single intercontinental missile fitted with

MIRVs could hold up to a dozen nuclear warheads, each one hitting a separate target. MIRVs provided each side with a way to skirt the requirements of the SALT treaty. To make matters worse, the SALT talks depended very much on the people involved. Nixon and Kissinger, with their anticommunist credentials, could sign arms treaties without suffering too much criticism for being "soft on communism." President Jimmy Carter, however, was a Democrat and could not escape the charge. He signed the SALT II agreement with Brezhnev in 1979, but the U.S. Senate refused to ratify it.

The second major détente treaty, the Helsinki Accords, came in 1975 and was signed by President Gerald Ford. This agreement did not address the arms race but did try to settle the question of Soviet-controlled governments in Eastern Europe. Ford and the West agreed to concede a sphere of influence to the USSR. But in exchange, the Soviets had to agree to the treaty's guarantees of human rights for Soviet citizens. The treaty represented a new willingness by American leaders to put pressure on the USSR for its abysmal treatment of political dissidents. The U.S. Congress passed the Jackson-Vanik Amendment in the same year, which linked American diplomatic and trade relations to human rights abuses. Countries that imprisoned or executed dissidents, censored the press, and outlawed religious worship would face stiff penalties in their business dealings with the United States.

After a few years of détente, the Cold War went from thaw right back to freeze when the Soviet Army invaded Afghanistan in December 1979. Carter and National Security Adviser Zbigniew Brzezinski knew about the invasion six months in advance, and they began supplying Afghan warlords with arms in preparation for the war. Nonetheless, Carter expressed shock and outrage when Soviet tanks rumbled across the border, and he immediately suspended American grain exports to the USSR. He also boycotted the 1980 Summer Olympics, held in Moscow. Carter's successor in the White House, Ronald Reagan, publicly referred to the Soviet Union as an "evil empire," and he refused to meet directly with three successive Soviet premiers. Détente was over.

Middle East Peace and Conflict

Created from Palestine in 1948 by a United Nations mandate, the state of Israel has always been under the microscope. Because the land in Israel is sacred ground to Jews, Christians, and Muslims, events there take on international importance. Even so, during the 1970s, Israel received more attention than usual, especially from the United States. The key moment came in the Yom Kippur War of 1973, which sent out shock waves that damaged the American economy. Amazingly, within a few years, Israel forged a peace agreement with one of its historic enemies, facilitated by President Carter.

In 1967, Israel fought a war with the three largest Arab nations on its borders and won several hundred square miles of territory from each. Stung by these

Hostage Crisis

If Gerald Ford's presidency was doomed to last only one term when he pardoned former president Richard Nixon for any Watergate crimes, then President Jimmy Carter was doomed to one term by the Iran Hostage Crisis. The crisis began on November 4, 1979, and did not end until 444 days later, on January 20, 1981. It was an outgrowth of the Iranian Revolution of 1979, which deposed Iran's hated Shah and installed a fundamentalist Shi'a theocracy. In the end, the Iranian revolutionaries brought down two leaders—the Shah and President Carter.

The Iranian monarchy was established in 1501. But events in the 20th century weakened it considerably. Like the Queen of England, the Iranian monarch was a symbolic leader. The country was ruled mostly by a prime minister. In 1953, the democratically elected prime minister, Mohammad Mossadegh, indicated plans to take government control of Iran's vast oil fields, which had been controlled by British and American companies. A CIA-engineered coup toppled Mossadegh and left Shah Mohammad Reza Pahlavi in sole control of the country. He remained on the U.S. payroll for the duration of his reign, and he became increasingly dependent on American arms to crush his internal foes. American policy makers continued to support the shah because he was a staunch anticommunist and his country bordered the Soviet Union.

But policy makers overlooked the growing Islamic rebellion fomenting inside Iran, which was supported by powerful religious leaders living in exile. The main exiled leader, Ruhollah Khomeini, had achieved the title of "ayatollah," the highest clerical office in the religion of Shi'a Islam. When the Shah left Iran in early 1979 to seek medical treatment for cancer, Khomeini returned to Iran in triumph. He initiated a revolution in which the Shah's cronies were purged from government and all western cultural influences were banned. A group of 300 idealistic university students, hoping to impress the ayatollah, stormed the U.S. embassy in the capital city, Tehran. They seized 66 Americans who were working there as diplomats, embassy staff, and guards. At first the students planned to exchange the hostages for the Shah, whom the revolutionaries wanted to try for tyranny. But the hostage crisis continued long after the Shah's death in July 1980. The ayatollah was enjoying the public relations value of the hostages too much to let them go.

Consequently, the crisis consumed the final year of Jimmy Carter's presidency. At first the public reacted favorably to Carter's orders to freeze Iranian assets in the United States, to deport some Iranian students, and to halt all oil imports from Iran. But when these measures failed to win release, public opinion turned against Carter. Angry demonstrators crowded the sidewalk outside the Iranian embassy and the White House. Bumper stickers displayed obscene insults to the Ayatollah Khomeini. ABC News began running a nightly program—eventually named "Nightline"—that covered the hostage story and kept a running tab of the number of days of their captivity. Carter authorized a commando raid on the embassy in April

Continued on next page

Hostage Crisis, Continued

1980. But a disastrous sandstorm in the desert outside Tehran caused a crash that killed several of the commandos and left the others with no choice but to abort the mission. Iranian Revolutionaries interpreted the sandstorm as divine intervention.

To his credit, President Carter continued to press for the hostages' release even after he had lost the 1980 election to Ronald Reagan. Carter's negotiators in Algeria reached an agreement with Iran that led to the release of the hostages on the very day that Ronald Reagan took the oath of office. Cheering crowds greeted the former hostages when they returned home, but for many Americans the long ordeal surpassed even the fall of Saigon as the low point in 1970s foreign policy. It also represented the first direct confrontation between the United States and religious fundamentalists in the Middle East. It would be the first of many.

losses and assailed by Arab nationalists and Muslim extremists, these three countries coordinated a surprise attack on Israel in October 1973 on the most solemn Jewish holiday of the year, Yom Kippur. The United States helped Israel repel the attack for several reasons. First, the United States had always supported Israel due to the millions of familial and political ties between American and Israeli citizens. Second, President Nixon and Henry Kissinger regarded Israel as an outpost of democracy in the Middle East, a region of monarchs and military leaders. Third, several of these Arab states, Syria and Egypt in particular, received support from the Soviet Union. United States support for Israel thus had a Cold War rationale.

Arab nations in the Middle East decided to punish the United States for supporting Israel in the Yom Kippur War. Working through OPEC, the Arab states cut off oil shipments to the United States. The embargo lasted several months, during which time the price of crude oil in the United States quadrupled, from around three dollars per barrel to around twelve. The price of gasoline doubled almost overnight. Motorists were shocked to pull up to service stations that had no gas to sell. Every product that moved by truck, boat, or plane increased in price to compensate for added fuel costs. Economists pointed to this "supply shock" as a major cause of high inflation rates that kept the American economy in a tailspin during the 1970s. Because of the oil embargo, resolving the Israel-Arab dispute moved to the top of the list of priorities for American presidents.

Of the three 1970s presidents who took on the task, Jimmy Carter had the most success. He convinced Israeli prime minister Menachem Begin and Egyptian president Anwar Sadat to come to the presidential retreat in Camp David,

U.S. president Jimmy Carter, Egyptian president Anwar Sadat, and Israeli prime minister Menachem Begin after the signing of the Camp David Accords on September 17, 1978. (Jimmy Carter Library)

Maryland. There Carter worked tirelessly with the two leaders to reach a peace agreement. Israel agreed to return the Sinai Peninsula to Egypt, and Egypt pledged never again to attack Israel. For the past 29 years, both sides have upheld their promises. In a March 1979 ceremony at the White House, Begin and Sadat signed the Camp David Accords. All three leaders took a political risk in so doing. Carter received praise for his role but criticism for focusing too much on the problems of Israel while the U.S. economy faltered. Begin faced near-revolt from his own political party for giving back the Sinai. Sadat suffered the worse backlash when he was assassinated in 1981 by Islamist extremists who considered the Camp David Accords a betrayal.

Perpetuating the Military-Industrial Complex

Despite the arms control treaties signed by the United States and the Soviet Union, both superpowers vastly increased their nuclear weapons stockpiles during the

1970s. In addition, both governments tried to crack down on internal dissent. In the United States, domestic surveillance began to resemble the heavy-handedness of the Soviet KGB. As both sides dropped the pretense of détente, the weapons industry in the United States went through a period of steady growth. With these changes, it became increasingly difficult for presidents such as Jimmy Carter to emphasize human rights over national defense.

The massive flow of money from Congress to the Pentagon to the defense industry had large effects on American society. For one, it changed where many Americans lived. American manufacturing plants were in steep decline during the 1970s. Foreign plants were making steel, electronics, and automobiles of comparable quality but lower prices, which drove many U.S. firms to fire workers and shut down factories. Journalists began to call the Midwestern states such as Ohio, Michigan, and Illinois the Rust Belt because their landscapes were full of abandoned factories rusting from disuse. But American military manufacturers boomed during the 1970s. Defense spending helped underwrite explosive population growth in Florida, Texas, Arizona, and California. A string of military bases and defense plants stretched from San Diego to Jacksonville, and journalists began calling this region of the country the Sunbelt. It might have been called the "gun belt."

The shift in population maintained the flow of defense dollars to the Sunbelt. Rust Belt refugees swelled the populations of Sunbelt states, which were generally more conservative politically than were Rust Belt states. Between the 1968 and 1984 elections, New York lost seven electoral votes while California gained seven. Sunbelt states tended to elect more Republicans than Democrats, and Republicans in Congress generally were quicker to approve funding for advanced weapons and new military installations. In this way, the political constituency of the military-industrial complex grew during the 1970s. There is no doubt that the arms race, the numerous proxy wars, and weapons sales to military dictators were all very good for business.

The term "military-industrial complex" was coined by President Eisenhower in his 1961 farewell address. He used the term because he feared that the alliance of government with defense contractors could lead to an erosion of democracy and civil liberties and keep the nation on a constant wartime footing. During the 1970s, Congress investigated revelations that proved Eisenhower prophetic. In 1974, *The New York Times* published a Seymour Hersh story that uncovered secret CIA programs that undermined foreign regimes. The tactics ranged from sabotage to assassination. The program, known inside the CIA as the "family jewels," played a role in the deaths of Zaire's Lumumba, South Vietnam's Diem, and the Dominican Republic's Trujillo; Cuba's Castro survived every assassination attempt, including an exploding cigar and a plot to spear-gun him while he was snorkeling.

The Senate set up a special committee chaired by Frank Church (D-Idaho) to investigate the Hersh articles. The Church Committee discovered a history of

The Nuclear Arms Race

During the 1970s, the United States added 5,250 nuclear warheads to its arsenal, and the USSR added 4,560 warheads to its arsenal. Yet, this was supposedly the decade of détente and arms control. What happened? Inside the Soviet Union, a power struggle resulted in the accession of Leonid Brezhnev. Brezhnev was a military hard-liner who ordered thousands of new weapons and hardened existing nuclear missile silos. Observers in the United States struggled to see all this. The Soviets were notoriously closed off to Westerners, so American experts poured over the annual photos of May Day military parades to learn about the latest Soviet hardware. U.S. analysts perceived, correctly as it turned out, that the Soviets were engaged in a massive arms build-up.

Calls for a swift American response were variations on a Cold War theme—that the Soviets had more of some weapon than did the United States. In the 1940s, leaders in the United States warned of a "bomber gap." In the 1950s, they warned of a "missile gap." In the 1970s, a group of Ford Administration analysts, including Defense Department analyst Paul Nitze and Harvard historian Richard Pipes, raised the alarm of a "throw-weight gap," which referred to a nuclear missile's size and explosive force. According to Ford's analysts, the Soviets were building bigger and more destructive missiles than ever. So even if the United States had more warheads, it had less firepower.

For the second half of the 1970s, then, national defense discussions focused on how to grow the U.S. nuclear arsenal so that the Soviets would not contemplate a first strike. The SALT treaty placed strict limits on the number of missiles the United States could maintain, but there were ways to observe the letter of the treaties while violating the spirit of arms control. Thus, the 1970s became a boom time for weapons research and development. Researchers perfected ways to fit up to one dozen warheads into each missile. New missiles launched from submarines, naval ships, and aircraft. The cruise missile could be guided in flight for improved accuracy. One ambitious plan was to replace old missiles with the MX, a missile that would travel underground on rails among several different launch silos spread over hundreds of square miles. The Soviets would never know exactly where the MX missiles were located. From 1970 to 1980, there was no slowdown in the pace of the nuclear arms race, and thus no time for the American public to exhale any sighs of relief.

covert operations within the CIA and the FBI. The agencies did more than meddle in other nation's affairs. They also spied on American citizens. Through its counterintelligence program, the FBI had tapped the phones of civil rights leaders, including Martin Luther King Jr.'s. The FBI also broke the law in order to arrest members of African American nationalist and Native American political organizations. Together, the two agencies had opened almost a quarter-million

Threats at Home

Terrorism was in the news in the 1970s when several militant groups appeared on the scene. They represented only a small part of American politics, occupying a space on the farthest fringes of left and right. But their actions received a large amount of coverage in the press. At the time, observers considered them left-overs of the 1960s. But following the terrorist attacks of the 1990s and early 2000s, the militant groups seemed more like early harbingers of a violent trend.

In some cases, armed radicals on the left were a holdover from the 1960s. The Black Panther Party for Self-Defense openly carried shotguns when they patrolled police officers in African American neighborhoods. The Weather Underground con-sisted mostly of white antiwar radicals who wanted to "bring the war home" through a series of bombings that they imagined would connect them to anti-colonial forces fighting overseas.

A similar group of California radicals formed the Symbionese Liberation Army (SLA) in 1973. Considering themselves revolutionaries against capitalism and im-perialism, the SLA went on a two-year crime spree that included the murder of the Oakland schools superintendent and the spectacular kidnapping of millionaire heiress Patty Hearst. The SLA apparently persuaded Hearst to join them because she participated in an armed bank robbery, which resulted in the shooting of two innocent bystanders. By 1975, the police had captured most SLA members and driven the rest into exile. Unlike the armed radicals of the 1960s, who were ad-mired by some, the SLA was uniformly scorned by the public. In the late 1970s, the SLA appeared in fictionalized form as the psychotic bad guys in a sequel to *Dirty Harry, The Enforcer* (1976) in which Clint Eastwood portrayed a San Francisco po-lice detective who apprehended violent radicals by riddling them with bullets.

The armed radical groups on the fringes of the political right were longer last-ing. Fleeing from the increasingly poor, increasingly nonwhite cities, the majority of white Americans moved to suburbs with high housing costs, residential zoning laws, and homeowners associations that kept out the poor, the brown, and the black. Radical white supremacists went a step further by moving deeper into the countryside and relying on firearms to exclude nonwhites. The Aryan Nations, for example, set up an armed compound in Hayden Lake, Idaho, in 1970. Borrowing its title from Adolf Hitler's ideal of racial hierarchy, Aryan Nations members stock-piled weapons in preparation for what they thought would be an inevitable war between the races. In this they revived a 19th-century prediction of the social Darwinists. There were several similar groups operating in rural areas with names such as the Posse Comitatus, the Minutemen, and the New Order.

In comparison to left-wing armed radicals, the right-wing armed radicals had a more lasting influence. They identified foreigners, Jews, and nonwhites as their enemies but also included the federal government because they perceived it to be protective of, or even controlled by, these groups. Some white supremacists of the 1970s even seriously planned to create a separate country out of the states of Washington, Oregon, Idaho, Montana, and Wyoming. Right-wing radicals were not limited to these states. For example, the Aryan Nations located a branch in Pennsylvania. Although they existed on the political fringes, their antigovernment rhetoric held some small appeal for the growing conservative movement that be-came increasingly powerful during the 1970s.

pieces of mail. Congress made many reforms in the wake of the Church Committee hearings. It endorsed President Ford's Executive Order outlawing assassination. It passed the 1978 Foreign Intelligence Surveillance Act, which required law enforcement to get a warrant from a judge before spying on a U.S. citizen. And it created a standing Senate Intelligence Committee to oversee the FBI and CIA.

POWER SHIFTS: CONSERVATIVE ACTIVISM

Challenges to Expansive Government: Decline of New Deal/Great Society Liberalism

The last presidential election before the 1970s showed how closely the electorate was divided. Republican Richard Nixon won a narrow victory with 43.5 percent of the vote, edging out Democrat Hubert Humphrey's 42.7 percent. Third-party candidate George Wallace, with 13.5 percent, represented something of a wild card. Wallace claimed Johnson's Great Society reforms led directly to the urban riots of the late 1960s and trampled on the "states' rights" tradition. This message appealed to working-class families in northern cities who had voted for Democrats since the New Deal. Wallace fared well in Midwestern primaries, which spelled trouble for Democrats. Along with the Midwest, the Democrats were losing their hold on the South. Many southern states had voted Republican or for Wallace in the 1964, 1968, and 1972 presidential elections. Liberals gradually lost control of Congress, the Electoral College, and ultimately, the very terms of political debate.

Nixon's contribution to the conservative movement was to arouse popular distrust of Great Society liberalism. Rather than try to undo Johnson's reforms—which would have been impossible, given Democrats' numbers in Congress—he quietly cut the budgets of federal agencies in charge of running the Great Society. He also undercut support for Great Society programs by labeling them as "welfare," a term that in the 1970s acquired scornful and derisive connotations. Instead of interstate highways and student loans or subsidies to defense contractors, "welfare" came to mean federal tax money for poor people (Matusow 1998, 204). Conservative critiques of welfare spending resonated with voters who were watching their incomes shrink during the inflationary 1970s.

The Great Society was designed to help not only the poor but also the nonwhite. It contained numerous "affirmative action" programs designed to help groups who had historically suffered discrimination in education and employment. Nixon took a stand against what he called "quotas." For example, Great Society legislation required that employers on construction sites that received federal funds must set aside a certain percentage of their workforce for minority applicants. Nixon criticized this as unfair, but he allowed his administration

Protesters march around the Detroit federal building during Supreme Court deliberations on the Allan Bakke case, October 3, 1977. Bakke claimed that he was deprived of admission to the University of California Medical School at Davis due to affirmative action. (Bettmann/Corbis)

to continue to run these programs because they pitted Democrats against each other. Blue-collar construction workers came to see as their political enemy the middle-class liberals who supported affirmative action quotas.

The political debate over affirmative action came to a climax in 1978 when the Supreme Court decided the case of *University of California Regents v. Bakke*. Allan Bakke was a white 32-year-old former Army officer who applied to 12 different medical schools. He was turned down by all 12, but he sued the University of California–Davis for setting aside a small number of seats for minority applicants, even if their test scores were low. The Supreme Court was unusually divided in the *Bakke* case. The 5–4 majority could not even agree on how to word a single written opinion. Although the Court ruled in favor of Bakke, the Court took pains to instruct colleges and universities to change their policies so that they would be constitutional. Nevertheless, conservatives celebrated what seemed like a legal defeat for affirmative action.

In this way "affirmative action" joined "welfare" in the category of terms that stood for liberals' misguided attempts at social reform. In an attempt to help the disadvantaged and the disenfranchised, the Democrats, many felt, had undermined meritocracy, the idea that one's abilities should matter more than one's ethnicity. By imposing quotas on certain industries, especially ones that had provided livelihoods to thousands of unionized working people, the Democrats seemed to be favoring race over ability. And by expanding the number of federal programs available to low-income families, the Democrats seemed to be offering handouts to the "undeserving poor." President Nixon's rhetoric and policies were designed to harden these impressions.

The careful racial posturing of Nixon's strategy reflected the Southernization and suburbanization of the electorate. Between 1950 and 1980, Sunbelt cities dramatically gained residents while Rust Belt cities dramatically lost residents. The population of Cleveland dwindled from 914,000 to 573,000 while Houston's exploded from 596,000 to 1.6 million people. Not all of this was a direct transfer.

Divisions in the Democratic Party

The Democratic Party did not go into complete eclipse during the 1970s. Indeed, in many cities and states, it still dominated the political process. There has not been a Republican mayor in Chicago since 1931, for example. But unlike the Republican Party, which was steadily unified by the energy of a conservative social movement, the Democrats were divided by the energy of the various movements of the 1960s and 1970s.

The Democrats began the 1970s trying to control the damage done at the 1964 and 1968 conventions. Members of the civil rights and antiwar movements were bitterly disappointed by the compromises to retain the loyalty of conservative Democrats from Southern states. In 1972, nominee Sen. George McGovern (D-S.D.) tried to bring the movement activists back into the party by pledging to end the war and grant amnesty to those who had evaded the draft. McGovern's campaign played right into the hands of the Republicans, who portrayed the Democrats as controlled by radicals.

The divides within the Democrats were deep, but nothing bridged them better than a common enemy, which Nixon provided after the 1972 election. The Watergate scandal revived the Democrats' political position, transforming even a former segregationist such as Sen. Sam Ervin (D-N.C.) into a political hero for doggedly pursuing the trail of White House crimes. With many voters still mad at the Nixon administration, Democrats gained seats in Congress in 1974 and 1976 and won back the presidency in 1976.

But the Watergate meteor soon fizzled out for the Democrats. The political, social, and economic trends were all in favor of the Republicans, and the Democrats could not settle on a winning strategy. Some felt that a recommitment to civil rights was the key, and they managed to get such language written into the 1976 party platform. But by then it was too late to rebuild the coalition of minorities, working-class whites, and middle-class liberals who had elected so many Democrats in the past. Republicans pointed knowingly to the "fairness" plank in the Democratic platform and translated it to mean more quotas for schools and businesses. Many working-class whites felt abandoned by a Democratic Party that seemed more interested in busing their children across town than in trying to secure their employment and their income. Large chunks of voters began breaking away from the Democrats and voting for Republicans. The press called these voters "Reagan Democrats."

The press also began writing obituaries for the Democrats after the 1980 election, in which Republicans won the White House and control of the Senate. But reports of the Democrats' death were greatly exaggerated. For all the divisions caused by the Vietnam War, affirmative action, and school busing, Democrats were still a large numerical force. In 1976, Jimmy Carter won the Southern states of Alabama, Arkansas, Kentucky, Mississippi, the Carolinas, and Tennessee. Four years later Reagan won them all, but by less than one percent of the popular vote. Thanks to the efforts of women, African American, and Latino activists, Democrats still controlled many of the largest city and state governments in the nation. The true damage suffered by the Democrats in the 1970s was not so much that they lost all their supporters but that they lost ideological coherence. The various groups that made up the party could no longer agree on what it meant to be a liberal. Republicans and conservatives were all too happy to define it for them.

Some of Cleveland's former residents settled in the suburbs ringing the city. In either case, Southern and suburban voters supported conservative candidates. Despite the fact that many Sunbelt industries depended heavily on federal defense contracts and military facilities, Sunbelt voters developed a disdain for the federal government.

Conservative Activism

At the beginning of the 1970s, it seemed unlikely that the Republican Party would benefit from a mass movement. Most movements of the 1950s and 1960s ended up promoting liberal reforms. Republicans were still seen by many voters as wealthy country club members and Chamber of Commerce businessmen. When Nixon ran for president in 1968 and 1972, he raised money not from the masses but from the "fat cats" who ran large corporations, such as Roy Ash, the chief of Litton Industries who became a White House adviser. Nixon did not do much to inspire average-income conservatives who felt alienated from government and who were dismayed by Watergate.

Nixon did succeed, however, in inflaming conservative intellectuals. They expected him to gut Lyndon Johnson's Great Society programs just on principle. When he allowed the Office of Economic Opportunity and Model Cities program to continue, conservative intellectuals cried foul. Even worse, Nixon was willing to meddle with the most basic function of the free market. Fearing that inflation could jeopardize his reelection, Nixon imposed mandatory wage-price controls on American businesses. Free market conservatives were appalled, but Nixon did not stop there. He angered many in the business community by taking the United States off the gold standard in 1971. He also angered many militarists by ending the draft in 1973. Liberals may have despised Nixon, but that did not mean that conservatives understood him any better.

With the accession of Gerald Ford, conservative intellectuals began implementing their ideals. From the academy to the White House came Donald Rumsfeld and Dick Cheney, who operated as Ford's chiefs of staff. Together with CIA director George H. W. Bush, these conservatives urged Ford to restore what they saw as the constitutional powers of the president. Ford defied the Democrat-controlled Congress by vetoing 64 bills in just over two years, only 12 of which were overturned, including Ford's veto of the Freedom of Information Act. Ford thwarted Congress's attempts to place price controls on oil. Ford also asserted the president's power to make war, an unpopular notion in the aftermath of Vietnam. Ford acted without Congress in ordering a bloody Marine raid to rescue the crew of the *S.S. Mayaguez,* a U.S. ship captured by Cambodian communists in 1975.

Unlike Nixon, Ford was willing to take a clear stand against liberal reforms of the early 1970s, much to the delight of free market advocates writing in the

Direct-Mail Campaigns

Fundraising was the foundation of the Republicans' rise to majority-party status at the end of the 1970s. Post-Watergate Democrats in Congress limited how much money any one person could donate to a campaign. The Republicans could no longer flip open Richard Nixon's Rolodex of "fat cats." New party leaders adopted the opposite strategy—appealing to the small cats. Republican Party chair William Brock, who lost his Senate seat in 1976, teamed up with *Conservative Digest* publisher Richard Viguerie to take advantage of new computer technology that made feasible direct-mail appeals to Republican voters. The letters attacked specific liberal reforms such as court-ordered bans on prayers in public schools, affirmative action programs, or the 1973 *Roe v. Wade* decision. The letters concluded with a request for a small donation, usually less than $100, to help the Republicans win elections and roll back the liberal measures.

Brock and Viguerie first tried their strategy in the 1978 midterm elections. Many Republicans criticized the program because it used up almost all of the party's discretionary funds. But the dividends were stunning. Brock and Viguerie spent $8 million on the 1978 mailings, which brought in $25 million in contributions. For the 1980 elections, the Republicans sent out even more mailings, at a cost of $12 million. Voters mailed back $54 million in contributions. The Party milked this new cash cow and used the funds to make Republican candidates more consistently conservative. Experienced moderates such as Richard Nixon and Nelson Rockefeller were tossed aside as outdated models. Instead, the Republicans recruited novice candidates to run for school boards, city councils, state legislatures, even Congress. In 1979–1980, the Republicans sent 10,000 trainee candidates to seminars that taught them the basics for running a campaign. More than 4,000 of them eventually qualified for Party funds and ran as candidates.

The direct-mail strategy was not only useful for running campaigns every two years. It also functioned to keep the Republicans in a constant state of campaign, endowing the Party with a recognizable brand: the small government, antiliberal party. During the debate over the Panama Canal Treaties, for example, which President Carter eventually won, direct mail raised the money and ire of grassroots conservatives who saw the treaty as an example of liberal weakness in foreign policy. The American Conservative Union raised $15,000 per day with its anti-treaty letter. A Republican National Committee letter signed by Ronald Reagan netted a hefty $700,000 and kept the name and stance of the future candidate fresh in voters' minds.

Wall Street Journal and the *National Review*. In a speech before the U.S. Chamber of Commerce, Ford denounced the Consumer Product Safety Commission as an unnecessary burden on businesses. Formed just three years earlier, the Commission was an attempt by Great Society liberals to keep dangerous products off the market. Most famously, consumer advocate Ralph Nader had demonstrated

Proposition 13

Almost all of the major forces changing American society and politics in the 1970s converged to bring about the passage of Proposition 13 in June 1978. The law was a voter initiative in California, a state that allowed voters to propose new laws and then vote them into effect by placing them on the ballot as propositions. Its passage by a 65 percent majority of California voters demonstrated the national importance of the growing Sunbelt, the strains of the economic crisis, and the power of grassroots conservative activists to put their concerns at the top of the national agenda.

Howard Jarvis was a newspaper man from Utah who moved to Southern California in the 1930s. After World War II, like many neonative Californians, he was worried about the state's explosive population growth. In particular, he watched in horror as his property tax bill got bigger every year. The reason for the higher tax was simple. Millions were flocking to the Sunbelt's booming economy and boosting the value of local real estate, especially in Southern California, where most towns and cities were hemmed in by oceans and mountain ranges. Jarvis put his own name on his grassroots group. The Howard Jarvis Taxpayers Association collected petition signatures to put Proposition 13 on the 1978 ballot.

Jarvis's campaign struck a nerve everywhere. Americans from all regions and walks of life faced a mounting tax burden in the 1970s, mostly due to inflation. As prices for consumer goods rose, salaries and wages also rose, often the automatic result of "cost-of-living adjustments" in employment contracts. Tax codes did not change quickly enough to keep up with inflation. A simple cost-of-living increase could bump a family up into a new tax bracket. In the new bracket, the family would be taxed at a higher rate, turning a raise into an effective pay cut. Like rising property values, "bracket creep" left millions of Americans convinced that taxes were too high.

Even though property taxes funded local schools and police, antitax voters were also motivated by what they perceived to be runaway spending in the federal government. Unemployment insurance, for example, seemed to tax hard-working citizens and sent the money to people who were out of work. Increasingly, middle-class white Americans such as Jarvis saw poor people as distant strangers. Welfare recipients were dark-skinned or Spanish-speaking, lived in ghettos, and bore too many children. Sympathy for the poor dried up in the parched 1970s economy. Voters were in a vindictive mood and the antitax revolt spread from California to Michigan, Idaho, Nevada, Massachusetts, Oregon, and Arizona. Howard Jarvis appeared on the cover of *Time* magazine raising his fist in triumph.

Once passed, Proposition 13 eviscerated municipal budgets in California by drying up local tax revenue. The average property tax bill fell by 57 percent. California's public school system, rated the best in the country in the 1960s, went into long decline and was ranked 49th by the 1990s. Police and fire departments fell desperately short of funds, requiring the state to devise a new revenue-sharing plan to prevent the collapse of public safety. The Proposition 13 campaign began

---

Proposition 13, Continued

as an attempt to fix the problem of rising housing costs in California, but in practice, the new law helped drive housing prices to new heights. Because only expensive construction brought in adequate tax revenues to fund services, local governments wrote zoning laws and master plans that made it nearly impossible to build low-income housing units. Proposition 13 benefited those who already owned a home but at the expense of everyone else trying to find one.

---

that several American car models had gas tanks that were likely to explode in accidents. The Commission had the power to keep unsafe products off store shelves, which included everything from cars with faulty seat belts to fire-prone children's pajamas. Ford helped make deregulation one of the main themes of the late 1970s. He called for the deregulation of investment firms, and his successor Jimmy Carter deregulated the trucking and airline industries.

Jimmy Carter won the election of 1976 on his personal honesty, which contrasted with Gerald Ford's complicity in the Watergate deceptions. Carter campaigned as an "outsider" to Washington. But once in power, he handled crises in a way that conservatives portrayed as stereotypically liberal. To alleviate shortages of heating fuel and the high price of oil, Carter created the Energy Department in 1977, which conservatives assailed as another government bureaucracy weighing down American businesses. In making appointments to federal agencies, Carter drew from the ranks of minorities, women, and liberal activists, such as "Nader's Raiders," who had been goading the government to regulate private industry. This played right into the hands of conservatives who described the Democrats as hostages to "special interest groups" and as overly eager to regulate the private sector. They made Carter the perfect foil for Reagan's anti-government campaign message.

The conservatives making these criticisms of liberalism were not just members of Congress. Throughout the 1970s, conservative intellectuals and philanthropists created a network of policy research centers, where scholars and analysts could examine government policies and offer remedies to the flaws they found. The Hoover Institution, the American Enterprise Institute, and the Heritage Foundation quickly became major players in policy debates of the 1970s. They had particular success in arguing that liberal reforms had expanded the amount of government spending, which increased the amount of money in circulation and drove up the inflation rate.

In the late 1970s, the intellectual conservatives at the federal level met up with the grassroots conservatives at the local level. The intellectuals' antiregulatory zeal matched the locals' antitax crusade, sparked by the passage of Proposition 13 in California in 1978. In Boston and Detroit, antibusing mobs surrounded high schools and threw rocks at buses from other neighborhoods. In state capitals, grassroots activists carried signs denouncing the Equal Rights Amendment. They found common cause with Republican candidates who called for an end to "activist judges" and "tax-and-spend liberals" who were engaging in "social experiments." But most importantly, the grassroots activists demonstrated that they could generate the financial contributions necessary to fund national campaigns.

Organizing the Christian Right

Direct mail helped unify Republican Party leaders with grassroots conservatives. A revived Christian Right was another force that arose in the 1970s and had an immediate impact on politics. The 1970s were hardly the first time in U.S. history that Christian activists had altered the course of national politics. The abolition and progressive movements stand out as examples. But the political issues of the 1970s turned the mobilized Christian Right voter into an implacable foe of liberalism.

In 1970, 20 percent of the national electorate identified themselves as evangelical Protestants, and they were predominately southerners who voted for Democrats. By the end of the 1970s, millions of Christian Right activists were campaigning for Ronald Regan, the Republican candidate. One of the key turning points was the Supreme Court's 1971 *Lemon v. Kurtzman* decision, which prohibited public funding for Catholic schools, and the Court's 1973 *Roe v. Wade* decision, which legalized some types of abortion. These decisions provided a common enemy for Catholics and fundamentalist Protestants. Historically, there had been much tension and distrust between Catholics and fundamentalist Protestants. But they both agreed that liberals in government had violated sacred religious principles when they partially legalized abortion and partially cut off funds for religious private schools.

Christian Right activists asserted that liberals violated the First Amendment guarantee of "free exercise" of religion. By 1975, the Christian Right had founded several organizations dedicated to furthering this argument, including National Conservative Political Action Committee, the Conservative Caucus, the Committee for the Survival of a Free Congress, and the Moral Majority.

The Christian Right added moral weight and additional resources to causes grassroots conservatives were already fighting. School busing, for example, had been denounced by conservatives as "forced integration." The Christian Right joined the battle after Jimmy Carter's IRS commissioner, Jerome Kurtz, made a point of investigating Christian academies. These sectarian private schools increased their enrollment from a few thousand in the 1960s to over one million by 1976. Kurtz suspected that Christian academies were escape hatches for white families who did not want to send their children to integrated public schools.

He required academies to prove they did not discriminate against nonwhite applicants or risk losing their tax-exempt status. The storm of protest was immense. Letters, some threatening, poured into the IRS from enraged parents and from Christian Right organizations. Kurtz eventually obtained Secret Service protection for himself and his wife. Christian Right lobbyists convinced their allies in Congress to call off the Kurtz investigations.

Christian activism permeated other political debates of the 1970s, such as the Equal Rights Amendment debate. Religious leaders widened the campaign against the ERA into a campaign against secular, liberal reforms in general, which included the women's movement. Across the street from the feminist-led 1977 International Women's Year Conference in Houston, anti-ERA protestors characterized the Conference as a liberal endorsement for "abortion, lesbianism, pornography, Federal control" (Crichtlow 2005, 246–247).

Delegate to the Republican National Convention wears anti-ERA pins and hat, July 1980. (Wally McNamee/ Corbis)

The rise of the Christian Right also abetted the conservative turn in foreign policy. Although the conservative takeover of American foreign policy was largely orchestrated by secular academics and journalists who called themselves "neoconservatives," they shared with the Christian Right a profound sense of American exceptionalism. Whether they believed in the inherent rightness of American actions because the United States was the cradle of democracy or because the United States was God's chosen country, voters responded positively to Ronald Reagan's use of the term "evil empire" to describe the Soviet Union. With that one phrase, Reagan banished the amoral realpolitik of the Nixon-Kissinger years and the moral-but-weak-kneed human rights focus of the Carter-Brzezinski years. Many in the Christian Right greeted the 1980 election as a millennial event.

Moral Majority

The Rev. Jerry Falwell founded the Moral Majority in 1979 as an umbrella organization to organize, publicize, and help fund numerous political action committees of the Christian Right. More importantly, the Moral Majority made Reverend Falwell the unofficial spokesman of the Christian Right. In 1956, Falwell began his preaching career when he founded the Thomas Road Baptist Church in his hometown of Lynchburg, Virginia. His first 35 congregants put $175 in the offering plate. In 1980, Falwell's church seated thousands and broadcast his sermons to millions of television viewers through "The Old Time Gospel Hour" and "The PTL Club." He also built a Christian college, Liberty University, and an amusement park called Heritage USA. These attractions helped make Lynchburg one of the busiest tourist spots in the country.

Like many evangelists, Falwell at first seemed most concerned with winning converts and saving souls. He was not explicitly political. But events of the 1970s, he said, gave him no choice but to use his enormous ministry to speak out against the evils of liberal government. Falwell allied with Catholic leaders to form an antiabortion movement that included Protestants and Catholics. He also made alliances with the growing conservative political network. Robert Billings Sr., for example, became the first executive director of Moral Majority in 1979 after he successfully led the National Christian Action Coalition in its efforts to protect Christian academies from IRS investigations.

Falwell's Moral Majority provided the conservative political movement with a source of volunteers, funding, and broadcasting that helped bring about the Republican electoral victory of 1980. Beyond that, the Moral Majority also provided the rhetoric and the crusading spirit of the "culture wars" that divided liberals from conservatives during the 1980s and 1990s. Claiming that liberals imposed their moral standards on others Falwell lashed out at liberals whose "degenerate lifestyles," best exemplified by feminists and homosexuals, posed a mortal threat to the "family values" of American Christians. In this way Falwell was one of the key transitional figures from the politics of the 1970s to the politics of the 1980s.

BIOGRAPHIES

Shirley Chisholm, 1924–2005

Congresswoman and Candidate for President

Women gained the right to vote in federal elections in 1920, but it was not until 1972 that the first woman ran a campaign to become the major-party candidate for president. That it was Shirley Chisholm surprised few at the time. In 1968, Representative Chisholm became the first African American woman elected to Congress, representing New York's 12th District. A Brooklyn native, Chisholm did not abide by custom that would have kept her in a lowly position as a Congressperson with the least seniority. In fact, she demanded reassignment after Democratic leaders placed her on the House Forestry Committee. After her reelection, she announced her plan to run for the Democratic nomination, and she made a strong showing with 152 delegate-votes at the 1972 convention. Her positions were similar to those of nominee George McGovern's, including an end to the military draft and a renewed federal effort to rebuild decaying cities.

Congresswoman Shirley Chisholm announces her candidacy for presidential nomination, January 25, 1972. (Library of Congress)

After 1972, Rep. Chisholm displayed her political savvy by making allies with the white supremacist Gov. George Wallace of Alabama. She was one of the few elected Democrats to visit him in the hospital as he recovered from an assassination attempt. With his support, Chisholm was able to push through Congress a reform of federal labor law by applying the minimum wage to domestic workers—nannies, housekeepers, and elder-care providers, all of whom had been left out of the 1938 legislation. The old law penalized women and minorities, who in many parts of the country made up the bulk of the domestic workforce. As her minimum-wage fight demonstrated, Chisholm was a woman in politics who strove for reforms that directly improved the lives of women, and especially women of color.

Tom DeLay, 1947–

Republican Lawmaker Tom DeLay's political career did not leave much of an impact on the 1970s, but it encapsulated the decade's conservative ideological triumph. His impact came much later, when the Republican Party finally dislodged the Democratic majority in Congress in 1995. But like many of the Republicans who ran Capitol Hill and the West Wing at the turn of the 21st century, he found in the 1970s a new formula for political success.

For most of the 1970s, DeLay did not work in politics. He ran a pest control business in the suburbs of Houston, Texas. The area was growing by leaps and bounds for two reasons. The OPEC crises had driven up the price of oil, which made Texas crude a hot commodity. Houston became one of the capitals of the Texas oil boom. (Another was Midland, hometown of future Republican president George W. Bush.) The other growth factor was the massive influx of Rust Belt refugees looking for oil business jobs, factory work, and construction jobs. For DeLay's extermination business, the resulting building boom meant plenty of work. But he chafed at the increasing federal restrictions on his firm. During the 1970s, the newly formed Environmental Protection Agency began the first major attempt to regulate toxic chemicals. The EPA sometimes resorted to an outright ban, such as on DDT and Mirex, which DeLay's firm used to kill fire ants, the scourge of the Texas lawn. The Mirex ban inspired DeLay to run for the state legislature as a Republican.

A few years earlier, such a decision would have been quixotic. As one voter told DeLay on the campaign trail, "It'll be a cold day in hell when a Republican wins in this county" (Dubose and Reid 2004, 36). Like most Southern states, the Democratic machine dominated Texas for decades. But 1978 offered DeLay and his partisans a chance to change this. It was the year of Proposition 13, and it was a midterm election year, a chance to capitalize on anti-Carter sentiment. The 1970s slump was entering a second recession, with millions of households paying record heating bills during the oil shortage of the 1977 winter. Even more profoundly, DeLay was running to represent some of Houston's most recent arrivals embittered by school desegregation and by the disappearance of factory jobs further north. DeLay's antiregulatory, antitaxation campaign struck a chord and he won a seat in Austin, along with several dozen others who were the first Republicans since Reconstruction to win their particular election.

DeLay's ascension to national office did not occur until 1985, but by then he had completed the spiritual journey necessary to make him the epitome of the young, 1970s-vintage conservative. DeLay became a born-again Christian, swearing off liquor and women. In just under a decade, DeLay had aligned himself with both strands of the resurgent party's most ardent supporters: the white, middle-class suburban, antiregulatory voters and the Christian evangelical voters who saw politics as a way to rescue America from moral degeneracy.

Harvey Milk, 1930–1978

California State Politician

Presumably, homosexuals have been active in American politics for a long time, but it was only during the "new politics" of the 1970s that a gay candidate could openly talk about his sexuality. One notable and tragically portentous example was Harvey Milk, who became the first openly gay member of the San Francisco Board of Supervisors in 1977 after three unsuccessful campaigns. Milk joined a board that already had African Americans and women serving on it, including future U.S. senator Dianne Feinstein. Milk represented a district that included the Castro, a neighborhood that took on a homosexual profile in the years after World War II.

Milk was already a popular politician in San Francisco and he used his seat on the board to raise his salience at the state level. When state senator John Briggs from Orange County sponsored a ballot initiative to bar homosexuals from teaching in public schools, Milk led the statewide campaign to defeat Proposition 6. Supervisor Milk toured the state and made numerous appearances at rallies and on television. In November 1978, the measure was rejected by a wide majority of California voters.

Milk was at the height of his career. It was cut short in a manner that symbolized the limits of electoral reform in the 1970s. Party rules and neighborhood demographics could change rapidly, but ingrained bigotry did not go away quite so quickly. Fellow supervisor Dan White had been frustrated during his brief tenure on the board, and he felt that the board's liberals, including Milk and Feinstein, formed a solid coalition to thwart him. On the morning of November 27, 1978, White assassinated Milk in his office and then murdered Mayor George Moscone, an ally of Milk. Milk's murder was atypical. Few other members of the "new politics" met the terrible fate of Harvey Milk. But his assassination seemed to symbolize a surging backlash against the efforts of both political parties—but especially the Democrats—to open political office to female and minority-group politicians.

Phyllis Schlafly, 1924–

Many people remember Phyllis Schlafly as the one-woman dynamo who defeated the Equal Rights Amendment. But long before she challenged feminists, Schlafly spent more than two decades fighting for recognition and influence within the Republican Party. A native of St. Louis, Missouri, Schlafly married a successful businessman and occasional political candidate who moved the family to the suburb of Alton, Illinois. While raising six children, Schlafly made her Alton home the base for a grassroots crusade to mold the Republican Party into a conservative force.

Schlafly's original nemesis was not feminism but communism. She saw the Soviet Union as an evil, atheistic, authoritarian monstrosity, dead set on world domination. Although millions of Americans shared Schlafly's view, she distinguished herself from wild-eyed conspiracy theorists who feared that communists had already infiltrated the U.S. State Department, military, entertainment industry, public libraries, public health system, and school system. Schlafly and her followers put no stock in such theories, but they were convinced that the liberals in power were weakening the nation's ability to withstand international communism. Accordingly, she struck hard at leaders for compromising with the

Soviets or for failing to maximize American military defenses. The liberals were not confined to the Democrats, she believed, but also included moderate and liberal Republicans such as Dwight Eisenhower, Richard Nixon, and Gerald Ford. She lambasted each one for allowing the Soviet Union to build long-range missiles, for recognizing the People's Republic of China, and for signing human rights agreements with the Soviets. In a series of detailed books coauthored by retired military generals, Schlafly argued that the post–World War II liberal establishment was squandering its chances to overwhelm dangerous foreign powers.

While Schlafly's defense-policy screeds circulated among a relatively small circle of conservatives, her 1964 book endorsing Sen. Barry Goldwater (R-Az.) for president, *A Choice Not an Echo,* put her on the map politically. Although Goldwater lost to Lyndon Johnson by a wide margin, Schlafly's book began the process of transforming the Republicans' image from the party of Wall Street to the party of Main Street. The Republican old guard still had enough clout to put Richard Nixon on the ballot in 1968 and 1972, but Schlafly built a national network of neighborhood conservatives that supported uncompromising candidates, such as Ronald Reagan who won the governorship of California in 1966. At first, Schlafly's network was most effective in local politics. In Orange County, California, for example, Eleanor Howe and Jan Pippinger took over the local school board because it had implemented a sex education curriculum in the local public schools, a shocking example, they felt, of liberals' willingness to undermine families.

In 1972, Schlafly became the chief spokeswoman for antiliberal rage when she founded the Eagle Forum, named after a biblical passage. The Eagle Forum had 50,000 members in the 1970s, and many thousands more subscribed to Schlafly's newsletter. Therefore, she was well placed to lead the fight against the Equal Rights Amendment when it passed Congress in 1972, even though antifeminism had not been Schlafly's focus. Nevertheless, she was able to characterize the ERA as a familiar foe—one more well-intentioned liberal reform. This one would bring down the institution of the family by removing the legal protections that American women enjoyed. Schalfly's Stop Taking Our Privileges (STOP-ERA) forces traveled state to state, testifying to legislators that the legal ramifications of mandated sex equality would be staggering: gay marriages, an epidemic of divorces, the end of child-support payments from separated fathers, women drafted into the military, and unisex restrooms to replace separate men's and women's rooms.

STOP-ERA dovetailed with Schlafly's larger project to remake the Republican Party because it proved that conservatives could win elections and gain wide popular support by attacking liberal reforms that "went too far," such as the ERA. The successful campaign also proved that women in politics could produce major results. Schlafly's defeat of the ERA was perhaps the most stunning political reversal of the 1970s, and it was orchestrated largely by a network of grassroots conservatives led by a woman.

George Wallace, 1919–1998

A combative campaigner from an impoverished background, Gov. George Wallace (D-Ala.) ran for president in 1968 and 1972 as a states' rights folk-hero. He first became prominent in 1963 when the Justice Department ordered the University of Alabama to begin admitting qualified African American students. Wallace refused, making a famous stand in the schoolhouse door, blocking federal marshals from escorting the first African American students into the registrar's office. His stand only lasted a few minutes. Once the television news crews packed up and left, he stepped aside and the students walked in. But the symbolic stand was enough. It validated his 1962 inaugural address promise to defend "segregation forever," and it won him the support of Alabama voters who resented the way civil rights leaders used their state—Birmingham in particular—to stage acts of civil disobedience.

The Democrats had written off Wallace as a relic of the Jim Crow era. But they did not realize how enthusiastically voters outside the South would respond to his tirades against federal government power. When many voters in Michigan and Ohio saw him standing in the schoolhouse door, they did not see the last of dying breed but a new kind of Democrat, one with the guts to slay his

Alabama governor George Wallace in 1968. A staunch segregationist, Wallace appealed to both northern and southern voters in his 1968 presidential bid. He ran as a "moderate" in the 1972 and 1976 Democratic primaries, even after an assassin's bullet left him paralyzed from the waist down in May 1972. (Yoichi Okamoto/Lyndon B. Johnson Library)

party's sacred cows. Wallace walked out of his party's convention in 1968 to form the American Independent Party. The move was hardly novel. Segregationists had been walking out of Democratic conventions since at least 1948. But none of them went on to win as many votes as did George Wallace. His genius was his ability to convince voters to vote for him as a form of protest. They could vote for him to protest civil rights reform or even to uphold the abstract principle of states' rights. But at bottom, voting for Wallace was a protest against a federal government that had once again forgotten the "forgotten man" of the New Deal. These forgotten voters packed Wallace rallies by the hundreds. As Wallace himself remarked, he appealed to white working-class voters in Northern states because he learned how to "speak Polish." It was a language the Democrats did not speak fluently.

For a third-party candidate, Wallace made a strong showing in 1968. He was on his way to a sequel in 1972 when an assassination attempt left him paralyzed from the waist down. He finished out his career as governor of Alabama.

REFERENCES AND FURTHER READINGS

Appy, Christian G. 1993. *Working-Class War: American Combat Soldiers and Vietnam*. Chapel Hill: University of North Carolina Press.

Bailey, Beth, and David Farber, eds. 2004. *America in the Seventies*. Lawrence: University Press of Kansas.

Bartlett, Randall. 1998. *The Crisis of America's Cities*. Armonk, N.Y.: M. E. Sharpe.

Blum, John Morton. 1991. *Years of Discord: American Politics and Society, 1961–1974*. New York: W. W. Norton.

Busch, Andrew. 2005. *Reagan's Victory: The Election of 1980 and the Rise of the Right*. Lawrence: University Press of Kansas.

Chafe, William H. 2007. *The Unfinished Journey: America since World War II*, 6th edition. New York: Oxford University Press.

Crichtlow, Donald T. 2005. *Phyllis Schlafly and Grassroots Conservatism: A Woman's Crusade*. Princeton, N.J.: Princeton University Press.

Cunningham, David. 2004. *There's Something Happening Here: The New Left, The Klan, and FBI Counterintelligence*. Berkeley: University of California Press.

Dubose, Lou, and Jan Reid. 2004. *The Hammer: Tom DeLay, God, Money, and the Rise of the Republican Congress*. New York: Public Affairs Books.

Edsall, Thomas, and Mary D. Edsall. 1991. *Chain Reaction: The Impact of Race, Rights, and Taxes on American Politics*. New York: W. W. Norton.

Ellsberg, Daniel. 2002. *Secrets: A Memoir of Vietnam and the Pentagon Papers*. New York: Viking Penguin.

Faludi, Susan. 1991. *Backlash: The Undeclared War against American Women*. New York: Anchor Books.

Farber, David. 2005. *Taken Hostage: The Iran Hostage Crisis and America's First Encounter with Radical Islam*. Princeton, NJ: Princeton University Press.

Fink, Gary M., and Hugh Davis Graham, eds. 1998. *The Carter Presidency: Policy Choices in the Post-New Deal Era*. Lawrence: University Press of Kansas.

Flippen, J. Brooks. 2000. *Nixon and the Environment*. Albuquerque: University of New Mexico Press.

Graham, Hugh Davis. 1990. *The Civil Rights Era: Origins and Development of National Policy, 1960–1972*. New York: Oxford University Press.

Greene, John Robert. 1995. *The Presidency of Gerald R. Ford*. Lawrence: University Press of Kansas.

Haldeman, H. R. 1995. *The Haldeman Diaries: Inside the Nixon White House, The Complete Multimedia Edition* CD-ROM. Santa Monica: Sony Imagesoft.

Herring, George. 1996. *America's Longest War: The United States and Vietnam, 1950–1975,* 3rd edition. New York: McGraw-Hill, 1996.

Hoff, Joan. 1994. *Nixon Reconsidered*. New York: Basic Books.

Horowitz, Daniel. 2005. *Jimmy Carter and the Energy Crisis of the 1970s: The "Crisis of Confidence Speech," A Brief History with Documents*. Boston: Bedford/ St. Martin's.

Hyland, William. 1987. *Mortal Rivals: Superpower Relations from Nixon to Reagan*. New York: Random House.

Jackson, John S., III, and William Crotty. 2001. *The Politics of Presidential Selection,* 2nd edition. New York: Longman.

Kaplan, Fred M. 1980. *Dubious Specter: A Skeptical Look at the Soviet Nuclear Threat*. Washington, DC: Institute for Policy Studies.

Kazin, Michael. 1995. *The Populist Persuasion: An American History*. New York: Basic Books.

Kotlowski, Dean J. 2001. *Nixon's Civil Rights: Politics, Principle, and Policy*. Cambridge: Harvard University Press.

Kruse, Kevin M. 2005. *White Flight: Atlanta and the Making of Modern Conservatism*. Princeton, NJ: Princeton University Press.

Lamb, Charles M. 2005. *Housing Segregation in Suburban America since 1960: Presidential and Judicial Politics*. New York: Cambridge University Press.

Lassiter, Matthew D. 2006. *The Silent Majority: Suburban Politics in the Sunbelt South*. Princeton, NJ: Princeton University Press.

Matusow, Allen J. 1998. *Nixon's Economy: Booms, Busts, Dollars, Votes*. Lawrence: University Press of Kansas.

Matusow, Allen J. 1984. *The Unravelling of America: A History of Liberalism in the 1960s*. New York: Harper & Row.

McGirr, Lisa. 2002. *Suburban Warriors: The Origins of the New America Right*. Princeton, N.J.: Princeton University Press.

Merrill, Karen R. 2007. *The Oil Crisis of 1973–1974: A Brief History with Documents*. Boston: Bedford/St. Martin's Press.

Miller, Stephen Paul. 1999. *The Seventies Now: Cultures of Surveillance*. Durham: Duke University Press.

Mohl, Raymond A., ed. 1993. *Searching for the Sunbelt: Historical Perspectives on a Region*. Athens: University of Georgia Press.

Phillips, Kevin. 1969. *The Emerging Republican Majority*. New Rochelle, N.Y.: Arlington House.

Reichley, A. James. 1992. *The Life of the Parties: A History of American Political Parties*. New York: The Free Press.

Rudenstine, D. 1996. *The Day the Presses Stopped: A History of the Pentagon Papers*. Berkeley: University of California Press.

Schlafly, Phyllis. 1964. *A Choice Not an Echo*. Alton, IL: Pere Marquette Press.

Schlesinger, Arthur M., Jr. 1989. *The Imperial Presidency*. Boston: Houghton Mifflin.

Schulman, Bruce. 2002. *The Seventies: The Great Shift in American Culture, Society, and Politics*. Cambridge, Mass.: Da Capo Press.

Shawcross, William. 1979. *Sideshow: Kissinger, Nixon, and the Destruction of Cambodia*. New York: Simon & Schuster.

Slocum-Schaffer, Stephanie A. 2003. *America in the Seventies*. Syracuse: Syracuse University Press.

Sugrue, Thomas. 1996. *Origins of the Urban Crisis: Race and Inequality in Postwar Detroit*. Princeton, N.J.: Princeton University Press.

Thernstrom, Abigail. 1987. *Whose Votes Count? Affirmative Action and Minority Voting Rights*. Cambridge: Harvard University Press.

Thompson, Kenneth W. 1988. *The Ford Presidency*. Lanham, Md.: University Press of America.

Vogel, David. 2003. *National Styles of Business Regulation: A Case Study of Environmental Protection*. Washington, DC: Beard Books.

Wattenberg, Ben J., and Richard M. Scammon. 1970. *The Real Majority*. New York: Coward-McCann.

People and Events in the 20th Century

THE 1900s

THE 1910s

THE 1920s

THE 1930s

THE 1940s

THE 1950s

THE 1960s

THE 1970S

The 1980s

THE 1990s

1970s Index

About the Author

Dr. Laurie Mercier is professor of history at Washington State University (WSU) in Vancouver, where she has taught since 1995. She received her Ph.D. from the University of Oregon. She has directed a number of public history projects, including the oral history program of the Montana Historical Society from 1981 to 1988 and the WSU digital archive *Columbia River Basin Ethnic History Archive* http://www.vancouver.wsu.edu/crbeha/. In addition to numerous articles, her publications include *Mining Women: Gender in the Development of a Global Industry, 1700–2000* (co-editor, Palgrave/Macmillan Press, 2005) and *Anaconda: Labor, Community, and Culture in Montana's Smelter City* (University of Illinois Press, Working Class in American History Series, 2001).